THE KILKENNY WAR DEAD

Tom Burnell

AND THE KILKENNY GREAT WAR MEMORIAL COMMITTEE

Acknowledgement.

The publication of the *Kilkenny War Dead* has been made
possible by a generous donation from R.E.

Tom Burnell and the Kilkenny Great War Memorial Committee
gratefully acknowledge the substantial contribution.

Go raibh míle maith agat.

ISBN 978-0-9930790-0-9

Published By
Tom Burnell

The Kilkenny War Dead

The Kilkenny War Dead

By
Tom Burnell

All proceeds from this book go the the Kilkenny Great War Memorial

"Nuair a théann an ghrian faoi, agus ar maidin, 'Cuimhnímis iad';- *At the going down of the sun, and in the morning, we will remember them.*

Foreword

The firing of two shots by Serbian nationalist Gravilo Princip in Sarajevo on the 28th of June 1914 killing Arch Duke Franz Ferdinand and his wife Sophie Chotek can be said to have occasioned the start of World War One. The causes of the war are complex and relate to issues like globalisation, militarism, complex mutual alliances and imperialism. But the consequences of the war were the death of over 700 men and women from County Kilkenny and the untold story of the thousands of combatants and non-combatants who returned to Kilkenny during and after those war years.

The so called blank check given by Germany to Austria-Hungary is recognised as a catalyst which allowed Austria-Hungary to declare war on Serbia on 28th of July. Europe was now caught up in the perfect storm. Allegiances between the central powers on one side and France-Russia and Great Britain on the other would cause mass mobilisation and war declarations. This culminated with the British declaring war on Germany on the 4th of August.

In the late summer of 1914 the political situation in Ireland was grave, and the headline news in Ireland and the United Kingdom was the threat of conflict in Ireland. This climaxed with the arming of the Irish National Volunteers when weapons were landed in Howth and Kilcoole between the 26th of July and the 2nd of August. However after the 4th of August the focus of Nationalist and Unionist plans would now be funnelled into supporting the European war effort in order to advance their different causes with the government of the time.

The mobilisation of the British Expeditionary Force in August 1914 necessitated all serving Kilkenny men, regardless of whether they were full time soldiers or members of their local Special Reserve Regiment, to rally to the colours. These soldiers were dispatched to France with some immediate haste and went into action on the 23rd of August near Mons in Belgium and were the first Kilkenny battle casualties. So many more Kilkenny men and women were killed during the war in places such as The Somme, Ypres, Gallipoli, Macedonia, Salonika, and on the high seas. They made the ultimate sacrifice with little or no idea of the strategic, operational or even tactical intent of their generals or higher commanders.

Inarguably, the true cause of the massive unprecedented casualty rate during the war was the inability of generals, who had received their military education studying wars of the Napoleonic era, employing the tactics and values of the Victorian gentleman in the battle field of the late 19th century in 1914. They were totally unable to comprehend the destruction caused on one hand by machines guns and artillery, and the lack of mobility caused by siege warfare fighting initiated by the introduction of barbed wire and entrenchment (the only way of becoming invisible to the enemy on the battlefield). The logistical pressures placed on all the armies lagged seriously behind the enhancement of firepower. This set the scene for events like the Somme offensive of 1916 where many Kilkenny soldiers died.

For all those interested in researching the Kilkenny casualties in the First World War this book is a an invaluable resource and becomes a testament to all the Kilkenny men and women who lost their lives. Regardless of whether they answered the bugle call, Redmond's call, or enlisted for any political, religious, family or personal reason, there is one known certainty, the events during, and immediately subsequent to, Easter Week 1916 ensured that very few returning survivors of the war were ever able to express their feelings or talk about their experiences; often hiding their active service for the rest of their lives as if it was some sort of terrible secret.

This comprehensive publication the product of detailed research allows the reader to now identify with the Kilkenny men and women who were lost in the First World War and importantly to identify information like service number, regiment on enlistment and crucially the location of grave or memorial where they are commemorated. In many cases there is supplementary information, available now in this book for so many of those listed affords the reader and the researcher a valuable insight into the lives of the casualty.

Lieutenant Laurence Scallan.
Military Historian and member of the
Kilkenny Military Heritage Project.

Kilkenny War Memorial Committee
Top left;- Betty Manning, Noel Bourke, Michael Gabbett, Michael McLoughin, Alice McDermott, Bernie Kirwan,
Bottom left;- John Joe Cullen, Jim Corcoran, Donal Croghan, Paddy Horohan. Missing from the photograph is Bernie Egan.

Kilkenny Great War Memorial Committee

The origin of the **Kilkenny Great War Memorial Committee** has its seed sown in the act of commemoration that the Irish Government held in different regions around the Country. Kilkenny Borough Council hosted one such event in Kilkenny Castle talking to the Mayor David Fitzgerald two members of the then committee expressed a wish to see names of the Kilkenny Soldiers on Limestone on a Memorial in Kilkenny.

We were asked to join a meeting in the Town Hall to a debate on the Commemoration Ceremony and there we put the proposal to the Borough Council, to the Mayor, and the Council to engage in a project to remember the Great War soldiers from Kilkenny who died.

After many meetings plans were unveiled for a 1.2m high Carved Limestone Plinth by Kilkenny Sculptor Aileen Anne Brannigan. This was to commemorate all those Kilkenny Citizens who had died in past wars including those men and women who had served with the United Nations. This beautiful monument unveiled in 2012 adds greatly to the heritage of our City, the desire persists to name in tablets of stone, the almost 800 Kilkenny men and women who died in World War 1.

Previous to 2012 a few people had begun remembering these Men and women, on 11th of the 11th Month 2011 a collection of photographs was compiled and uploaded to Utube. At this time also I was given the British War Medal of my Great- Granduncle a Gowran man, Private John Purcell 43129 1st Batt Royal Dublin Fusiliers. Further research led me to Yorkshire and I was again presented with the Dead Man's Penny from another relation and namesake John Purcell. The train of desire was firmly set to remember all the Kilkenny Soldiers and Nurses in stone in their home County.

By coincidence around this time Councillor Betty Manning had also made an appeal to the Borough Council to commemorate the Kilkenny men fallen in the Great War.Mr Noel Bourke was writing to the local papers proposing a similar project to be undertaken in Kilkenny.

Many Kilkenny War Dead are already commemorated in St Canice's Cathedral in Kilkenny but the list is not conclusive. St Canice's also holds one of the eight country wide text's listing the 49,000 all Ireland War Dead. It is illustrated by Harry Clarke Stained glass artist; of An Túr Gloine this is freely accessible to the public.

So from humble beginnings this committee of three set to finding like minded people whose wish also was to commemorate the Kilkenny fallen in WW1, those whose memory by our Nations bloody birth was erased by our National Amnesia.

Donal Croghan

Below is a record of the 787 Kilkenny men and women who died in the military and associated services during and just after the Great War. This list includes WW1 service personnel buried in Kilkenny from other locations. They died in the service of the British Army, the Australian Army, the New Zealand Army, the American Army, the Indian Army, the Canadian Army, the South African Army, the Royal Navy and the British Mercantile Marine, and the Nursing Services.

Sources;-
The Commonwealth War Graves Commission, Soldiers Died in the Great War. Soldiers of the Great War. The New Library and Archives Canada. The National Archives of Australia. Nominal Rolls of the New Zealand Expeditionary Force. De Ruvignys Roll of Honour, The War Graves of the British Empire, Commonwealth War Graves Commission registers for the Irish Free State, Irelands Memorial Records. The Tipperary War Dead, The Wexford War Dead, The Wicklow War Dead, The Offaly War Dead, The Waterford War Dead, The Kerry War Dead, University of St Andrews Roll of Honour, Souvenir of the Great Naval Battle, Call to Arms, Montreal's Roll of Honour, Croydon and the Great War, Artists Rifles Roll of Honour, Princes Patricia's Canadian Light Infantry, University of Edinburgh Roll of Honour, 1914-1919, Irish at the Front, New Zealand Roll of Honour, Irish on the Somme, Tenth Irish Division in Gallipoli, The National Roll of the Great War, London, Blackrock College Roll of Honour, South Irish Horse Casualties, The First Five Hundred, Great War Memorial in St Canice's Cathedral, Kilkenny. WW1 Irish Soldiers; Their Final Testament, Roll of the sons and daughters of the Anglican Church, The Roll of Honour, Five months on a German Raider, The Munster Express, RGA Enlistments—Ireland, WW1 Irish Soldiers wills, Irish Submariners (Barrie Downer), Lijssenthoek Cemetery Project, Our Heroes, Soldiers of the Great War (USA), The Distinguished Service Order, Bond of Sacrifice, King's County Chronicle, Public Records Office-Kew, the West Australian, The London Gazette, Flight, The Tipperary Star, The Kilkenny Journal, The Kilkenny People, 1901 and 1911 Census, The Carlow Sentinel, The Leinster Express, The Waterford News,"The Argus" (Melbourne),"The Poverty Bay Herald", Harrow Memorials, Volume 1; Harrow School Register, 1845-1925; Harrovian War Supplement,"The Times", The Nationalist and Leinster Times, The Enniscorthy Guardian, The Clare Journal.

Kilkenny placenames and variants to found in this book.

Ahenny. Aughavillar. Bagenalstown. Ballinamore. Ballinaugh. Ballycallan. Ballyconra. Ballyfoyle. Ballyhale. Ballyhall. Ballyraggett. Batts. Benchfield. Bennetsbridge. Bennettesbridge. Bennetts bridge. Birchwood. Bishops Hill. Bonnetstown. Butts. Callan. Callean. Callen. Carrickbeg. Carrigeen. Castle Comer. Castlecomer. Castlecolumn. Castlecomer. Castletown. Cleara. Clifton. Clomantagh. Clough. Conahy. Connetty. Connety. Coolcullen. Cowran. Craigmannan. Cuff's Green. Cuffs Grange. Cuffsgrange. Danes Fort. Danesfort. Desart. Donnimagen. Drumgoole. Dunamaggin. Dunbell. Dunbell. Dungarven. Dunkill. Dunnamaggan. Ferrybank. Fiddown. Freshford. Glenmore. Gores Bridge. Goresbridge. Gouran. Gowran. Graignamsena. Graigue. Graiguenamanagh. Graiguenanaugh. Green Hill. Hartlands. Hugginstown. Inistioge. Johnstown. Kells. Kilderry. Kilfane. Kilkenny. Killaloe. Killeasey. Killen. Kilmacon. Kilmacow. Kilmanagh. Kilmarcow. Kilmason. Kilree. Knocktopher. Knocktoplin. Lisdowney. Long Easter. Melinvat. Mooncoin. Moonteen. Mucalee. Muckalee. Newmarket. Newton. Newtownbarry. Orlingford. Ownin. Paulstown. Piltown. Pitt. Ratheash. Rosbercan. Rosbercon, Shankill. Skehana. Slieverue. Slievrue. Sliverue. St. Ganice's. St. John's. St. Peter's. St. Canice's. St. Dennis's. St. Mary's. St. Patrick's. Stoneyford. Templeorum. The Butts. Thomas Town. Thomastown. Tobernabrone. Tullaherin. Tullaroan. Urlingford. Windgap. Windgate.

Abbreviations;-

CWGC;- Commonwealth War Graves Commission.

ODGW;-Officers Died in the Great War.

SDGW;-Soldiers Died in the Great War.

IMR;-Ireland's Memorial Records.

Terminology;
Killed in Action; The soldier was killed during engagement with the enemy.

Died of wounds; The soldier was not killed outright and may have made it back to the Regiments Aid post or Casualty Clearing Station before he eventually died of his wounds.

Died at home; Death by drowning, suicide, accident or illness in the UK. Home in these cases means back in England and not necessarily where he lived. Many times I have come across this and it turned out to be that the soldier died in a UK hospital.

Died of wounds at home; The soldier was not killed outright and may have made it back to the Regiments Aid post or Casualty Clearing Station before he eventually died of his wounds back in the UK or Ireland.

Died; Can mean death by drowning, suicide, accident or illness.

A

Ackford, Thomas. Rank; Private. Regiment or Service: Royal Warwickshire Regiment. Unit; 1/7th Battalion. Service Number; 3233. Date of death; 14/06/1916. Age at death; 21. Born; Dublin City. Enlisted; Stratford-on-Avon. Killed in action. Brother of Robert, son of Ellen and Grandson of Helen Elizabeth Ackford. Son of Thomas and Ellen Ackford, of Chearsley, Aylesbury. Grave or Memorial Reference; Pier and Face 9 A 9 B and 10 B. Cemetery: Thiepval Memorial in France. I include him for your reference as he is commemorated on the Great War Memorial in St Canice's Cathedral, Kilkenny. 'To the Glory of God and in loving memory of the following members of the Diocese of Ossory who gave their lives for their country in the Great War 1914-1918'.

Allen, John Irwin. Rank; Private. Regiment or Service: Household Cavalry and Cavalry of the line including the Yeomanry and Imperial Camel Corps. Unit; 2nd King Edward's Horse. Service Number; 2313. Date of death; 03/11/1918. Age at death; 27. Born; King's Lyn, Norfork. Enlisted; Tooting, London. Died at home. Son of John and Frances C. Allen, of 100, Upper Tooting Rd., London. Grave or Memorial Reference; In the North East part. Cemetery: Kilkenny (St John) Church of Ireland Churchyard, Kilkenny.

Amery, James. Rank; Petty Officer. Regiment or Service: Royal Navy. Unit; (R. F. R. /Ch. /A/1116). H. M. Yacht "Kethailes.". Service Number; 129483. Date of death; 11/10/1917. Age at death;48. Born; Kilkenny. Husband of Rose Eliza Amery (born in Northampton), 39 Larches Lane, Wolverhampton. Grave or Memorial Reference; In the South West part. Cemetery: Llanaber (St Mary) Churchyard, Merionethshire.

Anderson, Edward Patrick. Rank; Private. Regiment or Service: King's Liverpool Regiment. Unit; 8th Battalion. Service Number; 307115. Date of death; 08/08/1916. Age at death; 36. Born; Melinavat,. County Kilkenny. Enlisted; Liverpoorl. Residence; Whitinsville, Mass, U. S. A. Killed in action. Grave or Memorial Reference; Pier and Face ID, 8B and 8C. Cemetery: Thiepval Memorial in France.

Aspell, Edward Patrick. Rank; Sergeant. Regiment or Service: Royal Irish Fusiliers. Unit; 8th Battalion. Service Number; 7396. Date of death; 10/08/1917. Born; Kilkenny. Enlisted; Kilkenny. Killed in action. Grave or Memorial Reference; Panel 42. Cemetery: Ypres (Menin Gate) Memorial in Belgium

Aylward, Edward. Rank; Sapper. Regiment or Service: Corps of Royal Engineers. Unit; Railways (263rd Railway Company.). Service Number; R/256524. Date of death; 13/04/1918. Age at death; 36. Born; Ballybricken, County Waterford. Enlisted; Waterford. Killed in action. Son of Thomas and Margaret Aylward, of 22, Southpark, Co. Kilkenny. Notes; Formerly he was with the Royal Irish Rifles where his number was 1676. Grave or Memorial Reference; On the West side. Cemetery: La Motte-Brebiere Communal Cemetery in France.

Aylward, Edward. Rank; Private. Regiment or Service: Irish Guards. Unit; 3rd Battalion. Service Number; 2255. Date of death; 28/10/1918. Born; Carlow, County Carlow. Enlisted; Dublin. Died at home. Grave or Memorial Reference; In the North East part. Cemetery: Coon Catholic Churchyard, County Kilkenny.

Aylward, Edward W. Rank; Private. Regiment or Service: Royal Dublin Fusiliers. Unit; 8th Battalion. Service Number; 23571. Date of death; 10/08/1917. Born; Thomastown, County Kilkenny. Enlisted; Kilkenny. Killed in action. Son of the late William and Elizabeth Aylward, of Thomastown, Co. Kilkenny. Grave or Memorial Reference; 1 F 52. Cemetery: Ypres Reservoir Cemetery in Belgium.

Aylward, William. Rank; Private. Regiment or Service: Royal Irish Regiment. Unit; 2nd Battalion. Service Number; 6186. Date of death; 19/10/1914. Born; Ballyhale, County Kilkenny. Enlisted; Waterford. Residence; Knocktopher. Killed in action. Kilkenny People, July, 1915. Death of a Gallant Leinster. Mrs Statia Aylward, Ballyhale, County Kilkenny, has been informed that her nephew, Private P. Ryan, of the 2nd Leinster Regiment, has been killed in action at the front. Deceased was a brave soldier and did service in India and had been 11 months in the firing line in the thick of all the heavy fighting and never received a wound till he was killed on the 6th June, near Hill 60. Kilkenny People, August, 1915. Ballyhale Soldier's Death. Mrs Statia Aylward, Ballyhale Cottages, Ballyhale, whose nephew, Private Patrick Ryan, of the 2nd Leinsters, was killed in action on the 6th June, has received letters of sympathy from his officers. Captain Louis Daly, B Company, 2nd Leinster Regiment, writes;--"Dear Mrs Aylward; Your nephew was the greatest loss to my Company and the regiment. He had been out since the start, never gave any trouble, was full of courage, and was in every way a wise, and excellent soldier. He was the type of a man who, given the opportunity, would earn distinction for himself and his Regiment, so it is mighty sad to have lost him. He was killed in action on June 6, at 9-30p. m., north of Ypres. A bullet got your nephew in the head, killing him instantly and painlessly, and to our great sorrow. He received Absolution with the rest of us in the evening. In any case he died for his country and doing his duty, so you need have no fear of his eternal salvation. No man can do more than to give his life for another, and he gave his for all of us. He is buried by a priest, Father Moloney, at La Brique, north of Ypres, and his grave is marked distinctly by a cross. In the course of another letter of sympathy, Lieutenant J. H. Monaghan, the officer commanding the deceased's platoon, said they all keenly felt his loss, as he,"was truly a gallant soldier who could be depended on to do his duty in an unflimching manner." Sergeant T. T. Geary, of the same regiment, on behalf of the N. C. O. 's and men, also extends his sympathy to Mrs Aylward, and says;-- "He died like an Irishman should, with his face to the enemy. I am glad to be able to tell you he was at Holy Communion the very day he was killed.". Grave or Memorial Reference; Panels 11 and 12. Cemetery: Le Touret Memorial in France.

Ayres, James Henry. Rank; Private. Regiment or Service: The Queen's (Royal West Surrey Regiment). Unit; 1st Battalion. Service Number; L/7915. Date of death; 27/08/1914. Age at death; 33. Born; Bow, Middlesex. Enlisted; Stratford, Middlesex. Residence; Hackney, Wick, Middlesex. Killed in action. Son of James and Elizabeth Ayres; husband of Sarah Emily Harvey (formerly Ayres, of "Benalla," Rowell Crescent, Kilkenny, South Australia. He is also listed in De Ruvigny's Roll of Honour with no new information or picture. Notes; Number listed as L/7915 (CWGC) 7915 (SDGW). Grave or Memorial Reference; I F 19. Cemetery: St Souplet British Cemetery in France.

B

Baker, Daniel. Rank; Munitions Worker. Regiment or Service: Munitions Factory in Wales. Date of death; 02/01/1917. Age at death;49. Born; Kilkenny. Died. Cemetery: Unknown

Bannan, James Charles. Rank; Private. Regiment or Service: Canadian Infantry (Alberta Regiment). Unit; 31st battalion. Service Number; 79897. Date of death; 06/11/1915. Age at death; 21. Son of Joseph Bannan of Jamesgreen, Kilkenny, Ireland. From de Ruvigny's Roll of Honour. son of Joseph Cope Bannan, of Kilkenny, Ireland. Ex-Sergeant, Royal Irish Constabulary, by his wife, Mary, daughter of Edward McElveny, ex-Inspector, M. D., Police. Born in Kilkenny, 24 February-1894. Educated at the Model National School there. Went to Canada, 10-March-1913, and after the outbreak of war enlisted at Calgary in October-1914. came over with the 2nd Canadian Contingent. Went to France 14-September-1915 and was shot by a sniper 06-November-1915. Irish Times. Bannan-November 6, 1915, killed in action in France, James Charles (Jim) 31st Battalion, 2nd Canadian Expeditionary Force, dearly loved youngest son of Joseph and Mary J Bannan, Kilkenny."Peace, perfect peace.". Notes; 79897 (CWGC) 79891 (Records). Grave or Memorial Reference; K 55. Cemetery: Kemmel Chateau Military Cemetery in Belgium. He is also commemorated on the Great War Memorial in St Canice's Cathedral, Kilkenny;-'To the Glory of God and in loving memory of the following members of the Diocese of Ossory who gave their lives for their country in the Great War 1914-1918'.

Bannon, Joseph. Rank; Private. Regiment or Service: Royal Irish Regiment. Unit; 4th Battalion. Service Number; 4483. Date of death; 12/12/1917. Age at death;22. Son of Michael Bannon, of Urlingford. Grave or Memorial Reference; Near the South West boundary. Cemetery: Urlingford Old Graveyard, County Kilkenny.

Barden / Burden, Thomas / Patrick. Rank; Private. Regiment or Service: Royal Irish Regiment. Unit; 2nd Battalion. Service Number; 4546. Date of death; 27/05/1915. Born; Thomastown, County Kilkenny. Enlisted; Thomastown. Residence; Moonteen, County Kilkenny. Died of wounds. Barden (CWGC, SDGW), Thomas Burden, Patrick (IMR). Barden, Patrick, (Kilkenny Journal). Kilkenny Journal, June, 1915. South Kilkenny Notes. Tribute to a Deceased Soldier. Addressing the congregation at 11 o'clock Mass in Thomastown church on Sunday, Rev. John O'Shea, C. C., asked their prayers for the repose of the soul of the late Private Patrick Barnes, a native of Moonteen, Thomastown, who died from the effects of gas poisoning while fighting with his regiment in France. Father O'Shea said he knew the deceased soldier very well, and he was a fine upright, decent young man. He had fallen a victim to the inhuman methods employed by the German forces in the present terrible war. Kilkenny People, June, 1915. Thomastown Soldier Gas Poisoned. Information was received from the War Office on Wednesday last by the relatives of Private Patrick Barnes, of the Royal Irish regiment, announcing his death from gas poisoning in France. The deceased soldier was about 21 years of age, and previous to rejoining his regiment was a popular and prominent member of the Thomastown Volunteers. He was a native of Moonteen, Thomastown, and was an only son. Much sympathy is felt for his mother in her sorrow. There is no Patrick Barnes or Patrick Burden in the 1911 Census for Kilkenny. There is a Thomas Barden in the Census and this man may be the same Thomas Barden listed above, as the date of death and type of death are the same. There is not a single instance of a Patrick Barnes dying in ww1 in any of the War Dead Databases for Australia, New Zealand, Canada, South Africa, India or the USA. There is one instance of a Thomas Leslie Barden dying in 1916, but this is a year out and he was from London. Grave or Memorial Reference; II A 7. Cemetery: Hazebrouck Communal Cemetery, Nord, in France.

Barnes, Henry. Rank; Fireman. Regiment or Service: Mercantile Marine. Unit; Ship;S. S."Ivernia" (Liverpool). Date of death; 01/01/1917. Age at death;36. Son of the late Henry Barnes, and Margaret Barnes, of Cloghssegg, Thomastown, Co. Kilkenny; husband of the late Kate Barnes. Born in Co. Tipperary. Cemetery: Tower Hill Memorial, London.

Barron, John. Rank; Private. Regiment or Service: Black Watch (Royal Highlanders). Unit; 4th Battalion. Service Number; 201364. Date of death; 03/09/1916. Born; Craigmannan, County Kilkenny. Enlisted; Dundee. Killed in action. Grave or Memorial Reference; Pier and Face 10 A. Cemetery: Thiepval Memorial in France.

Barron, William. Rank; Gunner. Regiment or Service: Royal Garrison Artillery. Unit; 38th Siege Battery. Service Number; 38573. Date of death; 17/07/1917. Age at death;24. Born; Ballyellen, County Carlow. Enlisted; Carlow. Died of wounds. Son of Mrs. James Barron, of Ballyellin, Goresbridge, County Kilkenny. Grave or Memorial Reference; In the North West corner. Cemetery: Ballyellin Cemetery, County Carlow. Also listed under Borris/Ballyellin on the Great War Memorial, Milford Street, Leighlinbridge, County Carlow.

Barry, John. Rank; Private. Regiment or Service: Royal Irish Regiment. Unit; 6th Battalion. Service Number; 2534. Date of death; 26/06/1916. Born; The Butts, Kilkenny. Enlisted; Kilkenny. Killed in action. Grave or Memorial Reference; I G 12. Cemetery: Dud Corner Cemetery, Loos in France.

Barry, William. Rank; Sergeant. Regiment or Service: Royal Irish Regiment. Unit; A Company, 2nd Battalion. Service Number; 2523. Date of death; 19/10/1914. Age at death;34. Born; St Canice's, Kilkenny. Enlisted; Tipperary. Residence; Kilkenny. Killed in action. Son of Patrick and Mary Barry (nee Fooley), of Butts Cross, Kilkenny; husband of Margaret Barry, of 11, Lord Edward St., Kilkenny. Grave or Memorial Reference; Panel 11 and 12. Cemetery: Le Touret Memorial in France.

RÉPUBLIQUE FRANÇAISE

ARRONDISSEMENT
de
BOULOGNE-sur-MER

ACTE Nº ....

NATIONALITÉ

.Anglaise.

EXTRAIT DU REGISTRE AUX ACTES DE DÉCÈS
de la Ville de CALAIS pour l'Année 1919

Le six février mil neuf cent dix neuf, trente cinq minutes
du matin en l'hopital général anglais numéro trente est
décédé C.BARTHOLOMEW , agé de vingt cinq ans, caporal au
deuxième "Dragoon guards" "C. squadron" de l'armée britanni-
que, numéro matricule deux mille six cent quarante et un,
domicilié à Kilkenny (Irlande) (sans autres renseignements)
Dressé le douze février mil neuf cent dix neuf, neuf heures
quarante minutes du matin sur la déclaration de Paul Lacogne,
trente ans, soldat interprête à l'armée anglaise, et de Vic
tor Poiret, cinquante deux ans, employé, domiciliés à Calais
Lesquels lecture faite ont signé avec Nous Henri, Charles,
Ravisse, adjoint au Maire de Calais, Officier de l'État Civil
par délégation

Suivent les signatures

Pour expédition certifiée conforme au registre et délivrée sur papier libre
pour renseignement administratif.

Calais, le ..six février..... mil neuf cent..... dix neuf..

Le Maire,

A.T. Calais

Bartholomew, Charles Frederick. Rank; Corporal. Regiment or Service: 2nd Dragoon Guards (Queen's Bays). Unit; C Squadron. Service Number; 2641. Date of death; 10/02/1919. Age at death; 25. Son of Sergeant. Maj. C. F. Bartholomew (late 3rd Battalion. Royal Sussex Regt) and Mrs. Mary Bartholomew, of Thomas St., Kilkenny. Grave or Memorial Reference; VIII C 2A. Cemetery: Les Baraques Military Cemetery, Sangatte in France.

Bateman, Fred/Frederick. Rank; Lance Corporal. Regiment or Service: Royal Welsh Fusiliers. Unit; 2nd Battalion. Service Number; 25719. Date of death; 26/10/1916. Age at death;19. Son of William and Margaret Bateman, of Green St., Kilkenny. Grave or Memorial Reference; II B 27. Cemetery: Grove Town Cemetery, Meaulte, France

Beehan, John. Rank; Private. Regiment or Service: Royal Irish Regiment. Unit; D Company, 2nd Battalion. Service Number; 4459. Date of death; 14/05/1915. Age at death; 20. Born; Urlingford. Enlisted; Johnstown, County Kilkenny. Residence; Urlingford. Killed in action. Son of Richard and Margaret Beehan, of Main St, Urlingford, Co. Kilkenny. Mobilized Aug., 1914, went to France Oct., 1914. Grave or Memorial Reference; Panel 33. Cemetery: Ypres (Menin Gate) Memorial in Belgium.

Bell, Charles Frederick James. Rank; Private. Regiment or Service: Royal Dublin Fusiliers. Unit; 7th Battalion. Service Number; 14162. Date of death; 16/08/1915. Born; Kilkenny. Enlisted; Dublin. Killed in Action in Gallipoli. Irish Independent; Mr C F J Bell, of the "Pals" Battalion of the Dublin Fusiliers, who has been killed in Gallipoli, was the younger son of the late Mr J Bell, Effra Road, Rathmines. Grave or Memorial Reference; Panel 190 to. Cemetery: Helles Memorial in Turkey.

Bellew, Richard Courtenay. Rank; Second Lieutenant. Regiment or Service: Irish Guards. Unit; 2nd Battalion. Date of death; 21/08/1917. Age at death; 19. Died of wounds. Son of the Hon. Richard and Mrs. Bellew, of Mt. Firoda Castlecomer. Ireland. Grave or Memorial Reference; IV G 1. Cemetery: Dozinghem Military Cemetery in Belgium.

Bennett, Thomas. Rank; Sergeant. Regiment or Service: Royal Irish Regiment. Unit; 1st Battalion. Service Number; 4047. Date of death; 13/07/1916. Born; St Mary's, Kilkenny. Enlisted; Kilkenny. Died in Salonika. Husband of Mary Bennett, of Knoppogue, Ballyduff, Co. Kerry. In his Will, dated 18-February1915, his effects and property were received by;- (Wife) Mrs Mary Bennett, Convent Street, Listowel, County Kerry, Ireland. Grave or Memorial Reference; 1375. Cemetery: Mikra British Cemetery, Kalamaria in Greece.

Image courtesy of Mary McEnery, Callan.

Bergin, Andrew. Rank; Sergeant. Regiment or Service: Machine Gun Corps. Unit; 90th Infantry. Service Number; 11383. Date of death; 14/10/1916. Born; Dunnamaggan County Kilkenny. Enlisted; Kilkenny. Killed in action. In his Will, dated 11-August-1916, his effects and property were received by;- (Sister) Miss Mary Bergin, Ballytobin, Callan, County Kilkenny, Ireland. Notes; Number listed as 11383. Formerly he was with the Royal Irish Rifles where his number was 4634. Grave or Memorial Reference; Pier and Face 5 C and 12C. Cemetery: Thiepval Memorial in France.

Bergin, James. Rank; Gunner. Regiment or Service: Royal Garrison Artillery. Unit; 266th Battery. Service Number; 78862. Date of death; 15/08/1917. Born; St Patrick's. Kilkenny. Enlisted; Kilkenny. Died of wounds. Grave or Memorial Reference; I B I. Cemetery: Duhallow A. D. S. Cemetery in Belgium

Bergin, John. Rank; Corporal. Regiment or Service: Royal Irish Regiment. Unit; 1st Battalion. Service Number; 3443. Date of death; 15/03/1915. Born; Callan, County Kilkenny. Enlisted; Tipperary. Residence; Callan. Killed in action. After his death his effects and property were received by;- (Wife) Mrs B Bergin, Haggards Green, Callan. Grave or Memorial Reference; Panel 44. Cemetery: Ypres (Menin Gate) Memorial in Belgium.

Bergin, John. Rank; Private. Regiment or Service: Leinster Regiment. Unit; 1st Battalion. Service Number; 8625. Date of death; 12/05/1915. Born; Kilkenny. Enlisted; Maryborough. Killed in action. Kilkenny Journal, October, 1915. Five Sons With the Colours. Mr John Bergin, Callan, has already given five sons to the fighting line. One son, John, was killed in France last March; William, Michael and Patrick have been to the front already, and James, who was drill instructor to the Inistioge I. N. V., has lately volunteered. Mr Bergin has also a son-in-law, James Hogan in the trenches. After his death his effects and property were received by;- (Brother) Mr Joseph Bergin, Cuffabara, Ballacollea, Queens County, Ireland. Grave or Memorial Reference; Panel 33. Cemetery: Ypres (Menin Gate) Memorial in Belgium.

Bergin, Patrick. Rank; Sergeant. Regiment or Service: Royal Irish Regiment. Unit; 2nd Battalion. Service Number; 4019. Date of death; 03/04/1918. Age at death; 26. Born; Kilkenny. Enlisted; Kilkenny. Residence; Callan. Died of wounds. Husband of Bridget Bergin, of 9, Green View, Green Lane, Callan, Co. Kilkenny. In his Will, dated 17-June-1917, his effects and property were received by;- (Wife) Mrs Bridget Bergin, Green St Callan, Kilkenny. Grave or Memorial Reference; I A 32. Cemetery: Le Cateau Military Cemetery in France.

Lieutenant Bernard, from De Ruvigny's Roll of Honour.

Bernard, Robert. Rank; Lieutenant. Regiment or Service: Royal Dublin Fusiliers. Unit; 1st Battalion. Date of death; 25/04/1915. Killed in action. Son of the Most Rev. and Rt. Hon. J. H. Bernard, D. D., and Maud, his wife, of Provost's House, Trinity College, Dublin. Educated at Marlborough College and Sandhurst. From De Ruvigny's Roll of Honour;-…2nd son of the Most Reverend John henry Bernard, D. D., D. C. L., Lord Archbishop of Dublin, by his wife, Maud, 2nd daughter of the late Robert Bernard, M. D., R. N., Inspector General of Hospitals and Fleets. Born in Dublin 20-December-1891. Educated at Arnold House, Llandulas, Marlborough College (where he was in the O. T. C.) and Sandhurst. Gazetted 2nd Lieutenant, Dublin Fusiliers 13-March-1912, and promoted Lieutenant 12-November-1913. He served in the 2nd Battalion at Gravesend, April to August-1912, and then joined the 1st Battalion in India, serving with them at Ahmednagar and Madras to November-1914, when the regiment returned home, afterwards proceeding to the Dardanelles. Lieutenant Bernard landed in one of then open boats on Sunday 25-April-1915, when many officers were killed and wounded. His Captain was wounded in the landing, so that he was left in command of his company for twenty-four hours, when they lay out under slight cover on "V" beach. The next morning the Dublin's and the Munster's were ordered to storm the village of Sedd-el-Bahr, which thet successfully accomplished. Lieutenant Bernard was killed when gallantly leading his men in a bayonet charge. Lieutenants Bernard and Andrews were together with about 20 men of the X and Y companies, and they took cover behind a wall five and a half feet high. They were being fired at from a house in the village. Andrews stood in a gap made by a shell and was directing the fire when he was killed. Lieutenant Bernard then called on the others to follow him, and saying "Come on, boys," he dashed through the gap, when he was shot dead by a Turkish rifleman. He and his brother officers were buried close to the beach in a large rectangular grave. Carlow Sentinel, May, 1915. Lieutenant Robert Bernard. The casualties announced on Monday include the name of Lieutenant Robert Bernard, younger son of the Bishop of Ossory, Ferns and Leighlin, and Mrs Bernard, the Palace, Kilkenny, who was killed in action on Sunday, 25th April. He was born 21st, December, 1891, and was gazetted from Sandhurst Second Lieutenant, Royal Dublin Fusiliers in March, 1912, and promoted Lieutenant November, 1913. On Sunday last, previous to the 11. 30 o'clock Service in St Canice's Cathedral, a muffled peal was rung by the members of the Change Ringers Society as a mark of respect to the memory of the deceased. Kilkenny People, May, 1915. The Late Lieutenant Robert Bernard. At a meeting of the County Kilkenny Relief Committee held in the Assembly Room, City Hall, on Monday last, the Mayor, Mt John Magennis, P. L. G., who resided, proposed the following resolution;-- "That we, the members of the Co. Kilkenny Relief Committee, respectfully tender to His Lordship the Right Rev Dr. Bernarg, Bishop of Ossory, and esteemed member of this committee, and expression of our sincere condolence and sympathy in the great loss he has sustained by the death of his gallant son, Lieutenant Robert Bernard, who nobly fell in action in the Dardanelles, and that this meeting be adjourned as a mark of respect." Very Rev. Dean Barry, D. D. P. P., V. F., Ballyragget, seconded the resolution which was passed in silence. From 'Our Heroes'. younger son of the Archbishop of Dublin, and Maud his wife, was born in Dublin, 21st December-1891. Educated at Arnold House, Landulas, and at Marlborough College, where he was a member of the O. T. C. Entered Sandhurst, January-1911. Gazetted to the 1st Battalion, Royal Dublin Fusiliers, March-1912. Promoted Lieutenant, November-1913. Served from October-1912 to November-1914, with his battalion in India. Killed in action, 26th-April-1915, at Sedd-el-Bahr, the day after the Dublin Fusiliers effected a landing at the extreme point of the Gallipoli Peninsula whilst gallantly leading his men. Irish Independent; Lieutenant Bernard's death, which we have already announced, has caused deep regret in Kilkenny, and a resolution of sympathy with his father, the Rt Rev. Dr Bernard, was passed at a meeting of the Kilkenny Charitable and Benevolent Societies, on the motion of Ald. M L Potter, J. P., and seconded by the Rev. J Carroll, C. C., St Canice's. Grave or Memorial Reference; Special Memorial A 26. Cemetery: V. Beach Cemetery in Turkey. He is also commemorated on the Great War Memorial in St Canice's Cathedral, Kilkenny…'To the Glory of God and in loving memory of the following members of the Diocese of Ossory who gave their lives for their country in the Great War 1914-1918'.

Blanchfield, Michael. Rank; Private. Regiment or Service: Royal Irish Regiment. Unit; 7th/8th Battalion. Service Number; 16504. Date of death; 17/08/1917. Age at death; 23. Born; Kilkenny. Enlisted; Kilkenny. Killed in action. Son of John and Annie Blanchfield, of Lord Edward St., Kilkenny. After his death his effects and property were received by;- (Mother) Mrs A Blanchfield, Lord Edward St, Kilkenny. Notes; Number listed as 16504 Formerly he was with the Royal Irish Regiment where his number was 1827. Grave or Memorial Reference; 4 XI D 26. Cemetery: Bedford House Cemetery in Belgium.

Bolger, Michael. Rank; Sergeant. Regiment or Service: Royal Irish Regiment. Unit; 6th Battalion. Service Number; 8183. Date of death; 12/08/1917. Born; Clough. County Kilkenny. Enlisted; Dublin. Died of wounds. In his Will, dated 01-June1917, his effects and property were received by his wife. Limerick Chronicle, May, 1917. Bolger ands Kelly—May 15, 1917, at St Mary's, Haddington Road, Dublin, by the Rev Father McGough, Sergeant M J Bolger, Royal Irish Regiment, third son of Patrick

Bolger, Charlesworth, Castlecomer, County Kilkenny, to May, fourth daughter of M J Kelly, 55 Beach Hill, Haddington Road, Dublin. Grave or Memorial Reference; IV E 9. Cemetery: Mendingham Military Cemetery in Belgium.

Bolger, Nicholas. Rank; Private. Regiment or Service: Royal Inniskilling Fusiliers. Unit; 7th Battalion. Service Number; 43187. Date of death; 09/10/1916. Age at death; 24. Born; Kilkenny. Enlisted; Kilkenny. Killed in action. Son of Bridget Bolger, of Bodal, Cuffe's Grange, Co. Kilkenny. After his death his effects and property were received by;- (Mother) Bridget Bolger, Bodal, Cuffsgrange, County Kilkenny, Ireland. Notes; Formerly he was with the Connaught Rangers where his number was 5623. Grave or Memorial Reference; E 2. Cemetery: Kemmel Chateau Military Cemetery in Belgium.

Bolger, Pierce. Rank; Private. Regiment or Service: Machine Gun Corps. Unit; 89th Company. Service Number; 36402. Date of death; 12/10/1916. Born; Graiguenamanagh, County Kilkenny. Enlisted; Dublin. Residence; Graiguenamanagh, County ilkenny. Killed in action. Brother of William Bolger, of Tinnahinch East, Graiguenamanagh, Co. Kilkenny. Grave or Memorial Reference; Pier and Face 5 C and 12 C. Cemetery: Thiepval Memorial in France. Also listed under Palatine/Urglin on the Great War Memorial, Milford Street, Leighlinbridge, County Carlow.

Bolger, William. Rank; Private. Regiment or Service: Irish Guards. Unit; 1st Battalion. Service Number; 4412. Date of death; 06/11/1914. Born; Graiguenamanagh, County Kilkenny. Enlisted; Dublin. Killed in action. Son of Patrick and Mary Bolger, of The Quay, Graiguenamanagh, Co. Kilkenny. Kilkenny People, December, 1915. Killed in Action. The relatives of Private William Bolger, a native of Graigue-na-managh, have been officially notified of his death in action. The deceased soldier who was attached to the Irish Guards, left England for France with the first British Expeditionary Force in August, 1914. He took part in the battle of Mons and was reported missing on the 6th of October of last year. It has now been learned that he was killed at the battle of Ypres. Private Bolger was a prominent member of the Graigue Temperance Band and the members of that body have learned of his death with keen regret. Grave or Memorial Reference; Panel 11. Cemetery: Ypres (Menin Gate) Memorial in Belgium.

Bolton, Henry. Rank; Private. Regiment or Service: Royal Irsh Regiment. Unit; 2nd Battalion. Service Number; 123236. Formerly he was with the Royal Dublin Fusiliers where his number was 29096. Date of death; 13/11/1918. Born; Bagenalstown, County Carlow. Enlisted; Carlow. Residence; Bagenalstown, County Carlow. Died of wounds. After his death his effects and property were received by;- (Wife) Mrs H Bolton, Clowater, Gores Bridge, County Kilkenny, Ireland. Grave or Memorial Reference; I C 33. Cemetery: Valenciennes (St Roch) Communal Cemetery in France. Also listed under Bagenalstown/Fenagh on the Great War Memorial, Milford Street, Leighlinbridge, County Carlow.

Booth, William. Rank; Private. Regiment or Service: Royal Irish Regiment. Unit; 2nd Battalion. Service Number; 7830. Date of death; 14/07/1916. Born; Castlecomer, County Kilkenny. Enlisted; Castlecomer. Killed in action. Grave or Memorial Reference; Pier and Face 3 A. Cemetery: Thiepval Memorial in France. He is also commemorated on the Great War Memorial in St Canice's Cathedral, Kilkenny…'To the Glory of God and in loving memory of the following members of the Diocese of Ossory who gave their lives for their country in the Great War 1914-1918'.

Lieutenant Bor, from 'Our Heroes.'

Bor, Thomas Humphrey. Rank; Lieutenant. Regiment or Service: Royal Naval Reserve. Unit; H. M. Submarine E. 5. Date of death; 11/03/1916. Son of Edward N. C. Bor and Mabel Bor, of Kilcoran House, Callan, Co. Kilkenny. From;- 'Our Heroes. 'Lieutenant T. H. Bor, R. N. R., was drowned at sea whilst on active service, about Marhc 11th, 1916. he was the eldest son of Mr and Mrs Bor, Bank of Ireland, Maryborough, and was educated at Kilkenny College. He entered the Mercantile Marine when 14 years of age and secured his captain's certificate at 22. On the outbreak of the war he offered his services and obtained a Commission in the Royal Naval Reserve. From De Ruvigny's Roll of Honour…. eldest son of Edward Norman Cavendish Bor, of the Bank of Ireland, Maryborough, Queen's County, by his wife, Mabel, daughter of Isaac Thornton of Waterford, solicitor. Born Tramore, County Waterford, 12th Feb, 1892. Educated in Kilkenny College, entered the Mercantile marine age the age of 14, and received his captain's certificate at the age of 22. Offered his services after the outbreak of war and was gazetted Lieutenant, Royal Naval reserve in September, 1914. He was employed in the Submarine Service from that time, his depot ship being H. M. S. Maidstone, and was lost in action 5th or 6th of March, 1916. His Captain wrote on 25 March, 1916; "We only know that the boat should have returned before dark on the 11th, and has never arrived. The two possibilities are that she either struck a mine, or was rammed by one of the German ships that we know passed over her patrol station on the night of the 5th or 6th. Your son had been here almost since the outbreak of war, and had done excellent service, and he was always keen.". From The Leinster Express;- Death of Lieutnenat Bor. The large circle of friends and acquaintances of

Mr E. N. C. Bor, agent of the bank of Ireland, Maryborough, were grieved to learn that his eldest son, Lieutenant Thomas H. Bor, had lost his life in the service of his country while on naval duty. Lieutenant Bor was educated in Kilkenny College, from whence he passed into the mercantile marine service. The fact that he was granted a captain's certificate at 22 years of age is sufficient evidence of Lieutenant Bor's ability, and of his special aptitude for the profession he adopted. While in the mercantile service he travelled practically over the whole world, having visited China, Japan, South Africa, New Zealand, etc. At the outbreak of the war Lieutenant Bor volunteered his services, and subsequently he received a Commission in the Royal Naval Reserve. He was only a few weeks Second Lieutenant, promotion following quickly on his connection with the Royal Navy, and the rank of Lieutenant was conferred upon him. Lieutenant Bor was actively engaged in the naval warfare, chiefly in connection with the most dangerous section of it—the submarine—and while thus engaged it is not revealing any secret to realise that his craft was instrumental in sending some enemy ships to the bottom. That he was an expert gunner is also evidenced by the fact that he fired an air-craft gun which injured a Zeppelin. Lieutenant Bor was a young man whose life was upright and blameless. He was beloved by his parents and all who knew him, it is regrettable that his brilliant, bu all to brief career---one which promised such a bright and useful future—should be prematurely destroyed. But his case is unfortunately only one of thousands that are grieved for to-day. The utmost sympathy is felt for Lieutenant Bor's family in their great sorrow. A second son of Mr Bor's is on active service in the army. The following telegram has been received by Mr E. N. C. Bor, Maryborough;. The Waterford News, 1916. Lieutenant T. H. Bor. Lieutenant T. H. Borr, R. N. R., whose death on active service has been notified, was the son of Mr. E. N. C. Bor, Bank of Ireland, Maryborough. He received his early education at Kilkenny College, and at the age of 14 entered the Merchantile Marine, receiving his captain's certificate at 22. At the outbreak of hostilities he offered his services to his country, was accepted, and got a commission in the Royal Navy Reserve. The deceased officer gave promise of a brilliant career. Mr. Bor was for many years stationed in Waterford, and his many friends will, we are sure, with him in his bereavement. Carlow Sentinel, April, 1916. Lieutenant T. H. Bor. The death on active service at sea is announced of Lieutenant T. H. Bor, R. N. R. Lieutenant Bor, who was 24 years of age, was the eldest son of Mr E. N. C. Bor, Agent of the Bank of Ireland, Maryborough, and formerly of Kilkenny. His brother, Lieutenant N. L. Bor, is at present in France serving with the Connaught Rangers. Grave or Memorial Reference; 22. Cemetery: Plymouth Naval Memorial, UK

Bourke, J. Rank; Private. Regiment or Service: The King's Liverpool Regiment. Service Number; 102328. Date of death; 23/09/1919. Age at death; 38. Grave or Memorial Reference; In the East part. Cemetery: St Patrick's Graveyard, County Kilkenny.

Bourke, John. Rank; Private. Regiment or Service: Household Cavalry and Cavalry of the line including the Yeomanry and Imperial Camel Corps. Unit; 2nd Dragoon Guards (Queen's Bays) attached to the 1st Life Guards. Service Number; 6488. Date of death; 14/12/1914. Age at death;30. Born; Kilkenny. Enlisted; Kilkenny. Died. Bourke, (SDGW, IMR) Burke, (CWGC), Son of John and Mary Burke, of Killiney, Co. Dublin; husband of Mrs. E. Burke, of 4, Reas Cottages, Islandbridge, Dublin. Grave or Memorial Reference; I C 5A. Cemetery: Wimereux Communal Cemetery, Pas de Calais, France.

Bowe, James. Rank; Private. Regiment or Service: Princess Patricia's Canadian Light Infantry (Eastern Ontario Regiment). Service Number; 51077. Date of death; 04/05/1915. Age at death; 38. Born; Kilkenny. Occupation on enlistment, Labourer. Age on enlistment; 38 years 1 months. Date of birth;23-October-1876. Next of kin details; Jim Bowe, Napier, New Zealand. Place and date of enlistment, 20-November-1914, Quebec. Height, 5 feet, 9 ½ inches. Complexion, dark. Eyes, blue. Hair, dark. Previous military experience; 11 months with the Imperial Light Horse. Supplementary information: Brother of Mrs. M. A. Fitzpatrick, of Coolcashin House, Johnstown, Co. Kilkenny, Ireland. Grave or Memorial Reference; Panel 10. Cemetery: Ypres (Menin Gate) Memorial in Belgium.

Bowman, Albert Aldridge. Rank; Sergeant. Regiment or Service: Hampshire Regiment. Unit; 12th (Service) Battalion. Service Number; 15418. Date of death; 25/04/1917. Born; Kilkenny. Enlisted; Waterford. Killed in action in the Balkans. Cemetery: Doiran Memorial in Greece.

Boyd, John. Rank; Corporal. Regiment or Service: Army Cyclist Corps. Service Number; 816. Date of death; 16/11/1918. Age at death; 19. Born; Kilkenny. Died of pneumonia at King George 5th General Hospital. Son of P Boyd, Patrick Street, Kilkenny. Husband of Birdget Boyd. Grave or Memorial Reference; RC 584. Cemetery: Grangegorman Military Cemetery, Dublin.

Boyle, William. Rank; Private. Regiment or Service: Royal Irish Regiment. Unit; 2nd Battalion. Service Number; 8674. Date of death; 05/07/1916. Born; Butts, County Kilkenny. Enlisted; Kilkenny. Killed in action. Son of Mary Boyle, of 7, Green St., Kilkenny, and the late Michael Boyle. Grave or Memorial Reference; Pier and Face 3 A. Cemetery: Thiepval Memorial in France.

Boyle/Boyne, Thomas. Rank; Private. Regiment or Service: Connaught Rangers. Unit; 1st Battalion. Service Number; 9167. Date of death; 05/11/1914. Age at death; 23. Born; Kilkenny. Enlisted; Tipperary. Residence; Kilkenny. Killed in action. Boyle (SDGW) Boyne (CWGC, IMR), Thomas. Boyle, P (Kilkenny People) : Son of Kate Boyne, of Dean St., Kilkenny, and the late Michael Boyne. Kilkenny People, December 1914. Killed in Action. Mrs McGuire, who resides in Dean Street, received official notification on Sunday last that her son (by her first husband) P. Boyle, a private in the Irish Guards, had been killed in action. It was the Irish Guards who cheered John Redmond before going to the war, and it was the Irish Guards who sang "God Save Ireland" as they delivered their famous charge. Grave or Memorial Reference; III B 13. Cemetery: Aubers Ridge British Cemetery, Aubers, Nord, France.

Brady, Michael. Rank; Sergeant. Regiment or Service: Welsh Regiment. Unit; 9th Battalion. Service Number; 32992. Date of death; 02/11/1916. Age at death;34. Enlisted; Weston-Super-Mare. Residence; Dunkill, County Kilkenny. Killed in action. Son of the late Michael Barry and of Margaret O'Shea, of Warrington, Kilkenny. Grave or Memorial Reference; XVII A 1. Cemetery: Mill Road Cemetery, Thiepval, Nord, France.

Brawders, Richard. Rank; Private. Regiment or Service: Canadian Machine Gun Corps. Unit; 2nd Battalion. Service Number; 428182. Date of death; 15/11/1917. Age at death; 26. Awarded the Military Medal and is listed in the London Gazette. Data from attestation papers;- What is your name?.... Richard Brawders. In what Town, Township or Parish, and in what Country were you born?....... Luffany, Kilkenny, Isle, Ire (sic). What is the name of your next of kin?....... (brother) Malcolm, Brawders. What is the address of your next of kin?....... 22 Phillips Street, Salem, Mass. What is the date of your birth?....... July-3-1893. What is your trade or calling?....... Labourer. Are you married?....... No. Are you willing to be vaccinated or re-vaccinated and inoculated?....... Yes. Do you now belong to the Active Militia?....... Yes, 11th I. F. Do you understand the nature and terms of your engagement?....... Yes. Are you willing to be attested to serve in the Canadian Over-Seas Expeditionary Force?....... engagement?....... Yes. Apparent age.... 22 years.... 9 months......Height.........5 Ft.... 6 ¾ Ins. Girth when fully expanded.... 40 Ins. Range of expansion......4 Ins. Complexion.........medium. Eyes....... grey. Hair.........light. Distinctive marks....... four vaccination marks on left arm. Date............... 20-March-1915. Son of John and Mary Brawders. Native of Mooncoin, Waterford, Ireland. Grave or Memorial Reference; XII B 16. Cemetery: Dozinghem Military Cemetery in Belgium.

Breen, Richard. Rank; Lance Corporal/Private. Regiment or Service: Royal Irish Regiment. Unit; 7th Battalion (South Irish Horse). Service Number; 7804. Date of death; 28/03/1918. Born; St Mary's, Kilkenny. Enlisted; Kilkenny. Died of wounds. In his Will, dated 01-August-1915, his effects and property were received by;- (Mother) Mrs Maryann Breen, Abbey St, Kilkenny, Ireland. Grave or Memorial Reference; Panel 30 and 31. Cemetery: Pozieres Memorial in France.

Breen, Thomas P. Rank; Private. Regiment or Service: South African Infantry. Unit; 3rd Regiment. Service Number; 3289. Date of death; 26/02/1916. Born;. Kilkenny People, March, 1916. A Brave Fallen Soldier, --The mother of the late Private T Breen, 3rd Battalion, South African Infantry regiment, who was killed in action in Egypt, has received a letter from Captain John Jackson, offering her the sympathy of the officers and men of the deceased's Company on her bereavement."We feel the loss of your son very much," he writes," for he was always cheerful no matter how irksome the duties may have been. The only satisfaction one has is that he fell in action. Our Company had a hard task before it, but I may say nothing would have stayed the attack. Our chief regret is that we lost so many of our brave men during the advance. Your son fell shortly after the advance commenced and just close to where I was.," Private Breen, we may mention, was a native of Kilkenny, and having been through the German West African campaign visited his mother s few months ago. Grave or Memorial Reference; B 157. Cemetery: Alexandria (Hadra) War memorial Cemetery in Egypt.

Brennan, Edward. Rank; Private. Regiment or Service: Leinster Regiment. Unit; 2nd Battalion. Service Number; 8380. Date of death; 09/06/1916. Age at death;30. Born; Castlecomer, County Kilkenny. Enlisted; Maryborough. Killed in action. Son of Edward and Elizabeth Brennan. Grave or Memorial Reference; II B 13. Cemetery: Ration Farm (La Plus Douve) Annexe in Belgium.

Brennan, Edward. Rank; Private. Regiment or Service: Australian Infantry A. I. F. Unit; 17th Battalion. Service Number; 7129. Date of death; 14/05/1918. Age at death; 31. Son of Martin McKeon Brennan and Catherine McKeon Brennan, of Moneenroe, Castlecomer, Co. Kilkenny, Ireland. Born, Castle Comer, Ireland. Occupation on enlistment, labourer. Age on enlistment; 29 years 5 months. Date of birth;27-March-1888. Next of kin details; (father) Mr Martin McKeon Brennan, Castle Comer, County Kilkenny, Ireland. Later changed to (widowed mother) Mrs C McKeon Brennan, Moneenroe, Castle Comer, County Kilkenny. Place and date of enlistment, 05-August-1917. Sydney. Weight, 11st 12 lbs. Height, 5 feet, 6 ¼ inches. Complexion, medium. Eyes, brown. Hair, brown. Grave or Memorial Reference; II D 5. Cemetery: Villers-Bretonneux Military Cemetery in France.

Brennan, James. Rank; Private. Regiment or Service: Royal Irish Regiment. Unit; 2nd Battalion. Service Number; 3565. Date of death; 06/11/1918. Born; Ballyhale, County Kilkenny. Enlisted; Tipperary. Residence; Ballyhale, County Kilkenny. Died of wounds. He won the Military Medal and is listed in the London Gazette. In his Will, dated May-1917, his effects and property were received by;- (Mother) Mrs Catherine Brennan, Ballyhale, County Kilkenny. Grave or Memorial Reference; I B 20. Cemetery: St Symphorien Military Cemetery in Belgium

Brennan, John. Rank; Private. Regiment or Service: Royal Irish Regiment. Unit; 2nd Battalion. Service Number; 8116. Date of death; 21/10/1914. Age at death; 35. Born; Kilmanagh, County Kilkenny. Residence; Callan. Killed in action. Son of Thomas and Catherine Brennan, of Ballintaggart, Callan; husband of Statia Brennan, of Ballintaggart, Callan, Co. Kilkenny. Grave or Memorial Reference; Panel 11 and 12. Cemetery: Le Touret Memorial In France.

Brennan, John. Rank; Corporal. Regiment or Service: Royal Irish Regiment. Unit; 3rd Battalion. Service Number; 9952. Date of death; 24/04/1916. Born; Gowran, County Kilkenny. Enlisted; Kilkenny. Killed in action at home. Son of Mrs. Mary Maddock, of Ballinaboola, Gowran, Co. Kilkenny. Born in Gowran, County Kilkenny. News, May, 1916. Amongst the list of casualties in the Royal Irish Regiment in connection with the Dublin rebellion…. The other names include;- Royal Irish Regiment, 992, Corporal J. Brennan, Gowran,. Grave or Memorial Reference; RC 722. Cemetery: Grangegorman Military Cemetery on Blackhorse Avenue outside the North-East boundary of Phoenix Park in Dublin.

Brennan, John. Rank; Lance Sergeant. Regiment or Service: Irish Guards. Unit; 1st Battalion. Service Number; 7476. Date of death; 27/04/1918. Born; Kilkenny. Enlisted; Kilkenny. Died of wounds. Grave or Memorial Reference; I B 32. Cemetery: Ebblinghem Military Cemetery in France.

Brennan, Joseph. Rank; Private. Regiment or Service: Australian Infantry A. I. F. Unit; 9th Battalion. Service Number; 1312. Date of death; 04/06/1915. Born; Kilkenny, Ireland. Died of wounds. Occupation on enlistment, Labourer. Age on enlistment; 20 years 3 months. Apprenticiship; 2 years, Butcher. Next of kin details; (mother) Mary Brennan, High Street, Kilkenny. Place and date of enlistment, 09-December-1914, Brisbane, Queensland. Weight, 145 lbs. Height, 5 feet, 6 ½ inches. Complexion, fair. Eyes, blue. Hair, light. His mother received a pension of £2 per fortnight from 04-September-1915. The newspaper following below is written by his brother Thomas who survived the war. Kilkenny People, June, 1915."No Fear of Death." Young Kilkenny Soldier's Splendid Letter. The following fine letter was been received by Mrs Brennan, newsagent, High Street, Kilkenny, from her son Tom, who is now with the Australian forces in Egypt."Joe," referred to in the letter is in the 9th Australian Infantry and was wounded in the Dardanelles. Both young men had been some years living in Australia. They are splendidly educated, and occupied excellent positions; but they relinquished everything—positions and prospects—to take a hand in the Great Adventure. It may be added that the third, and only other, son of Mrs Brennan is in the Cadet Corps of the Royal Irish regiment, and is at present training at Kilbride Camp;--8th June, 1915. My Dearest Mother—Excuse rough species of notepaper, as the commodity is priceless at present with me. I have now been weeks in the actual din of battle, and shall never compose lyrics to heroes any more—heroism is, after all, such a commonplace thing with the soldiers I have daily been communing with. I am in the best of health, dining sumptuously, living in a dugout worthy of the most scrutative "Red Eye" of leave days, and have had the pleasure of counting numerous shrapnel holes in my blankets, overcoat and various other articles of clothing without experiencing any corresponding cavities in my worthy hide. In fact, I look back on the past few weeks in this land of sunshine and classical antiquity as amongst the most pleasant I have ever spent, and certainly—what with bathing under shrapnel and cooking the daily repast on the empty shell cases of the monster—it is a most novel and delightful life. Joe took part in the glorious landing, and also in the biggest assault on our lines since, but was a victim to a shrapnel splinter and had two fingers fractured. He is away in hospital, and it is worthy of this bloodthirsty youngster that his great regret was that they couldn't keep him there to finish a few more of the heathens. For myself you may be easy in mind. I have been to Confession, and am fully ready for anything, and my only prayer is that I may do worthily what God chooses me for, and I have no fear for the pain or death it may entail. I have had a few narrow escapes. But was not abashed, as I knew my time had not come. If you can I would be glad if you would send a few papers, and also write often. Sincerest love to all, and especially to yourself. Your fond son. Tom Brennan. 3rd Reinforcement. 2nd Light Horse Field Ambulance. Australian A. M. C. Kilkenny People, September, 1915. Young Kilkenny Soldier Dies of Wounds. We regret to announce the death on July 4th, at the Hospital, Alexandria, from wounds received in action in the Dardanelles on may 19th, of Joseph Francis Brennan, third son of the Late Mr John Brennan and Mrs Brennan, newsagent and stationer, High Street, and grandson of the late Mr John Brennan, Watergate. He was a fine type of young Irishman, just 20 years of age. He and his brother Thomas emigrated to Australia some years ago, and both of them, being well educated and clever, occupied excellent positions in the Commonwealth. When the war broke out they joined the Australian Imperial Forces, and the deceased was serving with the 9th Infantry, 3rd Brigade. A third brother, who had been assisting his mother in the business in which she is engaged, volunteered some months ago, and is now at the front. We desire to tender to Mrs Brennan our deepest sympathy in her great bereavement. Kilkenny Journal, September, 1915. Kilkenny Soldier's Death. The news of the death of Mr Joseph F. Brennan, third son of Mrs Brennan, High Street, and grandson of the late Mr John Brennan, Watergate, will be received with much regret in Kilkenny city and county. Deceased, who was only twenty years of age, was attached to the 9th battalion, 3rd Brigade of the Australian Imperial Infantry. He was one of the first Australian contingent dispatched to the Dardanelles, having arrived there on the 25th April last. Shortly after the landing he was wounded in the hand and forehead by shrapnel, on May 19th, and died in Alexandria Hospital on the 11th July. Mrs Brennan has two other sons at the front, and an interesting letter from her son Thomas, who is attached to the A. M. C. is published in another column. We tender to her our deep sympathy in her sad bereavement. Kilkenny Journal, September, 1915. Deaths. Brennan. —On the 4th July, at the Hospital, Alexandria, Egypt, from wounds received in action at the Dardanelles on May 19th, Joseph Francis Brennan, 9th battalion, 3rd Brigade, Australian Imperial Infantry; third son of the late John Brennan, and Mrs Brennan, High Street, and grandson of the late John Brenan, Watergate. —R. I. P. From "The Argus" (Melbourne), 1915. Our Nameless Dead. (To those of our comrades who perished in the early stages of the fighting in the Dardanelles, and who, through decomposition and the pilferage of identification discs by enemy snipers, were unrecognisable, and were buried "nameless" on the hillside behind the trenchline where these lines were written). Comrade of Knapsack or bandolier. Tread light, we pray, when you pass this way, For sake of the brave ones slumbering here. Nameless in death to the Judgement Day. Tread light lest the tramp of your martial host, Or the rattle of rifle or bayonet-blade, Should ring down the night to their silent post, And rouse them too soon for the Grand Parade. Close-buried they lie, yet they perished lone, And Death scattered them wide on the war-torn track, And we found them far out, in their Fate, unknown, And rev'rent and sadly we brought them back. And we laid them to rest on this lonely slope. With the sward they had won for their funeral-pall, 'Neath the star-hung beacons of Faith and hope, While the night-wind whispered its sentry-call. And we fashioned a slab for each sacred tomb, And in rough-hewn letters their Tale engraved, While in grim salute came the far-in boom, Of the guns whose pathway their lives had paved, And we hollowed a space in the solemn stone, For the names they'd gloried, which none could tell, Save God, to whose Silence their souls had flown, And the cold earth which guarded His secret well. And we banished a tear as the final sod, Of the last sad sepulchre sank hone, For the anguished cries to a silent God, Of the dear ones left in the years to come—Of the mothers waiting in homes so vain, In the homes made lonely far o'er the sea, Where they'd list for the "step at the door again," And the fond embrace that could never be. And we wondered the while—when on History's page, With heroes' life-blood, their country's fame, Was lettered in fire, for each future age, To kindle ever in quenchless flame—What honoured place in that glorious tale, With their Nation's patriot dead would share, The comrades brave which Death's solemn veil, Left nameless, asleep in the silence there. 31-8-'15."Brentomnan." (The writer of the above fine verses, Mr T. Brennan, is in the Australian Medical Corps, attached to the Australian Light Horse in the Dardanelles. His brother, Mr Joseph Brennan, recently died in Alexandria from wounds received while taking part, with the Australian forces, in the fighting in the Peninsula. A third brother, Mr Anthony Brennan, is in the trenches in France, having joined the Royal

Irish Regiment some months ago. The three brothers are sons of Mrs Brennan, stationer and newsagent, Kilkenny. Thomas and Anthony Brennan survived the war. Kilkenny Journal, October, 1915. (Article below is a brother of Joseph Brennan in the Australian Army. Author). The Boy Soldier. A Singular Irish Example. Writing in the "Daily Mail" on "The Scandal of the Boy Soldier," Mr G. C. Curnock, hon, secretary of the National Service Organisation, cites the case of Private A. Brennan, son of Mrs M Brennan, High Street, Kilkenny, who joined the Army in Ireland in July, being then only aged 17 years and two months. The lad's mother stated that she was advised by the recruiting officer to give him "three months of it," as,"under no condition should he be sent to the front under nineteen," and the officer said he would alter the age on the form. When Brennan was ordered to the front, his mother forwarded his birth certificate to the Commanding Officer at Richmond Barracks, Dublin, who returned it saying that the boy had gone to France. In a letter to Mr P. O'Brien, M. P., Mr Tennant observes that it is contrary to the King's Regulations to alter the age on an attestation form, and regretted that the boy could not be discharged, adding however, that the Field-Marshal Commanding-in-Chief "is sending back all men who, in his opinion, are unable to stand the strain of active service."In a subsequent letter Mr Tennant said; "The question is one both of age and of the place where the soldier is serving," discharge being only claimable "for the solder serving in this country."But," he said,"apart from that, Private Brennan is ruled out by age." In Mr Curnock's opinion "Mr Tennant's reply is a mockery of justice," since,"if a boy was not fit to serve at 17 in this country, how can he be considered fit to face death in France or the Dardanelles.". Notes; Died of wounds (bullet wounds to the forehead and finger) received in action at the Egyptian Government Hospital, Alexandria. Grave or Memorial Reference; E 178. Cemetery: Alexandria (Chatby) Military and War Memorial Cemetery in Egypt.

Brennan, Nicholas. Rank; Lance Corporal. Regiment or Service: Irish Guards. Unit; 1st Battalion. Service Number; 8836. Date of death; 03/08/1917. Born; Liverpool. Enlisted; Liverpoorl. Residence; Cuffs Grange, County Kilkenny. Killed in action. Grave or Memorial Reference; IV A 17. Cemetery: Artillery Wood Cemetery in Belgium.

Brennan, Patrick. Rank; Sergeant. Regiment or Service: Leinster Regiment. Unit; 1st Battalion. Service Number; 2213. Date of death; 12/03/1915. Age at death;50. Born; Castlecomer, County Kilkenny. Enlisted; Heath Camp. Killed in action. Son of the late Mr. and Mrs. Patrick Brennan; husband of Mary Dooling (formerly Brennan), of Mooneerol, Castlecomer, Co. Kilkenny. In his Will, dated 01-January-1915, his effects and property were received by;- Miss Mollie Callaghan, Massford, Castlecomer, County Kilkenny, Ireland. Grave or Memorial Reference; Panel 44. Cemetery: Ypres (Menin Gate) Memorial in Belgium.

Brennan, Patrick. Rank; Private. Regiment or Service: Northumberland Fusiliers. Unit; 9th Battalion. Service Number; 48467. Date of death; 16/05/1917. Born; Ballyalln (sic), County Carlow. Enlisted; Dublin. Killed in action. Son of Mrs. A. Brennan, of Bevllafallen, Goresbridge, Co. Kilkenny. Notes; Formerly he was with the T. RES, where his number was TR/5/52621. Grave or Memorial Reference; I B 43. Cemetery: Highland Cemetery, Roclincourt, Pas-de-Calas, France.

Brett, John. Rank; Private. Regiment or Service: Irish Guards. Unit; 1st Battalion. Service Number; 9408. Date of death; 10/10/1917. Age at death;26. Born; Athlone, County Westmeath. Enlisted; Athlone. Killed in action. Son of Francis and Bridget Brett; husband of Margaret Brett, of Dunmore, Kilkenny. After his death his effects and property were received by;- (Wife) Mrs Margt Brett, Ballycumber, Kings County, Ireland. Grave or Memorial Reference; Panel 10 to 11. Cemetery: Tyne Cot Memorial in Belgium.

Bridgett, Martin. Rank; Private. Regiment or Service: Yorkshire Light Infantry. Unit; 1st Battalion. Service Number; 23212. Date of death; 04/10/1915. Born; Graignamsnea, County Kilkenny. Enlisted; Dublin. Killed in action. Notes; Formerly he was with the 12th Reserve Cavalry Regiment where his number was 13143. Grave or Memorial Reference; Panel 97 to 98. Cemetery: Loos Memorial in France.

Brien, Edward. Rank; Lance Corporal/Private. Regiment or Service: Royal Irish Regiment. Unit; 2nd Battalion. Service Number; 5336. Date of death; 27/03/1918. Born; Thomastown, County Kilkenny. Enlisted; Kilkenny. Residence; Thomastown, County Kilkenny. Died of wounds. He won the Military Medal and is listed in the London Gazette. Grave or Memorial Reference; II C 72. Cemetery: Honnechy British Cemetery in France.

Brien, William. Rank; Able Seaman. Regiment or Service: Royal Navy. Unit; H. M. S. Burwark. Service Number; 217440 (Po). Date of death; 26/11/1914. Age at death; 28. Born; Tipperary. Killed or died by means other than disease, accident or enemy action. Next of kin listed as Mother, Kate, Ormonde Slate, Quarries, Ahenna, Carrick-on-Suer, Kilkenny. Munster Express. News from the front. Our correspondent expresses his sorrow at having to announce the death of W. O'Brien who, poor fellow, went down of the battleship Bulwark. His bereaved mother in the Ormonde Quarries, received official news of his demise during the past week. It is an old saying that "one trouble never comes alone," for on the 20th ult, King Death visited her humble home and laid his wand on the poor woman's breadwinner in the person of Jim Brien, a Wexfordman, who for the past 35 years lived and worked in the valley. On Saturday, 22nd ult. His remains were conveyed by his fellow workmen and laid in their last resting place at Tullahought. He has three sons at the front. R. I. P. Notes; D. O. B. 08/02/1885. Cemetery: Portsmouth Naval Memorial, U. K.

Briscoe, Mervyn Whitby. Rank; Lieutenant. Regiment or Service: Royal Flying Corps. Unit; 6th Squadron Formerly he was with the Royal Field Artillery. Date of death; 23/06/1917. Limerick Chronicle, August, 1917. Briscoe—July 23, 1917, killed in action, Lieutenant Mervyn Whitby Briscoe, RFA, (attached RFC), seventh son of the late Edward Whitby and Mrs Briscoe, Harristown House, Piltown, County Kilkenny, aged 21 years. Waterford News;-By a very large circle of friends and acquaintances the death in action is much regretted of Lieutenant Mervyn Whitby Briscoe, R. F. A., after an exciting and varied career. Lieutenant Briscoe, who was killed on 23rd July, was but 21 years of age, and at the outbreak of war, he ran away from school and joined the R. H. A. as a private. Afterwards, he was commissioner by general Parsons to the R. F. A. Since the commencement of hostilities, he had been fighting, and served with the 16th Division. He was latterly attached to the Royal Flying Corps. The deceased officer has six other brothers serving at present, one of whom fought for the Germans in German South-West Africa in 1903, and was afterwards pioneering in the Belgian Congo. Lieutenant Briscoe was the seventh son of the late Mr E. W. Briscoe, Harristown House, Piltown, County Kilkenny, whose family were well known in the hunting field and were intimately associated with the late Lord Waterfords's family. From;- Poverty Bay Herald, Rōrahi XLII, Putanga 13603, 8 Huitanguru 1915, Page 4. Kilkenny Man's record. Eighteen son's in the Army. London, December 28.] The Briscoes of Kilkenny appear to hold the record for the number of soldiers in the army, as the following letter written to a London newspaper explains; I wish to contradict through your paper a statement regarding my son, Captain Edward Whitby Briscoe of the Eighteenth Royal Irish Regiment, which was published in a recent edition. He is not an Englishman, neither is he serving in an English Regiment, but in the crack corps of the British Army, the good old Eighteenth Royal Irish. He is a soldier by profession, and is only doing what thousands of Erin's son's are ever proud to do—fight for their flag and Empire. I have 18 sons who will all be with the colours if their country needs them, and my only regret is I haven't more. Edward W. Briscoe. Irish Independent;Dead Lieutenant M W Briscoe, RFA (Attached to the RFC) on July 23. at the age of 21, was the 7th son of Mrs Briscoe. Harristown House, Piltown, County Kilkenny. Irish Times. Briscoe-July 23, killed in action, Lieutenant Mervyn Whitby Briscoe, RFA (attached RFC.) son of the late Edward Whitby and Mrs Briscoe, Harristown House, Piltown, County Kilkenny. The Weekly Irish Times. Ireland's Roll of Honour. August 11, 1917. Lieutenant M W Briscoe, Royal Field Artillery (attached to the Royal Flying Corps), was killed in action on July 23rd. He was 21 years of age, and was the seventh son of the late Mr Edward Whitby and Mrs Briscoe, Harristown House, Piltown, County Kilkenny. Cemetery: Arras Flying Services Memorial. Pas-de-Calais, France. He is also commemorated on the Great War Memorial in St Canice's Cathedral, Kilkenny... 'To the Glory of God and in loving memory of the following members of the Diocese of Ossory who gave their lives for their country in the Great War 1914-1918'.

Broderick, James. Rank; Private. Regiment or Service: Royal Irish Regiment. Unit; 2nd Battalion. Service Number; 7618. Date of death; 03/09/1916. Born; Johnstown, County Kilkenny. Enlisted; Kilkenny. Residence; Johnstown, County Kilkenny. Killed in action. Harristown House, Piltown, County Kilkenny, Ireland, December 8, 1914. Grave or Memorial Reference; Pier and Face 3 A. Cemetery: Thiepval Memorial in France.

Brophey, Michael. Rank; Sergeant. Regiment or Service: South Lancashire Regiment. Unit; 1st/5th Battalion. Service Number; 2228. Date of death; 03/07/1915. Age at death;37. Born; Kilkenny. Enlisted; St Helen's, Lancashire. Killed in action. Son of Michael and Margaret Brophey, of Maddockstown, Kilkenny; husband of Sarah Smith, (formerly Brophey), of 2, Crispin St., St. Helens, Lancs. Grave or Memorial Reference; Panel 37. Cemetery: Ypres (Menin Gate) Memorial in Belgium.

Brophy, Andrew. Rank; Private. Regiment or Service: Royal Irish Regiment. Unit; 2nd Battalion. Service Number; 5037. Date of death; 14/07/1916. Age at death; 24. Born; New Ross, County Wexford. Enlisted; Kilkenny. Residence; Graiguenamanagh, County ilkenny. Killed in action. Son of Andrew and Mary Brophy of High St, Graiguenamanagh, Co. Kilkenny. In his Will, dated 04-January-1916, his effects and property were received by;- (Mother) Mary Brophy, High Street, Graiguenamanagh, County Kilkenny, Ireland. Grave or Memorial Reference; Pier and Face 3 A. Cemetery: Thiepval Memorial in France

Brophy, John. Rank; Private. Regiment or Service: Royal Irish Fusiliers. Unit; 1st Battalion. Service Number; 11703. Date of death; 11/06/1915. Born; Ballyraggett, County Kilkenny. Enlisted; Maryborough. Residence; Ballyraggett. Died of wounds. In his Will, dated 24-April-1915, his effects and property were received by;- (Sister) Miss Mary Brophy, Byrnesgrove, Ballyragget, County Kilkenny, Ireland. Grave or Memorial Reference; Panel 42. Cemetery: Ypres (Menin Gate) Memorial in Belgium.

Brophy, John. Rank; Sergeant. Regiment or Service: Royal Irish Regiment. Unit; 6th Battalion. Service Number; 4501. Date of death; 07/08/1917. Born; St Patrick's, Kilkenny. Enlisted; Kilkenny. Killed in action. After his death his effects and property were received by;- (Wife) Mrs Ellen Brophy, Upper Walker St, Kilkenny. Grave or Memorial Reference; I B 11. Cemetery: Potijze Chateau Grounds Cemetery in Belgium.

Brophy, William. Rank; Driver. Regiment or Service: Royal Army Cyclist Corps. Unit; Attached to the 16th Cyclist Battalion, Army Cyclist Corps. Service Number; TS/295. Date of death; 05/12/1918. Age at death;33. Born; Urlingford, County Kilkenny. Enlisted; Kilkenny. Died. Grave or Memorial Reference; I F 1. Cemetery: Sofia War Cemetery, Bulgaria.

Lieutenant Brown, from De Ruvigny's Roll of Honour.

Brown, Hubert William. Rank; Lieutenant. Regiment or Service: Royal Irish Regiment. Unit; 2nd Nigeria regiment, W. A. F. F. Date of death; 19/09/1914. Died of wounds. De Ruvignys Roll of Honour; -...son of the late John Mosse Brown. Born in Greenville, Waterford, 11-January-1890. Educated at Aravon, Bray; St Faughan's College, County Cork, and at Cheltenham College. Gazetted 2nd Lieutenant Royal Irish Regiment, 06-November-1909, and promoted Lieutenant, 09-March-1910. Served with the Indian Expeditionary Force, and died in September-1914 from wounds received in action while fighting in the Cameroons. The Irish Times. Brown-September 19, 1914, died of wounds in the -------. Hubert William Brown, Lieutenant, Royal Irish Regiment, youngest son of the late John Mosse (?) Brown, of Greenville, Waterford, aged 24 years. Cemetery: Lokoja Memorial, Nigeria. He is also commemorated on the Great War Memorial in St Canice's Cathedral, Kilkenny. 'To the Glory of God and in loving memory of the following members of the Diocese of Ossory who gave their lives for their country in the Great War 1914-1918'.

Brown, John. Rank; Private. Regiment or Service: Royal Irish Regiment. Unit; 1st Battalion. Service Number; 4797. Date of death; 15/03/1917. Age at death;47. Born; Ballyhale, County Kilkenny. Died after discharge. Cemetery: Unknown

Bryan, Alfred. Rank; Private. Regiment or Service: Royal Irish Regiment. Unit; 6th Battalion. Service Number; 7866. Date of death; 02/08/1917. Born; Durrow, Queen's County. Enlisted; Maryborough, Queen's County. Residence; Durrow. Killed in action. Grave or Memorial Reference; Panel 33. Cemetery: Ypres (Menin Gate) Memorial in Belgium.

Buckley, George. Rank; Private. Regiment or Service: Royal Irish Regiment. Unit; B Company, 2nd Battalion. Service Number; 7812. Date of death; 14/07/1916. Born; St John's, Kilkenny. Enlisted; Kilkenny. Killed in action. Son of Mrs. Jane Haide, of Barrack St, Kilkenny. Grave or Memorial Reference; Pier and Face 3 A. Cemetery: Thiepval Memorial in France

Buckley, John. Rank; Private/Lance Corporal. Regiment or Service: King's Own Yorkshire Light Infantry. Unit; 5th Battalion. Service Number; 2431. Date of death; 08/07/1916. Age at death; 37. Born; Thomastown, County Kilkenny. Enlisted; Doncaster. Died of wounds. Son of the late James and Mary Buckley, of Thomastown, Co. Kilkenny. Grave or Memorial Reference; I D 6. Cemetery: Puchevillers British Cemetery in France.

Buckley, Thomas. Rank; Private. Regiment or Service: Connaught Rangers. Unit; D Company, 1st Battalion. Service Number; 9382. Date of death; 26/04/1916. Age at death;29. Born; Kilkenny. Enlisted; Waterford. Residence; Thomastown, County Kilkenny. Killed in action. Son of James and Bridget Doyle. Grave or Memorial Reference; Panel 42. Cemetery: Ypres (Menin Gate) Memorial in Belgium

Buggy, James. Rank; Gunner. Regiment or Service: Royal Garrison Artillery. Unit; No 1 Depot. Service Number; 7458. Date of death; 18/04/1916. Age at death; 36. Born; Kilkenny. Died after discharge. Cemetery: Unknown

Burke, Edward. Rank; Private. Regiment or Service: Irish Guards. Unit; 2nd Battalion. Service Number; 9315. Date of death; 15/09/1916. Age at death;26. Born; Urlingford. Enlisted; Kilkenny. Killed in action. Son of Mrs. Mary Burke, of Graine, Urlingford, Co. Kilkenny. Grave or Memorial Reference; Pier and Face 7 D. Cemetery: Thiepval Memorial in France.

Burke, James. Rank; Driver. Regiment or Service: Royal Horse Artillery and Royal Field Artillery. Unit; 2nd Battery, 13th Brigade. Service Number; 34380. Date of death; 13/08/1916. Born; Kilkenny. Enlisted; Cork. Killed in action in Mesopotamia. Grave or Memorial Reference; XV C 2. Cemetery: Amara War Cemetery in Iraq.

Burke, John. Rank; Private. Regiment or Service: Royal Irish Regiment. Unit; 2nd Battalion. Service Number; 4574. Date of death; 19/10/1914. Born; Urlingford. Enlisted; Urlingford. Killed in action. Grave or Memorial Reference; Panels 11 and 12. Cemetery: Le Touret Memorial in France

Burke, Michael. Rank; Private. Regiment or Service: Connaught Rangers. Unit; 2nd Battalion. Service Number; 10312. Date of death; 14/09/1914. Born; Kilkenny. Enlisted; Kilkenny. Residence; Kilkenny. Killed in action. Son of Mrs. Mary Creede (formerly Burke), of Scotts Lane, Kilgenny, and the late Michael Burke. Cemetery: La Ferte-Sous-Jouarre-Memorial in France

Burke, Michael. Rank; Pioneer. Regiment or Service: Corps of Royal Engineers. Unit; 3rd Divisional Signal Company. Service Number; 32644. Date of death; 27/03/1916. Born; Kilkenny. Enlisted; Dublin. Killed in action. Notes; Formerly he was with the Royal Garrison Artillery where his number was 18760. Grave or Memorial Reference; I B 30. Cemetery: Birr Cross Roads Cemetery in Zillebeke, Belgium.

Burke, Michael. Rank; Private. Regiment or Service: Royal Dublin Fusiliers. Unit; 1st Battalion. Service Number; 5646. Date of death; 04/09/1918. Born; Kilkenny. Enlisted; Carlow. Residence; Kilkenny. Killed in action. Grave or Memorial Reference; Panel 10. Cemetery: Ploegsteert Memorial in Belgium

Burke, Thomas. Rank; Private. Regiment or Service: Welsh Regiment. Unit; 2nd Battalion. Service Number; 12099. Date of death; 10/03/1915. Age at death;48. Born; Dungarven, County Kilkenny. Enlisted; Aberdare. Residence; Dungarven. Killed in action at Festubert. After his death his effects and property were received by;- (Molly. no further information). Grave or Memorial Reference; Panel 23 and 24. Cemetery: Le Touret Memorial in France

Burke/Bourke, William. Rank; Private. Regiment or Service: Welsh Regiment. Unit; 13th Battalion. Service Number; 34717. Date of death; 10/07/1916. Born; Cuffs Grange, County Kilkenny. Enlisted; Bridgend. Residence; Caerau, Glam. Killed in action. Son of Michael and Margaret Burke, of Cuffe's Grange, Co. Kilkenny. Grave or Memorial Reference; Pier and Face 7 A and 10 A. Cemetery: Thiepval Memorial in France.

Burke/Bourke, William. Rank; Private. Regiment or Service: Royal Irish Regiment. Unit; B Company, 6th Battalion. Service Number; 184823. Date of death; 03/09/1916. Age at death;18. Born; Piltown, County Kilkenny. Enlisted; Carrick-on-Suir. Residence; Piltown. Killed in action. Burke (CWGC) Bourke (SDGW), Son of Mrs. Katherine Burke, of Dowling, Piltown, Co. Kilkenny. Grave or Memorial Reference; Pier and Face 3 A. Cemetery: Thiepval Memorial in France.

Burns, George Henry. Rank; Private. Regiment or Service: Machine Gun Corps. Unit; Infantry. Service Number; 72530. Date of death; 18/04/1918. Born; Kilkenny. Enlisted; Stratford. Killed in action. Notes; Formerly he was with th Somerset Light Infantry where his number was 6972. Grave or Memorial Reference; Panel 154 to 159 and 163A. Cemetery: Tyne Cot Memorial in Belgium.

Butler, Philip. Rank; Private. Regiment or Service: Royal Irish Regiment. Unit; 2nd Battalion. Service Number; 4391. Date of death; 19/10/1914. Born; Newtownbarry, Co Kilkenny. Enlisted; Graiguemanagh. Residence; Tinahely, County Wicklow. Killed in action. Grave or Memorial Reference; Panel 11 and 12. Cemetery: Le Touret Memorial in France.

Butler, William James. Rank; Private. Regiment or Service: Australian Infantry A. I. F. Unit; 1st Battalion. Service Number; 5979. Date of death; 03/10/1917. Age at death; 30. Killed in action. Son of Mrs. Bridget Butler, of Wildfield, Ballyfoyle, Co. Kilkenny, Ireland. Native of Tullabrin, Co. Kilkenny. Born, Kilkenny, Ireland. Occupation on enlistment, farm labourer. Age on enlistment; 29 years 3 months. Next of kin details; (mother) Bridget Butler, Wildfield, Ballyfoyle, County Kilkenny, Ireland. A pension of 40/- per fortnight was awarded to his mother from 23-April-1918. Place and date of enlistment, 06-March-1916. Coolamundra, N. S. W. Weight, 172 lbs. Height, 5 feet, 8 inches. Complexion, fair. Eyes, hazel. Hair, light brown. Wounded in action, shell wound to the leg and arm on 05-May-1916. Treated in Rouen and discharged to his unit after treatment on 31-May-1916. reported missing in action, later altered to Killed in action. Grave or Memorial Reference; XLII A 4. Cemetery: Tyne Cot Cemetery in Belgium

Butler, William Patrick. Rank; Private. Regiment or Service: Cheshire Regiment. Unit; 2nd Battalion. Service Number; 33826. Date of death; 17/09/1918. Age at death;35. Born; Kilkenny. Enlisted; London. Died in Serbia. Notes; Formerly he was with the Bedfordshire Regiment where his number was 29881. Grave or Memorial Reference; A 4. Cemetery: Plovdiv Central Cemetery in Bulgaria.

Byrne, James. Rank; Private. Regiment or Service: Leinster Regiment. Unit; 1st Battalion. Service Number; 6246. Date of death; 13/05/1915. Born; Callan, County Kilkenny. Enlisted; Aldershot, Hants. Died of wounds. Husband of Mary Phelan (formerly Byrne), of Bauntha, Callan, Co. Kilkenny. Grave or Memorial Reference; I1 25. Cemetery: Oxford (Botely) Cemetery, Oxfordshire, UK.

Byrne, John. Rank; Gunner. Regiment or Service: Royal Garrison Artillery. Unit; 22nd Siege Company. Service Number; 17742. Date of death; 04/03/1917. Age at death;38. Enlisted; Carlow. Residence; Kilkenny. Died after discharge. Cemetery: Unknown

Byrne, Martin. Rank; Private. Regiment or Service: Leinster Regiment. Unit; 2nd Battalion. Service Number; 1865. Date of death; 31/07/1917. Born; Kilkenny. Enlisted; Kilkenny. Residence; Kilkenny. Killed in action. In his Will, dated 02-March-1917, his effects and property were received by;- (Wife) Mrs Alice Byrne, Upper Patrick St. Waterford Rd. Kilkenny. Grave or Memorial Reference; Panel 44. Cemetery: Ypres (Menin Gate) Memorial in Belgium.

Byrne, Thomas. Rank; Private. Regiment or Service: Irish Guards. Unit; 1st Battalion. Service Number; 7851. Date of death; 09/09/1917. Age at death;30. Born; Kilkenny. Enlisted; Carlow. Killed in action. Son of James and Mary Byrne, of 44, Michael St., Kilkenny. Kilkenny Journal, August, 1915. Irish Guardsman and The "Kilkenny Boys." Private Thomas Byrne, Irish Guards, better known to his friends as "Cock" Byrne, and who will shortly be on his way to the seat of war, is not forgetful of his old associates in the Marble City, or the "Kilkenny boys," as he facetiously describes them I the subjoined note which he has addressed to the Editor of the "Kilkenny Journal";"Dear Sir—Just a line hoping all the Kilkenny boys are well. I'm going on very well here in the Irish Guards. I expect to be going to the front the 1st September. This Regiment is the best fighting regiment under his Majesty, and the smartest; they dread nothing; best at the bayonet charge. Please let the boys know I was asking for them. Yours Truly."Thomas Byrne." ("Cock."). From The Irish Guards, Volume 2, page 70 by Rudyard Kipling. ;-' It may have been he was the great and only "Cock" Burne or Byrne of whom unpublishable Battalion-history relates strange things in the early days. He was eminent, even among many originals—an elderly "old soldier," solitary by temperament, unpredictable in action, given to wandering off and boiling tea, which he drank perpetually in remote and unwholesome corners of the trenches. But he had the gift, with many others, of crowing like a cock (hence his nom-de-guerre), and vastly annoyed the unhumorous Hun, whom he would thus salute regardless of time, place, or safety. To this trick he added a certain infinitely monotonous tomtomming on any tin or box that came handy, so that it was easy to locate him even when exasperated enemy snipers were silent. He came from Kilkenny, and when on leave wore such medal-ribbons as he thought should have been issued to him—from the V. C. down; so that when he died, and his relatives asked why those medals had not been sent them, there was a great deal of trouble. Professionally, he was a "dirty" soldier, but this was understood and allowed for. He regarded authority rather as an impertinence to be blandly set aside than to be argued or brawled with; and he revolved in his remote and unquestioned orbits, brooding, crowing, drumming, and morosely sipping his tea, something between a poacher, a horse-coper, a gipsy, and a bird-catcher, but always the philosopher and man of many queer worlds. His one defect was that, though difficult to coax on to the stage, once there and well set before an appreciative audience, little less than military force could haul "Cock" Byrne off it. '. Grave or Memorial Reference; Panel 10 to 11. Cemetery: Tyne Cot Memorial in Belgium.

Byrne, Thomas. Rank; Private. Regiment or Service: Leinster Regiment. Unit; 2nd Battalion. Service Number; 4182. Date of death; 30/12/1917. Age at death; 36. Born; Thomastown, County Kilkenny. Enlisted; Maryborough. Died at sea. Son of Thomas and Bridget Byrne; husband of Margaret Kennedy (formerly Byrne), of New Rd., Birr, King's Co. Midland Tribune, January, 1918. It is announced that Private T Byrnes (sic), Burkes Hill, Birr, has been drowned at sea. King's County Chronicle, 1918. Birr Soldier drowned. On Sunday last the sad news was received by Mrs Byrnes (sic), Burke's Hill, that her husband, Pte Thomas Byrnes, Leinster Regiment, had been drowned on a voyage to Egypt, the ship being torpedoed. The official news stated that his body had been recovered. The late Private Byrne had about two years service, and was a fine stamp of a soldier. Much sympathy is felt with the bereaved wife and four children. Grave or Memorial Reference; C 47. Cemetery: Alexandria (Hadra) War Memorial Cemetery in Egypt.

Byrnes, Edward Patrick. Rank; Private. Regiment or Service: Army Service Corps. Unit; 3rd Base remount Depot. Service Number; TS/5577. Date of death; 25/01/1916. Born; Abbeyleix. Queen's County. Enlisted; Leith. Residence; Kilkenny. Died at Baconel. Nephew of Mr. J. Kirk, of Archestown, Durrow, Queens Co. After his death his effects and property were received by (Aunt) Miss Marey Byrnes, Archerstown, Durrow, Queens County, Ireland. Grave or Memorial Reference; II B 3. Cemetery: St Pierre Cemetery, Amiens in France.

Cahill, John. Rank; Private. Regiment or Service: Welsh Regiment. Unit; 12th Battalion. Service Number; 42085/ 42685. Date of death; 16/11/1917. Born; Kilkenny. Enlisted; Oldham, Lancs. Died of wounds. Notes; Transferred to 187th Company, Labour Corps. Number listed as 42085 (SDGW) 42685 (CWGC). Formerly he was with the Welsh Regiment (12th Battalion) where his number was 111999. Grave or Memorial Reference; XXVII A 5A. Cemetery: Lijssenthoek Military Cemetery in Belgium.

Cahill, John Nugent. Rank; Captain. Regiment or Service: Royal Irish Rifles. Unit; 13th Battalion. Date of death; 16/08/1917. Born; Kilkenny. Killed in action. Carlow Sentinel and Leinster Express, August-1917. Captain J. N. Cahill. Captain J. N. Cahill, Royal Irish Regiment (attached Royal Irish Rifles), was killed in action on the 16th August. He was the eldest son of Molonel J. N. Cahill, Ballyconra, County Kilkenny. Captain Cahill's colonel writes of him;- " He was hit leading his company like the gallant soldier he was. We were all so fond of him, and I always considered him as good a company commander as there was in----, and he had trained and led one of the best companies going. We buried him that night at dark, and I will get a proper cross put up as soon as possible." He was a great favourite with everyone who knew him. A good, all-round sportsman, he was a fine rider across a country, and was well known with the Kilkenny Hounds and other packs in the South of Ireland.". Kilkenny People, January, 1918. Death of Colonel J. N. Cahill. We regret to announce the death of Colonel John Nugent Cahill, J. P., Ballyconra House, Ballyragget, which occurred on Wednesday. He was the fourth son of Mr Michael Cahill, D. L., and joined the Royal Irish Regiment early in life. His eldest son, captain J. N. Cahill, joined his father's regiment and was killed on active service on August 16-1917. Colonel Cahill was a fine sportsman and was exceedingly popular with all classes in the County Kilkenny. He was an extensive land agent in the old days, and always maintained friendly relations with the tenantry. His daughter is the wife of Mr E. J. McElligott, K. C., one of the leaders of the Munster Bar. Carlow Sentinel, January, 1918. Death of Colonel John Nugent Cahill. The announcement of the death of Colonel J. N. Cahill, which occurred on Wednesday last will be received with very genuine regret in Kilkenny and the adjoining counties, where, for many years he was a prominent figure in the public life of the country. He wad the fourth son of the late Michael Cahill, D. L., of Ballyclera House, Ballyragget, County Kilkenny, and was educated at Stoneyhurst College. Early in life he joined the 4th Royal Irish Regiment at, which he subsequently commanded for many years. He married in 1889, Emily, daughter of the late Mr Henry Hodges, of Beaufort, Rathfarnham, and is survived by three sons and four daughters. His eldest son, the late Captain J. N. Nugent Cahill, joined his fathers regiment eight years ago and was killed on active service on the 16th August, 1917. Colonel Cahill was a very fine sportsman, and was exceedingly popular with all classes. Irish Independent; Cahill—August 16, 1917, killed in action while gallantly leading his men, Captain J N Cahill, Royal Irish Regiment, attached to the Royal Irish Rifles, Lough, Three Castles, County Kilkenny, aged 27, eldest son of Colonel J N Cahill, Ballyconra House, Ballyragget, and dearly loved husband of Maisie N Cahill. R. I. P. Irish Times. Cahill-March 21, killed in action, Lieutenant P L Cahill, Munster Fusiliers, son of the late Colonel Cahill, and Mrs Cahill, Ballyconra House, Ballyraggett, County Kilkenny. The Weekly Irish Times. Ireland's Roll of Honour. April 6, 1918. Lieutenant P L Cahill. -Lieutenant (Acting Captain) Cahill, Royal Munster Fusiliers, was killed in action on the 20th March. He was the second surviving son of the late Colonel J Nugent Cahill, Ballyconra House, Ballyragget, and was in his twenty fourth year. he was in Canada when the war broke out, and at once joined a Canadian cavalry regiment, subsequently getting his commission in the Munsters. Since 1915, he had been almost continuously on active service in France and Belgium. Lieutenant Cahill, was a man of fine physique, and was an adept at all outdoor sports. His eldest brother, Captain J V Cahill, was killed in France in August, 1917. Waterford News, August, 1917; Captain J N Cahill, Royal Irish Regiment (attached Royal Irish Rifles), was killed in action on the 16th August. He was the eldest son of Colonel J N Cahill, Ballyconra, County Kilkenny. Captain Cahill's Colonel writes of him;-"He was hit leading his company like the gallant soldier he was. We were all so fond of him, and I always considered him as good a company commander as there was in ---, and he had trained and led one of the best companies going. We buried him that night at dark, and I will get a proper cross put up as soon as possible." "Johnnie" Cahill was a great favourite with everyone who knew him. A good all-round sportsman, he was a fine rider across a country, and was well known with the Kilkennt Hounds and other packs in the South of Ireland. Grave or Memorial Reference; Panel 138 to 140 and 162 to 162A and 163A. Cemetery: Tyne Cot Memorial in Belgium.

Cahill, Patrick Leopold. Rank; Lieutenant. Regiment or Service: Royal Munster Fusiliers. Unit; 4th Battalion. Date of death; 21/03/1918. Age at death; 24. Killed in action. Son of Emily Nugent Cahill, of Ballyconra House, Ballyragget, Co. Kilkenny, and the late Colonel John Nugent Cahill. Kilkenny People, April, 1918. Kilkenny Officer Killed. Lieutenant (Acting Captain) Cahill, Royal Munster Fusiliers, was killed in action on the 20th March. He was the second surviving son of the late Colonel J. Nugent Cahill, J. P., Ballyconra House, Ballyragget, and was in his twenty-fourth year. He was in Canada when the war broke out, and at once joined a Canadian Cavalry Regiment, subsequently getting his commission in the Munsters. Since 1915 he had been almost continuously on active service in France and Belgium. Lieutenant Cahill was a man of fine physique, and was an adept at all outdoor sports. His eldest brother, Captain J. N. Cahill, was killed in France in August, 1917. At a meeting of the Committee of the North Kilkenny Coursing Club at Lisdowney, the Rev. E. Brennan, P. P., presiding, the following vote of condolence was passed in silence, on the proposition of Mr Joseph Fitzpatrick, seconded by Mr George Kenny;-- "That we wish to convey to Mrs Cahill and family, of Ballyconra House, our heartfelt sympathy in their sad bereavement, caused by the death of Lieutenant Cahill, killed in action on March 20th." The meeting adjourned as a mark of respect without transacting any business. Irish Independent; Cahill-Lieutenant P L Cahill, Munster Fusiliers, third son of the late Colonel Cahill and Mrs Cahill Bally----- House, Ballyragget, County Kilkenny, killed in action, March 21, 1918. Limerick Chronicle, April, 1918. Roll of Honour. Lieutenant (Acting Captain) Cahill, Royal Munster Fusiliers, was killed in action on the 20th March. He was the second surviving son of the late Colonel J Nugent Cahill, Ballyconra House, Ballyragget, and was in his 24th year. He was in Canada when the war broke out, and at once joined a Canadian cavalry regiment, subsequently getting his commission in the Munsters. Since 1916 he had been almost continuously on active service in France and Belgium. Lieutenant Cahill was a man of fine physique, and was an adept at all outdoor sports. His eldest brother Captain J N Cahill, was killed in France in August, 1917. Limerick Chronicle, April, 1918. Cahill—March 21, 1918, killed in action, Lieutenant P L Cahill, Munster Fusiliers, third son of the late Colonel Cahill and Mrs Cahill, Ballyconra House, Ballyraggett, County Kilkenny. Grave or Memorial Reference; III F 6. Cemetery: Epehy Wood Farm Cemetery, Epehy in France.

Campbell, Alexander. Rank; Rifleman. Regiment or Service: Royal Irish Rifles. Unit; 2nd Battalion. Service Number; 6983. Date of death; 27/10/1914. Born; Kilkenny. Enlisted; Newtownards, County Down. Residence; Belfast. Killed in action. Grave or Memorial Reference; Panel 42 and 43. Cemetery: Le Touret Memorial in France

Cantley, Alexander Alfred. Rank; Private. Regiment or Service: Canadian Infantry (Central Ontario Regiment). Unit; 15th Battalion. Service Number; 27049. Date of death; 29/04/1915. Born; Kilkenny. Enlisted; Valcartier. Killed in action. Occupation on enlistment, Prospector. Date of birth; June 1st, 1886. Height, 5 feet, 8 inches. Complexion, medium. Eyes, blue. Hair, brown. Next of kin listed William Cantley, County Kilkenny. Place of birth, County Kilkenny. Date of birth, June-02-1886. Occupation on enlistment, Prospector. Place and date of enlistment, 18-September-1914, Valcartier. Address on enlistment, 28 yrs 3 mths. Height, 5 feet, 8 inches. Complexion, medium. Eyes, blue. Hair, brown. He is listed in the 1901 Census living in Blanchfield. Son of William and Elizabeth, brother of Sarah, Mary, William, Helena, and Robert Cantley.

Limerick Chronicle, July, 1915. Cantley, April 29, 1915, killed in action in France. Private Alexander Alfred Cantley (Sandy), 15th battalion, 48th Highlanders, 1st Canadian Contingent,., aged 27 years, son of William and Mrs Cantley, of Blanchville, Dunbell, County Kilkenny. Irish Times. Cantley-April 29, 1915, killed in action in France, Private Alexander Alfred Cantley (Sandy), 15th Battalion, 48th Highlanders, 1st Canadian Contingent, aged 27 years, son of William and Mrs Cantley, of Blackvilla (?), Dunbell, County Kilkenny. Grave or Memorial Reference; Panel 18-24-26-30. Cemetery: Ypres (Menin Gate) Memorial in Belgium. He is also commemorated on the Great War Memorial in St Canice's Cathedral, Kilkenny...'To the Glory of God and in loving memory of the following members of the Diocese of Ossory who gave their lives for their country in the Great War 1914-1918'.

Cantlon, William Robert. Rank; Gunner. Regiment or Service: Royal Garrison Artillery. Unit; 231st Siege Battery. Service Number; 157977. Date of death; 23/12/1917. Age at death;33. Enlisted; Liverpool. Residence; Kilkenny. Died of wounds. Son of the late Philip and A. Cantlon, of Ballyellen, Goresbridge, Co. Kilkenny. Irish Times. Cantlon-December 23, Gunner William Robert Cantlon, Siege Battery, RGA., BEF., died from wounds received in action, son of Philip and Mrs Cantlon, Ballyellis, Goresbridge, County Kilkenny. The Weekly Irish Times. Ireland's Roll of Honour. February 9, 1918. Gunner William Robert Cantlon, Siege Battery, Royal Garrison Artillery, who died on 23rd December, 1917, of wounds received in action, was the youngest son of Mr and Mrs Philip Cantlon, Ballyellin, Goresbridge, County Kilkenny. Grave or Memorial Reference; II B 43. Cemetery: Bleuet Farm Cemetery in Belgium. Also listed under Borris/Ballyellin on the Great War Memorial, Milford Street, Leighlinbridge, County Carlow.

Carolan/Corolan, John. Rank; Private. Regiment or Service: Royal Irish Regiment. Unit; 6th Battalion. Service Number; 7800. Date of death; 02/08/1917. Born; St Patrick's, Kilkenny. Enlisted; Kilkenny. Killed in action. Caralon (CWGC, SDGW) Corolan (IMR), Son of John and Cecilia Carolan, of "Greenfield," Kells Rd., Kilkenny. After his death his effects and property were received by;- (Father) John Carolan, Greenfield Kells Road, Kilkenny, Ireland. Event of his death to (Sister) Mary Ann and (Brother) Daniel Carolan, Greenfield Kells Road, Kilkenny, Ireland. (Brother) James Carolan, New Street, Kilkenny, Ireland. Son of John and Cecilia Carolan, of "Greenfield," Kells Rd., Kilkenny. Grave or Memorial Reference; I A 11. Cemetery: Aeroplane Cemetery in Belgium.

Carpendale, George. Rank; Fireman. Regiment or Service: Mercantile Marine. Unit; S. S."Formby" (Glasgow). Date of death; 16/12/1917. Age at death;35. The ship was lost with all hands and never located during a fierce storm. Son of Elizabeth Carpendale and the late George Carpendale; husband of Mary Carpendale (nee Stephens), of 40, Ferrybank, nr. Waterford, Co. Kilkenny. Born at Leicester. Cemetery: Tower Hill Memorial in the UK. He is also listed on the Formby-Coningbeg Memorial, Adelphi Quay in Waterford City

Carr, Albert. Rank; Private. Regiment or Service: Royal Irish Regiment. Unit; 7th Battalion, Formerly he was with the Army Service Corps where his number was 320212 and 2673 while he was with the South Irish Horse. Service Number; 25109. Date of death; 19/01/1918. Born; Kilmoganny, County Kilkenny. Enlisted; Carrick-on-Suir, County Tipperary. Residence; Kilmoganny. Died of wounds. Grave or Memorial Reference; P VI E 6A. Cemetery: St Sever Cemetery Extension, Rouen in France. He is also commemorated on the Great War Memorial in St Canice's Cathedral, Kilkenny…'To the Glory of God and in loving memory of the following members of the Diocese of Ossory who gave their lives for their country in the Great War 1914-1918'.

Carroll, James. Rank; Private. Regiment or Service: Royal Munster Fusiliers. Unit; 6th Battalion. Service Number; 2901. Date of death; 09/08/1915. Age at death;22. Enlisted; The Curragh Camp, County Kildare. Residence; Kilmacow, County Kilkenny. Killed in Action in Gallipoli. Son of William and Ellen Carroll, of Lower Kilmacow, Waterford (sic), Co. Kilkenny. Grave or Memorial Reference; Panel 185 to 190. Cemetery: Helles Memorial in Turkey.

Carroll, Michael. Rank; Sergeant. Regiment or Service: Royal Irish Regiment. Unit; 1st Battalion. Service Number; 10184. Date of death; 10/03/1918. Born; St John's, Kilkenny. Enlisted; Kilkenny. Killed in action in Palestine. In his Will, dated 28-December-1917, his effects and property were received by;- (Aunt) Mrs Bridget Fitzpatrick, 13 Usher's Island, Dublin, Ireland. Grave or Memorial Reference; J 85. Cemetery: Jerusalem War Cemetery, Israel.

Cashin, Edward. Rank; Private. Regiment or Service: Royal Irish Regiment. Unit; 1st Battalion. Service Number; 10106. Date of death; 10/03/1918. Born; Kilmacow. Residence; Kilmacow, County Kilkenny. Killed in action in Palestine. Notes; Born Kilmacow, County Kilkenny (Soldiers died in the Great War), Kilmacow, County Waterford (The Commonwealth War Graves Commission). Grave or Memorial Reference; A 68. Cemetery: Jerusalem War Cemetery, Israel.

Clancy, Michael. Rank; Private. Regiment or Service: Royal Irish Regiment. Unit; 1st Battalion. Service Number; 3230. Date of death; 24/04/1915. Born; Windgap, County Kilkenny. Enlisted; Tipperary. Residence; Carrick-on-Suir, County Tipperary. Killed in action. Mrs Mary Conway, Bawnriegh, Carrick on Suir, County Kilkenny. Witnessed by;- Lawrence O'Shea. Will executed by;- Mary Conways Parents, Lawrence and Johanna O Shea. Of same address. Grave or Memorial Reference; Panel 33. Cemetery: Ypres (Menin Gate) Memorial in Belgium

Clark, Ellis. Rank; Lieutenant. Regiment or Service: Lancashire Fusiliers. Unit; 1st Battalion. Date of death; 25/04/1915. Age at death;29. Killed in action. Son of George William and Sarah Clark, late of Stockport; husband of C. M. Clark, of 13, Lower Pembroke St., Dublin. Kilkenny People, May, 1915. Gallant Officer Killed in Action. We regret to announce the death of Lieutenant Ellis Clark, who was killed in action in the Dardanelles on Saturday, 1st May. Lieutenant Clark was for a considerable time stationed in Kilkenny, and prior to his departure became engaged and shortly afterwards was married to Miss Kitty English, who was then manageress of the "Kilkenny People" newspaper and stationary department. To Mrs Clark and her only child we extend our sincere sympathy. Her many friends in Kilkenny join in this sad tribute of respectful sorrow on the loss of her gallant husband who, had he not fallen in battle, would assuredly have obtained higher distinction in the service. Kilkenny People, May, 1915. Deaths. Clark. —Killed in action at the Dardanelles on the 1st May, second Lieutenant Ellis Clark, 1st Lancashire Fusiliers, aged 29 years, son of the late George Clark, Stockport. —R. I. P. Notes; Date of death listed as 01/05/1915 (ODGW) 25/04/1915 (CWGC). Grave or Memorial Reference; I 96. Cemetery: Lancashire Landing Cemetery in Turkey.

Claydon, George. Rank; Company Sergeant Major. Regiment or Service: Royal Irish Regiment. Unit; 6th Battalion. Service Number; 1690. Date of death; See notes. Age at death; 45. Born; Kentish Town, Middlesex. Enlisted; Kilkeny. Residence; Walthamstow, Essex. Killed in action. Son of George and Elizabeth Claydon, of 82, Blyth Rd., Lea Bridge Rd., Leyton, London. Notes; Date of death 03/07/1916 (SDGW), 03/09/1916 (CWGC). Grave or Memorial Reference; Pier and Face 3 A. Cemetery: Thiepval Memorial in France.

Cleary, Patrick. Rank; Private. Regiment or Service: Royal Irish Regiment. Unit; 2nd Battalion. Service Number; 11547. Date of death; 30/08/1917. Age at death;18. Born; Johnstown, County Kilkenny. Enlisted; Kilkenny. Died of wounds at home. Son of Patrick and Mary Cleary, of Upper John St., Kilkenny. In his Will, dated 03-April-1917, his effects and property were received by;- (Father) Mr P Cleary, Kilmangh, County Kilkenny. Grave or Memorial Reference; Screen Wall. War Plot. Cemetery: Bristol (Arnos Vale) Roman Catholic Cemetery, UK.

Cleary, William. Rank; Lance Corporal. Regiment or Service: Welsh Regiment. Unit; 18th Battalion. Service Number; 54142. Date of death; 19/07/1917. Born; Kilmacow, County Kilkenny. Enlisted; Cardiff. Killed in action. Grave or Memorial Reference; I D 12. Cemetery: Fins New British Cemetery, Somme in France.

Cleere, John. Rank; Private. Regiment or Service: South Lancashire Regiment. Unit; 2nd Battalion. Service Number; 7490. Date of death; 20/09/1914. Born; Ballingarry, County Kilkenny. Enlisted; Ballingarry. Killed in action. Cemetery: La Ferte-Sous-Jouarre-Memorial in France.

Cleere, Richard. Rank; Private. Regiment or Service: Canterbury Regiment, N. Z. E. F. Unit; 1st Battalion. Service Number; 49526. Date of death; 05/04/1918. Age at death; 24. Killed in action on the Somme. Son of Piree and Kate Cleere, of Brounstown Kilkenny, Ireland. Occupation on Enlistment, Hospital Attendant. Next of kin details, Mrs Cleere, Kilkenny, Ireland (mother). Embarked with the 27th Reinforcements Canterbury Infantry Regiment, C Company, New Zealand Expeditionary Force on 12-June-1917 in Wellington, New Zealand aboard the 'Tahiti' bound for Devonport, England. Cemetery: Grevillers (New Zealand) Memorial in France.

Cleeve, John. Rank; Private. Regiment or Service: Irish Guards. Unit; 1st Battalion. Service Number; 1453. Date of death; 01/11/1914. Born; Ballyhale, County Kilkenny. Enlisted; Dublin. Residence; West Hamstead, Middlesex. Killed in action. Grave or Memorial Reference; Panel 11. Cemetery: Ypres (Menin Gate) Memorial in Belgium.

Clowry, James. Rank; Private. Regiment or Service: Royal Dublin Fusiliers. Unit; 1st Battalion. Service Number; 5647. Date of death; 25/08/1915. Born; Kilkenny. Enlisted; Carlow. Residence; Kilkenny. Killed in action. In his Will, dated 06-June-1915, his effects and property were received by;- (Mother) Mrs M Clowry, 3 Callan Road, Kilkenny. Grave or Memorial Reference; Panel 97 to 101. Cemetery: Helles Memorial in Turkey.

Coady, James. Rank; Private. Regiment or Service: The King's Liverpool Regiment. Unit; 12th Battalion. Service Number; 3/10716. Date of death; 29/01/1915. Age at death;34. Born; Kilkenny, Leinster. Enlisted; Liverpool. Residence; Kilkenny. Died at home. Son-in-law of Mrs. J. Murphy, of Ballyellen, Goresbridge, Co. Kilkenny. Notes; Number listed as 3/10716 (CWGC) 10716 (SDGW). Grave or Memorial Reference; R 298. Cemetery: Aldershot Military Cemetery, UK.

Coady, John. Rank; Private. Regiment or Service: Royal Irish Regiment. Unit; 3rd Battalion. Service Number; 9019. Date of death; 01/12/1917. Age at death; 33. Born; Ballinakill, County Kilkenny. Enlisted; Maryborough, Queen's County. Residence; Ballinakill. Died at home. Son of Margaret Coady, of Chapel St., Ballinakill, and the late Michael Coady. Grave or Memorial Reference; In the South East part. Cemetery: Ballyoskill Catholic Churchyard, County Killenny.

Coady, Simon. Rank; Private. Regiment or Service: Royal Irish Regiment. Unit; 1st Battalion. Service Number; 4580. Date of death; 16/03/1915. Born; Graiguenamanagh, County Kilkenny. Enlisted; Thomastown. Residence; Graiguenamanagh, County ilkenny. Killed in action. After his death his effects and property were received by;- (Mother) K Coady, MainStreet, Graugue na Managh. Grave or Memorial Reference; Panel 33. Cemetery: Ypres (Menin Gate) Memorial in Belgium.

Coady/Cody, Edward. Rank; Private. Regiment or Service: Connaught Rangers. Unit; 5th Battalion. Service Number; 11057. Date of death; 14/12/1915. Born; Kilkenny. Enlisted; Kilkenny. Residence; Thurles, County Tipperary. Died in Salonika. Coady (SDGW, IMR) Cody (CWGC), Edward. Notes; Before his commission he was No 6834, Warrant Officer 1st Class in the Royal Irish Regiment. Cemetery: Doiran Memorial in Greece.

Image courtesy of Tom Brett.

Coady/Cody, John. Rank; Second Lieutenant. Regiment or Service: Connaught Rangers. Unit; Attached to the 2nd Battalion, Royal Irish Regiment. Date of death; 21/08/1918. Age at death;37. Killed in action. Kilkenny People, June 1917. Soldier's Distinction—Regimental Sergeant-Major J Cody, whose wife resides at Duncannon, County Wexford, has been awarded a special certificate " in recognition of gallant conduct and devotion to duty in the field on April 5". Notes; Born Croix de Geurre (Belgium). Son of the late James and Margaret Coady; husband of Florence Mary Dounes (formerly Coady), of Duncannon, Waterford. From an article in an unknown Wexford newspaper; Lieut Cody Killed; Regret was felt in Duncannon when the sad news arrived to Mrs Cody that her husband, Lieut Cody, had been killed in action. The deceased Officer was promoted only a few months ago from the ranks for conspicuous bravery on the field. Besides his service on the Western Front he had also seen service formerly in South Africa where he also won distinction for bravery. While gallantly leading his platoon on 22nd of August last on the Lys sector he fell. Lieut. Cody belonged to a Kilkenny family, but had recently married a Duncannon Lady. From an article in the Free Press, 1918; The promotion of Mr John Coady to commissioned rank has been a source of gratification to his many friends in Duncannon. A Kilkenny man by birth, he married a Duncannon lady and made it his future home. When war broke out he was Regimentals Sergeant Major to the R. I. R., and has since been awarded the parchment, certificates, and Belgian Croix de Guere for bravery in the field. He has been awarded a commission in the Connaught Rangers as a further testimony to his gallantry. Cemetery: Vis-En-Artois Memorial in France.

Coburn, Thomas Notely. Rank; Sergeant. Regiment or Service: Leinster Regiment. Unit; 2nd Battalion. Service Number; 3590. Date of death; 11/11/1916. Born; Clonegale, County Carlow. Enlisted; Edenderry, King's County. Residence; Kildare. Died of wounds. Coburn, Thomas Notley (CWGC). Coburn, Notely (SDGW). Irish Times. Coburn-In proud and loving memory of Thomas Notley Coburn, Sergeant Leinster regiment, who was killed in action, in France, on November 11, 1916, ---and dearly loved son of J C and Mrs Coburn, Newport, County Tipperary;-The golden evening brightens in the West. Soon, soon to faithful warriors comes the rest; Sweet is the calm of Paradise, the blest. The Weekly Irish Times. Ireland's Roll of Honour. December 16, 1916. Sergeant Thomas Notley Coburn, Leinster Regiment, killed in action on 11th November, 1916, was one of the three brothers on active service and took part in the battles of Hooge, Hill 60 and Ypres. He was a son of Mr and Mrs J C Coburn, Carbury, County Kildare, and a brother of Mr George Coburn, 72 Tyrconnell Road, Inchicore, Dublin. (I include Seargent Notely Coburn as he is commemorated on the Great War Memorial in St Canice's Cathedral, Kilkenny. 'To the Glory of God and in loving memory of the following members of the Diocese of Ossory who gave their lives for their country in the Great War 1914-1918'. Author). Listed on the memorial under Sergeant Thomas N. Coburn. The Irish Times. Coburn-In proud and loving memory of Thomas Notley Coburn, Sergeant Leinster regiment, who was killed in action, in France, on November 11, 1916, ---and dearly loved son of J C and Mrs Coburn, Newport, County Tipperary;-The golden evening brightens in the West. Soon, soon to faithful warriors comes the rest; Sweet is the calm of Paradise, the blest. The Weekly Irish Times. Ireland's Roll of Honour. December 16, 1916. Sergeant Thomas Notley Coburn, Leinster Regiment, killed in action on 11th November, 1916, was one of the three brothers on active service and took part in the battles of Hooge, Hill 60 and Ypres. He was a son of Mr and Mrs J C Coburn, Carbury, County Kildare, and a brother of Mr George Coburn, 72 Tyrconnell Road, Inchicore, Dublin. Grave or Memorial Reference; I L 8. Cemetery: Maroc British Cemetery, Grenay in France.

Cody, James. Rank; Private. Regiment or Service: Welsh Regiment. Unit; 10th Battalion. Service Number; 15796. Date of death; 10/02/1916. Born; Thomastown, County Kilkenny. Enlisted; Perth, Glamorganshire. Killed in action. Grave or Memorial Reference; III D 7. Cemetery: Le Touret Military Cemetery, Richebourg-L'Avoue in France.

Cody, Joseph Francis. Rank; Bombardier. Regiment or Service: Royal Garrison Artillery. Unit; 77th Siege Battery. Service Number; 63171. Date of death; 25/09/1917. Born; Kilkenny. Enlisted; Manchester. Killed in action. Grave or Memorial Reference; I J 39. Cemetery: Voormezeele Enclosures No 1 and No 2 in Belgium.

Cody, Thomas. Rank; Fireman. Regiment or Service: Mercantile Marine. Unit; S. S. Leinster. Date of death; 10/10/1918. Age at death;39. Steamship Leinster was hit by a German Torpedo and sank with the loss of over 400 people. It was the greatest maritime disaster in Irish Waters. Date of Death:10-October-1918. Age at Death, 39. Son of Thomas and Bridget Cody (nee Curran); husband of Mary Cody (nee Malone), of 13, Clarinda Park N., Kingstown, Co. Dublin. Born at Kilkenny. Cemetery: Tower Hill Memorial, London.

Coffee, Francis Warren. Rank; Second Lieutenant. Regiment or Service: Royal Irish Rifles. Unit; 5th Battalion. Date of death; 16/08/1917. Age at death; 28. Born; Kilkenny. Residence; Dublin. Killed in action. Son of Francis Richard Coffee, of 8, Fairfield Park, Rathgar, Dublin, and the late Evelyn Coffee. Born 20-November-1888 at Whitechurch, Kilkenny. Son of Francis Richard and Evelyn Warren Coffee (nee Warren). Entered Trinity College in 1906. From 'Irish Life' October-1917;- … was killed in an advanced position whilst gallantly leading his men forward during an attack on the enemy's lines on August 16th, 1917, was the eldest and only surviving son of Mr F. R. Coffee, Inspector, Board of Works, of 8 Fairfield Park, Rathgar. He was educated at Bishop Foy's School, Waterford; Fermoy College, and Trinity College. He was gazetted to the Royal Irish Rifles in October 1915, proceeded to France in June 1916 and went through the Somme campaign of that year. He again arrived in France in January last and was on active service there until his death. '. Irish Times. Coffee-August 16, killed in action, Francis Warren Coffee, Second Lieutenant Royal Irish Rifles, eldest and only surviving son of Francis R Coffee, Inspector Board of Public Works, 8 Fairfield Park, Rathgar, Dublin. The Irish Times, August 16, 1922. Roll of Honour. In Memoriam. Coffee-In very dear and loving memory of Frank, Second Lieutnenat, Royal Irish Rifles, killed in action, near Ypres, August 16th, 1917. Irish Times. Coffee-In fond memory of Frank, Second Lieutenant, Royal Irish Rifles, killed in action, August 16th, 1917. —"D.". The Weekly Irish Times. Ireland's Roll of Honour. September 1, 1917. Second Lieutenant Francis Warren Coffee, Royal Irish Rifles, killed in action on August 16th, was the eldest and only surviving son of Mr F R Coffe, Inspector, Board of Works, 3 Fairfield Park, Rathgar, Dublin. The Weekly Irish Times. Ireland's Roll of Honour. September 22, 1917. Second Lieutenant Francis Warren Coffee, Royal Irish Rifles, killed in action on August 16th, received his education at Bishop Foy's School, Waterford, and Fermoy College, and entered Trinity College, Dublin, in April, 1906. He received his commission on 27th October, 1915, and proceeded abroad in June, 1916. After an absence on leave he again returned to the front in January, 1917, since when he had been engaged in various active operations. He was the eldest and only surviving son of Mr F R Coffee, Inspector, Board of Works, 8 Fairfield Park, Rathgar, Dublin. Grave or Memorial Reference; 138 to 140 and 162 to 162A and 163A. Cemetery: Tyne Cot Memorial in Belgium. He is also listed on the Bishop Foy School Memorial located in Christ Church Cathedral (Church of Ireland), Henrietta Street, Waterford.

Colclough, Harry Henry William. Rank; Private. Regiment or Service: Irish Guards. Unit; 1st Battalion. Service Number; 5768. Date of death; 14/09/1917. Age at death;21. Born; Clomantagh, County Kilkenny. Enlisted; Kilkenny. Killed in action. Son of Robert Edward and Sarah Jane Colclough, of Tubrid, Barna, Woodsgift, Co. Kilkenny. In his Will, dated 08-August-1917, his effects and property were received by;- (Father) Mr Robert Colclough, Tubrid, Barna, County Kilkenny. Notes; Name listed as Harry (CWGC) Henry (SDGW, IMR) William. Grave or Memorial Reference; I F 40. Cemetery: Bleuet Farm Cemetery in Belgium. He is also commemorated on the Great War Memorial in St Canice's Cathedral, Kilkenny…'To the Glory of God and in loving memory of the following members of the Diocese of Ossory who gave their lives for their country in the Great War 1914-1918'.

Coleman, Edward. Rank; Private. Regiment or Service: Northumberland Fusiliers. Unit; 8th Battalion. Service Number; 5667. Date of death; 06/08/1917. Age at death; 37. Born; Kilkenny. Enlisted; Newcastle-on-Tyne. Killed in action. Husband of Elizabeth J. Coleman, of 12, Ridley Gardens, Swalwell, Co. Durham. Grave or Memorial Reference; Panels 19 to 23 and 162. Cemetery: Tyne Cot Memorial in Belgium

Colfer/Colter, Patrick. Rank; Sergeant. Regiment or Service: Irish Guards. Unit; 1st Battalion. Service Number; 7762. Date of death; 22/04/1917. Age at death;25. Born; Shankill. County Kilkenny. Enlisted; Manchester, Lancashire. Residence; Shankill, County Kilkenny. Died of wounds. Colfer (CWGC, IMR) Colter (SDGW), Patrick. Son of Peter and Kate Colfer, of Shankill, Whitehall, Co. Kilkenny. Grave or Memorial Reference; O IX I 1. Cemetery: St Sever Cemetery Extension, Rouen in France.

Colles, Richard Bertram. Rank; First Lieutenant. Regiment or Service: Royal Navy. Born;. An article in the King's County Chronicle, 1915. An Irish force in the Great Battle. The point of view of the individual fighter, the man actually engaged in the conflict, what he saw and what he did, has been depicted simply yet graphically in a letter from a Sergeant in the 1st Royal Irish Rifles, who was in he battle of Neuve Chapelle. The personal note runs right through his narrative. It is a tale of the deeds of men and not merely of big guns."It was there," he says,"We lost Col. Laure, capt. And Adjutant Wright, Captains Briscoe and Colles, Lieuts. Hutcheson, Barrington, Lang, and Gilmour; total officers killed 10, wounded 8—which only left us four officers— Major Baker, Capt. Tee, Lieuts, Gaitland and Browne. The rank and file lost 130 killed; 24 died of wounds, 280 wounded, and 40 missing; total casualties 474. Up to the battle our losses were the heaviest in the Brigade, and the second heaviest in the Division. The colonel lost his life charging the German trenches with B Co, and two latoons of D Co., Major Wright who was commanding ? Co., got wounded. Myself and seven riflemen managed to get to a trench on the left of the German position. To get to this trench we had to cross by a river which was about 100 yards wide. Lieut. Lang tried to cross by a road, but was riddled by machine gun fire. He was a very plucky officer. I tried the river, I was spotted by a few German rifleman, but I moved as quickly as possible across, the rest of my platoon following; all of No's 1 and 2 sections (about 24 men) being killed, with the exception of two riflemen. Owing to the heavy fire the remainder of the platoon could not get across. Lieut. Hutcheson got over safely, but on arrival at the trench was shot through the brain by a bullet which came through the parapet of the trench. Sergt. Cunningham and Corporal, Holmes attempted to cross but the former was severely wounded, the latter killed. Co Sergt-Major Kendrick jumped up and ordered the remainder of the company to advance, but was instantly shot through the heart. He was very brave and cool under fire; he was a great loss to us, and there was no reason to doubt that had he been in command from the beginning we would have got over with less casualties. Sergt. Rees was seriously wounded. Captain. O'Sullivan ordered the advance to be stopped. I was left with seven riflemen of ours, 2 German prisoners, wounded and unwounded; also 12 of the Notts and Derbys wounded. When the Colonel was killed he was trying to cross on the right. Th adjutant was killed about the same time while studying a map. Both were very plucky officers; they were proud of us as we were proud of them. Our won artillery shelled us by mistake, although messages were repeatedly sent to them that they were doing us harm, bot owing to the terrific fire the messages never got there. At the same time the German artillery were dropping shells behind us, thereby preventing the Lincolnshire Regiment from supporting us. It is my opinion that had every regiment moved forward as we did there is no doubt we would have taken Lille. But as there were numerous obstacles to surmount, such as barbed wire, etc., probably this could not be done. Lieut. Gilmore was killed while on outpost duty; he was a brave officer. Major Baker ordered the regiment to retire, the Lincolns creeping forward and taking our places, myself taking the wounded who could walk and the German prisoners back with me. Capt. Laynon joined us in the billets. He was shot through the head the first night we went into the trenches. Capt. Cinnamond was wounded in the leg. Company Sergt-Major Moutung (?) was killed in a charge on the first day. Sergt. Riordan, Corpl. Gordon, and 12 riflemen were blown to pieces near a wood. A man named Phipps who was in front of me, was struck by a shell, portions of his flesh and equipment striking me in the face, but I pushed on as fast as I could, as it is the safest plan under such circumstances, and as luck would have it, I am quite safe. Lieuts. Barrington, Lang and Hutcheson were very brave, and were it not for these and half a dozen non-commissioned officers and a few dare-devil riflemen, Neuve Chapelle would never have been taken. No words of command were used. Some officer jumped up and shouted ;rush' and everybody got down and waited for someone else to take the lead. Victoria crosses were earned by the dozen. When you saw those men, all fear left you, and you were automatically following their example. Remember out regiment took Neuve Chapelle. What was an obstacle to others we overcame and I can safely say there were very few regiments who would have beaten the Royal Irish Rifles at that battle. All I have related here I have seen with my own eyes. On the third day of the battle I was in a position on the German flank, and could see their movements, I tried to semaphore across to our chaps, but owing to the heavy fire the messages could not be heard. My object in sending you this letter is to see that our regiment gets its due. We had plenty of Michael O'Learys at Neuve Chapelle, and men who had been at Mons and the Aisne say that this battle beat the other two into one. Sergt. Buckley got his legs blown off, and eventually died of wounds; he was a brave chap, but did not get his due. Our regimental stretcher bearers did good work being right up to the firing line all the time. From the "Times." Colles. —On the 13th November, at 4, Lion-gate-Gardens, Richmond, Surrey, Richard Bertram Colles, R. N., late First Lieutenant and Navigating Officer, H. M. S."Espiegle," dearly-loved second son of R and S Colles, Millmount, Kilkenny, aged 28. Irish Times. Colles-November 13, 1914, t 4 Lion Gate Gardens, Richmond, Surrey, of fever, contracted while on foreign service. Richard Bertram Colles, R. N., late First Lieutenant Navigating Officer, H. M. S., Espiegle, dearly-loved second son of R and S Colles, Millmount, Kilkenny, aged 28. Cemetery: Memorial in St Canice's Cathedral, Kilkenny. 'To the Glory of God and in loving memory of the following members of the Diocese of Ossory who gave their lives for their country in the Great War 1914-1918'.

Collins, Patrick. Rank; Private. Regiment or Service: Connaught Rangers. Unit; 5th Battalion. Service Number; 11055. Date of death; 05/12/1915. Age at death;19. Born; Kilkenny. Enlisted; Kilkenny. Residence; Kilmoganny, County Kilkenny. Died in Salonika. Son of Denis and Margaret Collins, of Rogerstown, Kilmoganny, Co. Kilkenny. After his death his effects and property were received by;- (Mother) Mrs M Collins, Rogers Town, Kilmoganny, County Kilkenny, Ireland. Grave or Memorial Reference; A 50. Cemetery: Alexandria (Chatby) Military and War Memorial Cemetery in Egypt.

Comerford, John. Rank; Private. Regiment or Service: Irish Guards. Unit; 1st Battalion. Service Number; 2802. Date of death; 26/10/1914. Age at death; 26. Born; Castlecomer, County Kilkenny. Enlisted; Dublin. Killed in action. Son of Edward and Mary Comerford. Grave or Memorial Reference; Panel 11. Cemetery: Ypres (Menin Gate) Memorial in Belgium.

Comerford / Commerford, James. Rank; Corporal. Regiment or Service: Leinster Regiment. Unit; 1st Battalion. Service Number; 10173. Date of death; 21/04/1915. Age at death;21. Born; Castlecomer, County Kilkenny. Enlisted; Maryborough. Killed in action. Comerford (CWGC, IMR) Commerford (SDGW), James. Son of Nicholas and Julia Comerford, of Deir Park, Castle Comer, Co. Kilkenny. Grave or Memorial Reference; Panel 44. Cemetery: Ypres (Menin Gate) Memorial in Belgium.

Connell, Cornelius. Rank; Private. Regiment or Service: Royal Irish Regiment. Unit; 6th Battalion. Service Number; 2532. Date of death; 03/09/1916. Born; St John's, Kilkenny. Enlisted; Kilkenny. Killed in action. After his death his effects and property were received by;- (Father) Mr Thomas Connell, 22 Maudlin Street, Kilkenny, Ireland. Grave or Memorial Reference; Pier and Face 3 A. Cemetery: Thiepval Memorial in France.

Connell, Denis. Rank; Private. Regiment or Service: Royal Irish Regiment. Unit; 6th Battalion. Service Number; 7827. Date of death; 09/09/1916. Born; Castlecomer, County Kilkenny. Enlisted; Castlecomer. Killed in action. Son of Michael and Margaret Connell, of Love Lane, Castlecomer. Co. Kilkenny. Grave or Memorial Reference; Pier and Face 3. Cemetery: Pier and Face 3 A.

Connell, Martin. Rank; Private. Regiment or Service: Royal Irish Regiment. Unit; 6th Battalion. Service Number; 7172. Date of death; 09/09/1916. Age at death; 39. Born; Callan, County Kilkenny. Enlisted; Kilkenny. Residence; Callan. Killed in action. Husband of Johanna Connell, of Mill Street Callan, Co. Kilkenny. Grave or Memorial Reference; Pier and Face 3 A. Cemetery: Thiepval Memorial in France.

Connell, Michael. Rank; Private. Regiment or Service: Connaught Rangers. Unit; 5th Battalion. Service Number; 3787. Date of death; 24/08/1915. Age at death;23. Born; Kilkenny. Enlisted; Carlow. Residence; Kilkenny. Died of wounds in Gallipoli. Son of Thomas and Catherine Connell, of 22, Manalin St., Kilkenny. After his death his effects and property were received by;- (Father) Thomas Connell, Maudlin St, Kilkenny, Ireland. Kilkenny People, June 1916. Kilkenny Soldier's Letter. (Passed by Censor). Balkan States, 12-04-1916. Dear Mr Keane—I take the liberty of writing to you to let you know if you would be so kind as to spare a space in your valuable paper for this letter. Being an old reader of the "Kilkenny People" I will try and let the readers at home know, through you, of the doings of the "People's" readers abroad. I have been through the landing on the 6th August, 1915, at Suvla Bay, where, I am sorry to say, we lost a few Kilkenny boys. From there we found ourselves on the Serbian frontier facing the Germans, Bulgars, Austrians and Turks. We, however gave them to understand that they were "up against" Irishmen, much to their surprise; but they came on in overwhelming numbers. Still there was no Kilkennyman coming down from the mountains wounded, but unfortunately the frost and snow proved too masterful for a couple of Kilkenny lads, who had got frost-bitten, but they proved themselves men and passed on with a smilw on their lips to hospital, and as they passed you could hear their "pass-word"—"Up the Black and Amber!" To mention the names of these brave lads—I only think it will serve to gather them some praise, which they highly deserve. Their names are;-- John Sheridan,"Dido" Kenny, as we used to call him, from Walkin Street Upper, and the renowned "Cock" Byrne's brother James, who got wounded through the thigh. All belong to the Connaught Rangers. Well, the "Kilkenny People" has been a great welcome to us, Kilkenny boys, both in Gallipoli and in the Balkans, and every post that comes the cry is. "Did you get the 'People'?" Our division is the 10th Irish Division, which bore the brunt at the landing and saved the day in Serbia, and which all the papers gave praise to on that memorable retreat. We are now nine months on active service, and don't expect to get leave before we finish the Huns up out here. I may mention that the boys from the city and county have been very lucky out here, thank God. I also may mention the names of the heroes who fell at Svla Bay, viz., Sergeant Michael O'Keeffe, late of Greensbridge and Privates K. Meehan, of Garden Row, and W. O'Connell, from Maudlin Street. Their memory is still fresh with us, and I trust that the people at home offer up a prayer for their happy repose. The English papers may boast of the deeds of valour performed by the Australian forces, but let them compare them with the magnificent dash of the Irish regiments and see who comes first. I think I will draw this letter to a close by saying that all the boys from city and county are "in the pink," and all hope to be back again soon, with the help of God. I enclose a few verses I composed by the help of Private J. Hogan, 3909, of the 4th Battalion., on thinking of the landing at Suvla Bay. I conclude by sending my best wishes for the success of your valuable paper. —I am, sir, yours sincerely. No 78, Corporal P. Staunton. A Company, 5th Royal Irish regiment, 10th Division, Salonika Field Force. The Landing at Suvla Bay. 'Twas on the 6th of August, on a bright and sunny day. We landed at the Dardanelles, some thousands of miles away. We knew not what before us lay, but we hear the shot and shell. And many an Irish soldier there that day now lives no more to tell. It was a bright and glorious day which we will never forget. When the Connaughts and the 5th Royal Irish went through that Vale of Death. It was death by fire, and water going through the Suvla tide. But those gallant sons of Erin their enemy defied! I will raise a glass, filled to the brim, of Smithwick's sparkling ale, and drink to the health of the boys that live who fought and did no quail. And whenever I hear the sound of guns and the clamour of war and din. I never will forget Gallipoli and the struggle I there was in. Kilkenny Journal, September, 1915. Kilkenny Soldier Killed. Much regret has been caused in Kilkenny by the news of the death of Lance Corporal Michael O'Connell, Connaught Rangers, son of Mr Thomas O'Connell, Maudlin Street, who was informed of the sad event in a letter from the Rev. Fr. Knapp, O. P., chaplain, Alexandria Hospital, Egypt. Father

Knapp states that the brave young soldier was brought to hospital on the 21st August, suffering from very serious wounds, and he died on the 24th August, having received the last sacraments. He was but twenty three years of age, and prior to his enlistment was engaged as assistant in the London and Newcastle tea Company's premises in High Street. He had been at the Dardanelles for five weeks before receiving his fatal wound. Widespread sympathy is extended to his bereaved father, who has three other sons serving in the Army—one at the front and two in training. Notes; Number listed as 5/3787 (CWGC) 3787 (SDGW). Grave or Memorial Reference; J 71. Cemetery: Alexandria (Chatby) Military and War Memorial Cemetery in Egypt.

Connell/O'Connell, Richard. Rank; Private. Regiment or Service: Royal Irish Regiment. Unit; 7th Battalion. Service Number; 7424. Date of death; 29/09/1918. Age at death; 18. Born; St John's, Kilkenny. Enlisted; Kilkenny. Died of wounds. Connell (CWGC) O'Connell (SDGW), Son of Thomas and Catherine Connell, of 22, Manalin St., Kilkenny. After his death his effects and property were received by;- (Father) Thomas Connell, Maudlin St, Kilkenny, Ireland. Notes; Formerly he was with the Royal Irish Regiment where his number was 9656. Grave or Memorial Reference; IV A 47. Cemetery: Bucquoy Road Cemetery, Ficheux in France.

Major Connellan, from 'Our Heroes.'

Connellan, Peter Martin. Rank; Major. Regiment or Service: Hampshire Regiment. Unit; 1st Battalion. Date of death; 20/10/1914. Age at death;32. Killed in action near Armentieres. Son of Major J. H. Connellan, D. L., of Coolmore, Co. Kilkenny; husband of Winifred Bollam (formerly Connellan), of Belline, Piltown, Co. Kilkenny. Killed in action near Armentieres. From 'Our Heroes'. was the only son of Major J. H. F. H. Connellan, Coolmore, Thomastown, County Kilkenny, who was formerly a Captain in the Hampshire Regiment. Major P. Connellan was gazetted 2nd Lieutenant in January, 1901, a first Lieutenant in November, 1903, and Captain in 1907. he served at Aden in 1903-4, and took part in the operations in the interior. He acted as Brigade Signalling Officer to the Aden Boundary Delimitation Column, and in 1909 Adjutant of the third Battalion of the Hampshire regiment, and acted as Adjutant in the Special reserve from January, 1911, to January, 1914. Harrow Memorials, volume 1; Harrow School Register, 1845-1925; Harrovian War Supplement. Major Peter Martin Connellan, Hampshire Regiment. The only son of the late Major J H F H Connellan, JP, DL and Mrs Laura Connellan of Coolmore, Thomastown, Ireland. Educated at Harrow from 1895-1898. Joined the Hampshire Regiment in 1901. Served on the Aden Boundary Delimination Column in 1903-1904. Promoted to Captain in 1907. Awarded the Royal Humane Society's Medal for saving a man on his regiment from drowning in 1909. Became Adjutant of the 3rd Battalion in 1911. In 1911 he married, Winifred, 3rd daughter of the late Arthur E Niblett, of Haresfield Court, Gloucester. Embarked for France at Southampton on 21 Aug 1914. After the retreat from Mons, General Hunter-Weston sent forward his name for "special reward and promotion.". Appointed company commander and Acting Major and given command of a company. Killed in action near Armentieres on 20 October 1914. He was mentioned in John French's despatch on the same day. Kilkenny People, November 1914. Late Major P. M. Connellan. Thomastown Magistrates Sympathy. At the Thomastown Petty Sessions on Tuesday last, the Chairman 9Mr P. C. Creaghe, R. M.) said;--Before beginning the business of the court I desire to say that my three brother magistrates and I regret that we are the only representatives of a generally large bench of magistrates here, but such as we are we would like to express in the most public way possible our deep sympathy with Major J. H. Connellan and his family, and young Mrs Connellan, widow of Major Peter Connellan. I am sure that everyone must feel as we do here to-day, the deepest sympathy with him in this great trial that has been sent to him. Major Peter Connellan has died a glorious death which any of us—if we were given a choice how to die—would certainly choose; he died for the sake of the Empire and his country. But death always leaves its sting, always leaves its bereavement and sorrow, and in the bereavement and sorrow that has fallen on Major Connellan and his family, we as brother magistrates, wish to offer him our sincere sympathy and condolence. Kilkenny People, November 1914. Death of Captain P. M. Connellan. The grim realities of the terrible war now being waged on the Continent were brought home to us in no uncertain manner on Monday morning last, when news was received in Kilkenny of the death of Captain Peter Martin Connellan, who was killed in action at the front. The deceased was the only son of our respected fellow-countryman, Major J. H. Connellan, J. P., D. L., Coolmore House, Thomastown, who is beloved and respected by all classes of the community and to whom profound sympathy is expended. The late Captain Connellan, who belonged to the 1st battalion of the Hampshire Regiment, had already distinguished himself in the battles of the Marne and Aisne, and at Mons. At the latter place his regiment suffered very severely, many officers and men being lost, and the deceased officer was appointed local Major of his Battalion. His remarkable acts of bravery and intrepidity of character merited for him mention in General French's despatches and a recommendation for special promotion. Needles to say, this fact was learned in the county with much pleasure, and many were the congratulations which were extended to Major Connellan of the success of his only son. And this fact renders the painful news that we announce today of his death all the more poignant. Seldom before has the bitter truth of the old decree—" In the midst of life we are in death"—thrust itself upon us. It is sad to think that a life so full of promise should be taken away so suddenly, and the regret wich the sad event has evoked is profound and universal. The late Captain Connellan—who by the way held the Royal Humane Society's medal for saving the life of a drowning soldier-married in 1911, Winifred, third daughter of the late Arthur Nebitt, Esq., formerly of Haresfield Court, Gloucester, but leaves no family. In common with all classes and creeds in the county we extend to Major Connellan our respectful sympathy in the terrible loss he has sustained, and trust that he will find consolation in the fact that his great grief is shared by all. Kilkenny Journal, September, 1915. Sympathy With Major J. H. Connellan, D. L. Much sympathy is felt for Major J. H. Connellan, D. L., Coolmore House, Thomastown, on the death of his nephew—Captain O'Hara, R. M. —who died from wounds received in action at the Dardanelles. Deceased officer was only in his 22nd year. De Ruvigny's Roll of Honour. only son of Major James Hercules Fitzwalter Henry Connellan, of Coolmore, Thomastown, County Kilkenny, J. P., D. L., formerly Hon. Col. 5th Royal Irish regiment and Capt. Hampshire regt., by his wife, Laura Elizabeth, daughter of Richard Ussher Roberts. Born at Sale, Chester, 19-February-1882. Educated at Harrow and was gazetted 2nd Lieutenant to the 1st Hampshires (then in India), 08-January-1901, being promoted Lieutenant, 30-November-1903, and Captain, 09-May-1907. he served in Aden, 1903-4, took part in the operations in the hinterland, and acted as signalling officer to the brigade under Brig. -Gen. Scallan with the Boundary Delimitation Commission, and was present at the attack by Arabs on the camp at Awabil, also in the expedition against the Kotalbis. He was Adjutant to the 1st Battalion, Hampshire Depot and 3rd battalion, from 23-January, 1911 to January-1914, when he rejoined the 1st Battalion, at Colchester. The Battalion left for the front in the 11th Brigade, 4th Division, in the third week of August-1914, and was closely engaged in covering the British retirement from Mons, the Division earning the war approval of the Commander-in-Chief. Captain Connellan bore a very conspicuous part in holding the railway line near Coudry on 26-August, being under heavy fire all day in a most exposed position, also in the retirement on Ligny, and subsequent engagements. On 07-September-1914, he was promoted Temporary Major (a rank which he continued to hold until he fell), and given the command of his Battalion, which he retained during the engagements at the Marne and the Aisne. After being relieved by the French near Buez-le-Long on 04-October the Brigade was engaged in the neighbourhood of Armentieres, to the north-east of which Major Connellan fell (shot through the neck by shrapnel) on 20-October, when second in command of his Battalion. He was buried at Pont-de-Nieppe. Major Connellan was twice mentioned in Despatches (London Gazette, 09-October-1914 and 17-February-1915), and especially recommended for promotion and reward by his Brigadier, who described his as one of his best commanders and a born soldier. He was a keen sportsman, a fine rider, very fond of hunting and salmon fishing, also of games, was a member of the Battalion polo team, and a good player of hockey, tennis, Badminton, etc. he held the Bronze Medal of the Royal Humane Society for saving one of the men of his Regiment from drowning. Major Connellan married at St Thomas' Church. (Bond of Sarcrifice carries a similar article) Winchester, 18-October-1911, Winifred (New Empress Club), 3rd daughter of the late Arthur

Niblett, formerly of Baresfield Court, Co. Gloucseter. Irish Times. Connellan,-Killed in action, Captain Peter Martin Connellan, Hampshire Regiment, only son of Major J H Connellan, D. L., Coolmore, County Kilkenny. Grave or Memorial Reference; I B 20. Cemetery: Pont-De-Nippe Communal Cemetery, Nord, France.

Connolly, Patrick. Rank; Private. Regiment or Service: Durham Light Infantry. Unit; 11th Battalion. Service Number; 16202. Date of death; 05/09/1916. Born; Kilkenny. Enlisted; Newcastle. Residence; Kilkenny. Died of wounds. Mr Shannon, C. P. S., said he desired to be associated with his worship's remarks. Grave or Memorial Reference; Pier and Face 14 A and 15C. Cemetery: Thiepval Memorial in France.

Connolly, William. Rank; Fireman. Regiment or Service: Mercantile Marine. Unit; S. S."Formby" (Glasgow. Date of death; 16/12/1917. Age at death;26. Son of the late William and Mary Connolly. Born at Milepost, Co. Kilkenny. Head Constable Connell—On behalf of the police, I wish to be permitted as associate myself with your worship's kindly reference to Major Connellan's death. Mr S. C. Webb, solicitor—On behalf of the solicitors profession I would like to associate myself with everything that your worship has said, and to say that we wish to extend our heartfelt sympathy to Major Connellan and Mrs Connellan in their very terrible bereavement. Cemetery: Tower Hill Memorial UK.

Connor, John. Rank; Sergeant. Regiment or Service: Machine Gun Corps. Unit; Infantry, 76th Company. Service Number; 53668. Date of death; 07/06/1917. Born; Abbeyleix. Queen's County. Enlisted; Shanbally. Residence; Kilkenny. Killed in action. Notes; Formerly he was with the Leinster Regiment where his number was 3677. Grave or Memorial Reference; V F 15. Cemetery: Wulverghem-Lindenhoek Road Military Cemetery in Belgium.

Connors, James. Rank; Private. Regiment or Service: Royal Irish Regiment. Unit; 1st Battalion. Service Number; 3593. Date of death; 15/03/1915. Born; Clonmel. Enlisted; Tipperary. Residence; Kilkenny. Killed in action. After his death his effects and property were received by;- (Wife) Mrs J Connors, Jacob Street, Kilkenny. Grave or Memorial Reference; Panel 33. Cemetery: Ypres (Menin Gate) Memorial in Belgium.

Conroy, James. Rank; Private. Regiment or Service: Royal Irish Regiment. Unit; 2nd Battalion. Service Number; 7790. Date of death; 14/07/1916. Age at death; 20. Born; Marshalstown, County Wexford. Enlisted; Kilkenny. Killed in action. Son of Michael and Annie Conroy of New St, Kilkenny. Grave or Memorial Reference; Pier and Face 16 C. Cemetery: Thiepval Memorial in France.

Second Lieutenant Considine, from Bond of Sacrifice.

Considine, Christopher Daniel. Rank; Second Lieutenant. Regiment or Service: Royal Dublin Fusiliers. Unit; 5th Battalion attached to the 2nd Battalion. Date of death; 24/05/1915. Age at death;27. Killed in action. Son of the late Sir Heffeman (sic) Considine, C. B., M. V. O., D. L., of Derk, Pallasgreen, County Limerick. Bond of Sacrifice, Volume 2. was the third son of the late Sir Heffernan Considine, C. B., M. V. O., D. L., of Derk, County Limerick, and Emily, daughter of the late John Hyacinth Talbot, M. P., D. L., of Castle Talbot, and Ballytrent, County Wexford. He was born on the 21st December, 1887, at "New Park," County Kilkenny, and was educated at Beaumont College, Old Windsor, where he was a member of both the Cricket and Football XI's, and rowed for the College VIII. He was also a fine sportsman and was good at all games. He volunteered for service at the outbreak of the war, receiving his commission as 2nd Lieutenant, in August, 1914, in the 5th Battalion, Royal Dublin Fusiliers. Early in May, 1915, he was ordered to the front in Flanders, where he was attached to the 2nd Battalion of his regiment. He was killed near Ypres by a shell early in the morning of the 24th May, 1915, during a strong German attack, which was delivered under dense clouds of poisonous gas. He gave his life in a noble attempt to save his Major, who had been gassed. He was buried by the Germans, with his men, where he fell, near "Shell Trap Farm." A Chaplain to the Forces wrote of him; "I knew him for a brave officer and a true gentleman even in the few days I was with him, and his death was just like what I knew of him. (?) Under a murderous artillery and machine-gun fire he tried to bring the Major Commanding his company out of danger. Your dear brother was killed instantaneously and the major died shortly afterwards. It was a fine and chivalrous thing to do, worthy of the man and of the old regiment. I don't think anyone who wasn't with them could understand the full heroism of our officers, men like your brother. The horrors of gas and heavy artillery and raking machine-gun fire seemed to matter nothing to them. They did the right thing, coolly and collectively, in the face of certain death. They died like a Christian gentlemen.". Kilkenny People and Limerick Chronocle, June, 1915. Second Lieutenant C. D. Considine, who was killed in action near Ypres on May 25, was the third son of the late Sir Heffernan Considine, of Derk, County Limerick, and was educated at Beaumont College, Windsor, where he greatly distinguished himself at all outdoor sports. He was gazetted to the 5th Battalion, Royal Dublin Fusiliers on the 15th of last August, and was transferred to the 2nd Battalion in Flanders on May 2nd. He is also listed in 'Our Heroes' with no new information. His brother, Captain Heffernan James Considine, from Limerick also died during the Great War. Irish Independent; 1915. Officers in the Casualty Lists. Lieutenant T J Considine, Dublins, wounded, is the second son of Sir Heffernan Considine C B., Derk., County Limerick, former Resident Magistrate and deputy Inspector General R. I. C., who has already lost a son in the war. Irish Times. Considine-Killed in action near Ypres, on May 23, 1915, Second Lieutenant C D Considine, 5th Battalion, Royal Dublin Fusiliers, third son of the late Sir Heffernan Considine, of Derk, County Limerick. A brother;-The Weekly Irish Times. Ireland's Roll of Honour. February 24, 1917. Lieutenant Talbot J Considine, Royal Dublin Fusiliers, wounded on 23rd January, and is still in hospital. He was seriously wounded in June, 1915, and only returned to the front on 5th January, 1917. He is the second son of the late Sir Heffernan Considine, C. B., of Derk, Pallasgreen, County Limerick, formerly deputy Inspector General, R. I. C. Lieutenant Considine's brother, Second Lieutenant C D Considine, Royal Dublin Fusiliers, was killed in action on 24th May, 1915; another brother, Lieutenant F A Considine, Royal Munster Fusiliers, was wounded on 24th August, 1916. His eldest brother, Captain Heffernan Considine, M. C., Royal Irish Regiment, was killed in action on 27th October, 1916, and his youngest brother, Lieutenant J P Considine, being unfit for military service, is a voluntary ambulance driver at the front. Freeman's Journal, 25/06/1915. Late Lieutenant Considine. -Great sympathy is felt by the people of East Limerick with the Considines of Derk, whose brother, a Lieutenant in the Royal Dublin Fusiliers, was recently killed in action in France. Grave or Memorial Reference; Panel 44 and 46. Cemetery: Ypres (Menin Gate) Memorial in Belgium.

Conville, Patrick. Rank; Gunner. Regiment or Service: Royal Garrison Artillery. Unit; 4th Siege Battery. Service Number; 18348. Date of death; 17/08/1917. Age at death; 37. Born; Clough, Castlecomer, County Kilkenny. Enlisted; Dublin. Killed in action. Son of John and Eliza Conville, of Co. Kilkenny; husband of Mary Conville, of 27, Rialto Cottages, South Circular Rd. Grave or Memorial Reference; I B 23. Cemetery: Duhallow A. D. S. Cemetery in Belgium. Duhallow Advanced Dressing Station was a front line casualty clearing station for soldiers wounded in this (Ypres) sector. It was named after a Southern Irish Hunt.

Conway, James. Rank; Private. Regiment or Service: Royal Army Service Corps. Unit; 1st Reserve Motorised Transport Depot. Service Number; M2/130587. Date of death; 01/09/1915. Born; Waterford. Enlisted; Dublin. Residence; Waterford. Died at home. Notes; 01/09/1916 (Soldiers died in the Great War and Irelands Memorial Records) 01/09/1915 (Commonwealth War Graves Commission). Grave or Memorial Reference; Near the South West boundary. Cemetery: Ferrybank Catholic Churchyard, Kilkenny.

Conway, James. Rank; Private. Regiment or Service: Royal Irish Regiment. Unit; 2nd Battalion. Service Number; 7538. Date of death; 07/06/1917. Age at death; 33. Born; Windgap, County Kilkenny. Enlisted; Clonmel, County Tipperary. Residence; Ballinaugh. County Kilkenny. Killed in action. Son of Martin and Bridget Sheehan Conway, of Ballinalinagh, Tullahought, Co. Kilkenny. Munster Express, July, 1917. Death of a Young Irish Hero. With feelings of deep sympathy we chronicle the demise of Private James Conway, Ballygown, Ponsonby, Tullahought. James Conway was second son of Mr Martin Conway, and came of an old and respected stock in Windgap parish. Private Conway joined the colours of the R. I. Regiment some two years ago last March. He was through the battles of the Dardanelles and Salonika, and received a few days leave to visit his parent, brother, and sisters. After being convalescent from malaria he was again called on to join his comrades on the western front when on that eventful morning, June 7th last, at the great drive of Messines, he was mortally wounded and died on the same day. A Vote of sympathy was received by his father from the King and Queen. Private Conway was a member of the Tullahought National Volunteers during their brief existence. He was a fairly good athlete and a jolly, jovial, genial soul, and is very much regretted by his numerous friends and companions. He was about 28 years of age. To his father, brother and sisters we offer our condolences. R. I. P. Munster Express, July, 1917. In memory of a dear friend and comrade, Private Jim Conway, late of Ballalinagh, was killed in action on June 7th "somewhere in France."."Munster Express, July, 1917. In memory of a dear friend and comrade, Private Jim Conway, late of Ballalinagh, was killed in action on June 7th "somewhere in France." "Somewhere in France" is a nameless grave, but under the blood-stained sod is only the casket that shrined a soul which is now at home with God; "Somewhere in France" as sister's tears rain down on a painted face; He was all that they had, but duty called the last of a noble race. His cheery whistle at morningtide, the lilt of an Irish song-The stormy flash of the bright blue eyes when we heard of a tale of wrong. The open hand for the needy, the ready help for the weak. The sunny smile, and the loving words, he never more will speak. This his life's rosary-memory tell, the bright decades one by one. While his sisters clasps a little cross, and whispers,"Thy will be done." They know he is safe for evermore, beyond the mishaps of chance.
In a better land, there they'll meet poor Jim, who sleeps now "somewhere in France." Sent by Val. D. Coughlan, Curragawn, Carrick-on-Suir. Grave or Memorial Reference; I A 3. Cemetery: Wytschaete Military Cemetery in Belgium.

Conway, William. Rank; Private. Regiment or Service: Leinster Regiment. Unit; 2nd Battalion. Service Number; 10740. Date of death; 12/04/1917. Age at death;25. Born; Windgate, County Kilkenny. Enlisted; Carrick-on-Suir. Killed in action. Son of Patrick and Catherine Conway, of Knockroe, Carrick-on-Suir. After his death his effects and property were received by;- (Mother) Mrs Catherine Conway, Carrick on Suir, County Tipperary, Ireland. Notes; Formerly he was with the Royal Irish Regiment where his number was 11518. Grave or Memorial Reference; IV A 17. Cemetery: Lievin Communal Cemetery Extension in France.

Cook, Charles. Rank; Private. Regiment or Service: Northumberland Fusiliers. Unit; 25th Battalion. Service Number; 847. Date of death; 22/02/1919. Age at death; 31. Born; Dunnamaggin, County Kilkenny. Residence; Kilmoganny, County Kilkenny. Died after discharge. Notes; Died after discharge at the Royal Hospital, Chelsea. Cemetery: Unknown

Cooke, Patrick. Rank; Fireman. Regiment or Service: Mercantile Marine. Unit; S. S."Formby" (Glasgow). Date of death; 16/12/1917. Age at death;30. Son of William and Anastasia Cooke; husband of Anne Cooke (nee O'Connor), of Slieverue, Co. Kilkenny. Born at Slieverue, Co. Kilkenny. Cemetery: Tower Hill Memorial UK.

Cooke, William Henry. Rank; Company Sergeant Major. Regiment or Service: Royal Engineers. Unit; 12th Labour Company. Service Number; 163345. Date of death; 20/02/1917. Age at death; 48. Born; Stafford. Enlisted; Belfast. Died in Salonika. Grave or Memorial Reference; D XVII 6. Cemetery: Pieta Military Cemetery in Malta.

Lieutenant Corbett-Wilson, from Bond of Sacrifice.

Corbett-Wilson, Denys. Rank; Lieutenant. Regiment or Service: Royal Flying Corps. Unit; 3rd Squadron. Date of death; 10/05/1915. Age at death;32. Killed in action. Son of the late W. H. C. Wilson, Barrister-at-Law, and Ada Caroline Wilson (nee Corbett), of 124, Knightsbridge, London S. W. Known to all as 'CW'. Bond of Sacrifice, Volume 2. had not served in the Army before the declaration of war. After leaving Eton, where he was educated, he took up various country pursuits, being a keen sportsman and an intrepid rider to hounds. He was a member of the Kilkenny Hunt for many years, and was well known in that county and with most of the South of Ireland packs. He took up aviation in 1911 and gained his pilot's certificate in that year at the Blériot School at Pau, and in April, 1912, he flew from England to Ireland, being the first aviator to fly across St George's Channel. He afterwards spent most of his time flying as an amateur, both in the United Kingdom, and France. He was the only son of the late W. H. C. Wilson, S. W., his mother—Ada Caroline—being a daughter of the late Charles I. Corbett, Esq., of Imber Court, Thames Ditton, Surrey, where the subject of this memoir was born on September 24th, 1882. With such a record of sport and aviation it is not surprising that in August, 1914, on war breaking out, Lieutenant Corbett-Wilson offered his services, and in that month he was gazetted 2nd Lieutenant in the Special Reserve, Royal Flying Corps. On the 9th October he was appointed Flying Officer and six days afterwards, on October 15th, he flew to France on a Blériot military monoplane, and served in No 3 Squadron throughout the winter in the neighbourhood of Bethune, being promoted Lieutenant in November, 1914. On May 10th, 1915, the day he was killed, he and an observer, Lieutenant N. Woodwiss, were flying over the enemy's lines in a Morane-Parasol, making a reconnaissance in the direction of Fournes, when both officers and the machine were struck by a German shell. At first, as they did not return, it was thought that they had probably been brought down and captured, and they were therefore reported as "missing." On the following day, however, a German flying machine passed over our line, and the aviators courteously dropped a message that a British Parasol machine had been struck by a shell from their artillery, and both pilot and observer had been killed instantly. Lieutenant Corbett-Wilson rendered most valuable service when in France and Belgium, and sustained at the seat of war the reputation he had gained in Ireland, and especially at Jenkinstown when he resided there and where he was known as the "intrepid Kilkenny aviator." His unfailing efficiency in the performance of his duty, his cheery disposition and quiet courage had been noticed by all, particularly in No 3 Squadron, where his death was greatly regretted. One comrade writes; "I do not know a more gallant officer, we all feel his loss terribly". While another refers to Lieutenant Corbett-Wilson's "utter insensibility to personal danger" ad "an inspiration to us all, he did not know what fear was, and always did his work splendidly". It is probable that Lieutenant Corbett-Wilson's daring had also been noticed and admired by the enemy, as the German message politely added that he and his companion were being "buried in the cemetery to the east of Fournes," where both these brave aviators now rest. Kilkenny People, May, 1915. The following is the copy of the letter received by Mrs Corbett-Wilson. Dear Mrs Corbett-Wilson. — You will have heard by now of the sad death of your son. He was killed by a shell while doing a reconnaissance over Fournes. A German aviator dropped a message yesterday to say that he and his observer, Woodiwin, were both killed instantly, and were being buried at a cemetery at Fournes. When we advance I will try to locate the spot and mark it. I cannot say how sorry I am to have lost your son. He was as gallant a fellow as I knew, and will be much missed by us all. His kit is being sent to Cox and Co., Charing Cross. Allow me to offer you my sincerest sympathy — Yours sincerely, T. E. Lewis, Major. Kilkenny Journal, May, 1915. Mr Corbett-Wilson. Kilkenny has suffered a painful shock within the past few days, from the effects of which it will take long to right itself, even though the cause of it proves — and we sincerely hope it does — not to be real. It was brought about by the news that Flight Lieutenant D. Corbett-Wilson., Kilkenny's airman, who recently took up his duties at the front, had been missing. The painful feeling which this intelligence had created, was intensified on it being learned that the gallant airman had died from the effects of wounds. However, as we go to Press, the sad news is lacking official confirmation. Kilkenny Journal, May, 1915. Kilkenny Airman's Fate. The Officer Commanding the 3rd Squadron Royal Flying Corps, to which Lieutenant Corbett-Wilson. — Kilkenny's famous airman — was attached, reports that on May 10th he proceeded on a reconnaissance in a Morane Parasol, taking as observer second Lieutenant N Woodiwiss. Neither officer returned, and they were reported as missing. Next day a german aviator dropped a message in the British lines, saying that on the 10th a British Parasol machine had been struck by a shell near fournes. Both pilot and observer, the message said, had been killed instantly, and they were being buried in

Fournes Cemetery. The time, place and type of machine specified leave no doubt that the victims were Lieutenant Corbett-Wilson and his observer. Both of them were only sons. The many friends and admirers of this popular airman will be glad to know that he sustained at the front the reputation he had won in Ireland. To his commanding and brother officers he had endured himself by his quiet courage, his unfailing efficiency in the performance of his duties, and his cheery personality."I do not know a more gallant officer," wrote one; and another, telling how he will be missed in the squadron, says;- "His utter insensibility to personal danger was an inspiration to us all.". Kilkenny Journal, January, 1915. Mr D Corbett-Wilson. Appointed Lieutenant in Royal Flying Corps. The "London Gazette" of last Friday night announced that Mr D. Corbett-Wilson has been appointed a Lieutenant in the Royal Flying Corps (Military Wing). This is interesting in view of the fact that the recipient is an Irishman, his home being at Jenkinstown, County Kilkenny. He is a wealthy man, and over five years ago too up aviation with enthusiasm. He was the first airman to land in Ireland from Britain. Starting from near Fishguard early in 1910 he safely landed at Enniscorthy, and after a rest proceeded to his home. He was so pleased with the way he was treated by the people of Enniscorthy that he returned there soon afterwards and gave a fine exhibition of flying. This was the first occasion upon which anything in the nature of exhibition work had been seen in this country, and he followed it up by giving many demonstrations in the South of Ireland, and also at his home in Jenkinstown. He bears a sort of charmed life. He has been in many different situations, but he has never had a serious mishap. On one occasion at Hendon his machine went wrong at a great height and suddenly dived towards the earth. Those who witnessed the accident felt that another airman was about to be added to the long roll of Hio Jacets (?). But no. When a hundred feet from the earth the machine righted itself, and cool and collected as usual, the pilot glided into the aerodrome."A petrol burn," he declared," is very painful." His hands were severely injured as the result of an explosion, but he was such an optimistic patient that he was on the wing again before the week was out. At Jenkinstown, when he was entertaining the local people, he had to land in a plantation. He escaped with a few scratches. Since he took to aviation the career of Mr Corbett-Wilson has naturally been followed with the keenest interest by his mother, who has been present at almost all his demonstrations in Ireland. There is a wonderful affection between the two. When he landed in Enniscorthy in 1910 his first thought was his mother, to whom he sent a cheerful message, and when he was about to start for the final stage of his lourney he said; "I am flying home to mother; won't she be delighted." She was, and she insisted that evening that the people of Kilkenny should share her delight, for she prevailed on her aviator son to circle over the marble City. The new flying officer is regarded in aviation circles as one of the most careful of men, though daring to a degree. He has studied the science of aeronautics to the smallest amount. King's County Chronicle, 1915. Lieut D Corbett-Wilson, Royal Flying Corps, who was killed on May 10 while making a reconnaissance, was the only son of Mrs Corbet-Wilson, Jenkinstown, County Kilkenny. He was the first aviator to fly the Irish Sea. Kilkenny People, October, 1915. The Late Mr Corbett-Wilson. Lieutenant Corbett-Wilson of the Royal Flying Corps, who was killed in action in the air in Belgium, left estate valued at £35, 236. lieutenant Corbett-Wilson was the well known Kilkenny airman and the first to fly from England to Ireland. Kilkenny People, May, 1915. Corbett-Wilson Killed in Action."Kilkenny's Own" Flying man meets Heroic Death. Tribute From His Commanders."Never Knew What Fear was.""As Gallant a Fellow as

I Knew." The "Times" of Sunday, May 15, had the following paragraph in its "Roll of Honour";--Lieutenant Denys Corbett-Wilson, Royal Flying Corps, who was killed on Monday, May 10th, while making a reconnaissance over Fournes, was the only son of Mrs Corbett-Wilson, of 3, Basil Mansions, London, S. W. He became a Lieutenant in the Special Reserve in October last, and was appointed to the Royal Flying Corps in the following month. The death of the gallant aviator, Denys Corbett-Wilson, has evoked intense regret in Kilkenny City and County alike. For some years he resided at Darver, Jenkinstown, with his respected mother, for whom the deepest sorrow will be felt in her great bereavement, and he it was who first made the Kilkenny public acquainted with the marvels of the science of aviation. For an entire season he flew several times weekly—very often several times daily—from his home at Darver over the city and around the big circuit of the county, until "Corbett-Wilson and his flying machine" became household words. Other aviators, not more skilful and certainly not more daring—for that were impossible—could not be tempted beyond the classic grounds of Brooklands or Hendon, where opportunities for spectacular flying, garnished with laudatory newspaper paragraphs, snapshots in the illustrated papers, bouquets from actresses and big money prizes, were numerous. Corbett-Wilson was no poseur, but a genuine sportsman, absolutely without "side," pretence or bombast. He found in Kilkenny a community that he liked, he got to know them while hunting with the Kilkenny Hounds, and he often said that he never wished for a better lot of fellows. As a mark of appreciation of his skill and daring, and many of his great kindness in providing so many fine treats for the people of Kilkenny, Mr Corbett-Wilson was presented, during his residence amongst us, with a valuable souvenir—a beautiful silver model of an aeroplane—the testimonial fund being subscribed to by large numbers in the city and county. Corbett-Wilson, it must not be forgotten, was the first aviator who flew from Great Britain to Ireland. Others had attempted the feat but failed, notably Robert Loraine, the actor, who flew to within a short distance of the shore, where his machine came to water. The Weekly Irish Times. Ireland's Roll of Honour. May 29, 1915. Lieutenant Denys Corbett-Wilson. The Officer Commanding the 3rd Squadron Royal Flying Corps, to which Lieutenant Corbett-Wilson was attached, reported that on May 10th, he proceeded on a reconnaissance in a Morane Parasol, taking as observer Second Lieutenant N Woodiweiss. Neither officer returned, and they were reported as missing. Next day a German aviator dropped a message in the British lines, saying that in the 10th a British parasol machine had been struck by a shell near Fournes. Both pilot and observer, the message said, had bee killed instantly, and they were being buried in Fournes Cemetery. The time, place, and type of machine specified no doubt that the victims were Lieutenant Corbett-Wilson and his observer. Both of them were only sons. The many friends and admirers of this popular airman will be glad to know that he sustained at the front the reputation he had won in Ireland. To his commanding and brother officers he had endeared himself by his quiet courage, his unfailing efficiency in the performance of his duties, and his cheery personality."I do not know a more gallant officer," writes one; and another, telling how he will be missed in the Squadron, says—"His utter insensibility to personal danger was inspiration to us all.". Grave or Memorial Reference; XV M 38. Cemetery: Cabaret-Rouge British Cemetery, Souchez in France.

Corcoran, Nicholas. Rank; Lance Corporal/Private. Regiment or Service: Royal Irish Regiment. Unit; 1st Battalion. Service Number; 10181. Date of death; 09/03/1918. Born; Callan, County Kilkenny. Enlisted; Kilkenny. Residence; Callan. Died of wounds in Palestine. Grave or Memorial Reference; M 65. Cemetery: Jerusalem War Cemetery, Israel.

Corr, David. Rank; Private. Regiment or Service: Leinster Regiment. Unit; 1st Battalion. Service Number; 20168. Date of death; 17/10/1918. Age at death;23. Born; Danesfort, County Kilkenny. Enlisted; Kilkenny. Died in Egypt. Son of Patrick and Mary Corr, of Ballybur Castle, Cuffs Grange, Co. Kilkenny. In his Will, dated 15-June-1918, his effects and property were received by;- (Mother) Mrs Mary Corr, Ballyburr Cuffs Grange, County Kilkenny, Ireland. Kilkenny People;-Corr—October 17th, 1918, at Alexandria, of malaria, after 3 years service, Priavte David P. Corr, beloved son of the late Patrick and Mary Corr, Ballybur Castle, Cuffsgrange; aged 23 years. Notes; Formerly he was with the Royal Field Artillery where his number was 100348. Grave or Memorial Reference; B 182. Cemetery: Deir El Belah Cemetery, in Israel.

Costigan, Michael. Rank; Private. Regiment or Service: Royal Irish Regiment. Unit; 2nd Battalion. Service Number; 3824. Date of death; 15/10/1914. Born; St John's, Kilkenny. Enlisted; Tipperary. Residence; Waterford. Killed in action. Grave or Memorial Reference; Panel 11 and 12. Cemetery: Le Touret Memorial in France.

Costigan, Patrick. Rank; Private. Regiment or Service: Connaught Rangers. Unit; 5th Battalion. Service Number; 4/5205. Date of death; 08/06/1918. Born; Thomastown, County Kilkenny. Enlisted; Waterford. Residence; Carrick, County Tipperary. Died in Egypt. Notes; Number listed as 5205 (SDGW) and 4/5205 (CGWC). Grave or Memorial Reference; C 76. Cemetery: Alexandria (Hadra) War memorial Cemetery in Egypt.

Costigan, William. Rank; Private. Regiment or Service: Royal Irish Regiment. Unit; 2nd Battalion. Service Number; 9700. Date of death; 03/09/1916. Age at death; 23. Born; Muckalee, County Kilkenny. Enlisted; Kilkenny. Residence; Coolcullen, County Kilkenny. Killed in action. Son of Michael and Ellen Costigan, of Coolcullen, Bagnalstown, Co. Kilkenny. Kilkenny People, September, 1916."Killed in Action."Private William Costigan, son of Mr Michael Costigan, Coolcullen, who was in the Royal Irish Regiment, having enlisted as a voluntary recruit about two years ago, was "killed in action," on the 3rd September. He was a young man, fired with a young Irishman's love of his own country, and under the belief that his own country would be served best by his action. Grave or Memorial Reference; Pier and Face 3 A. Cemetery: Thiepval Memorial in France.

Coughlan, Harry. Rank; Private. Regiment or Service: Canadian Infantry (Eastern Ontario Regiment). Unit; 38th Battalion. Service Number; 639839. Date of death; 26/04/1918. Age at death;23. Next of kin listed as (sister), Caroline Coughlan, Invercargill, New Zealand. Place of birth, Kilkenny, Ireland. Date of birth, 30-09-1894. Occupation on enlistment, Clerk. Place and date of enlistment, Ottowa, Ontario, 02-March-1916. Height, 5 feet, 8 inches. Complexion, fair. Eyes, blue. Hair, light brown. Cemetery: Vimy Memorial in France.

Coughlin, Luke. Rank; Private. Regiment or Service: Machine Gun Corps. Unit; Infantry. 101st Company. Service Number; 13684. Date of death; 01/07/1916. Age at death; 27. Born; Hawick. Enlisted; Kilkenny. Residence; Kilkenny. Killed in action. Husband of Kathleen Coughlin, Kilkenny. Grave or Memorial Reference; Pier and Face 5 C and 12 C. Cemetery: Thiepval Memorial, France.

Coulter, Robert. Rank; Sapper. Regiment or Service: Royal Engineers. Unit; Signals. Service Number; 152133. Date of death; 13/12/1918. Age at death;33. Son of Anne and the late John A. Coulter, of 16, Milton Avenue, Highgate, London. Born at Inistioge, Co. Kilkenny, Ireland. De Ruvigny's Roll of Honour. . Postal Section (Telegraphs), Royal Engineers. Son of the late John Alexander Coulter, of Tramore, County Waterford, Schoolmaster, by his wife, Anne, daughter of the late James Coulter, of Pettigo, County Donegal. Born in Inistioge, County Kilkenny, 18-May-1883. Educated at Hughes Academy, Belfast. Was a Civil Servant, joined the Civil Service Volunteers in 1906, and subsequently the London Yeomanry. Enlisted in the Royal Engineers, 07-March-1916. Served in british and German East Africa from the following July, and died at Lindi, German East Africa, 13-December-1918, of Spanish influenza contracted while on active service. Buried in Lindi European Cemetery, He married at St Mary Magdalene's, Holloway, N., 26-July-1911, Daisy Elizabeth, daughter of Henry Martin Payne, and had a son, Robert Stanley, born 21-August-1912. Grave or Memorial Reference; 5 F 22. Cemetery: Dar Es Salaam War Cemetery in Tanzania.

Cox, James. Rank; Lance Corporal. Regiment or Service: Royal Irish Regiment. Unit; Depot. Service Number; 9366. Date of death; 07/11/1915. Age at death; 25. Born; Thomastown, County Kilkenny. Enlisted; Kilkenny. Residence; Clonmel. Died at home. Son of Mrs. Ellen Cox, of Maudlin St. Thomastown. Kilkenny Journal, November, 1915. Death of Private James Cox, Thomastown. The death occurred on Sunday night last at the residence of his mother, Maudlin Street, Thomastown, of Private James Cox from pneumonia, following wounds received in action in France. The deceased soldier, who was only 24 years of age had been through the whole of the present campaign, his regiment—the 1st Battalion of the Royal Irish, being first at the front since the outbreak of the war. Private Cox was slightly wounded at the Battle of Mons, but continued in the firing line until last March, when he was invalided home, suffering from frost bite. He returned to the front in May, and was again wounded at St Eloi in France, in August, portion of the hip being blown away. He was treated in a London hospital for two months, and at the end of October was given a fortnight's leave to visit his relatives in Thomastown, at the expiration of which, it is stated, he was under orders to rejoin his regiment. On his arrival at Thomastown it was too evident that his health was completely shattered, and towards the end of last week pneumonia set in, and despite all that Dr J. P. Barry, Inistioge, and Dr T. J. O'Gorman, Stonyford, could do he expired on Sunday night. He was the sole support of his widowed mother, with whom as well as for his older relatives much sympathy is felt. On Monday evening the remains were removed to the Thomastown parish church, where the Rosary was recited for the repose of the soul of the deceased soldier. On Tuesday the remains were interred in the family burial place at Thomastown, the funeral being largely attended by the gentry and general public of the district. A reworded, shorter article on Private Cox in the Kilkenny People, November, 1915. Grave or Memorial Reference; Panel 5 (Screen Wall). Cemetery: Grangegorman Memorial in Dublin.

Crampton, Thomas. Rank; Private. Regiment or Service: Royal Irish Fusiliers. Unit; 9th Battalion. Service Number; 24927. Date of death; 16/08/1917. Age at death;21. Born; Kilkenny. Enlisted; Enniskillen. Residence; Mountcharles, County Donegal. Killed in action. Son of William and Elizabeth Crampton, of the Club House Hotel, Carlow. Grave or Memorial Reference; Panel 140 to 141. Memorial. Cemetery: Tyne Cot Memorial in Belgium.

Cranny, John. Rank; Private. Regiment or Service: Royal Irish Regiment. Unit; 2nd Battalion. Service Number; 7751. Date of death; 03/09/1916. Born; Kilkenny. Enlisted; Kilkenny. Killed in action. Grave or Memorial Reference; Pier and Face 3A. Cemetery: Thiepval Memorial in France.

Croke, J. Rank; Private. Regiment or Service: Worcestershire Regiment. Unit; 4th Battalion. Service Number; 5242257. Date of death; 29/06/1921. Son of Mrs. Anne Croke, of 4, Walshers Place Ballybricken, Co. Waterford. Grave or Memorial Reference; 6 (Screen Wall). Cemetery: Grangegorman Memorial in Blackhorse Avenue in Dublin.

Croke/Cooke, Michael. Rank; Corporal. Regiment or Service: Royal Irish Regiment. Unit; 2nd Battalion. Service Number; 10300. Date of death; 15/05/1915. Age at death; 20. Born; Mooncoin, County Kilkenny. Enlisted; Waterford. Killed in action. Croke (CGWC) Cooke (SDGW), Michaell. Son of Catherine O'Brien (formerly Croke), of Mooncoin, Co. Kilkenny, and the late James Croke. In his Will, dated 05-August-1914, his effects and property were received by;- (Mother) Mrs Js O' Brien, Banack St, Mooncoin, Waterford, Ireland. Grave or Memorial Reference; XXVII A 9. Cemetery: New Irish Farm Cemetery in Belgium.

Cuddihy, William. Rank; Private. Regiment or Service: Welsh Regiment. Unit; 17th Battalion. Service Number; 18161. Date of death; 24/04/1917. Born; Newmarket, County Kilkenny. Enlisted; Pentre, Glamorganshire. Residence; Donnimagen, County Kilkenny. Died of wounds. Grave or Memorial Reference; IV J 1. Cemetery: Fins New British Cemetery, Somme in France.

Culbert, Patrick. Rank; Private. Regiment or Service: Royal Dublin Fusiliers. Unit; 1st Battalion. Service Number; 17959. Date of death; 15/06/1915. Born; Kilkenny. Enlisted; Inverkeithling. Residence; Wicklow. Killed in Action in Gallipoli. Grave or Memorial Reference; XI E 10. Cemetery: Twelve Tree Copse Cemetery in Turkey.

Cullen, James Joseph. Rank; Private. Regiment or Service: Household Cavalry and Cavalry of the line including the Yeomanry and Imperial Camel Corps. Unit; Reserve Regiment, Corps of Lancers. Service Number; L/15524. Date of death; 01/11/1918. Born; St John's, Kilkenny. Enlisted; Dundalk. Residence; Farnderg, near Dundalk. Died at home. Notes; Number listed as L/15524 (CWGC) 15524 (SDGW). Grave or Memorial Reference; Near the North boundary. Cemetery: St Patrick's Graveyard, County Kilkenny.

Cullen, John. Rank; Private. Regiment or Service: Royal Irish Regiment. Unit; 1st Battalion. Service Number; 4078. Date of death; 03/05/1915. Age at death; 25. Born; Bagenalstown, County Carlow. Enlisted; Kilkenny. Residence; Graiguenamanagh, County ilkenny. Killed in action. Son of John and Julia Cullen, of High St., Graiguenamanagh; husband of Mary Cullen, of High St., Graiguenamanagh, Co. Kilkenny. Grave or Memorial Reference; Panel 33. Cemetery: Ypres (Menin Gate) Memorial in Belgium.

Culleton, John. Rank; Private. Regiment or Service: Connaught Rangers. Unit; 2nd Battalion. Service Number; 10524. Date of death; 14/11/1914. Born; Kilmacow, County Kilkenny. Enlisted; Waterford. Residence; Kilmacow, County Kilkenny. Killed in action. Grave or Memorial Reference; Panel 42. Cemetery: Ypres (Menin Gate) Memorial in Belgium.

Culleton, Thomas. Rank; Lance Corporal/Private. Regiment or Service: Royal Irish Regiment. Unit; 1st Battalion. Service Number; 8675. Date of death; 30/12/1917. Born; Bagenalstown, County Carlow. Enlisted; Carlow. Residence; Bagenalstown, County Kilkenny (sic). Died at sea. The Nationalist and Leinster Times, June, 1916. Soldiers Furlough. Thomas Culleton, Bagnalstown, is home on eight days furlough, having been twice wounded at the front by a bullet and a piece of shrapnel. He stated that there were times when they have been as near as 50 yards from the German trenches. Cemetery: Chatby Memorial Cemetery in Egypt. Also listed under Bagenalstown/ Fenagh on the Great War Memorial, Milford Street, Leighlinbridge, County Carlow.

Culleton / Cullerton, Thomas. Rank; Private. Regiment or Service: Leinster Regiment. Unit; 2nd Battalion. Service Number; 3491. Date of death; 15/03/1916. Age at death;23. Born; Gores Bridge, County Kilkenny. Enlisted; Maryborough. Killed in action. Culleton (CWGC and the Great War Memorial, Milford Street, Leighlinbridge, County Carlow), Culleton (SDGW+IMR), Thomas. Son of William and Ellen Culleton, of Near Grange, Goresbridge, Co. Kilkenny. Grave or Memorial Reference; I K 5. Cemetery: Menin Road South Military Cemetery in Belgium.

Cullinan, Joseph. Rank; Private. Regiment or Service: Royal Irish Regiment. Unit; 1st Battalion. Service Number; 5/1448. Date of death; 28/12/1917. Born; Callan, County Kilkenny. Enlisted; Kilkenny. Residence; Callan. Killed in action in Palestine. In his Will, dated 12-January-1917, his effects and property were received by;- (Wife) Mrs J Cullinan, address on second will, Haggardsgneen, Callan, County Kilkenny,. Notes; Number listed as 1449 (SDGW) 5/1448 (CWGC). Grave or Memorial Reference; A 30. Cemetery: Jerusalem War Cemetery, Israel.

Cummins, John. Rank; Private. Regiment or Service: Royal Dublin Fusiliers. Unit; 2nd Battalion. Service Number; 24594. Date of death; 30/05/1917. Born; Kilkenny. Enlisted; Ammanford. Residence; Cork. Killed in action. Grave or Memorial Reference; Bay 9. Cemetery: Arras Memorial in France.

D

Dalton, Richard. Rank; Private. Regiment or Service: U. S. Army. Unit; 115th Infantry Regiment, 29th Division. Date of death; 14/10/1918. Age at death; 29. Born; Knocktopher, County Kilkenny. Enlisted; New York. Grave or Memorial Reference; Plot H, Row 8, Grave 32. Cemetery: Meuse-Argonne American Cemetery, Romagne, France.

Daly, Edward. Rank; Private. Regiment or Service: Irish Guards. Unit; 1st Battalion. Service Number; 4298. Date of death; 25/10/1914. Age at death;21. Born; Ballycallan, County Kilkenny. Enlisted; Kilkenny. Killed in action. Son of James Daly, of Baleven, Ballycallan, Kilkenny. After his death his effects and property were received by;- (Wife) Mrs J Connors, Jacob Street, Kilkenny. Kilkenny People, July, 1915. Ballycallan Soldier's Bravery. Corporal Patrick Daly of Ballycallan, was engaged in the last battle in which one company of the Irish Guards lost 700 men. His brother Edward was killed in another battle. The brave Kilkenny Guardsman is now Sergeant Daly. Grave or Memorial Reference; Panel 11. Cemetery: Ypres (Menin Gate) Memorial in Belgium.

Daly, John. Rank; Private. Regiment or Service: Royal Irish Regiment. Unit; 5th Battalion. Service Number; 43. Date of death; 16/08/1915. Age at death; 34. Born; Hugginstown, County Kilkenny. Enlisted; Waterford. Residence; Newmarket, County Kilkenny. Killed in Action in Gallipoli. Son of John Daly, of Newmarket, Knocktopher, Co. Kilkenny. Grave or Memorial Reference; Panel 55. Cemetery: Helles Memorial in Turkey

Darcy, James. Rank; Lance Corporal. Regiment or Service: Royal Irish Regiment. Unit; 2nd Battalion. Service Number; 2589. Date of death; 10/11/1918. Age at death;27. Enlisted; Kilkenny. Killed in action. Son of T. Darcy and the late Mary Darcy, of Thomas St., Kilkenny. In his Will, dated 17-July-1918, his effects and property were received by;- (Aunt) Mary Darcy, Thomas St, Kilkenny, Ireland. Buried beside Private Patrick Shanahan from Carrickbeg, County Tipperary who died on the same day. Grave or Memorial Reference; In the South-East part. Cemetery: Spiennes Communal Cemetery, Mons, Hainaut in Belgium.

Darcy, Matthew. Rank; Gunner. Regiment or Service: Royal Garrison Artillery. Unit; 112th Heavy Battery. Service Number; 70468. Date of death; 15/11/1917. Born; Danesfort, County Kilkenny. Enlisted; Kilkenny. Residence; Kilree, County Kilkenny. Died at home. Will, dated 11-October-1916, his effects and property were received by;- (Father) Mr Richard Darcy, Kilree, County Kilkenny, Ireland. Grave or Memorial Reference; VIII I 103. Cemetery: Boulogne Eastern Cemetery in France

Darcy, Patrick. Rank; Private. Regiment or Service: Irish Guards. Unit; 1st Battalion. Service Number; 4672. Date of death; 04/02/1915. Age at death;18. Born; Thomastown, County Kilkenny. Enlisted; Thomastown. Died of wounds. Son of Patrick and Mary Darcy, of Thomastown, Co. Kilkenny. Kilkenny People, March, 1915. Young Thomastown Soldier Dies of wounds. Mr Patrick Darcy, Newtown, Thomastown, has received a message from the War Office notifying him of the death of his eldest son, Private Patrick Darcy, at the general hospital, Boulogne, on the 4th February, as a result of wounds received in action at the front. Accompanying the notification was a note from Lord Kitchener assuring Mr Darcy of the true sympathy of their Majesties the King and Queen in his sorrow. The sad intelligence was received in Thomastown and surrounding district with much regret, for young Darcy was exceeding popular in his native parish. Deceased, who had only reached his 20th year, joined the Irish Guards about two years ago, and was attached to the 1st Battalion of that regiment, which has earned such enviable fame during the present war. Darcy had been practically through the whole campaign. He was wounded at the battle of the Aisne and was invalided home; being treated in one of the military hospitals in England for some weeks. On his recovery he again left for the front, and had been through the thick of the fight up to a month ago when he received wounds which culminated in his death. At the different Masses in Thomastown on Sunday prayers were offered up for the repose of his soul. A similar article can also be found in the Kilkenny Journal, February, 1915. Grave or Memorial Reference; III B 85. Cemetery: Boulogne Eastern Cemetery in France.

D'Arcy, Edmund. Rank; Private. Regiment or Service: Royal Irish Regiment. Unit; 1st Battalion. Service Number; 7091. Date of death; 14/02/1915. Born; Kilkenny. Enlisted; Kilkenny. Killed in action. Grave or Memorial Reference; Panel 33. Cemetery: Ypres (Menin Gate) Memorial in Belgium

Darcy/D'Arcy, James. Rank; Lance Corporal. Regiment or Service: Leinster Regiment. Unit; 1st Battalion. Service Number; 5062. Date of death; 03/04/1915. Age at death;42. Born; Johnstown, County Kilkenny. Enlisted; Maryborough. Died of wounds. Son of James and Julia Darcy, of Crosspatrick, Johnstown, Co. Kilkenny. Grave or Memorial Reference; I B 23. Cemetery: Le Touquet-Paris Plage Communal Cemetery in France.

Darcy/D'Arcy, Thomas. Rank; Private. Regiment or Service: Nottinghamshire and Derbyshire Regiment. Unit; 1/6th Battalion. Service Number; 2276. Date of death; 30/09/1915. Born; Kilkenny. Enlisted; Bakewell, Derbyshire. Killed in action. Grave or Memorial Reference; I B 2. Cemetery: Chester Farm Cemetery, Ieper, West-Vlaanderen, Belgium.

Davidson, William. Rank; Sapper. Regiment or Service: Canadian Railway Troops. Unit; 3rd Battalion. Service Number; 229269. Date of death; 19/05/1917. Age at death;39. Born; Kilkenny. Enlisted; Winnipeg, Manitoba. Son of Thomas Davidson, Ballyneil, Newross, Kilkenny. Irish Times. Davidson-May 19, killed in action, William Davidson, son of Thomas Davidson, Ballyneal, Tullogher, New Ross. Grave or Memorial Reference; I B 14. Cemetery: Le Targette British Cemetery, Neuville-St, Vaast in France.

Dawson, Michael. Rank; Private. Regiment or Service: Welsh Regiment. Unit; 1st Battalion. Service Number; 14636. Date of death; 25/05/1915. Born; Kilmason, County Kilkenny. Enlisted; Tonypandy. Residence; Clydach vale, Glamorganshire. Killed in action. Grave or Memorial Reference; Panel 37. Cemetery: Ypres (Menin Gate) Memorial in Belgium

Day, William Edward. Rank; Unknown. Regiment or Service: Royal Field Artillery. Service Number; 33999. Date of death; 17/12/1918. Age at death;37. Discharged from Military Service in July-1917. Date of Death:17-December-1918. Address; Walkin Street, Kikenny. Husband of Julia Day (Nee Bourke) who died 18-July-1957, aged 76. Cemetery: St Patrick's Cemetery, Kilkenny.

Day/Daye, Richard. Rank; Private. Regiment or Service: Royal Irish Regiment. Unit; 2nd Battalion. Service Number; 6443. Date of death; 09/05/1915. Age at death; 50. Born; Mooncoin. Enlisted; Waterford. Residence; Mooncoin. Killed in action. Notes; Previously he was with the Royal Irish Regiment where his number was 11393 Born Mooncoin, County Kilkenny (Soldiers died in the Great War), Mooncoin, County Waterford (Irelands Memorial Records). Grave or Memorial Reference; Panel 33. Cemetery: Ypres (Menin Gate) Memorial in Belgium.

Deely, John. Rank; Sergeant. Regiment or Service: Royal Irish Regiment. Unit; 3rd Battalion. Service Number; 2280. Date of death; 09/10/1915. Age at death;48. Born; Adare, County Limerick. Enlisted; Kilkenny. Residence; Ballyfoyle, County Kilkenny. Died at home. Son of the late John Deely, of Rathkeale, Co. Limerick: husband of Mary M. Deely, of Webbsborough, Ballyfoyle, Co. Kilkenny. Grave or Memorial Reference; About 27 yards West of entrance. Cemetery: Dunmore Catholic Churchyard, Kilkenny.

Deevy, Daniel. Rank; Private. Regiment or Service: Royal Irish Regiment. Unit; 2nd Battalion. Service Number; 4507. Date of death; 30/04/1915. Born; Castlecomer, County Kilkenny. Enlisted; Kilkenny. Residence; Castlecomer. Died. Kilkenny People, June, 1915. Kilkenny and the War. Further Deaths Reported from France and Germany. Another Death in the German Prison. Our Castlecomer correspondent writes;--I regret very much to have again to record another death amongst the Castlecomer young men who are prisoners of war in Germany, the sad case this time being young John Nolan, eldest son of Mrs John Nolan, Love Lane, Castlecomer, and who was a Private in the Royal Irish Regiment. Mrs Nolan received the following letter from Rev. R. Warren, C. C., Chaplain;-Limburg, Lahn, 24th May, 1915. Dear Mrs Nolan, --I sincerely regret to have to announce to you the death of your son, John Nolan, which took place here after a brief illness. His death is due to consumption, which crept rapidly into the poor boy's constitution. His death is greatly regretted amongst his poor companions, who long for the day soon to come when they may see Ireland once more. Your son received all the consolations which Our Holy Mother the Church gives to her children, before he left this world. I sympathise with you in your sad bereavement. —Very truly yours. R. Warren. This is the second death in this prison, and moreover they are the death of two men (D. Deevy and J. Nolan) whose constitutions and general physique were always of the best when in Castlecomer. Oh! The Germans will have a lot to aN. S. W. er for on the accounting day, for one can only draw the one conclusion from such events, and that is that starvation diet is very nearly the rule of the German prisons. May his soul rest in peace. Kilkenny People, May, 1915. Death of Kilkenny Soldier in Germany. News has been received in Castlecomer from Limburg that Private Daniel Deevy of the Royal irish Regiment, who was taken prisoner, has died therein, and this news will be heard with much regret by all who knew the young man, who was a blacksmith by trade, was well known around Castlecomer and was always popular. His was a sad lot, away from his home and a prisoner. May we hope that in the new land his lot is brighter and that his soul has found peace and happiness. Grave or Memorial Reference; III K 4. Cemetery: Niederzwhren Cemetery in Germany.

Deevy, John. Rank: Lance Corporal. Regiment or Service: Australian Infantry. Unit: 48th Battalion. Date of Death: 06/08/1916. Service Number: 3037. Age at Death: 50. Born: Dysart Bridge, Castlecomer Co Kilkenny. Enlisted: Queensland. Killed in Action. Supplementary Information: Husband of Norah Deevy, Gladstone Street, Rockhampton. Son of John Deevy. Brother of Miss May Deevy, Terminus Hotel, Rockhampton. Brother of Private M Deevy, Service Number: 3059 47th Battalion12th Infantry Brigade, 4th Australian Division. Grave or Memorial Reference: 1 B 4 Cemetery: Sunken Road Cemetery, Contalmaison.

Delahunty, John. Rank; Private. Regiment or Service: Irish Guards. Unit; 2nd Battalion. Service Number; 10793. Date of death; 09/10/1917. Age at death;27. Born; Kilkenny. Enlisted; Whitehall, Middlesex. Residence; Inishtioge, County Kilkenny. Killed in action. Son of Michael and Mary Delahunty, of Inistioge, Co. Kilkenny. In his Will, dated 26-November-1916;-£30 to (Mother) Mrs M Delahunty. £30 to (Father) Michael Delahuntey. Remainder of money to (Sister and Brother) Katty Delahunty and Paddy Delahunty. Watch and gold chain to Maggie Delahunty. Grave or Memorial Reference; Panel 10 to 11. Cemetery: Tyne Cot Memorial in Belgium.

Delaney, Christopher. Rank; Private. Regiment or Service: Royal Irish Regiment. Unit; 1st Battalion. Service Number; 4721. Date of death; 15/05/1915. Age at death; 29. Born; St Mary's, Kilkenny. Enlisted; Kilkenny. Killed in action. Son of Michael and Bridget Delaney, of Garden Row, Kilkenny. After his death his effects and property were received by;- (Mother) Mrs B Delany, Garden Row, Kilkenny. Grave or Memorial Reference; Panel 33. Cemetery: Ypres (Menin Gate) Memorial in Belgium.

Delaney, Joseph Patrick. Rank; Private. Regiment or Service: Household Cavalry and Cavalry of the line including the Yeomanry and Imperial Camel Corps. Unit; 18th (Queen Mary's Own Royal) Hussars. Service Number; 5564. Date of death; 02/11/1914. Born; Kilkenny. Enlisted; Carlow. Residence; Ballyraggett. Killed in action. Grave or Memorial Reference; Panel 1. Cemetery: Ploegsteert Memorial in Belgium.

Delaney, Michael. Rank; Private. Regiment or Service: Welsh Guards. Unit; 1st Battalion. Service Number; 1541. Date of death; 25/07/1916. Age at death; 26. Born; Kilkenny. Enlisted; Cardiff, Glamorganshire. Killed in action. Son of William Delaney, of Upper Patrick St., Kilkenny. Grave or Memorial Reference; II K 3. Cemetery: Brandhoek Military Cemetery in Belgium.

Delaney, Patrick. Rank; Private. Regiment or Service: Royal Dublin Fusiliers. Unit; 2nd Battalion. Service Number; 5569. Date of death; 01/07/1916. Born; Ballingarry, County Tipperary. Enlisted; Carlow. Residence; Kilkenny. Killed in action. Son of John Delaney, of Maudlin St, Kilkenny. Grave or Memorial Reference; I D 94. Cemetery: Sucrerie Military Cemetery, Colinclamps in France.

Delaney, Patrick. Rank; Company Sergeant Major. Regiment or Service: Royal Dublin Fusiliers. Unit; 1st Battalion. Service Number; 9364. Date of death; 28/09/1918. Died of wounds. Won the D. C. M. and the Military Medal and he is listed in the London Gazette. Son of Michael Delaney, of Collier's Lane, Kilkenny. In his Will, dated 01-June-1916, he is named Richard Delaney, and his effects and property were to shared equally between (Father, Mother, Sisters). Mr Michael Delaney, Basket Maker, Jordan Road, Kilkenny, Ireland. Kilkenny Journal, October, 1915. Kilkenny's "Roll of Honour."Private Patrick Delaney, 1st Battalion, Royal Dublin Fusiliers, who has been wounded in action, is now in a convalescent home in Lancashire, having had his arm amputated. With a letter to his father, Mr Michael Delaney, Colliers Lane, Kilkenny, he enclosed a photo of the heroic chaplain, Father Finn, and the place where he was buried, with six hundred of the "Dublins." Private Delaney refers in the highest terms to the bravery of Father Finn."He was a father to the lot of us," he states,"We had many a chat with him about old Ireland and Home Rule. He was the bravest of the brave. He died looking after the dying and wounded. He was a great man and a worthy son of gallant Tipperary. I would like to hear from Christie. Please God, he is all right." His brother, Private Christie Delaney, 4th Battalion, Royal Irish Regiment, about whom he inquires, was killed in action at the battle of Hooge, Ypres, on the 15th May last. Grave or Memorial Reference; I. H. 4. Cemetery: Beach Cemetery, Anzac, Turkey. He is also commemorated on the Great War Memorial in St Canice's Cathedral, Kilkenny…'To the Glory of God and in loving memory of the following members of the Diocese of Ossory who gave their lives for their country in the Great War 1914-1918'.

Dempsey, William. Rank; Private. Regiment or Service: Royal Irish Regiment. Unit; 2nd Battalion. Service Number; 11027. Date of death; 23/04/1916. Age at death;18. Born; Dunamaggin, County Kilkenny. Enlisted; Kilkenny. Residence; Callan. Killed in action. Son of William and Judith Dempsey, of Dunamaggin, Callan, Co. Kilkenny. Grave or Memorial Reference; I B 14. Cemetery: Foncquevillers Military Cemetery in France.

Dennehy, Patrick James. Rank; Lance Corporal. Regiment or Service: Royal Berkshire Regiment. Unit; 8th Battalion. Service Number; 18274. Date of death; 21/04/1918. Age at death; 25. Born; Tullamore. Enlisted; Reading. Residence; Dublin. Killed in action. Son of James and Anna M. Dennehy, of 32, John St., Kilkenny. In his Will, dated 12-October-1915, his effects and property were received by;- (Uncle) James Dennehy, Mount Verdant, Kilkenny, Ireland. A note on his will says ' Alias

Joseph Byrne'. Grave or Memorial Reference; Panel 56 and 57. Cemetery: Pozieres Memorial in France.

Denton, Thomas James. Rank; Private. Regiment or Service: Queen's Own (Royal West Kent Regiment). Unit; 1st Battalion. Service Number; S/8699. Date of death; 07/01/1915. Age at death;19. Born; Kilkenny. Enlisted; Tunbridge Wells, Kent. Residence; Tunbridge Wells. Died of wounds. Son of Thomas and Susannah Denton, of 42, Granville Rd., Tunbridge Wells, Kent. Born at Kilkenny. Notes; Number listed as 8699 (CWGC) S/8699 (SDGW). Grave or Memorial Reference; Div. 14. I. 7. Cemetery: Ste. Marie Cemetery, Le Havre in France.

Dermody, John/Joseph. Rank; Gunner. Regiment or Service: Royal Horse Artillery and Royal Field Artillery. Unit; 115th Brigade. Service Number; 6409. Date of death; 28/09/1915. Age at death; 32. Born; St Peter's, Kilkenny. Enlisted; Dublin. Died of wounds. Dermody, John (CWGC, SDGW) Joseph (IMR). In his Will, dated 23-October-1914, his effects and property were received by;- Margaret Lennon, C/o Mrs Mahony, Blackmill St, Kilkenny. Grave or Memorial Reference; L 2 3. Cemetery: Hoddesdon Cemetery, Hertfordfshire, UK.

Deveraux, Michael. Rank; Private. Regiment or Service: Irish Guards. Unit; 1st Battalion. Service Number; 3927. Date of death; 01/11/1914. Age at death;29. Born; Kilkenny. Enlisted; Carlow. Killed in action. Son of Michael and Bridget Devereux, of Canal Lodge, Kilkenny. Grave or Memorial Reference; Panel 11. Cemetery: Ypres (Menin Gate) Memorial in Belgium.

Devereux, William Patrick. Rank; Sapper. Regiment or Service: Royal Engineers. Unit; 14th Signals. Service Number; 58571. Date of death; 20/08/1915. Age at death; 23. Born; Kilmacon, County Kilkenny. Enlisted; Waterford. Residence; Ferrybank, County Kilkenny. Died of wounds. Son of Patrick and Margaret Devereux, of Mount Sion, Ferrybank, Waterford. Grave or Memorial Reference; III C 21A. Cemetery: Lijssenthoek Military Cemetery in Belgium.

Lieutenant Devine;-The Weekly Irish Times, December 8, 1917.

Devine, Patrick. Rank; Lieutenant. Regiment or Service: Australian Infantry A. I. F. Unit; 9th Battalion. Date of death; 03/11/1917. Son of Patrick and Elizabeth Devine; husband of Eva M. Devine, of 4, Brighton Terrace, Terenure Rd., Dublin, Ireland. Native of Skeaghnasteen, Co. Kilkenny, Ireland. Previous experience; 5 years, 3 months R. I. C., 1 year, 4 months Queensland Police Force. Treated for shellshock when he was blown up by a shell at Pozieres and unconscious for half an hour, 24-July-1916. Carried on until the next day and then collapsed. Killed in action by a bullet through the head. Date of birth; 17-March-1886. Next of kin details; (father) Patrick Devine, Skeaghvasteen, Goresbridge, County Kilkenny. His widow, Mrs Eva Mary Devine, 4 Brighton Buildings, Terenure Road, Dublin, received a pension of 70/- per fortnight from 08-January-1918. Irish Times. Devine-November 3, killed in action, Lieutenant P J Devine, Australian Imperial Force, son of Mr P Devine, Goresbrodge, County Kilkenny, and husband of Eva M devine, 4 Terenure Road, North, Dublin. The Weekly Irish Times. Ireland's Roll of Honour. November 24, 1917. Lieutenant P J Devine, Australian Imperial Force, was killed in action on November the 3rd. He was the third son of Mr P Devine, of Goresbridge, County Kilkenny. The Weekly Irish Times. Ireland's Roll of Honour. December 8, 1917. Image above from The Weekly Irish Times, December 8, 1917. Lieutenant P J Devine, Australian Forces, killed in action, was the husband of Mrs Eva M Devine, 4 Terenure Road, North, Dublin, and son of Mr P Devine, Goresbridge, County Kilkenny. The Weekly Irish Times. Ireland's Roll of Honour. December 8, 1917. Lieutenant P J Devine, Australian Imperial Forces, who was killed in action on 3rd November, 1917, was the third son of Mr P devine, Goresbridge, County Kilkenny, and husband of Mrs Eva M Devind, 4 Terenure Road,

North, Rathgar, Dublin. Irish Times. Devine-November 3, killed in action, Lieutenant P J Devine, Australian Imperial Force, son of Mr P Devine, Goresbrodge, County Kilkenny, and husband of Eva M devine, 4 Terenure Road, North, Dublin. Grave or Memorial Reference; Panel 7 - 17 - 23 - 25 - 27 - 29 - 31. Cemetery: Ypres (Menin Gate) Memorial in Belgium.

Devlin, Thomas. Rank; Private. Regiment or Service: Royal Irish Regiment. Service Number; 2899. Date of death; 01/11/1918. Age at death; 35. Born; Castlecomer, County Kilkenny. Enlisted; Tipperary. Residence; Kilkenny. Died at home. Son of James and Eliza Devlin, of Ballyhemon, Castlecomer, Co. Kilkenny. Kilkenny People, December 1914. Back for the War. He has no fear of the ultimate whipping of the Germans. From the base of operations we have again seen Mr Tom Devlin, who got home for a few days after being one of the escort in charge of German prisoners who were brought to Templemore. Tom is looking fit and well, and shows no sign whatever of being downhearted. Kilkenny People, June, 1915. From the Firing Line. I have recently had letters from some of our Castlecomer young men who are at the front. Privates Devlin and Campion, and I am glad to be able to say they are in good fighting form, and they add that those from the locality—who are at the front are also in good form, and are not one bit "downhearted." I have also learned that those of our young men who have been taken prisoners are also in good health, and that Sergeant P. Holden has been transferred from one prison to another and that in the latter there is no Castlecomer man but himself. Lance Corporal William Connery, of the Leinsters, of whom, brilliant work in France I write a couple of weeks ago, is again back to the fighting line, and I am sure he will again give a good fighting account of himself and bring credit to Castlecomer and to Ireland in the coming battles. Notes; Transferred to the Labour Corps where his number was 229697. Grave or Memorial Reference; 330. Cemetery: Durrington Cemetery, Wiltshire.

Dickie, David. Rank; Farrier Quartermaster Sergeant. Regiment or Service: Royal Horse Artillery and Royal Field Artillery. Unit; 2nd/1st Berkshire Battery/Territorial Force. Service Number; 9. Date of death; 07/10/1916. Age at death;54. Born; Kilmarnock. Enlisted; Reading. Died at home. Long Service and Good Conduct Medal. Father of David Edward Dickie, of 6, Body Rd., Reading. Born at Kilmarnock, Ayrshire. Served in the South African Campaign. Munster Express. Roll of Honour. The English papers to hand chronicle the death of Quartermaster Sergeant Farrier Dickie, R. H. A. The deceased soldier had seen a long period of service, and obtained the King's and Queen's Medals in connection with the South African Campaign, and also the medal for long service and good conduct. He resided at 36 Howard Street, Reading. His wife was formerly a native of Graiguenamanagh, County Kilkenny. Miss Mary Healy, a member of a highly respected family in the district. The funeral, with full military honours, took place at Reading. The body was borne on a gun-carriage, attended by a number of the deceased's comrades and representatives of other branches of the service. The widow, her children and her brothers were the chief mourners, and to them will go forth the deep sympathy of our readers in the Graiguenamanagh district. Cemetery: Tilehurst (St George) Church Burial Ground in Berkshire.

Lieutenant Colonel Dobbs, from 'Our Heroes.'

Dobbs, George Eric Burroughs. Rank; Lieuteant Colonel (Bt. Major) and Acting Lieutenant Colonel. Regiment or Service: Royal Engineers. Unit; Signal Corps (A. D. Signals). Date of death; 17/06/1917. Age at death; 32. Died of wounds. Chevalier of the Legion of Honour. Son of Joseph and Mary Dobbs, of The Chalet, Temple Road Dublin. Native of Castlecomer, Co. Kilkenny. 'Our Heroes'. who has been awarded the Cross of the legion of Honour for distinguished service, is a son of Mr Joseph Dobbs, of Coolbawn House, Castlecomer, and entered the service as 2nd Lieutenant in March-1904, obtaining his promotion as Lieutenant in 1906. De Ruvigny's Roll of Honour. son of Joseph Dobbs, of the Chalet, Temple Road, Dubolin, J. P., by his wife, Mary Agusta, daughter of Willam Harte, C. E. Born in Castlecomer, County Kilkenny, 21-July-1884. Educated at St Stephens Green School, Dublin, and Shrewsbury. Was gazetted 2nd Lieutenant 1904. Served in South Wales, Devon, Singapore and limerick. On the outbreak pf war served with the Expeditionary Force in France and Flanders. Promoted Captain in 1914, Brevet Major in 1915, and temporary Lieutenant Colonel in November 1916. Was appointed to be Assistant Director of Signals with a corps, and died of wounds in a casualty clearing station, 17-June-1917, having been hit by a shell whilst returning from prospecting a new cable trench in the front line. Buried at Poperinghe. He was awarded the Legion of Honour for valuable services in keeping up communication during the Retreat from Mons, and was three times mentioned in Despatches (London Gazette, 19-October-1914 and 01-January-1916) by F. M. Sir John (now Lord) French, and (London Gazette, 15-May-1917) by F. M. Sir Douglas Haig, for gallant and distinguished service in the field. He was a well known Rugby football player, and played for England in 1903-6 against Wales and Ireland. Limerick Chronicle, March, 1915. Dear Mrs Henn,--Still another sack of most wonderful and useful comforts. Ever so many thanks. The men are delighted with the things, and there is great competition for the various articles. —Yours very sincerely, Eric B Dobbs, Major, Royal Engineers. Mrs Milton Henn hopes that her kind friends will continue their help, and now that socks are urgently needed at the front, send her contributions either of money, socks, or wool, to get socks knitted. She has sent out about 130 pairs of socks already, also mufflers, body belts, mittens, but those latter articles are no longer needed. Mrs Milton Henn, has been buying with the small sum in hand quinine, borax, and potash tablets; also carbolic soap, carbolic Vaseline, leather boot laces, curry powder, mustard, and matches; also chocolate. Contributions of any of the above will be gratefully received and forwarded to the front in the next parcels. Pipes, tobacco, and cigarettes will be most acceptable, and duly acknowledged in the Limerick Chronicle. Kilkenny People, November 1914. The Legion of Honour. Conferred on a Castlecomer Soldier. The cross of the legion of Honour has been bestowed on Lieutenant G. E. B. Dobbs, R. E., in recognition of his bravery in the battlefield. Lieutenant Dobbs is a native of this county, being son of Mr Joseph Dobbs, Coolbawn House, Castlecomer. Irish Independent; Rugby International Killed. Lieutenant Colonel E B Dobbs, (RE) who is reported killed in action, played for England v Ireland at Rugby in 1906. he was born in Dublin 33 years ago. Serving in France since the retreat of Mons, he was thrice mentioned in despatches. Irish Independent; Lieutenant Colonel G Eric B Dobbs, R. E., Chevalier of the Legion of Honour, died of wounds, son of Mr Joseph Dobbs, The Chalet, Temple Road, and Liscarrig, Greystones, formerly of Castlecomer. Grave or Memorial Reference; XIII A 25. Cemetery: Lijssenthoek Military Cemetery in Belgium. He is also commemorated on the Great War Memorial in St Canice's Cathedral, Kilkenny…'To the Glory of God and in loving memory of the following members of the Diocese of Ossory who gave their lives for their country in the Great War 1914-1918'. Listed on the memorial under Lieutenant Colonel Eric Dobbs.

Dobbyn, Michael. Rank; Private. Regiment or Service: Royal Irish Regiment. Unit; 6th Battalion. Service Number; 1885. Date of death; 06/06/1916. Age at death;28. Born; Kilmacow, County Kilkenny. Enlisted; Dungarvan. Killed in action. Son of Michael and Mary Dobbyn, of Kilmacow, Co. Kilkenny, husband of E. Dobbyn, of 39, Queen St, Portlaw, Co. Waterford. Grave or Memorial Reference; Panel 44. Cemetery: Loos Memorial in France.

Doheney, Philip. Rank; Private. Regiment or Service: Royal Irish Regiment. Unit; 2nd Battalion. Service Number; 8433. Date of death; 24/05/1915. Born; Tullaroan, County Kilkeny. Enlisted; Kilkenny. Residence; Tullaroan. Killed in action. Grave or Memorial Reference; Panel 33. Cemetery: Ypres (Menin Gate) Memorial in Belgium.

Doherty, Patrick. Rank; Guardsman. Regiment or Service: Guards Machine Gun Regiment. Unit; 4th Battalion. Service Number; 1062. Date of death; 09/08/1917. Born; St John's, Kilkenny. Enlisted; Kilkenny. Killed in action. Notes; Formerly he was with the Irish Guards where his number was 7803. Grave or Memorial Reference; X E 2. Cemetery: Artillery Wood Cemetery in Belgium.

Donovan, James. Rank; Private. Regiment or Service: Canadian Infantry (Quebec Regiment). Unit; 13th Battalion. Service Number; 4040061. Date of death; 02/10/1918. Age at death; 34. Born; London, England. Son of John and Mary Donovan; husband of Anna Donovan, of Carrenroe Cottage, the Rower, Thomastown, Co. Kilkenny, Ireland. Native of Highgate, London, England. Occupation on enlistment, Bar Tender. Address on enlistment; 95 Scott Street, Quebec, P. Q. Age on enlistment; 30 years 6 months. Date of birth;14-May-1887. Next of kin details; (wife) Anna Donovan. Place and date of enlistment, 13-January-1918, Quebec. Height, 5 feet, 5 ½ inches. Complexion, dark. Eyes, hazel. Hair, black. Grave or Memorial Reference; C 57. Cemetery: Queant Communal Cemetery British Extension in France.

Donovan, Patrick. Rank; Private. Regiment or Service: Australian Infantry A. I. F. Unit; 9th Battalion. Service Number; 1753. Date of death; 25/02/1917. Age at death;31. Born; Callan, County Kilkenny. Killed in action in France. Unit embarked from Brisbane, Queensland, on board HMAT A15 Star Of England on 08-April-1915. Educated; Christian Brothers (Catholic) School, Callan, Ireland. Served in Gallipoli, Egypt and on the Western Front. Killed in action in France. Occupation on enlistment, Labourer. Age on enlistment; years months. Address on enlistment; c/o Mrs Mackay, Federal Hotel, Rockhampton, Queensland. Next of kin details; Phillip Donovan, Castle Callas, Kilkenny, Ireland. Place and date of enlistment, 12-January-1915. Weight, 154 lbs. Height, 5 feet, 6 ½ inches. Cemetery: Australian National Memorial, Villers-Bretonneux Memorial in France

Dooley, John. Rank; Private. Regiment or Service: Royal Irish Regiment. Unit; 5th Battalion. Service Number; 7698. Date of death; 05/02/1916. Age at death; 34. Born; Thomastown, County Kilkenny. Enlisted; Waterford. Residence; Thomastown, County Kilkenny. Died at home. Son of Patrick and Johanna Dooley of Columbine CottageThomastown. Waterford News, 1915. Kilkenny Soldier's Death. The death occurred in a London hospital of Private John Dooley, Royal Irish Regiment, as the result of a disease contracted while serving with his regiment in France. A native of Maudlin-street, Thomastown, he had previously been in the army and was discharged with a pension as medically unfit some seven years ago. At the outbreak of the war he volunteered for active service and was accepted. The remains were conveyed from London to Thomastown on yesterday and the interment took place today. The War Office, in appreciation of his services to king and Country, paid all expenses in connection with his removal from London. Grave or Memorial Reference; Panel 5 (Screen Wall). Cemetery: Grangegorman Memorial in Dublin.

Dooley, John. Rank; Driver. Regiment or Service: Royal Horse Artillery and Royal Field Artillery. Service Number; 89759. Date of death; 13/02/1920. Age at death;45. Born; Ballyragget, County Kilkenny. Died after discharge. Son of Edward and Julia Dooley, Donoughmore, Ballyragget, County Kilkenny. Cemetery: Unknown

Dooley, Michael. Rank; Private. Regiment or Service: Connaught Rangers. Unit; 6th Battalion. Service Number; 5559. Date of death; 16/12/1917. Born; Kilkenny. Enlisted; Kilkenny. Residence; Kilkenny. Killed in action. Grave or Memorial Reference; D 2. Cemetery: Ronssoy Communal Cemetery, Somme, France.

Doran, John. Rank; Private. Regiment or Service: Loyal North Lancashire Regiment. Unit; 10th Battalion. Service Number; 3369. Date of death; 17/07/1916. Age at death;28. Born; Tipperary. Enlisted; Blackburn. Residence; Kilkenny. Killed in action. Son of Ellen Doran, of Green's Hill, Kilkenny, and the late James Doran. Grave or Memorial Reference; III G 31. Cemetery: Pozieres British Cemetery, Ovillers-La Boisselle in France

Dougherty, John Edward. Rank; Private. Regiment or Service: Royal Irish Regiment. Unit; 6th Battalion. Service Number; 3380. Date of death; 09/09/1916. Age at death; 22. Born; St John's, Kilkenny. Enlisted; Fermoy, County Cork. Residence; Huddersfield. Killed in action. Son of Edward and Mary Ann Dougherty, of 47, Bradford Rd., Huddersfield. Grave or Memorial Reference; Pier and Face 3 A. Cemetery: Thiepval Memorial in France.

Dowdall, William. Rank; Gunner. Regiment or Service: Royal Garrison Artillery. Unit; 5th Battery. Service Number; 28111. Date of death; 24/07/1920. Age at death;37. Born; Kilkenny. Grave or Memorial Reference; Panel 4 and 61. Cemetery: Basra Memorial in Iraq.

Dower, James. Rank; Sapper. Regiment or Service: Labour Corps. Unit; 652nd Home Service Employment Coy. Service Number; 163344. Date of death; 06/07/1918. Age at death; 48. Born; Killen, County Kilkenny. Enlisted; Waterford. Residence; Ballinamore, County Kilkenny. Died at home. Husband of A. Dower, of Ballinamona, Ferrybank, Waterford. Born at Kilea. Notes; Formerly he was with the Royal Engineers where his number was 348305. Grave or Memorial Reference; In the North West part. Cemetery: Kilbride Graveyard in County Kilkenny.

Dowling, Bernard. Rank; Private. Regiment or Service: Royal Irish Regiment. Unit; 2nd Battalion. Service Number; 6450. Date of death; 30/11/1917. Age at death;41. Born; Kilkenny. Died after discharge. Cemetery: St Patrick's Graveyard, County Kilkenny.

Dowling, John. Rank; Private. Regiment or Service: Labour Corps. Service Number; 364286. Date of death; 17/01/1918. Age at death; 49. Enlisted; Kilkenny. Died at home. Husband of Mary Dowling, of 10, Lord Edward St., Kilkenny. Formerly he was with the Royal Irish Regiment where his number was 6923. Listed in the CWGC under his R.I.Regiment number. Grave or Memorial Reference; In the South East part. Cemetery: Kilkenny (St John) Catholic Churchyard, Kilkenny.

Dowling, Lawrence. Rank; Private. Regiment or Service: Royal Dublin Fusiliers. Service Number; 10039. Date of death; 22/04/1916. Age at death;31. Born; Gowran, County Kilkenny. Died after discharge. Cemetery: Unknown

Dowling, Matthew. Rank; Private. Regiment or Service: Welsh Regiment. Unit; 9th Battalion. Service Number; 18617. Date of death; 26/01/1917. Born; Gowran, County Kilkenny. Enlisted; Bargoed. Residence; Dungarven,County Kilkenny. Died of wounds. Grave or Memorial Reference; II J 6. Cemetery: Sailly-Au-Bois Military Cemetery in France.

Dowling, Patrick. Rank; Private. Regiment or Service: Royal Welsh Fusiliers. Unit; 10th Battalion. Service Number; 34197. Date of death; 27/09/1917. Born; Kilkenny. Enlisted; Aberdare. Died of wounds. Grave or Memorial Reference; V F 16. Cemetery: Dozinghem Military Cemetery in Belgium

Dowling, Patrick. Rank; Sergeant. Regiment or Service: Royal Irish Regiment. Unit; 2nd Battalion. Service Number; 10931. Date of death; 21/03/1918. Age at death; 21. Born; Newton, County Kilkenny. Enlisted; Kilkenny. Residence; Bonnetstown, County Kilkenny. Killed in action. Son of Edward and Ellen Dowling, of The Lodge, Orchardton, Kilkenny. Grave or Memorial Reference; Panel 30 and 31. Cemetery: Pozieres Memorial in France

Dowling, Pierce. Rank; Private. Regiment or Service: Middlesex Regiment. Unit; 4th Battalion. Service Number; L/10042. Date of death; 14/10/1914. Born; Kilkenny. Enlisted; Dublin. Killed in action. In his Will, dated 08-September-1914, his effects and property were received by;- Mrs N Boyce. De Ruvigny's Roll of Honour;-Dowling, P., Private, No 10042, 4th Battalion Middlesex Regiment. Son of Patrick Dowling, of New York, U. S. A. Served with the Expeditionary Force; killed in action 14-October-1914. Grave or Memorial Reference; Panels 31 and 32. Cemetery: Le Touret Memorial in France.

Downey, Michael Joseph. Rank; Private. Regiment or Service: King's Shropshire Light Infantry. Unit; 5th Battalion. Service Number; 11502. Date of death; 08/04/1917. Born; Castlecomer, County Kilkenny. Enlisted; Ludlow. Residence; Castlecomer. Killed in action. Son of the late Martin and Mary Downey, of Firoda (Lower), Castlecomer, Co. Kilkenny. Grave or Memorial Reference; Bay 7. Cemetery: Arras Memorial in France.

Doyle, Matthew. Rank; Private. Regiment or Service: Australian Army Medical Corps. Unit; 8th Field Ambulance. Service Number; 10063. Date of death; 25/09/1917. Age at death;29. Born; Graigue. Kilkenny. Son of William and Catherine Doyle, of Upper Main St., Graiguenamanagh, Co. Kilkenny, Ireland. Occupation on enlistment, State School Teacher. Age on enlistment; 26 years 11 months. Next of kin details; (mother) Catherine Doyle, Uper main Street, Graig-Na-Managh, County Kilkenny. She received a pension of 40/- per fortnight from 11-December-1917. Place and date of enlistment, 02-September-1915. Townsville, Queensland. Weight, 9st 6 lbs. Height, 5 feet, 7 inches. Complexion, dark. Eyes, grey. Hair, black. Died of multiple wounds received in action on the Menin Road at the 3rd Field Ambulance. The day he died was known as Black Friday. Nationalist and Leinster Times, 1917. Sergeant (sic) Matthew Doyle. The many friends of Matthew Doyle, formerly of Graiguenamanagh, who fell in action in France on September 25th, while serving with his Regiment there, will deeply regret the very sad occurrence. This young fellow was trained some years ago for the teaching profession in this country and, having spent some time in Edenderry Boys School, he at the suggestion of his Australian friends determined to parade his calling under the Southern Cross. Getting on remarkably well in his new home, and maintaining his former prestige as a teacher with his characteristic unselfishness, he in obedience to the call of his adopted country threw up a lucrative position and in company with his brother and several other young teachers, took service in the Army Service Branch of the Australian Imperial Forces. Having spent some time in preliminary training, his unit was drafted to Egypt and after a short stay there, was subsequently ordered to the front. Here he passed through many hazardous actions, as his letters to home indicated. But alas, the end came too soon, for he fell, as he lived, trying to succour others. To his sorrowing mother, sister, and brothers the greatest sympathy is extended, while the vast circle of his relations in the Counties of Carlow, Kilkenny and Wexford, as well as in Australia, will be grieved to hear of his young life cut away so swiftly. Grave or Memorial Reference; Panel 31. Cemetery: Ypres (Menin Gate) Memorial in Belgium.

Doyle, Michael. Rank; Private. Regiment or Service: Irish Guards. Unit; 2nd Battalion. Service Number; 7793. Date of death; 27/09/1915. Age at death; 25. Born; Tullaherin, County Kilkenny. Enlisted; Kilkenny. Killed in action. Son of Patrick and Kate Doyle, of Kilfane, Thomastown, Co. Kilkenny. After his death, his effects and property were received by;- Mr Patrick Doyle, Kilfane, Thomastown, County Kilkenny, Ireland. Kilkenny People, November, 1915. A Popular Kilfane Athlete Killed in Action. The parents of Private Michael Doyle, a native of Kilfane, Thomastown, have received notification from the officer commanding the Irish Guards that their son was killed in action at the battle of Loos on the 27th September. Private Doyle had been a member of the Welsh police force for about two years, and volunteered for active service in the month of April last. He joined the Irish Guards, and has been in the trenches since May. He was a splendid type of Irish manhood. Previous to joining the Welsh police force he was a noted athlete, and was a prominent competitor at the different G. A. A. sports held in the County Kilkenny and adjoining counties. Much sympathy is felt for his parents and relatives in their sad bereavement. 12/11/1915. Freeman's Journal. Popular Thomastown Athlete Killed in Action. The parents of Private Michael Doyle, a native of Kilfane, Thomastown, have been officially informed of the death of their son, who was killed in action in France on the 27th September. The deceased soldier was a member of the Welsh Police Force for a number of years. He volunteered for the front last April, and joined the Irish Guards, and had been in the trenches since May. Previous to joining the Welsh Police Force Private Doyle was a well-known athlete and long-distance runner. He was the leading mile runner in the County Kilkenny for a number of years. Grave or Memorial Reference; Panel 9 and 10. Cemetery: Loos Memorial in France

Doyle, Patrick. Rank; Private. Regiment or Service: Royal Irish Regiment. Unit; 2nd Battalion. Service Number; 5938. Date of death; 19/10/1914. Age at death;32. Born; Thomastown, County Kilkenny. Enlisted; Waterford. Residence; Thomastown, County Kilkenny. Killed in action. Son of Mrs. Ellen Mulcahy, of Masudlin St., Thomastown, Co. Kilkenny. Grave or Memorial Reference; VIII H 4. Cemetery: Cabaret-Rouge British Cemetery, Souchez in France

Doyle, William. Rank; Gunner. Regiment or Service: Royal Garrison Artillery. Unit; 122nd Heavy Battery. Service Number; 15201. Date of death; 17/03/1918. Born; Kilkenny. Enlisted; Nas. Residence; Thomastown, County Kilkenny. Died at home. In his Will, dated June-1917, his effects and property were received by;- (Sister) Mr M Evans, Island House, Thomastown, County Kilkenny, Ireland. Grave or Memorial Reference; Special Memorial. Cemetery: Grangegorman (Cork) Memorial Headstones. Alternative Commemoration - buried in Cork Military Cemetery.

Drea, Kieran. Rank; Private. Regiment or Service: Royal Irish Regiment. Unit; 2nd Battalion. Service Number; 5258. Date of death; 06/07/1918. Age at death;36. Born; Cuffsgrange, County Kilkenny. Enlisted; Kilkenny. Residence; Cuffsgrange. Died. Son of John Drea. After his death, his effects and property were received by;- (Sister) Mrs Bridget Murphy, Cuffs Grange, County Kilkenny. Grave or Memorial Reference; 302. Cemetery: Sedan (St Charles) Communa Cemetery, Ardennes, France.

Dreeling, Edward. Rank; Lance Corporal. Regiment or Service: Royal Irish Regiment. Unit; 2nd Battalion. Service Number; 9953. Date of death; 14/07/1916. Age at death; 30. Born; Gowran, County Kilkenny. Enlisted; Kilkenny. Residence; Gowran. Killed in action. Son of John and Mary Dreeling, of Closhwilliam. Cowran, Co. Kilkenny. In his Will, dated 16-September-1914, his effects and property were received by;- (Mother) Mrs Mary Dreeliing, Clashwilliam, County Kilkenny, Ireland. Grave or Memorial Reference; Pier and Face 3 A. Cemetery: Thiepval Memorial in France.

Dreeling, Nicholas. Rank; Private. Regiment or Service: Irish Guards. Unit; 2nd Battalion. Service Number; 7071. Date of death; 09/10/1917. Age at death;33. Born; Gowran, County Kilkenny. Enlisted; Kilkenny. Killed in action. Husband of Julia Dreeling, of Sheafield, Gowran, Co. Kilkenny. After his death his effects and property were received by; (Wife) Julia Dreeling, Sheafield Gardens, Killiney. His Last Will and Testament was witnessed by;- James O Keffe, 19 Mill Cottage Gds, Anamoe?. Grave or Memorial Reference; VIII F 6. Cemetery: Artillery Wood Cemetery in Belgium.

Dryden, Robert. Rank; Lance Corporal. Regiment or Service: Royal Dublin Fusiliers. Unit; 1st Battalion. Service Number; 27215. Date of death; 24/04/1918. Age at death; 22. Born; Thomastown, County Kilkenny. Enlisted; Carlow. Residence; Thomastown, County Kilkenny. Killed in action. Son of Alfred and Mary Dryden, of Field House, Triangle, Halifax. Grave or Memorial Reference; Panel 78 and 80. Cemetery: Pozieres Memorial in France. He is also commemorated on the Great War Memorial in St Canice's Cathedral, Kilkenny…'To the Glory of God and in loving memory of the following members of the Diocese of Ossory who gave their lives for their country in the Great War 1914-1918' and he is also listed on the Great War Memorial, Milford Street, Leighlinbridge, County Carlow.

Dudley, Harry/Henry Pemberton. Rank; Second Lieutenant. Regiment or Service: Leinster Regiment. Unit; 3rd Battalion. Date of death; 03/09/1916. Age at death;36. Killed in action. Son of Henry N. Dudley, M. D., and Mary E. Dudley (nee Pemberton), of Durrow, Queen's Co. Previously wounded when serving as Lance Corporal with the 7th Battalion. Royal Dublin Fusiliers, in Gallipoli, Aug, 1915. De Ruvignys Roll of Honour. 3rd son of the late Henry, N, Dudley, M. D., formerly of Kinnitty, Kings County, and afterwards of Durrow, Queens County by his wife, Mary Elizabeth (2 Burdett Ave, Sandycove) daughter of John Pemberton, of Blackrock, Dublin. Born in Kinnitty, 8 May, 1880. Eductaed by private tuition, Lanly School, and Dublin. On the outbreak of war he returned home from Singapore, and joined the 7th (Service) Battalion, of the Royal Dublin Fusiliers; went to the Dardinelles, and was severely wounded at Suvla Bay, August 1915. On his recovery was gazetted, 2nd Lieut, 3rd Leinster Regiment, Nov, 1915. Proceeded to France, July, 1916, where he was attached to the 2nd Royal Irish Regiment, and was killed in action near Guillemont, 3rd Sept, 1916. The Leinster Express;-September-1916. Roll of Honour. Dudley—September 3, 1916, killed in action, Henry Pemberton, Second Lieutenant, Leinster regiment (attached Royal Irish Regiment), third son of the late H. N. Dudley, 2 Burdett Avenue, Sandycove, Kingstown, aged 36 years. Second Lieutenant H. P. Dudley. The death in action is reported of Second Lieutenant Harry P, Dudley ("Hunt"), third son of the late Dr Dudley, formerly of Kinnitty, King's County, and of Mrs Dudley, of 2 Burdett Avenue, Sandycove. At the outbreak of the war he gave up a fine position in Singapore to come home and serve his country in the field. He joined the 7th ("Pals") Battalion of the Dublin Fusiliers, and was severely wounded at Suvla Bay. On his recovery he was gazetted Second Lieutenant to the Leinster Regiment, and in July proceeded to France, where he was attached to the Royal Irish Regiment. A fine all-round athlete, he gained many trophies, chiefly for lawn tennis and swimming. Notes; Attached to the 2nd Battalion Royal Irish Regiment. Grave or Memorial Reference; XIV K 6. Cemetery: Delville Wood Cemetery, Longueval in France.

Duggan, John. Rank; Private. Regiment or Service: Leinster Regiment. Unit; 1st Battalion. Service Number; 9235. Date of death; 24/04/1915. Born; Kilkenny. Enlisted; Cork. Killed in action at Ypres. Son of William and Mary Duggan, of 44, Maylors St., Cork. In his Will, dated 22-April-1915, his effects and property were received by;- (Sister) Miss May Duggan, Cullohill, Rathdowney, Queens County. Grave or Memorial Reference; Panel 44. Cemetery: Ypres (Menin Gate) Memorial in Belgium

Duggan, Martin. Rank; Private. Regiment or Service: Royal Irish Regiment. Unit; 7th Battalion. Service Number; 25239. Date of death; 12/12/1917. Born; Windgap, County Kilkenny. Enlisted; Carrick-on-Suir. Residence; Windgap. Killed in action. Notes; Number listed as 1787, South Irish Horse. Grave or Memorial Reference; II H 33. Cemetery: Templeux-Le-Guerard British Cemetery in France.

Duggan, Michael. Rank; Private. Regiment or Service: The King's Liverpool Regiment. Unit; 1st/8th Battalion. Service Number; 5559. Date of death; 08/09/1916. Age at death; 23. Born; Killown, Ireland. Enlisted; Liverpool. Residence; West Derby, Liverpool. Killed in action. Son of John and Margaret Duggan, of Poulrone, Piltown, Co. Kilkenny. In his Will, dated 10-August-1916, his effects and property were received by;- (Mother) Mrs John Duggan, Poulrone, Piltown, County Kilkenny, Ireland. Munster

Express;- Dec 23, 16...Killed in France some time since and for whose soul prayers were offered up by the congregation at Mass on Sunday last. Private Duggan, was the third son of Mr John Duggan, Poulrone, and brother of Mr J Duggan, Knickeen. Private Duggan served his apprenticeship to the hardware business in Carrick-on-Suir. Returning home afterwards he remained some time there, when the spirit of travel inspired his young mind and he set sail for the United States. Not content with the habits and ways of the Yank he returned once more to his native shore, when he worked on a home farm for a period. He again emigrated to Great Britain where he enlisted and gallantly fell in Flanders. To the father, mother, brothers and sisters we offer our condolence. R. I. P. Grave or Memorial Reference; Pier and Face 1 D 8 B and 8 C. Cemetery: Thiepval Memorial in France.

Duggan, Michael. Rank; Private. Regiment or Service: Welsh Regiment. Unit; 14th Battalion. Service Number; 11911. Date of death; 05/08/1917. Age at death;36. Born; Ballyhale, County Kilkenny. Enlisted; Pentre, Glamorganshire. Killed in action. Husband of Mrs. E. A. Duggan, of 37, Park Rd., Cwmpark, Treorchy, Glamorganshire. Grave or Memorial Reference; Panel 37. Cemetery: Ypres (Menin Gate) Memorial in Belgium.

Duggan, Patrick. Rank; Private. Regiment or Service: Irish Guards. Unit; 2nd Battalion. Service Number; 11662. Date of death; 13/09/1917. Born; Tullaroan, County Kilkeny. Enlisted; Kilkenny. Residence; Kilkenny. Killed in action. Grave or Memorial Reference; Panel 10 and 11. Cemetery: Tyne Cot Memorial in Belgium.

Duggan, Thomas. Rank; Lance Corporal. Regiment or Service: Royal Irish Regiment. Unit; 6th Battalion. Service Number; 8667. Date of death; 26/06/1916. Age at death;17. Born; Templeorum, County Kilkenny. Enlisted; Carrick-on-Suir. County Tipperary. Residence; Piltown, County Kilkenny. Killed in action. Son of Edward and Ellen Duggan, of Belline, Piltown, Co. Kilkenny. In his Will, dated 10-March-1916, his effects and property were received by;- Mrs Duggan, Belline, Piltown, County Kilkenny, Ireland. Munster Express;-In memory of Lance Corporal Thomas Duggan, Belline, who was killed in action on June 25th, 1916. In the heart of old Kilkenny lies a a spot so fair, Although I see it but in memory, happy thoughts yet linger there. Oh sweet Belline, green woods are thine, thy shady paths are fair. In Spring when notes of warbles ring, 'tis lively to be there. Oh, sweet Belline, neat walks are thine, with mossy banks so fair. In bygone days I loved to rove with my old fond comrades there. Far-famed Belline, green fields are thine, with pasture rich and rare. But I left them for the battlefield and they are so lovely there. When the shot and shell were flying upon the battlefield. Our Irish boys were bravely fighting the British flag to shield. When the shot and shell were firing upon the battlefield. Like a brave young hero I was fighting, when a German shot I had to yield. In a deep dug trench the pale June sun is shedding its radiant light, And is shining down on souls that soon will speed their eternal flight. Among the dying a young hero lay, his captain was near at hand. He said when I am passed away, please send news to my native land. Just write to my sweet mother, say we'll meet with God above—Tell father, sister and dear brothers, I send them all my last true love. God guard them safe in Ireland is their dying brother's prayer. Who could send no letter to them, nor sunny lock of nut-brown hair. Though they will weep o'er fate to-day, let their hearts beat high with pride, For in a cause more nobler than which I fell, none ever have fought or died. In a soldier's grave, by war, comrades, my body was laid to rest. Far, far away, from holy Ireland, and all I loved there bestSo fare thee well, dear old Belline, farewell dear friends of yore. I hope we'll meet in that bright land above, where we will part no more. Mary Flynn. Belline. Grave or Memorial Reference; I G 13. Cemetery: Dud Corner Cemetery, Loos in France.

Lieutenant Duggan from the Kilkenny People.

Duggan, Thomas Alphonsus. Rank; Second Lieutenant. Regiment or Service: East Lancashire Regiment. Unit; 7th Battalion. Date of death; 13/11/1916. Killed in action. Son of Mr. R. Duggan, of William St., Kilkenny. Killed in action. Image above from the Kilkenny People. Irish Independent; Duggan-Killed in action on 13th November, Lieutenant T A Duggan, East Lancs, son of Richard Duggan, J. P., Kilkenny, Requiem Office and High Mass at 11 o'clock at St Mary's Cathedral on to-morrow (Tuesday) 21st inst. Kilkenny People, April, 1915. Popular Young Citizen gets Commission. Mr Tom Duggan, son of Mr Richard Duggan, J. P., the Monster House, has been appointed to a Commission in the East Lancashire Regiment, and has proceeded to Devon for training. Mr Duggan is a law student at the National University, and has gained many distinctions in his academic career. Kilkenny People, February, 1916. Second Lieutenant T. A. Duggan, 10th East Lancs., second son of Mr Richard Duggan, J. P., the Monster House, Kilkenny, who was seriously wounded on December 17 in France, a bullet entering the right ear and passing out through the left eye. He had a brilliant career ay Clongowes and the National University, he is at present in the Research Hospital in Cambridge, where he is making a speedy recovery and soon expects to be fit enough to come home. Lieutenant Duggan is only 21 years of age. Waterford News;-During last weekend, Lieutenant Thomas Duggan, son of Mr. Richard. Duggan, Monster House, Kilkenny, was on a visit to some friends in the city. Lieutenant Duggan received a severe injury to his left eye in action some time ago. Kilkenny People, December, 1915. Gallant Kilkenny Officer Wounded. Lieutenant T. A. Duggan "Sniped" in the Trenches. Mr Richard Duggan, J. P., the Monster House, received a wire from the War Office on Monday that his son, Second Lieutenant T. A. Duggan, 10th Battalion,

East Lancashire Regiment (attached to the 7th Battalion), who has been fighting in Flanders for nearly three months, has been wounded. A letter followed on Tuesday morning from the Sister in charge of the French Hospital where Lieutenant Duggan is being treated, stating that he was severely wounded in the face, that he was suffering no pain, was going on as well as could be expected, and that she hoped to soon be able to send news of a more reassuring character. Kilkenny People, December, 1915. Tribute from his Company Commander. Captain G, B. Tyser, commanding A Company, 7th East Lancs, in a letter to Mr Richard Duggan on December 18, writes."You will no doubt, have been notified officially about your son's bad luck in getting hit yesterday. Recent heavy rains have naturally caused a good deal of settlement in comparatively recently dug ground, and parapets in parts of the trenches are lower than they should be, consequently some spots are not very safe on account of snipers, especially for a fine tall fellow like your son. He was walking along the trench, and passing one of these low places—at that point his whole head would have been visible if he stood up—the sniper was evidently waiting for someone to pass. He has not been out long, but everyone, officers and men, liked him, as he always took the rough with the smooth in the same quiet, genial way; and since he has been in my Company I have, on two occasions, shared a dug-out with him and found him an excellent companion under some rather rough conditions. I can only say I am extremely sorry he has been hit, and can only offer you and him my most sincere sympathy and wish him as speedy a recovery as possible." College and University Record. Lieutenant Duggan, who is only in his 1st year, is a Clongownian, and for part of his time in that famous College was Second Captain. An enthusiastic cricketer (like his father) he played against Phoenix in his 16th year and scored 67. He was a keen student and an Intermediate exhibitioner and prizewinner. Passing to the National University, he won the Delany Scholarship, and was reading a Law course when he got his Commission on the 20th March last. Kilkenny People, November, 1916. Lieutenant T, A. Duggan. Killed in Action. Most Unselfish and Gallant."Did not know what fear meant."We deeply regret to announce that Lieutenant T. A. Duggan, East Lancashire Regiment, was killed in action in France at Midday on Monday, November 13. His father, Mr Richard Duggan, J. P., the Monster House, received a telegram from the War Office on the evening of Thursday, November 16, conveying the sad news. On November 22, Mr Duggan received the following telegram."Buckingham Palace, November 22-1916." "R. Duggan, Esq., William Street, Kilkenny. —The King and Queen deeply regret the loss you and the Army have sustained by the death of your son in the service of his country. Their majesties truly sympathise with you in your sorrow. —Keeper of the Privy Purse."The manner in which this fine young Kilkennyman met his death in a foreign land is told in the following letter, received on Thursday morning. November 23, from the Captain of his Company, and the manner in which as a faithful and devoted Irish catholic he prepared for his death is told in the succeeding letter, received on the same morning from the Catholic chaplain who knew him intimately and loved him dearly, as indeed did everyone who came under the influence of his engaging and charming personality;--Letter from his Captain. 7th Battalion, East Lancashire Regiment. My Dear Mrs Duggan—I have taken the liberty of opening the enclosed letter to your son in order to get your address that I might be able to tell you about the way he died. Your son was, for the time being, in command of "A" Company. He was leading two platoons to attack a position when he was shot by a rifle bullet and died in a few seconds. As I believe he lost consciousness at once I am confident that is end was painless, and this will, I hope, be some consolation to you in your bereavement as it is to me in mine. You may perhaps be a little surprised that I talk of it as my bereavement when I am a perfect stranger to you, but in the two months I had known your son I had formed a real affection for him. He was the most unselfish and gallant boy I ever knew, and is as great a loss to me privately as he is to the Regiment as a soldier. We must be comforted that he died as he would have wished, fighting for his Ireland, of which he was so fond. You should receive from the Adjutant his effects, and of these, I expect, the little things from his pockets should arrive fairly soon. I should say that your son's men buried him as decently as they could, and the location of the grave should eventually be recorded by the Graves Registration Committee. With my deepest sympathy to you and his father, I am, yours sincerely. R. W. Palmer (Captain). Letter from the Chaplain. November-16-1916. Dear Mr Duggan — I suppose you have by this time heard of the death of your son. I did all I could to get a wire to you on Tuesday but regulations would not alow me to do so. None was more sorry than I was when I heard he had been killed. As I suppose you know, I knew him when in the hospital at Le Treport. I can say without a doubt that there was no better officer in the brigade to which I am attached. He was loved and respected by all. All say there was no braver soldier; he did not know what fear meant. He never missed Communion when it was possible to receive. He was at Mass. Three Sundays out of four for the past four weeks and received Holy Communion each time. A very strange thing happened last Sunday. As his Battalion came to service I missed the officers. I asked the sergeant in command why the officers were absent; I told him to let one of the men fall out and go and tell the officers to come. The man returned and said all the officers had to attend a conference. Just that moment your son came to me and said "we have a meeting of officers at 10. 45."At that time it was about 10 a. m. he asked me not to preach as he wanted to get Holy Communion. I did so. I gave him Holy Communion and told him to go as soon as he received, and, strange to say, he and another were the only two who came to Mass that morning. I saw him again at 3 p. m., as the Battalion was going into action, and gave him absolution. So you have the grand consolation that his death must have been a most holy one. In conclusion, I ask you, to accept my earnest sympathy in your great bereavement. —J. J. Leech, C. F. --------Thomas Alphonsus Duggan was the second son of Mr Richard Duggan, J. P., the Monster House, Kilkenny and of the late Mrs Duggan, who belonged to a family that for generations has been respected an honoured in this county, the Shellys of Callan. He had but just completed his 22nd year. Handsome, well proportioned, athletic, he was physically as fine a type of young Irishman as it was possible to meet; and — a rare combination — his intellectual gifts were no less remarkable than his physical fitness and power. Add to this, that he was a clean living, high thinking young fellow — and to none more so than to the justly esteemed lady who has been a mother to him in the highest and noblest sense of the sacred word — and to the religion whose consolations, as the noble letter from his chaplain printed above most touchingly shows, soothed his dying moments, and one can form some ideas of all that his death means to the sorrowing ones who are left to mourn his loss. He received his early education, as so many other Kilkenny boys have done, at the Christian Schools, James's Street, afterwards passing to St Kieran's College. He then went to the famous Jesuit School at Clongowes, where he soon gave unmistakable evidence of all those brilliant qualities that — had the hand of Providence not intervened — justified the prediction that a future rich in achievement as it was in its promise awaited him. He won Exhibitions in the Junior and Middle Grades of the Intermediate. During one of his years at Clongowes he was second Captain of the school. He passed from Clongowes to the National University, where he won the Delaney Scholarship of £40 a year for three years. The bent of his mind directed him towards the higher branch of the legal profession and he was reading his law course up to the time that he got his commission in the Army. While a student at the University he was Captain of the university Hall, Stephens Green. Both at Clongowes and the University he distinguished himself as an all-round athlete, but cricket was his forte, and as a cricketer his performances marked him out as a first-class man. Playing for his school against Phoenix he ran up a splendid score of 67 runs in one hard-fought match. During vacation he frequently played for Kilkenny and in one match against Pembroke he defended his wicket for over two hours, and although he only scored 7 runs himself, his stonewalling tactics enabled his fellow batsmen to win out the game, an achievement that at first seemed hopeless. The information above is just a small part of a half page newspaper article on Lieutenant Duggan. For more see The "Kilkenny People" of November-16-1916. Irish Independent;Duggan-Killed in action on 13th November, Lieutenant T A Duggan, East Lancs, son of Richard Duggan, J. P., Kilkenny. Requiem Office and High Mass at 11 o'clock at St Mary's Cathedral on to-morrow (Tuesday) 21st inst. Grave or Memorial Reference; A 29. Cemetery: Grandcourt Road Cemetery, Grandcourt, Somme, France.

Duke, Alexander Mark. Rank; Gunner. Regiment or Service: Royal Horse Artillery and Royal Field Artillery. Unit; A Battery, 7th Reserve Brigade. Service Number; 261338. Date of death; 30/10/1918. Age at death;27. Born; Maryborough, Queen's County. Enlisted; Kilkenny. Died at home. Son of Mrs. Helen Duke, of 21, William Street, Kilkenny. Grave or Memorial Reference; In the South West part. Cemetery: Kilkenny (St Mary) Church of Ireland Churchyard, County Kilkenny. He is also commemorated on the Great War Memorial in St Canice's Cathedral, Kilkenny…'To the Glory of God and in loving memory of the following members of the Diocese of Ossory who gave their lives for their country in the Great War 1914-1918'.

Dullard, James. Rank; Private. Regiment or Service: Royal Irish Regiment. Unit; 3rd Battalion. Service Number; 8293. Date of death; 26/02/1915. Born; St Canice's, Kilkenny. Enlisted; Clonmel, County Tipperary. Died at home. Kilkenny People, March, 1915. Military Funeral in the City. On Monday last the funeral took place from the Military Barracks to St John's, R. C. cemetery, of Private James Dullard, Royal Irish Regiment. The deceased, who was a native of the city, was aged about 28 years, and served 10 ½ years, after which he retired and lived in England for some time. Immediately on the outbreak of the war the deceased was recalled to the colours and sent to the front, where he received a wound in the thigh. The deceased partly recovered from the effects of the wound, but unfortunately, complications set in, and he passed peacefully away on Friday evening last. The funeral left the Military Barracks at 2 o'clock on Monday, the gun carriage conveying the coffin, ehich was covered with a Union Jack, being drawn by a number of the "A" Battery, R. F. A., at present stationed in Kilkenny, which furnished the funeral party, of whom Captain Mackesy was in charge, Second Lieutenant Campbell and Adams being also present. There were a fairly large attendance of the general public. The last prayers at the graveside having been recited by the Rev. M. Holohan, Adm., St John's, the Buglers sounded the "Last Post," after which the remains were laid to rest. A brother of the deceased in the same regiment is a prisoner of war in Germany. Kilkenny Journal, March, 1915. Kilkenny Soldier's Death. Buried with Military Honours. Private James Dullard, Walkin Street, Kilkenny, who had served with the 18th Royal Irish regiment since the outbreak of the war, and had taken part in all the glorious actions fought by that famous regiment up to two months ago, when he was severely wounded and allowed home to recuperate, died in the military hospital, Kilkenny, on Friday last. The deceased was son of the late Mr Edward Dullard, Walkin Street., who served the greater part of his life in the Army, winning many war distinctions and decorations, and whose greatest pleasure in his latter years was in relating his thrilling experiences during the many campaigns in which he was engaged, and in displaying the different medals and decorations he had won. His military ardour was imbued in his three sons, all of whom joined the Army at an early age, and at the outbreak of the present war, were amongst the first to respond to the call of King and Country. The military funeral which was accorded the deceased to St John's cemetery on Monday last, was most impressive in its melancholy significance, bringing to the minds of the large numbers that were present to pay their last respects to the deceased, the many brave deeds that are being performed by our countrymen—yes, our own townsmen—many of whom, alas, have found an unknown and forgotten grave on the battlefields of

Belgium and France. The coffin, which was placed on a gun-carriage, covered with the Union Jack, was drawn by six men of the 235th Battery, R. F. A, and the cortege was composed of about 100 men of the same Battery, under the command of Captain McAssey and Lieutenants Campbell and Adams. As the coffin was lowered in the grave the buglers sounded "The Last Post" and a hero of Mons was laid to rest in his native soil. A number of spectators assembled at different points along the route to the cemetery, and their comments on the smart and reverential bearing of the military were highly complimentary. The soldiers marched in perfect alignment and gave proof of the excellence of the instruction they have received under the capable supervision of their officers in Kilkenny. Grave or Memorial Reference; About 9 yards West of East entrance. Cemetery: Kilkenny (St John) Catholic Churchyard, Kilkenny.

Dullard, Martin. Rank; Private. Regiment or Service: Royal Irish Regiment. Unit; 6th Battalion. Service Number; 2530. Date of death; 09/09/1916. Born; St Mary's, Kilkenny. Enlisted; Kilkenny. Died of wounds. After his death, his effects and property were received by;- (Wife, child and mother) Wife's address, Mrs Martin Dullard, Saint Rochs, Walkin Street, Kilkenny, Ireland. Grave or Memorial Reference; I A 30. Cemetery: Dive Copse British Cemetery, Sailly-Le-Sec in France.

Dullard, Nicholas Michael. Rank; Private. Regiment or Service: Leinster Regiment. Unit; 1st Battalion. Service Number; 6108. Date of death; 24/04/1915. Age at death; 35. Born; Kilkenny. Enlisted; Kilkenny. Died of wounds. Son of Nicholas and Bridget Dullard; husband of Mary Dullard (nee Byrne), of 2, Callan Rd., Kilkenny. In his Will, dated 07-April-1915, his effects and property were received by;- Mrs Maria Dullard, Callan Road, Kilkenny. Kilkenny Journal, May, 1915. Kilkenny Soldier's Killed in Action. News has been received that Private Nicholas Dullard, Walkin Street., was killed in action recently. Private Dullard, who belonged to the 2nd Battalion, Dublin Fusiliers., took part in the battle of Mons, and on recovering was again sent to the firing line. Private M. Keating and P. Holden, of this city, have also been killed in action. (There is no P. Holden in any of the War Dead Databases listed as having died in 1915, Author). Kilkenny People, May, 1915. Death of a Kilkenny Soldier. How he Met his Death."Never Flinched fro his Duty."Interesting Letter to his Wife. Notification has been received in the City by his wife of the death in action of Private Nicholas Dullard of the Leinster Regiment. The deceased was fatally wounded on the 23rd pf last month, and the brave manner in which he met his death is graphically described in the letter of condolence which his wife has received from the Sergeant of his platoon, Sergeant J. Matthews, a Callan man. The deceased had served for over seven years in South Africa, was all through the Boer War and had been engaged in all the principal engagements. His death is much regretted in the City as the deceased was a most popular young man. He leaves a young widow and child to mourn his loss. The following letter has been received by his wife;--"In the Trenches."24-4-1915. Dear Mrs Dullard—I deeply regret to have to inform you of the death of your husband—No 6108, Pte N. Dullard, of my platoon, who was killed in action about 4 a. m. on the morning of the 23rd. We were holding a trench and your husband was on watch duty. The enemy who were only about 60 yards away from us opened a rapid fire. Upon your husband's vigilance depended the lives of many and though bullets were falling fast he never flinched from the duty entrusted to him. It was in the performance of his duty that he was wounded through his right breast, the bullet passing through his right lung. His comrades and

I dressed the wound and carried him to the temporary hospital behind the firing line where he was attended to by the doctor. He lived throughout the day but died in the evening from the effects of the wound received. Dear Mrs Dullard, I am a Callan man and your husband and I were the warmest friends for many years when we soldiered together in different foreign lands. His death has grieved me very much and is much regretted by the officer, N. C. O. 's and men of his platoon. Before he left me his last words were "Oh, my dear wife and child" and he entrusted to me a photograph of yourself and baby and asked me to write if anything should happen. This photo I am forwarding at the earliest opportunity. Dear Mrs Dullard, the news of his death will be a great shock to you, but well may you and his countrymen be proud of him. He gave up his life in a fearless manner; he has died like many more brave Irishmen keeping up the traditions of the county that gave him birth and doing his duty to his God and country. He is laid to rest in a little graveyard some distance from the firing line and a cross has been erected to his memory with a simple inscription,"Killed in action." On behalf of the N. C. O. 's and men of his platoon, I tender to you in this great hour of sorrow our deep sympathy in the loss you have sustained. May God in heaven rest his soul—Believe me, yours respectfully. (Sergeant) J. Matthews. Notes; Name listed as Nicholas (SDGW, IMR) Michael (CWGC). Grave or Memorial Reference; Panel 44. Cemetery: Ypres (Menin Gate) Memorial in Belgium.

Dunne, Edward. Rank; Sergeant. Regiment or Service: Royal Irish Fusiliers. Unit; 8th Battalion. Service Number; 17706. Date of death; 27/04/1916. Born; Kilkenny. Enlisted; Kilkenny. Residence; Ballyraggett, County Kilkenny. Killed in action. Grave or Memorial Reference; Panel 124. Cemetery: Loos Memorial in France.

Dunne, James. Rank; Private. Regiment or Service: Irish Guards. Unit; 2nd Battalion. Service Number; 6353. Date of death; 27/09/1918. Age at death; 21. Born; Skehana, County Kilkenny. Enlisted; Waterford. Killed in action. Son of Patrick and Esther Dunne, of Inch, Burtown, Athy, Co. Kildare. In his Will, 13-July-1915, his effects and property were received by;- Esther Dunne, Moat Sign Field, Athy, County Kildare. The Nationalist and Leinster Times. October, 1915. Dunne-Private John (sic) Dunne, 2nd Battalion, Irish Guards, killed in action in France, 27th September, aged 21, youngest son of Patrick Dunne, Inch, Forest, Athy. Inserted by his father, mother, brothers and sisters. He is gone but not forgotten. May he rest in peace. Grave or Memorial Reference; Panels 9 and 10. Cemetery: Loos Memorial in France.

Dunne, John. Rank; Private. Regiment or Service: Royal Irish Regiment. Unit; 2nd Battalion. Service Number; 9651. Date of death; 14/07/1916. Born; Graiguenamanagh, County Kilkenny. Enlisted; Carlow. Residence; Graiguenamanagh, County ilkenny. Killed in action. Grave or Memorial Reference; Pier and Face 3 A. Cemetery: Thiepval Memorial in France.

Dunne, John. Rank; Private. Regiment or Service: South Lancashire Regiment. Unit; D Company, 2nd Battalion. Service Number; 7258. Date of death; 04/03/1917. Age at death; 43. Born; Kilkenny. Enlisted; Kilkenny. Died. Son of Luke and Mary Dunne, of Patrick Street, Kilkenny. Grave or Memorial Reference; III A 9. Cemetery: Niederzwehren Cemetery in Germany.

Dunne, Martin. Rank; Gunner. Regiment or Service: Royal Garrison Artillery. Unit; 23rd Heavy Battery. Service Number; 6940. Date of death; 24/08/1916. Age at death; 34. Born; Dungarvan, County Waterford. Enlisted; Seaforth. Residence; Piltown, County Kilkenny. Killed in action. Son of Thomas and Bridget Dunne, of Grange, Mooncoin, Waterford. Native of Dungarven, Co. Waterford. Grave or Memorial Reference; II A 12. Cemetery: Contalmaison Chateau Cemetery in France.

Dunne, Richard. Rank; Private. Regiment or Service: Royal Irish Regiment. Unit; 2nd Battalion. Service Number; 6640. Date of death; 24/05/1915. Born; St Patrick's, Kilkenny. Enlisted; Kilkenny. Killed in action. Brother of Thomas Dunne below. Grave or Memorial Reference; Panel 33. Cemetery: Ypres (Menin Gate) Memorial in Belgium.

Dunne, Thomas. Rank; Private. Regiment or Service: Royal Dublin Fusiliers. Unit; 1st Battalion. Service Number; 9886. Date of death; 30/06/1915. Age at death; 25. Born; Kilkenny. Enlisted; Carlow. Residence; Kilkenny. Killed in Action in Gallipoli. Son of John and Margaret Dunne, of 40, Waterford Road, Kilkenny. Kilkenny Journal, July, 1915. Kilkenny Soldier Killed in Action. Mrs Margaret Dunne, Waterford Road, has received intimation from the authorities of the death of her son, Private Thomas Dunne, Dublin Fusiliers, who was killed in action at the Dardanelles. Up to about three months ago Private Dunne was serving in India, where he had been for five years. His brother, Richard, a private in the Royal Irish Regimen, was killed in action in May last. Grave or Memorial Reference; Panel 190 to 196. Cemetery: Helles Memorial in Turkey.

Dunne, William. Rank; Private. Regiment or Service: Royal Irish Regiment. Unit; 2nd Battalion. Service Number; 3153. Date of death; 14/11/1918. Died in King Georges Hospital, Stanford Street. In his Last Will and Testament his effects and property were received by;- (Father) Jeremiah Dunne, New Buildings Lane, Kilkenny. Notes; Battalion listed as 2nd Battalion (Will) and Depot (CWGC). Grave or Memorial Reference; XII C 20. Cemetery: Brookwood Military Cemetery, UK.

Dunphy, Victor Louis. Rank; Private. Regiment or Service: Canadian Infantry. Unit; 43rd battalion. Service Number; 153679. Date of death; 21/09/1916. Age at death; 33. Born; Mount Sion, Kilkenny. Enlisted; Winnipeg, Manitoba. Son of Edward Dunphy, Mount Sion, Kilkenny. Irish Independent; Dunphy—September 21, 1916, killed in action, Victor Louis, Canadian Cameron Highlanders, son of Edward and Mrs Dunphy, Mount Sion, Kilkenny, aged 33. Cemetery: Vimy Memorial, France.

Dunphy/Dumphy, James. Rank; Private. Regiment or Service: Connaught Rangers. Unit; 1st Battalion. Service Number; 10427. Date of death; 26/04/1915. Age at death; 21. Born; Kilkenny. Enlisted; Waterford. Residence; Kilkenny. Killed in action. DUNPHY (CGWC, IMR) DUMPHY (SDGW), JAMES. Son of Mrs. Hannah Dunphy, of Dunkitt, Kilmacon, Co. Kilkenny. Grave or Memorial Reference; Panel 42. Cemetery: Ypres (Menin Gate) Memorial in Belgium.

Dunphy, John. Rank; Lance Corporal. Regiment or Service: Royal Irish Rifles. Unit; C Company, 2nd Battalion. Service Number; 10051. Date of death; 21/09/1914. Age at death;21. Born; Castlecomer, County Kilkenny. Enlisted; Carlow. Killed in action. Son of Eliza Dunphy, of Kilkenny St., Castlecomer, Co. Kilkenny, and the late Robert Dunphy. After his death, his effects and property were received by;- (Mother) Mrs Dunphy, Kilkenny St, Castlecome, County Kilkenny. If deceased than (Brother) Patrick Dunphy of same address. Cemetery: La Ferte-Sous-Jouarre Memorial in France.

E

Eagleton / Egleton, Thomas. Rank; Lance Corporal. Regiment or Service: Irish Guards. Unit; 2nd Battalion. Service Number; 6379. Date of death; 17/12/1917. Age at death; 32. Born; Birr, King's County. Enlisted; Birr. Died of wounds. Won the Military Medal and is listed in the London Gazette. De Ruvigny's Roll of Honour. Son of Michael Eagleton, Newbridge Street, Birr, Kings County by his wife Bridget, daughter of Thomas McGuinness of County Kilkenny. Born 26th April 1894. Educated Presentation Brothers School, Birr, was a shop assistant, enlisted 2nd Jan, 1915. Served with the Expeditionary Force in France and Flanders from 1st May following and was killed in action on the Somme 5th December, 1917. Buried 5 and a half miles North East of Combles. His Captain wrote; " He was deeply regretted by the NCOs and men of No 1 Coy". He was awarded the Military Medal in November 1917, for bravery in discharge of duty. King's County Chronicle, 1916, Pte Thomas Eagleton, Irish Guards, was gassed in France, and is now in England. His father, Mr Michael Eagleton resides at Newbridge Street, Birr. King's County Chronicle, March, 1916. Thomas, son of Mr Michael Eagleton, an employee of the Urban Council, has also seen active service with the Irish Guards. He was 'gassed' in France, but happiny a strong constitution enabled him to shake off the effects of the Huns 'fiendish' invention. He is now at the Depot. King's County Chronicle, December, 1917. Sincere sympathy is felt with the bereaved parents, Mr and Mrs Michael Eagleton, Newbridge Street, Birr, who last week received the sad news that their son (whose photo we reproduce above) had died of wounds received in action. Although not more than a boy in years, he was physically a splendid type of soldier, and his death is much regretted. He joined the army about three years ago, and had been previously gassed, but recovered, and was again sent to France, where he met his death. King's County Chronicle, December, 1915. In Memory of Lance Corporal Tom Eagleton. Irish Guards. Died of wounds in France, Dec. 5th, 1917. At home in Ireland is grief, deep grief;The mother's wailing is keen and loud, And the hard-won stripe brings scant relief, If its threads are sewn in a crimson shroud. O! Lord, look down on the old green land, Where homes are telling this tale of woe; A loved one dead, on a foreign strand, His blood small price for the ruby's glow. O! Tom, alanna, with heart of mirth, And quizzical face full of Irish fun;Your clay now gathered to stranger earth, And neighbours weep for the neighbour's son. Full brave, my boy, have you played your part;A host of valour is Ireland's fame—Your soul of humour cheered ev'ry heart, And comrades brighten'd to hear your name. No more the hearth-fire's flame shall light, To laughter sweet at your song and jokes, And with mother's eyes grow glad and bright With love and pride at each note you woke But swiftly passes the evening dream, The mem'ry sweet of those mirthful hours;Yet to fond hearts they will ever seem, Scant-laden with love's choicest flowers. But, oh, the carnage and the strife That took you from our midst, mó croidhe;The God who gave your spirit life, May hold you in love's mystery. Maire Ní Bruin,10, Newbridge St, Birr. Notes; Date of death 05-December-1917 (CWGC, SDGW) 17-December-1917 (IMR). Grave or Memorial Reference; V D 17. Cemetery: Rocquigny-Equancourt Road British Cemetery, Equancourt in France.

Egan, Michael. Rank; Private. Regiment or Service: Irish Guards. Unit; 1st Battalion. Service Number; 4255. Date of death; 01/11/1914. Age at death;22. Born; Ballyraggett, County Kilkenny. Enlisted; South Shields, Durham. Residence; South Kensington, Middlesex. Killed in action. Brother of, Mrs. I. Garrett, of 2, Torquay Villas, St. Osyth Rd., Clacton-on-Sea, Essex. In his Will, 06-July-1914, his effects and property were received by;- (Sister) Johanna Egan, 21 Rosary Gardens, South Kensington, England. Executor;- Joanna Egan. Grave or Memorial Reference; Panel 11. Cemetery: Ypres (Menin Gate) Memorial in Belgium.

ROLL OF HONOUR.

MEMORIAL SERVICE.

Waterford Cathedral,

THURSDAY, 25th JANUARY, 1917.

The following are the Names of men connected with the City and District who have given their lives for King and Country :—

Private PERCY A. ALEXANDER.
Private RUPERT BELL.
Lieut. TREVOR BENSON.
Private WILLIAM BRIEN.
Sergeant WILLIAM BOBBIN,
Sergeant WILLIAM BURNS.
Gunner S. COUCH.
Lieut. MAURICE C. DAY.
Lieut. ROBERT NEWPORT DOBBYN.
Lieut. WILLIAM AUGUSTUS NELSON DOBBYN.
Capt. GERALD EWAN ELLIOTT.
Lieut. CHARLES FARRAN.
Lance-Corporal NOEL FERNIE, D.C.M.
Capt. JOHN KIRWAN GATACRE.
Major HAROLD B. GALLOWAY.
Private WILLIAM GAMBLE.
Private THOMAS HUGHES.
Chief Petty Officer G. L. LINDSAY, R.N.
Lieut. ERIC A. THISELTON LINE.
Lieut. HUBERT MALCOMSON.
Corporal LLEWELLYN, MALCOMSON.
Commander JOHN S. PENROSE, R.N.
Seaman A. RANDALL, R.N.
Captain FRANK R. ROBERTSON.
Doctor GEORGE WATERS, R.N.

" Blessed are the dead which die in the Lord."

Captain Elliott, courtesy of Eddie O'Sullivan, Waterford.

Elliott, Gerald Ewen/Even. Rank; Captain. Regiment or Service: Gloucestershire Regiment. Unit; B Company, 1st/6th Battalion. Date of death; 21/06/1916. Killed in action. Son of the late J. C. and M. E. M. Elliott. Munster Express. Waterford Officer killed in action. Captain Gerald Ewen Elliott, Gloucester Regiment, was killed in action July 21st leading his company. He was aged 26, seventh son of the late J. C. Elliott, J. P., Rathcurby, County Kilkenny, and Mrs Elliott, Hollywood Gardens, Waterford. The following facts relating to the death of Captain Gerlad Ewen Elliott have been received by the Elliott family in a letter from the doctor of his battalion;- "He died like a gallant gentleman at the head of his company. He wore his best clothes and started his charge with bright buttons and clean gloves. From the accounts of his brother officers and men he was right ahead when he was first shot through the thigh and stomach. His servant tried to get him back, but he would sit up to cheer his men on, and he received another shot through the head. His battalion has lost a very fine officer and I have lost a very dear friend. I wish I could have been present at his funeral, but I was far too busy looking after his wounded men." Previous to the war he served eight years in the Territorials and volunteered for foreign service at the outbreak of the war. Irish Independent, July/August-1916; Captain G E Elliott, Gloucesters, killed in action, was the youngest son of the late Mr J C Elliott, J. P., Rathcurby, County Kilkenny, and Mrs Elliott, Hollywood Gardens, Waterford. He had been at the front for 18 months. A Captain in the RAMC writes that "Captain Elliott died like a gallant gentleman at the head of his company.". Irish Independent;Captain G E Elliott, Gloucesters, killed in action, was the youngest son of the late Mr J C Elliott, J. P., Rathcurby, County Kilkenny, and Mrs Elliott, Hollywood Gardens, Waterford. He had been at the front for 18 months. A Captain in the RAMC writes that "Captain Elliott died like a gallant gentleman at the head of his company.". Grave or Memorial Reference; Pier and Face 5 A and 5 B. Cemetery: Thiepval memorial in France

England, Thomas Ernest. Rank; Rifleman. Regiment or Service: Royal Irish Rifles. Unit; 22nd Entrenching Battalion. Service Number; 130. Date of death; 27/03/1918. Age at death;22. Born; Portadown, County Armagh. Enlisted; Belfast. Residence; Mount Verdant, County Kilkenny. Died of wounds. Son of William John and Elizabeth England, of Mount Verdant, Kilkenny. In his Will, dated 26-September-1916, his effects and property were received by;- (Mother) Mrs W J England, Mt Verdant, Kilkenny. Kilkenny People, April, 1918. Died of Wounds. Rifleman Thomas E. England, Royal Irish Rifles, who died from wounds received in France on the 27th March, was the third son of Mr and Mrs England, Mount Verdant, Kilkenny. Mr England is the respected secretary of Messrs. E. Smithwick and Son, St. Francis Abbey Brewery. Mr T. E. England served continuously with the Ulster Division, having been in France since October, 1915. The Irish Times, March 26, 1921. Roll of Honour. In Memoriam. England-In proud and loving memory of Thomas Ernest (Tom), Royal Irish Rifles (Ulster Division), beloved third son of William John and Mrs England, Kilkenny, who died 27th march, 1918, from wounds received in action at Berbancourt. We thank God for every remembrance of him. Inserted by his parents, brothers, and sisters. The Irish Times. England-In proud and loving memory of my dear brother, Tom, who died on March 27th, 1918, from wounds received in action. Remember what he was with thankful heart. The bright, the loved, the tender, and the true. Remember where he is-from sin apart. Present with God, yet not estranged from you. Madge. Irish Times. England-March 27, died from wounds received in action, Thomas Ernest England, Royal Irish Rifles, son of William John and Mrs England, Kilkenny. Grave or Memorial Reference; Panel 74 to 76. Cemetery: Pozieres Memorial in France.

F

Fannon, Patrick. Rank; Gunner. Regiment or Service: Royal Garrison Artillery. Unit; 108th Heavy Battery. Service Number; 19814. Date of death; 25/03/1918. Age at death; 34. Born; Urlingford. Enlisted; Templemore. Residence; Urlingford, County Kilkenny. Killed in action. Son of James Fannon, of Graigue, Urlingford, Co. Kilkenny. Grave or Memorial Reference; Panel 10. Cemetery: Pozieres Memorial in France.

Farrell, Edward. Rank; Private. Regiment or Service: Connaught Rangers. Unit; 2nd Battalion. Service Number; 6915. Date of death; 20/12/1914. Born; Kilkenny. Enlisted; Kilkenny. Residence; Kilkenny. Killed in action. Grave or Memorial Reference; Panel 43. Cemetery: Le Touret Memorial in France.

Farrell, Larry Michael. Rank; Private. Regiment or Service: 1st Canadian Mounted Rifles Battalion. Service Number; 425546. Date of death; 15/09/1916. Age at death; 19. Born; Curraghmore, Kilkenny. Enlisted; Brandon. Son of Robert and Johana Farrell, of Virden, Manitoba. Cemetery: Vimy Memorial, France

Farrell, Patrick. Rank; Gunner. Regiment or Service: Royal Horse Artillery and Royal Field Artillery. Unit; 2nd Reserve Battery. Service Number; 88660. Date of death; 05/08/1918. Age at death;51. Born; Kilkenny. Died after discharge. Cemetery: unknown

Faussett, Robert Clifford. Rank; Lieutenant. Regiment or Service: Royal Field Artillery. Date of death; 16/11/1916. Age at death; 25. Born; Mitchelstown, County Cork. Died of wounds. Son of William B Fausset (R. I. C.), Clancoole Road, Ballymodan, Cork, who is buried in the same cemetery. Grave or Memorial Reference; E. 6. 173883. Cemetery: Brompton Cemetery, London.

Feeney, Mildred Eleanor. Rank; Nurse. Regiment or Service: Voluntary Aid Detachment. Date of death; 08/11/1918. Born; Kilkenny in 1890. Lived at Patrick Street, Kilkenny with her family, Father-Peter John Carr Feeney n(Bank Manager), Mother-Edith Eleanor Feeney. Died at the Naval Hospital, Chatham. Cemetery: Unknown.

Fenton, Frederick. Rank; Driver. Regiment or Service: Royal Horse Artillery and Royal Field Artillery. Unit; Trench Mortar Battery, 119th Brigade. Service Number; W/1898. Date of death; 12/03/1917. Age at death; 33. Born; Kilkenny. Enlisted; Cardiff, Glamorganshire. Died. Husband of Eveline Lavinia Fenton, of 2, Penedre, Llandaff, Cardiff. Grave or Memorial Reference; II B 10. Cemetery: Mendinghem Military Cemetery in Belgium.

Lance Corporal Fernie, courtesy of Eddie Sullivan, Waterford.

Fernie, Noel/Robert Noel. Rank; Lance Corporal. Regiment or Service: Royal Irish Regiment. Unit; C Company, 2nd Battalion. Service Number; 10518. Date of death; 19/10/1914. Age at death;17. Born; Kilmacow, County Kilkenny. Enlisted; Waterford. Residence; Tramore. Killed in action. Son of John Fernie, of Rosemount, Tramore, Co. Waterford. In his Will, 06-August-1914, his effects and property were received by;- (Mother) Mrs E B Fernie, Rosemount, Tramore, Co Waterford, Ireland. Waterford News. 1914. Waterford man mentioned in Despatches. On Monday last there was published a long list of names of officers, non-commissioned officers, and men brought forward for special mention for services in the field from the beginning of the campaign to October 8th. The list included the name of Private N. Fernie, of the 2nd Royal Irish Regiment, son of Mrs Fernie, fruiterar, High Street. Waterford News. 1914. Medals for Waterford soldiers. Amongst the names of the soldiers to whom the medal for distinguished conduct in the field has been awarded we notice the name of Private N Fernie (now Lance Corporal), of the 2nd Battalion Royal Irish Regiment. Mr Fernie is son of Mrs Fernie, High Street, and was recently mentioned in despatches. He receives the medal for having at Vailly repeatedly shown great coolness and gallantry when conveying messages under heavy fire. We understand that Private J. Doherty, Royal Irish Regiment, another of the soldiers to whom the medal has been awarded, is also a Waterford man. Notes; Private (SDGW), Lance Corporal (CWGC). Grave or Memorial Reference; 11 and 12. Cemetery: Le Touret Memorial in France. He is also listed on the Waterford and District Roll of Honour. Located in Christ Church Cathedral (Church of Ireland), Henrietta Street, Waterford.

Bernard Osborne Ffield.

Sub-Lieutenant Ffield, from De Ruvigny's Roll of Honour.

Ffield, Bernard Osborne. Rank; Flight Sub-Lieutenant. Regiment or Service: Royal Naval Air Service. Date of death; 24/12/1914. Age at death; 20. Son of John Bernard and Beatrice Ffield, of Crooked Walls, Harvington, Evesham, Worcs. From De Ruvigny's Roll of Honour. Ffield, Bernard Osborne, Flight Sub-Lieut., R. N. Eldest son of Bernard Ffield of the Old Bank House, Coleshill, Warwickshire, Manufacturer, by his wife, Beatrice, elder daughter of the late William Hays, of Nevern Square, S. W., and Kileraggan, County Kilkenny. Born in London, 17-August-1894. Educated at Wimbleton College. Gazetted Sub-Lieutenant, R. N. A. S., 09-September-1914 and received his brevet from the Royal Aero Club on 10 December following. On 21-December-1914 he was coming down form a height of about 2, 000 feet after a good flight at the Royal Naval Air Station, when, at about 200 ft from the ground, the machine was seen to take a sudden vertical dive to earth, and was so smashed that it was impossible to ascertain what had gone wrong. He died the same evening, Christmas Eve, after receiving the Last Rites of the Church. A senior brother officer wrote of him; "He was quite the best of all the others who had gained their certificates some three weeks before him. I watched most of his flights as I had to look after the flying. He was one of the neatest men I have seen; he was so beautifully gentle with his hands and that is one of the secrets of a good pilot.". Grave or Memorial Reference; C 9 20387. Cemetery: Hendon Cemetery and Crematorium, Middlesex, UK.

Finn, William. Rank; Private. Regiment or Service: Royal Munster Fusiliers. Unit; 1st Battalion. Service Number; 5213. Date of death; 28/01/1917. Born; Thomastown, County Kilkenny. Enlisted; Ballyvonare, County Cork. Residence; Kilmallock. Killed in action. Son of Mr. J. Finn, of Thomastown, Kilmallock, Co. Limerick. Grave or Memorial Reference; I 11. Cemetery: Pond Farm Cemetery in Belgium,

Finnegan / Finnigan, Patrick Phair. Rank; Lance Sergeant. Regiment or Service: Royal Inniskilling Fusiliers. Unit; 7th Battalion. Service Number; 16522. Date of death; 28/04/1916. Born; Woodlawn, County Galway. Enlisted; Enniskillen. Died of wounds. Waterford News;-Kilkenny Soldier's Fate. The sad news has reached Kilkenny of the death of Sergeant P. P. Finnegan, Inniskilling Fusiliers, as a result of gas poisoning. Sergeant Finnegan, whow as a native of Kilkenny, was some years ago attached to the reporting staff of the "Kilkenny Journal," and at the time he volunteered for active service he was pursuing his career in journalism in Omagh, where he took an active part in the formation of the local branch of the National Volunteers. Grave or Memorial Reference; I E 27. Cemetery: Philosophe British Cemetery, Mazingarbe in France.

Fitzgibbon, Gerald John. Rank; Captain. Regiment or Service: Royal Dublin Fusiliers. Unit; 10th Battalion. Date of death; 20/11/1917. Age at death;23. Born; Kilkenny. Killed in action. Son of Bridget, brother of Mary Bridget, Onah C, Elizabeth M, Daniel, Maria P (a male), Peter, Francis C, and Maurice P Fitzgibbon. Listed in the 1911 Census in Cappawhite, Tipperary. Limerick Chronicle, December, 1917. Roll of Honour. Captain Gerald FitzgibbonWe regret to record the death of Captain Gerald J Fitzgibbon, Royal Dublin Fusiliers, who was killed in action at the battle of Cambrai on the 20th ult. This gallant officer who was only 24 years of age, was nephew of Mr M J Fitzgibbon, Oak Ville, New Street, and so late as the end of October was home on a brief visit to his relatives and friends/ he was held in affectionate regard by his comrades, who describe him as a "fine brave man, and a daring soldier." The sympathy of very many friends in Limerick will be extended to his bereaved relatives. The Weekly Irish Times. Ireland's Roll of Honour. December 15, 1917. His relatives in Limerick have received intelligence of the death of Captain Gerald J Fitzgibbon, Royal Dublin Fusiliers. He was killed in action on the 20th November last. Captain Fitzgibbon was in his twenty fourth year. He was a nephew of Mr M J Fitzgibbon, Oakville, New Street, Limerick, and was home on a brief visit to his relatives last October. In a letter from his regiment, Captain Fitzgibbon is described as "a fine, brave man, and a daring soldier.". Grave or Memorial Reference; G 4. Cemetery: St Leger British Cemetery in France

Lieutenant Fitzgibbon from 'Our Heroes.'

Fitzgibbon, Michael Joseph. Rank; Lieutenant. Regiment or Service: Royal Dublin Fusiliers. Unit; 7th Battalion. Date of death; 15/08/1915. Killed in action at Suvla Bay. Rank listed as Lieutenant (CWGC) Temporary Lieutenant (IMR+ODGW+MIC).

To give you a description of the landing that was forced at Suvla Bay on August 6th. The 10th Irish Division, under Gen. Mahon were instrumental in its forcing. At dawn on the morning of the 6th several transports pulled into Suvla Bay. This bay is very shallow, and ships cannot approach the beach nearer than a few miles, so troops had to be transferred to lighters. There were nearly 1,000 men on each lighter. As they approached the shore at several points they were under a terrible shrapnel and machine gun fire. Several shells burst over some of the boats, wounding and killing a great many. Of course you know there is a considerable strain on troops when they are subject to shell fire for the first time, and especially when they are cramped up together like sardines in a tin on the decks.

It is a kind of relief to make a rush for the beach, even though you are drenched with water (for the boats could not come right in) and the shells are bursting in hundreds overhead. There is a high slope at Lala Baba. Lala Baba is a steep hill entirely on its own in the very centre of Suvla. At the back of it extends the Salt Lake, which is of a kind of marshy nature, partially dried up in the dry seasons. Though it is supposed to be impassable I have seen ambulance wagons cross it. Lala Baba from the shore protected the troops very much from shrapnel fire. Here the whole brigade kept up a withering rifle and machine gun fire for several hours in order to facilitate the troops to land at Suvla Bay Point, which is a promontory running out into the sea. I will give you a half idea of the position in a rough sketch.

The objective was Chocolate Hill. We could not advance on our front owing to the salt lake, so we had to make a semicircular advance on the Chocolate Hill fort, in which we suffered terribly. We advanced all day under cover of the very effective fire of the navy and the small twelve pounder guns that followed up our advance. I will not trouble you to listen to the horrible sights and experiences I witnessed during that terrible advance, for it would fill dozens of columns. But at 6. 30 p. m., or rather in the French way (as the whole of the British army now in the Dardanelles recognise officially the French term) —at 18. 30 o'clock, we got the order to "prepare to charge." Then there was glistening of bayonets as they were pulled from their scabbards, and the supports arrived and filled up the gaps of the killed and dying.

Then the order came. It came with a great roar from the right, which mounted above the roar of the artillery, to be sent back with a ring of encouragement from the Australians on the hills of Anzec. Then the withering hail of bullets that descended from the fort above did not stop us, although it made gaping holes in the line. The church of the Irish Division was made at 19 o'clock, and the fort on Chocolate Hill had fallen, and we captured large quantities of shells which they could not remove in their hasty retreat. We held Chocolate Hill and remained there for nine days. We were then relieved so as to get a rest on the beach—I mean a sleep. But when we arrived at Suvla beach we were ordered immediately to support another Division which the Turks were by overwhelming forces trying to break through.

You can see on this rough sketch Suvla Point and the range of hills that run parallel with the shore on the extreme left, well up at the very end, the four arrows indicate the trench line. Well, that is the exact spot where one of the bloodiest battled on that side of the peninsula was fought. We seemed to have the advantage of the ground, for we were op over the Turks and they were situated right underneath us, about ten yards away from our trenches, where they were protected by great overhanging cliffs. Then the Turks were armed with hand grenades, which they were able to use with deadly effect on us. We, on the other hand, had no grenades, and had no way to get them properly except through a flanking movement, and that could only be done by getting around at the back of their lines.

It was a desperate attempt, and we had to crawl along the beach in the dark, and at dawn we got the order to charge the Hill I shall not go into details about the charge. But this I must say, I saw brave officers fall since we landed in the Dardanelles-men who stand up to give the order to their men and fell without a murmur. But this I can say, one of the bravest I have seen fall was Captain Fitzgibbon, of D Company of the 7th Royal Dublin Fusiliers. He died at the head of that charge with a blackthorn stick in his hand, and as he lay dying with a bullet in his breast, his last words were; "Go on boys! Go on."—I remain, yours faithfully,J. J. Tivnan.

Midland Reporter and Westmeath Nationalist, September, 1915. Castlerea News (County Roscommon). The Late Captain Michael J Fitzgibbon. When the news was made known at Castlerea that Captain Michael J Fitzgibbon had fallen at the Dardanelles on the 15th of August, it caused profound sorrow—a sorrow that was not confined to his own immediate family—but also extended to many in Castlerea, who shared his friendship, as well as to the townspeople in general, for in his short life he made a marked impression on those with whom he came in contact. The quiet humour of his voice, his kindly sympathies, his rare modesty, his courteousness to everyone he came across, these, his less known characteristics, will remain in the memories of his friends. To-day his body sleeps in far-off Gallipoli, and one's heart is heavy for him, who has fallen on the battlefield.

Although we know that for him the strife is over, he is gone to his long peaceful rest, but still his memory will be cherished long by the host of friends he has left behind him, and who now pray that God may give the gallant young soldier a place of light and peace, and may comfort his sorrow stricken parents, brothers, sisters, and other relatives in their hour of sorrow. Midland Reporter and Westmeath Nationalist, August, 1915. Captain Fitzgibbon Killed at Dardanelles. Mr John Fitzgibbon, M. P., Castlerea, has been informed that his son, Captain M Fitzgibbon, 7th Dublin Fusiliers, was killed in action at the Gallipoli Peninsula on the 15th August. Captain Fitzgibbon was 29 years of age the day he was killed, and prior to his receiving his commission as Lieutenant in the Fusiliers on volunteering, was a law student. He left recently with his division, and before his departure was gazetted captain. He was only a week at the Dardanelles when he was killed.

Irish Independent; Roll of Honour. Fitzgibbon—Killed in action at the Dardanelles 15th August, Captain Mico Fitzgibbon, 7th Battalion Dublin Fusiliers, aged 29 years, son of John Fitzgibbon, M. P., Castlerea. Solemn requiem Mass in Castlerea Church on tomorrow (Wednesday) September 1st, at 10. 30. a. m.   08/09/1915.

Freeman's Journal. The Ballinrobe District Council have adopted a resolution of sympathy with Mr John Fitzgibbon, M. P., on the death of his son, Captain M Fitzgibbon, who was killed in action. The chaplain attached to the Division has written Mr Fitzgibbon, M. P., stating that on the morning of the 15th August, Captain Fitzgibbon received Holy Communion, and rendered splendid services in the collection and arrangement of the troops for the recap[tion of the Blessed Sacrament. This intimation has brought the greatest consolation to Mr and Mrs Fitzgibbon and family.

King's County Independent, September, 1915. The Roll of Honour. Two Castlerea Officers. The Late Capt. Fitzgibbon. Tribute to his Bravery. Lance-Corporal's Touching Letter. The following letter has been received by Mr John Fitzgibbon, M. P., from Lance-Corporal P. J. Madden, 5th Royal Irish Fusiliers. No. 17527, Queen's F. I. Ward, 5th Royal Irish Fusiliers, Graylingwell, War Hospital, Chichester, Sussex, September 1st, 1915.

Dear Mr. Fitzgibbon, --You may feel surprised to get a letter from the above address, but I wish to send my sincere sympathy to yourself, Mrs Fitzgibbon and you family on the death of your son, and I assure the loss of such a gallant Captain will not alone be felt among the Dublin Fusiliers, but in the whole 10th Irish Division. The shelling was so severe and the fighting so incessant, we lost most of our officers in the landing. Captain Fitzgibbon was one of the few left to head the Irish Troops, and he set a fine example of pluck and courage to his junior officers and men, and cheered us on to victory when we captured Chocolate Hill, and a line of trenches on the evening of August 6th at the point of the bayonet.

After that charge we were all exhausted, and as the fighting grew quieter the inclination to sleep was almost irresistible, yet owing to the nearness of the enemy it was dangerous, and every man was ordered to "stand to arms". All night long Captain Fitzgibbon kept sending messages to Headquarters and receiving replies. I heard after his idea was to keep passing messages down the lines, so that no man could sleep. He was successful. No man slept. On August 10th, the night I was wounded, the Connaught Rangers and Inniskillings relieved the Dublin and Irish Fusiliers who had slept four days in the firing line, and were allowed to base for a rest. Captain Fitzgibbon and Captain Lennon were all right then, and were not due back in the firing line till Sunday morning, so it must be in the now famous charge of the 16th August the gallant Captain fell.

It was a pity, but a still greater loss, as the losing of such men as Captain Fitzgibbon will not hasten the end of this dreadful war, which I am sure you can never forget. When the history of this war comes before the public that landing and taking of Suvla Bay will be mentioned, and a tribute of recognition will be paid to the two brave Captains from Castlerea, who took the lion's share of the work in pulling their men through. Captain Fitzgibbon did not fall into the hands of the Turks alive. He met with a hero's death, leading his men to victory, envied by most soldiers and regretted by all. Trusting you will accept my deepest sympathy. —I remain, yours very sincerely, P. J. Madden, Lance Corporal, J. Fitzgibbon, Esq., M. P. in the world.

It is Ireland's fight as well as the fight of the other Allies concerned. This noble, young man has truly given his life for Ireland and amongst those whose memories we revere as having died for Ireland's sake do we class the noble-hearted son of our beloved and revered Chairman, and I propose that we pass a resolution of sympathy with him in his great sorrow. Mr Tully—I beg to second that vote of sympathy. I am very often in sharp division with our Chairman, and to second the resolution might come better from me as one who was very often divided with him on various matters.

But, in the presence of death there is no division or dissention amongst us and we all join in offering our sympathy to our Chairman in the great affliction that had befallen him. In the case of parents nothing could be more afflicting than the loss of a son and especially one in the prime of manhood. Captain Fitzgibbon, a young gentleman of great ability and was bound to become famous, for, in the course of a few short months he was promoted to the rank of Captain, from that of a Lieutenant. I am certain if he was spared he would reach a very high position indeed. We feel very deeply for Mr and Mrs Fitzgibbon in their terrible affliction. Mr Shanly—I am very sorry, indeed, that the occasion has arisen for me to have tp associate myself with such a resolution. Mr Heverin, Secretary---I wish, as an official of the Council, to express my own sympathy and the sympathy of my brother officials with Mr and Mrs Fitzgibbon, and all the members of the family on the death of their brave son who, as the Chairman has nicely put it, gave up his life for his country.

Mr Mapother, in that beautiful language which few can imitate, says he has given up his life fighting against barbarous methods and barbarians. Captain Fitzgibbon and many others are helping not only the cause of Ireland, but also the cause of civilised humanity. I could not speak of Captain Michael Fitzgibbon in anything but the highest terms of praise, and in expressing my deep sorrow at his untimely death I echo the feelings of the other Co Council officials. Captain Fitzgibbon, at one time, followed the legal profession, and put aside the law to take up arms and fight in a good cause. He did his bit and we are sorry for Mr John Fitzgibbon and the members of his family.

Mr O'Keeffe (Accountant) —I join with Mr Heverin in offering my sympathy to our Chairman, who has always been held in the highest esteem by the officials. On the motion of the Chairman, seconded by Mr Tully, the resolution of sympathy was passed in silence with Mr Fitzgibbon, on the death of his son, Captain Michael Fitzgibbon. Castlerea Guardian. Sympathy. Mr P Conry presided at the weekly meeting of the Castlerea Board of Guardians on Saturday. The other members present were;-- Messrs. M. G. Sweeney and Mr M. H. Grogan. Mr P. A. Flanagan, Clerk was also in attendance. The minutes of last meeting having been read and signed, Mr M. H. Grogan said—Mr Chairman and gentlemen, we have all heard with regret of the death of our townsman, Captain Fitzgibbon.

Indeed, it is very sad that at the very first engagement of his active military life he met his death. I am sure had it been his fate to live through this horrible war, he was one who would reach a very high rank in military circles, for he possessed all the qualities that make a brave soldier. This meeting is very small. I know that every member of our Board was aware that this day's meeting would be adjourned in respect to the memory of the late Captain Fitzgibbon. Our colleagues absence from the meeting today is due to sharing with us in our sympathy with the Chairman and his family. I propose;--That we, the Castlerea Board of Guardians, have heard with deep regret of the death of Captain Michael Fitzgibbon, who was killed in action in the Dardanelles. That we tender to his father, Mr John Fitzgibbon, M. P. and the other members of his family, our sincere sympathy in their sad affliction, and as a mark of respect to the deceased soldier, we do adjourn the Board meeting without transacting any business. Copy of this resolution to be forwarded to Mr Fitzgibbon. Mr M. G. Sweeney—I second that resolution. It is with deep regret we learn of the early death of Captain Michael Fitzgibbon. He was a promising young gentleman studying for the law, and had he been spared there was a splendid career before him. It was with deep regret we all heard of his death. Chairman—We all sincerely regret his early death. He was a brave young man, who wished to serve his country by joining the army when he considered it his duty. Clerk—He joined at the very beginning of the war. He is also listed on the Tullamore Roll of Honour.

Our Heroes; Captain M J Fitzgibbon was the youngest son of Mr John Fitzgibbon, M. P., Castlerea, and previous to the outbreak of the war was a law student, but immediately volunteered and obtained his commission in the 7th Battalion, Royal Dublin Fusiliers in August, 1914, and sailed with his regiment for Gallipoli, where he fell in the action on August 15th last. Captain Fitzgibbon was a very popular young officer, and admired for his many sterling qualities.

Kilkenny People, August, 1915. Roll of Honour. Death of Captain Michael Fitzgibbon, R. D. F. Notification has been received from the War Office of the death in action at the Dardanelles on August 15 of Captain Michael Fitzgibbon. Of the 7th Royal Dublin Fusiliers. The gallant officer was third son of Mr John Fitzgibbon, M. P., and brother of Mrs R. Duggan, Kilkenny. Captain Fitzgibbon was 29 years of age the day he was killed, and at the outbreak of war was a law student. He applied for a Commission and was attached as Second Lieutenant to the Dublin Fusiliers. Some few months after he was propmoted to a Lieutenancy, and was gazetted Captain prior to his leaving for the Gallipoli Peninsula a few weeks ago. He was only about a week in the firing line when he was killed. The deceased, who was a very promising young officer, was educated at Clongowes Wood College and was apprenticed to the firm of Messrs Hoey and Denning, solicitors, Dublin.

He was well known and extremely popular amongst a large number of people in Kilkenny, and very sincere regret has been occasioned both here and in his native Castlerea, where he was universally esteemed for his many sterling qualities, by his early demise. Sacrificing a life of ease for the more strenuous and perilous life of the battlefield, it is sad to think that a life so full of promise should be snatched away at an age when the future held so much. The sympathy of all classes, with whom we desire to join, goes out in unstinted measure to his bereaved father, who has long been one of the pillars of the National cause in the West, and to his sister, the wife of one of our most respected citizens, Mr R. Duggan, J. P., Monster House, and to the other members of his bereaved family, in the great affliction that God has thought well to send them.

Kilkenny Journal, August, 1915. Killed in Action. Brave Irish Officer's Death. Captain Michael Fitzgibbon, who was killed in action at the Dardanelles on the 15th August, was third son of Mr John Fitzgibbon, M. P., and brother of Mrs Duggan, William Street Kilkenny. Captain Fitzgibbon, who was a fine type of an Irish soldier, was law student, and on the outbreak of war he volunteered his services. He received a commission and was attached to the Royal Dublin Fusiliers. After a period of four months he was promoted Lieutenant, and his distinguished conduct in the field of battle secured a further promotion, he having been gazetted Captain a short time before his death.

He was educated at Clongowes Wood College, and was apprenticed to Messrs. Hoey and Denny, solicitors, Dublin. Kilkenny Journal. September, 1915. The Late Captain Fitzgibbon. The Ballinrobe District Council have adopted a resolution of sympathy with Mt John Fitzgibbon, M. P., on the death of his son, Captain M. Fitzgibbon, who was killed in action. The chaplain attached to the Division has written Mr Fitzgibbon, M. P., stating that on the morning of the 15th August Captain Fitzgibbon received Holy Communion, and rendered splendid services in the collection and arrangement of the troops for the reception of the Blessed Sacrament. This intimation had brought the greatest consolation to Mr and Mrs Fitzgibbon and family.

Kilkenny Journal, September, 1915. Irish Officers. The Late Captain M. J. Fitzgibbon. At the meeting of the Castlerea Board of Guardians on Saturday, Mr P Conry, V. C., presiding. Mr M. H. Grogan, D. C., Co-C, said they had all heard with deep regret of the death of their townsman, Captain Michael Fitzgibbon, son of their esteemed Chairman, Mr John Fitzgibbon, M. P. It was very sad that in the first engagement of his active military life Captain Fitzgibbon met his death, Had it been his fate to live through this horrible war he would have reached a very high rank in military circles. He possessed all the qualities that make a brave soldier. He proposed a resolution tendering to the bereaved father and the other members of his family sincere sympathy in ther sad affliction. This was seconded by Mr M. G. Sweeney, J. P., and as a mark of respect to the deceased soldier the Board meeting was adjourned without transacting any business.

King's County Chronicle, September, 1915. The news of the death of Captain Fitzgibbon, son of Mr John Fitzgibbon, M. P., Castlerea, and brother-in-law to Mr Malachy Scally, T. C., Tullamore, was received in Tullamore with deep regret. Captain Fitzgibbon on the 15th August, which was his 29th Birthday. He joined the 'Pals' battalion of the Dublin Fusiliers last year after the outbreak of the war, and was promoted to the rank of Captain shortly before leaving for the Dardanelles a few weeks ago when he paid his last visit to Tullamore. Tullamore Urban Council passed a resolution of condolence with Mr John Fitzgibbon, M. P., and Mr Malachy Scally in their bereavement, and the latter has received numerous letters of sympathy.

King's County Independent, September, 1915. The Late Captain M Fitzgibbon. Public Sympathy. Roscommon County Council. At the meeting of the Finance Committee of the Roscommon County Council on Thursday, Mr T. A. P. Mapother, J. P., D. L., presiding, when the paying orders had been signed, the Chairman said; A duty devolves upon me which is really the saddest duty that ever devolved upon me as a member of this Council ever since the Council was established, and it is to ask you to join in a resolution of sympathy with our beloved and respected Chairman in the severe affliction that has befallen him.

No doubt, in the freshness of a grief like this mere words of comfort and sympathy can have very little soothing effect at present, but when time has exercised its healing influence I hope that in future it will be a source of some gratification to our dear friend to know that in his trouble he has the heartfelt sympathy of all members of this Council. He will also have for his comfort the knowledge of the fact that his son has given his life is as noble a cause as any in which any nation or people were ever engaged, I might say, with the whole history of the world. He has given his life in the cause of Justice and humanity against an aggressive ad tyrannical power that is endeavouring to resuscitate on the face of the earth barbarism and barbarian methods of ancient times, which in our day of civilisation we thought we would never see again. In that cause our friend's son has given his life.

He has given that life for Ireland as truly as any of these men whose memories are revered in the pages of Irish history (hear, hear), because the interest of Ireland in the war now raging is truly as great as that of any other Nation in the world. It is Ireland's fight as well as the fight of the other Allies concerned. This noble, young man has truly given his life for Ireland and amongst those whose memories we revere as having died for Ireland's sake do we class the noble-hearted son of our beloved and revered Chairman, and I propose that we pass a resolution of sympathy with him in his great sorrow. Mr Tully—I beg to second that vote of sympathy. I am very often in sharp division with our Chairman, and to second the resolution might come better from me as one who was very often divided with him on various matters. But, in the presence of death there is no division or dissention amongst us and we all join in offering our sympathy to our Chairman in the great affliction that had befallen him. In the case of parents nothing could be more afflicting than the loss of a son and especially one in the prime of manhood. Captain Fitzgibbon, a young gentleman of great ability and was bound to become famous, for, in the course of a few short months he was promoted to the rank of Captain, from that of a Lieutenant. I am certain if he was spared he would reach a very high position indeed. We feel very deeply for Mr and Mrs Fitzgibbon in their terrible affliction.

Mr Shanly—I am very sorry, indeed, that the occasion has arisen for me to have to associate myself with such a resolution. Mr Heverin, Secretary---I wish, as an official of the Council, to express my own sympathy and the sympathy of my brother officials with Mr and Mrs Fitzgibbon, and all the members of the family on the death of their brave son who, as the Chairman has nicely put it, gave up his life for his country. Mr Mapother, in that beautiful language which few can imitate, says he has given up his life fighting against barbarous methods and barbarians. Captain Fitzgibbon and many others are helping not only the cause of Ireland, but also the cause of civilised humanity. I could not speak of Captain Michael Fitzgibbon in anything but the highest terms of praise, and in expressing my deep sorrow at his untimely death I echo the feelings of the other Co Council officials.

Captain Fitzgibbon, at one time, followed the legal profession, and put aside the law to take up arms and fight in a good cause. He did his bit and we are sorry for Mr John Fitzgibbon and the members of his family. Mr O'Keeffe (Accountant) —I join with Mr Heverin in offering my sympathy to our Chairman, who has always been held in the highest esteem by the officials. On the motion of the Chairman, seconded by Mr Tully, the resolution of sympathy was passed in silence with Mr Fitzgibbon, on the death of his son, Captain Michael Fitzgibbon.

'People' newspaper; Mr John Fitzgibbon, M. P., has been informed that his son, Captain Michael J Fitzgibbon, 7th Dublin Fusiliers, has been killed in action in the Dardanelles. Captain Fitzgibbon was 29 years of age on the day that he was killed. Pri. 17/01/1916.

Freemans Journal. Days of Glory and Tragedy. Officer's. Thrilling Account. Stories of Piety and Valour. Mass on The Hillside. The Battle-Eve Rosary. The following letter has been received by Mr Matthew Keating, M. P., from an officer in the 10th (Irish) Division. It gives the first connected account of the part played by the Division in the operations at Suvla Bay, and forms a most moving record of what will always be regarded as one of the most thrilling episodes in the military annals of the Irish race. It contains "the live human details of the fighting," which Sir Ian Hamilton said in his recent despatch he was unable to ascertain, and gives some vivid glimpses of the glory and tragedy of the work of the Irish troops. —December, 1915. Dear Mr Keating-What time Liverpudlian and Cunarder were lecturing the Irish peasants on the duties of patriotism, and their sad defection therefrom, our friend J tells me he was passing through the heart of the Empire to find the Liverpool proceedings find ready echo in the London Press. We Irish know, alas, too well that stream of emigration, begun in Black '47, has flowed during the intervening years, steadily at all seasons, but strongest of all, for obvious reasons, after the harvesting in the autumn. And yet in the autumn of this year of war the number of those who left our shores was, I think, the smallest on record.

Now, if there were amongst these peasants a small remnant which is not thus accounted for, an if that small remnant were cowardly-mind I do not grant it—Oh, the pity of it, Iago!" that such expressions as "Irish slackers' and "runaways" should be so freely bandied about, whilst our Irish lads, where the fight was fiercest in van or rear, were drenching the battlefields with their blood "from Dunkirk to Belgrade," and further afield still, by the Aegean Sea, in distant Gallipoli. With the Gallipoli campaign fresh in memory, I could not help thinking that if the happenings along these fronts were only known, these people would have judged the Irish peasants in a more chastened mood, and-I shall do them the justice of thinking-would have paused before casting the stone at "Irish runaways."

It was at such a time I recalled my promise to write something about the 10th (Irish) Division. When I reflected how coldest silence enshrouds their glorious deeds, how prominently they figure on the roll of honour, and how conspicuously absent they were from the roll of honours, I could no longer delay its fulfilment, and now proceed to tell such flabby things as the Censor may endure, and, as a foreward, let me give you the letter of an Irish father, of over 70 years, to his boy on the eve of going to the front.

It is worthy of a place in war literature, and may be taken as evidence of the spirit with which Ireland flung herself into the battle line. 'Willy, my Sear Son- I have your letter. It does not need a very long answer, as you wish. Besides my hands are feeble for writing. My next word is, Be sure, before you leave for expected was, to go to your duties. Keep your soul right with God and you need fear nothing. This is more important than anything in this world, and don't neglect you fathers advice. Now about other things, I never liked that man called the Kaiser. He wears a moustache with the points turned up-like a rhinoceros-to rip you. It would be a bad job for us if he won. Don't let him. And I don't think he will win. Now God bless you and your comrades and your purpose, and keep at all times a light heart. -Your old warm hearted, Father. '

Another piece of advice suggested itself to the old man, which he embodied in a post-script- 'That Kaiser is no more in the battlefield than you are, and if you get a chance at him, at 2,000 yards rifle range, pot him, and have no scruple about it—Father. 'Whilst we have such fathers we need not despair of our race. Of such are heroes made. General Bryan Mahon. And now to come to the 10th (Irish) Division. I speak naturally most of what was going on in my own small section of the line. We may dismiss the formative period of the Division briefly. It was drawn together by the name and personality of a brilliant Irish soldier. Lieutenant General Sir Bryan Mahon. As we campaigned with him in Suvla respect grew into admiration, and admiration deepened into affection. Only those can gauge the depth of that affection who witnessed the dismay which fell on all ranks when General; Mahon withdrew from us at Suvla. Happily the parting was brief.

I find an entry in my diary dated July 8th, 1915, made at Basingstoke, where we trained after leaving the Curragh, and whence we proceeded to the front. 'Had view of the Munster lines. About an hour and a half before they marched out quite a crowd of them played pitch and toss, with as much zest and concentration as if it were the only thing which mattered. Heads went up when the coins were in the air, and every head bent earthwards with drill-like precision to ascertain eventualities' It was such a scene as one often sees at a cross road in Ireland. On board ship the same light hearted spirit found expression at the game of card, the concert and the band performance. One would never suspect, looking at the cheery lads, that a great European war was raging, and that they were under way to take a hand in it.

It may be of interest to note here that the songs oftenest heard were "When Irish Eyes" and "The Little Grey Home in The West. At Mudros, on quitting the transport, we bade adieu to all the comforts of civilisation. We bivouacked with mother earth for our bed and starry heavens for our canopy. Henceforth our fate was bully beef and biscuits, and we had to fight for every mouthful of those war rations. The housefly gentle at home, was here unspeakably fierce and aggressive. He, together with the blue bottle, waged relentless war upon us, making meals and sleep a difficulty, and both of them were held largely responsible for the stomach troubles, which were nearly everyone's portion at Lemnos. I think, though our next move was to the front, everyone was glad when the order came to leave that dreadful island.

The last night there was one to live in memory. One had often seen in pictures the bivouac by night. Here it was in the life. The camp fires blazed. In their light you could discern the rifles stacked at well defined distances, the men in groups, their cheery faces ruddy with the glow. The canvas however, does not bring out the joke and song and frolic which were the order of the night. Davis's lines came into ones head, as he saw these fine Munster lads given up to the fun of the passing hour-You'd swear they knew no other mood-Than mirth and love in Tipperary. Lest we should forget the reality of things, a small dark cloud had gathered in the north east, which brought out in relief the flashes of the guns thundering at Achi Baba.

Under First Fire. We embarked on August the 6th, and under cover of the darkness stole to our unknown destination. That a stiff task confronted us we were led to expect from the orders. Every man was to take with him three days iron rations, and only the clothes in which he stood. We found ourselves riding at anchor in Suvla Bay at 4 30 a. m, and soon received a warm greeting from the enemy guns, which we returned in kind. Our ships were within range. My diary shows wherein we found comfort-'We are within range on board, but these are so many targets we shall be unlucky to suffer. ' And indeed, here was an education in things naval for the man who had time to pursue it. The masts in the bay were like trees in the forest. All sorts and conditions of craft were there-the large battleship, cruiser, monitor, destroyer, transport, trawler, down to the light steam tender in which embarkation was effected.

The Division was thus disposed of. The 29th Infantry Brigade, consisting of the 5th Connaught Rangers, 6th Leinsters, 6th Royal Irish Rifles, and 10th Hants took the field at Anzac, at the point marked "X" on the map, a few days before us. It did not operate as a brigade, but each regiment was used in aid of the Dominion troops and Gurkhas, as occasion demanded. This, of course, took away from its laurels as a Brigade. In this area the Connaught Rangers covered themselves with glory. One incident is eloquent of the spirit of the 29th. A dangerous parapet had to be sealed with a view to capturing an important position. Colonel Jourdaine called for volunteers. A veteran Ranger gave the lead."I have two sons in France with the Gallant Conduct Medal, I don't see why their old dad should not have one, too." He spoke nobly, as befitted his last utterance.

The 6th Leinsters are credited with hewing their way to the top of Sari Bair-Hill 971,--the occupation of which was the objective of this campaign. Here we bade adieu to the 29th Brigade. Though only three or four miles from us, they never came under divisional command, and were as effectually separated from us as if they were fighting in Flanders. For pace certain statesmen, there is other standard of distance in Gallipoli than linear measurement, as, I think, is now well known. The 31st Infantry Brigade was composed of the 5th and 6th Royal Inniskilling Fusiliers, and the 5th and 6th Royal Irish Fusiliers. They, together with half of the 30th Brigade-namely, the 6th and 7th Royal Dublin Fusiliers, landed at Niebrumesa (?) Point marked "XX" on the map. They were heavily shelled in the stream tenders which took them ashore. Napoleon's soldier carried the famous marshal's baton in his knapsack.

Many of our poor fellows did not know the value of the water bottle which they slung so carelessly over their shoulders. It does not require an effort of the imagination to picture some of them, in their happy go lucky vein, landing with their water bottles half filled (Be it recorded here parenthetically that Byrne of the 6th Dublins, King of the Quartermasters, besides regulation allowance, filled every available vessel and took it ashore, with a presence which of itself deserved a decoration. Later we find him provisioning, not only his regiment, but the whole Division, (utinam si sic omnes'). Be that as it may, very soon not a man of them was ignorant of its value.

Before the morrow's sun had set, liquid gold, drop for drop, would not have purchased the contents of the water bottle, were such exchange possible. The scorching August heat and the incessant fighting on the burning sands, which in these early days mainly, formed the floor of our operating area, produced a very agony of thirst, and the piteous cry of the wounded was often hear,"Water! Water!" Taking Chocolate Hill. The line of advance of all brigades was dominated by the Turkish guns in position on the hills, which formed a semi-circle whose extremities ran into the sea. From extremity to extremity measured about eight miles, from the sea line to the centre of the hills about five. The air was fragrant with thyme.

The surface generally presented a flat appearance. Its only growth, with the exception of corn very sparingly sown, was a prickly shrub, mostly of the holly type in miniature, bearing something resembling the acorn. The coast gave little or no cover. Within this enclosed area the 10th Division operated. After dis-embarkation the Royal Dublins, Inniskillings, and Irish Fusiliers marched over the bare promontory to Lala Baba (route marked "I" on the map) under heavy shrapnel fire. They right-turned sharply and faced the immediate objective-the hill called by the Turks Yilghin Burnu, by us Chocolate Hill, from its burnt appearance after shell fire. In extended order they advanced up the Salt Lake-route marked 2 on the map. At this season the Salt Lake is fairly dry under foot. Its surface glistens with the salt crystals deposited thereon.

There was no cover-not a rock, not a shrub- and the advance was right under the enemy guns. It was such as to put the mettle of the bravest troops to the test. As the shrapnel burst over them, comrades fell on every side, but ranks never wavered for a moment. A veteran officer of many campaigns remarked to me "These boys are wonderful, they march under shell fire like seasoned troops. Why, they were as calm as if on parade at the Curragh. Chocolate Hill went down that Saturday evening of the landing before the fierce onslaught of the Dublins. Thus blooded, with the 31st Brigade they occupied the hill due south of Burnt Hill, officially known as Hill W, if my memory serves me right. For military reasons they fell back on Chocolate Hill and dug themselves in. This position they held in the face of great opposition till Friday morning, August 13th, when, after incessant fighting and toil, which knew no sleep, they marched over route marked 3 on the map to rejoin the other half of the 30th Brigade. The Munsters. This second half of the 30th Brigade was made up of two battalions the 6th and 7th Royal Munster Fusiliers. They landed at Suvla Bay, at point marked "XXX" on the map.

A few hours later in Suvla Bay the Pioneer regiment, that is the Royal Irish Regiment, under the command of Lord Granard, also landed. These three regiments formed the entire command of General Mahon during those early days. The artillery of the Brigade went to Cairo. To return to the Munster landing. A German aeroplane hovered like a bird of prey over the lighters, treating them to bombs, which fell harmlessly into the sea. As the lighters crunched upon the sand, about 25 yards from the water line, everyone was congratulating his neighbour on the calm passage. The men jumped into the sea, and, wading ashore, fell in, to find, just as they left the beach, that the Turks had sown contact mines in profusion, first one and then another, and yet another terrific explosion sending poor fellows to their doom.

As yet without experience in the workings of explosives, all of us thought it was shell fire, and that the aeroplane had given range. Disembarkation from the lighter ceased. Everyone remained at his post awaiting the finishing stroke from the Turkish guns. After a brief delay, which seemed an eternity, word of command was given to continue the disembarkation. It was carried out in the most orderly way. These raw levies of the previous autumn formed up as coolly as if they were on their native sod. Fighting started straight off. They fought their way along the hill Karakol Dagh against an enemy in a very strong natural position, and by Friday evening they had to bivouac ready for their old comrades in arms, the 6th and 7th Dublin Fusiliers, between the heights of Karakol Dagh and the Gulf of Saros.

The Inniskillings and Irish Fusiliers arrived, to the best of my belief, the previous day. I witnessed these regiments drag their weary limbs over the ridge of Karakol Dagh. The drawn face and haggard look told of that dreadful week, into which more privation and suffering had been compressed than fall to the lot of most men in a lifetime. Their faces were begrimed with smoke and sweat. The clay of the trenches showed on their hands and through the unshaven beard and close-cropped head, for Water was still too scarce for washing purposes. How many inquiries were made about the water supply? How many comments on the virtues of water, which would have gladdened the heart of a total abstinence advocate. Never did eiderdown prove as soft as mother earth, when they sank down upon it exhausted, to sweet oblivion of their cares, and, perchance to dream of their 'Little Grey Home in the West. ' Whatever about their dreams, their first waking moments were for it. On all manner of odd writing desks, butt end of rifles, rocks, letters were written. One poor mother just at this time got a letter from her son with a bullet through it.

A comrade wrote a letter explanatory. After her boy had finished a letter to her, he put it into his breast pocket. A bullet pierced it and his heart! A human document this, in the inhuman thing called 'war. ' It was a comfort to that mother that her lads last thoughts on earth were for her, and I have no doubt he also told her, and it lit up the gloom of the home that he had been to confession. It will bring solid comfort to the bereaved ones to know …this campaign in Gallipoli…Communion on the day they fell, or certainly a few days previously."Fighting in Hell To-Day." Our Lady's Day (August the 15th) was ushered in with Mass and Holy Communion. Was it not the anniversary of the ---Ford which too began with Mass and then Hugh O'Neill charged to victory in the name of God and Our Lady! Like a bolt from the blue came to order to fall in for battle about 1 p. m. The objective was the capture of Kiretck Tepe Sirt.

Some very human grumbling was heard about the lack of water, loss of kit, etc., but never a grumble about fighting. The men fell in cheerily, and, as each regiment moved out to the attach, the Catholics fell out and received absolution from the Chaplain. The Royal Irish Fusiliers marched out after the Munsters and Dublins. The Royal Irish regiment also took part in the fray, and in this, as in all other engagements, with its gallant commanding officer, it shared to the full all the perils of the campaign. The Dublin, Munster, and Irish Fusiliers (one Battalion) advanced in the direction indicated by the arrow head, and on the sea side of the hill that is between Karakol Dagh and the Gulf of Saroe. The advance of the 5th and 6th Inniskillings and a battalion of the Royal Irish Fusiliers was along the same hills in the other side, whilst their right down on the palins was supported by a brigade of the 54th Division.

There was ----the heaviest encounter of the Suvla campaign. After two hours an advance of twenty yards was not established, so much were our movements dominated by the Turkish position, so deeply the fire. I quote from my diary 'The fighting is hell to-day from 1 15 p. m. up to now 7 15 p. m., when it rages as heavily as ever. ' The attack culminated in a bayonet charge that evening. It was with difficulty that the men in reserve were kept in the trenches. They could not be kept off the parapets (the sailors were in the rigging of the war ships) when their comrades were rushing the h—ls, and delivering a bayonet charge to the accompaniment of a wild Irish cheer.

The hill was taken, and crest after crest went down before that magnificent charge. The dawn of Monday, 16th August, found the enemy strongly reinforced, and he delivered a succession of counter attacks. The nature of the intervening ground was such as to make rifle fire impossible. The two armies were almost locked in embrace so close were they. Our fellows tried by lifting their rifles over the crest of the intervening hillocks to discharge them at random, but without result. The struggle now resolved itself into a fight with hand grenades. Our supply was exhausted, and from 4 a. m. to 10 a. m. the enemy was kept at bay with stones, and –hurling back such hand grenades as reached us unexploded. Major Harrison decided on a bayonet charge. A withering fire from the Maxims made advance impossible. Very few of the attacking party returned. Major Harrison was amongst the fallen.

After repeated attacks, the Turks acknowledged defeat towards noon, though the fighting continued into Wednesday. The Roll Call. During those days I can recall scenes worthy of a place beside the "Roll Call." I had not the heart to use the camera. Our loss was enormous. Colonel Cox was the only Commanding Officer left in the 30th Brigade- a brave officer worthy of any command Colonel Downing- a name to conjure with in the Division- was wounded. Healy and Whyte, bravest of the brave, were also wounded, whilst Harrison, Fitzgibbon, Richards, Preston, O'Duffy, Jeffson, Nesbitt,

Dunne, and Cullinane were killed. This was thinning the already thin ranks, for at the Salt Lake we had lost Jennings, McGarry, Staunton, O'Carroll, Clery, Hickman, with Captain Carroll and O'Carroll, Carter, and Martin wounded. Swift wrote to his friend, Wogan, the Chevalier of Inn—o—told fame—"I cannot but admire those gentlemen of Ireland, who, with all the disadvantages of being exiles and strangers, have been able to distinguish themselves by their valour and conduct in son many parts of Europe.

I think above all other nations." Words as true to-day as when Swift wrote them. These gentlemen of Ireland of our day in handing down the glorious tradition of Irish valour have added to the lustre. The colours of some of there regiments engaged bore the proud motto 'Spectamur Agendo'-a challenge to all and sun dry to judge them by their deeds. It might well have been the motto of all these Irish regiments, for any of them can make the challenge. These things could not be without paying a heavy toll in blood. Only a very small fraction of our officers, even thus early, remained; the loss in the ranks was also vey heavy; but our Irish boys had proved the stuff they were made of. Eleven months in training and they had to their credit achievements worthy of the olden glories of the Irish Brigade-"Long as honour shineth, Or mercy's soul at war repineth, So long shall Erin's pride, Tell how they lived and how they died." "Soldiers could not do better" was the burden of General Mahon's message to the 30th and 31st Infantry Brigades which formed his Division-a tribute warmly endorsed by all who had seen their work.

"And these are the men," quoth a senior officer,"who would not be trusted with Self Government,' and yet another "I shall be a Home Ruler henceforth."Rosary on The Hillside. Thursday, the 19th of August, found all that was left of the 30th Brigade, in a place of comparative safety-miscalled a rest camp-not far from the Munster landing place, between the Gulf of Saros and the hills, which fall almost sheer into it. Worn out, though there were, they had in self preservation to dig themselves in on their arrival in their new bivouac. When fatigue duty was finished the chaplain appeared on the evening of Thursday. You should see how the men rushed around him from every direction. More impressive than ceremonial in stateliest cathedral was the simple recital of Our Lady's Rosary on the hillside overlooking the sea.

That evening after the Rosary the chaplain gave them absolution. It was a scene which, though often repeated, never palled. When opportunity offered, Holy Communion was also given, generally in the evening when things had quieted down a little. The Pope had disposed with the fast before Holy Communion. The men scattered at once when they had 'received." We often met in fear and trembling, and it was not safe to tarry. What a beautiful sight the trenches then presented. Here is one poor fellow trying to read his thanksgiving from his prayer book in the fading light, another tells his beards, another has his head buried in his hands. Silence reigns save for the shrieking of the shells overhead, and all are on bended knee, paying homage to Him Who is Lord of life and death. I would not envy the man who could contemplate such scenes unmoved. Friday night found them on the wing again to take part in the grand assault delivered all along the Turkish position on Saturday, August the 21st.

Their route lay by the seashore to Lala Baba. The attack opened with artillery fire about 2 p. m. on Saturday. The earth trembled with the thunder from the ships and the land guns. Other divisions had now arrived and marched past in thousands. But this time the Turk had his wire entanglements, fresh guns were in position, and he awaited the attack with calm. By the way, the general verdict on the Turk was that he fought cleanly. We caught him at his best in that game of war. Ave et Vale! The remainder of our time in Suvla was spent in the trenches. By day and night we dug new trenches, defending lines of trenches which are usually held by thrice our number. Every day had its toll of casualties from shellfire and sniper, till the Division left the Peninsula during the nights of 30th October and 1st of November, embarking for Lemnos from Lala Baba.

We left that desolate land with gladness, but our joy was tempered with sorrow, as we thought of our brave comrades who were sleeping their last sleep by the Sea of Saros-I had almost written the Sea of Sorrows- and the slopes of Chocolate Hill. May Turkish earth lie lightly on them, for never breathed a cheerier, braver lot. Ave et Vale! I give you extracts from my diary, under date October 1st and 2nd-'Lomnos, the place of horrors in August, is a Paradise in October" "Felt when I heard we were coming here we would be as happy in Gallipoli. Absence of the eternal booming of guns makes Lemnos a Paradise." "The bugle call is heard again and gives us homely feeling" From here in the early part of October, we set sail for Salonika, after getting reinforcements. By the time you may have heard of some of our doings in our new campaign. Before I finish, I must pay a well-deserved tribute to the Royal Army Medical Corps. No nobler men took part in the expedition than they. Without one thought for self, brave even to rashness, no pen can tell what relief they brought to the sufferers. I have seen them –moved-hardly a medical officer was Irish-to the very depths of their being on coming from the marquee, after operating on our brave lads.

Time and again I heard "I often was told there was no soldier like the Irish, I know it now," for they carried their wounds as bravely as they fought. These gallant officers infused their fine spirit into the stretcher-bearers and orderlies, so that, once and all-and they came from the Three Kingdoms-they were proud to be attached to the Irish Division. I raise my hat to them from officer commanding to the humblest private. One simple tribute, I was in the front trench of the Dublins. A man had been wounded and the familiar cry "stretcher-bearers" was passed along the trench.

The Medical officer appeared with his gallant men."Do you know" asked one Dublin Fusilier "the men who will get all the honours of this ware?" "Who" I replied "These Medical Corps men" was the reply. Good judges of brave men are these Dublin boys. And dull indeed of perception would be he who was not impressed with the familiar sight of the Medical officer midst shot and shell behind the firing line, out in the open, performing an operation as calmly as if he were in the theatre of a hospital. The deep religious spirit manifested by all denominations was a feature worthy of notice. There was a fine response to the generous efforts of the Chaplain, canon McClean-the doyen of their number- I can vouch for it, amidst a storm of shell, on returning from his duties in the trenches, was equal to halting to dilate on the beautiful plumage of a bird, which was startled by his approach, and Father O'Farrell, the junior of that body, was able to crack a joke to the same grim accompaniment. Need I say hope our poor Irish boys responded to their chaplains call.

You were reminded of the fervour of a "mission" at home when you heard the deep toned response in the Rosary,"Holy Mary! Mother of God, pray for us sinners, now and at the hour of our death." Lovingly did they gather round the rude altar, hastily improvised by willing hands. Reverently they knelt in the Divine Presence, during the celebration of the sacred Mysteries. It was all so reminiscent of a closed page in their forefathers history. Religion in that supreme hour was to them as to their fathers a comfort and a stay! Official Silence What a pity when the heavy casualty list appeared that no one also told how these brave lads fought and died. That story would have brought balm to many a crushed heart at home. In a sense the home folk were the greatest sufferers. For one thing, theirs was an agony long drawn out, the sufferings of those fallen in battle if intense, was brief. Again their agony was not mitigated by the excitement the exhilaration of the fight, and of the home folk, the women suffered most.

The men had their duties to distract them, and one nail drives out another, but the mothers and wives when after a long period of suspense the worst had happened, were a prey to their own and thoughts, almost every object in the home suggesting some tender remembrance of the childhood and boyhood of the dead. Besides giving solace to the afflicted at home, if our rulers only knew it they had in the bare recital of these heroic deeds their most potent agency for recruiting. The young blood of the nation would have been fired. Beside that tale the oratory of the recruiting platform would have been the emptiest nothing. We too, at the front saw the newspapers and noted the silence, but we were not down in spirits. Whatever left us, good cheer did not. We found comfort in the thought of our gallant commander, we were proud of him; he must have been gratified by the affection, he knew we bore him. All of us had the calm of mind which comes from the consciousness of duty done faithfully and fearlessly. Such was our frame of mind sans honours, sans honourable mention, sans any mention at all, saying that mention which "darkly as in a glass" associated our efforts with failure. Some of us thought of the days of Napier-Napier had won the battle of Meanee against overwhelming odds.

All his troops were native with the exception of one Irish regiment. He wrote in his diary after the battle –I quote from memory-"once during the fight the men paused to cheer me. They gave me three cheers after the battle. I do not know what honours if any, her Majesty, the Queen may bestow on me, but I do know she has none to give which can compare with the cheers of these Tipperary men. Magnificent Tipperary!' Napier wanted no honours for himself that his men would not share, for later his doubts were removed and he was able to write "Now I can wear my Grand Cross with ease, for while my officers sat uncomfortably on my shoulder. Now I can meet corporal Tim Kelly, and Delaney, the bugler without a blush."

After Suvla there was no disparity of honours for our commander to reproach himself with not a solitary "mention" was given to the 10th Division. For the rest, our brave fellows felt that they were striking a blow for the old 'and. For her sake toil and privation, suffering and death itself were sweet. They had caught up the old time spirit."If death should come, that martyrdom, Were sweet endured for you, Dear land, Were sweet endured for you" And now I have fulfilled my promise, and don't thank me for this letter. Thank Liverpudlian and Cunarder. They dragged out of sluggish me this unworthy appreciation of the 10th Irish Division. The Press Bureau see no sufficient reason to stop the publication of this material,. But the responsibility for the accuracy must rest with the publisher.

'People' newspaper; Mr John Fitzgibbon, M. P., has been informed that his son, Captain Michael J Fitzgibbon, 7th Dublin Fusiliers, has been killed in action in the Dardanelles. Captain Fitzgibbon was 29 years of age on the day that he was killed. Prior to receiving his commission in the Dublin Fusiliers he was a law student. He was Gazetted Captain on 6th March 1915 (his records in the CWGC and SDGW give his rank as Lieutenant). Deep regret is felt in Castlerea for the gallant young officer, who was greatly admired for his many sterling qualities. This officer is a brother to Mrs Duggan of Monster House, Kilkenny and Father Fitzgibbon. He was also brother-in-Law to Mr Richard Duggan, of Monster House, Kilkenny. See full newspaper article on Lieutenant Duggan in The "Kilkenny People" of November-16-1916 where Captain Fitzgibbon is listed as a relation.

Kilkenny Journal, September, 1915. The Late Captain Fitzgibbon. The Ballinrobe District Council have adopted a resolution of sympathy with MrJohn Fitzgibbon, M. P., on the death of his son, Captain M. Fitzgibbon, who was killed in action. The chaplain attached to the Division has written Mr Fitzgibbon, M. P., stating that on the morning of the 15th August Captain Fitzgibbon received Holy Communion, and rendered splendid services in the collection and arrangement of the troops for the reception of the Blessed Sacrament. This intimation had brought the greatest consolation to Mr and Mrs Fitzgibbon and family.

Westmeath Independent, September, 1915. Roll of Honour. The Late Captain M Fitzgibbon. On Wednesday at 10. 30 o'clock in St Patrick's Church, Castlerea, a memorial service consisting of Solemn Office and Requiem High Mass was celebrated for the repose of the soul of the late Captain Michael ("Mice") Fitzgibbon, of the 7th Battalion Dublin Fusiliers, who was killed in action at the Dardanelles on the 10th of August. Deceased was son of Mr John Fitzgibbon, and Mrs Fitzgibbon, Castlerea, to whom, and the other members of their family, the deepest sympathy goes out on the death of their gallant son.

This sympathy is not confined to Mr Fitzgibbon's friends in the West, or all over Ireland, but, no doubt, will be shared by the Irish exiles beyond the Atlantic, where Mr Fitzgibbon is so well and popularly known for his life long struggles in the cause of the people. Captain Fitzgibbon was only 29 years of age when he met his death, and when the sad news was made known in Castlerea it caused intense sorrow amongst many acquaintances, who will always treasure an affectionate remembrance of the amiable and popular young gentlemen who has passed away. The attendance at the solemn ceremonies was extremely large, the spacious church being crowded, not only by the townspeople, but by large numbers from the surrounding districts…. the article continues with a long list of attendees. Michael is listed twice in the Tullamore Roll of Honour printed in the King's County Independent in February-1917. There are many other articles in newspapers from the midlands and the west concerning his death, too many to publish here, author.

King's County Independent, 1915. Killed in Action. Captain M. Fitzgibbon. Mr John Fitzgibbon, M. P., and Mrs Fitzgibbon will have the heartfelt sympathy of the people of Connaught, and, more especially, of Roscommpn and Mayo, on the death of their son, Capt, M. M. Fitzgibbon, 7th Dublin Fusiliers, who was killed in action at the Dardanelles on August 15th, which, by coincidence, was his 29th birthday. Captain Fitzgibbon was well known in his active district of Castlerea, and also in Tullamore, where, as a law student, has spent some years as an apprentice to Messrs, Hoey and Denning, solicitors.

He was probably the most popular member of his very popular family, and amongst his many acquaintances in Tullamore his death will be very sincerely mourned. He was a young man of brilliant intellect, and he had before him a very successful career in the legal profession, but he surrendered this to aN. S. W. er the call. He was gazetted as Lieutenant in the Dublin Fusiliers, and before the departure of the Division for the Mediterranean, he was promoted to the rank of captain. He was just a week on Turkish soil when he was killed. We desire to join in the common expression of sympathy with his bereaved parents, and to her relatives in their great loss. A photograph of the late Captain Fitzgibbon will appear in our next issue. Royal Irish Fusiliers. No. 17527, Queen's F. I. Ward, 5th Royal Irish Fusiliers, Graylingwell, War Hospital, Chichester, Sussex, September 1st, 1915. Dear Mr. Fitzgibbon, --You may feel surprised to get a letter from the above address, but I wish to send my sincere sympathy to yourself, Mrs Fitzgibbon and you family on the death of your son, and I assure the loss of such a gallant Captain will not alone be felt among the Dublin Fusiliers, but in the whole 10th Irish Division.

The shelling was so severe and the fighting so incessant, we lost most of our officers in the landing. Captain Fitzgibbon was one of the few left to head the Irish Troops, and he set a fine example of pluck and courage to his junior officers and men, and cheered us on to victory when we captured Chocolate Hill, and a line of trenches on the evening of August 6th at the point of the bayonet. After that charge we were all exhausted, and as the fighting grew quieter the inclination to sleep was almost irresistible, yet owing to the nearness of the enemy it was dangerous, and every man was ordered to "stand to arms". All night long Captain Fitzgibbon kept sending messages to Headquarters and receiving replies. I heard after his idea was to keep passing messages down the lines, so that no man could sleep. He was successful. No man slept.

On August 10th, the night I was wounded, the Connaught Rangers and Inniskillings relieved the Dublin and Irish Fusiliers who had slept four days in the firing line, and were allowed to base for a rest. Captain Fitzgibbon and Captain Lennon were all right then, and were not due back in the firing line till Sunday morning, so it must be in the now famous charge of the 16th August the gallant Captain fell. It was a pity, but a still greater loss, as the losing of such men as Captain Fitzgibbon will not hasten the end of this dreadful war, which I am sure you can never forget. When the history of this war comes before the public that landing and taking of Suvla Bay will be mentioned, and a tribute of recognition will be paid to the two brave Captains from Castlerea, who took the lion's share of the work in pulling their men through. Captain Fitzgibbon did not fall into the hands of the Turks alive. He met with a hero's death, leading his men to victory, envied by most soldiers and regretted by all. Trusting you will accept my deepest sympathy. —I remain, yours very sincerely, P. J. Madden, Lance Corporal,

J. Fitzgibbon, Esq., M. P. of our beloved and revered Chairman, and I propose that we pass a resolution of sympathy with him in his great sorrow. Mr Tully—I beg to second that vote of sympathy. I am very often in sharp division with our Chairman, and to second the resolution might come better from me as one who was very often divided with him on various matters. But, in the presence of death there is no division or dissention amongst us and we all join in offering our sympathy to our Chairman in the great affliction that had befallen him. In the case of parents nothing could be more afflicting than the loss of a son and especially one in the prime of manhood. Captain Fitzgibbon, a young gentleman of great ability and was bound to become famous, for, in the course of a few short months he was promoted to the rank of Captain, from that of a Lieutenant.

I am certain if he was spared he would reach a very high position indeed. We feel very deeply for Mr and Mrs Fitzgibbon in their terrible affliction. Mr Shanly—I am very sorry, indeed, that the occasion has arisen for me to have tp associate myself with such a resolution. Mr Heverin, Secretary---I wish, as an official of the Council, to express my own sympathy and the sympathy of my brother officials with Mr and Mrs Fitzgibbon, and all the members of the family on the death of their brave son who, as the Chairman has nicely put it, gave up his life for his country. Mr Mapother, in that beautiful language which few can imitate, says he has given up his life fighting against barbarous methods and barbarians. Captain Fitzgibbon and many others are helping not only the cause of Ireland, but also the cause of civilised humanity. I could not speak of Captain Michael Fitzgibbon in anything but the highest terms of praise, and in expressing my deep sorrow at his untimely death I echo the feelings of the other Co Council officials.

Captain Fitzgibbon, at one time, followed the legal profession, and put aside the law to take up arms and fight in a good cause. He did his bit and we are sorry for Mr John Fitzgibbon and the members of his family. Mr O'Keeffe (Accountant) —I join with Mr Heverin in offering my sympathy to our Chairman, who has always been held in the highest esteem by the officials. On the motion of the Chairman, seconded by Mr Tully, the resolution of sympathy was passed in silence with Mr Fitzgibbon, on the death of his son, Captain Michael Fitzgibbon.

Midland Reporter and Westmeath Nationalist, August, 1915. Captain Fitzgibbon Killed at Dardanelles. Mr John Fitzgibbon, M. P., Castlerea, has been informed that his son, Captain M Fitzgibbon, 7th Dublin Fusiliers, was killed in action at the Gallipoli Peninsula on the 15th August. Captain Fitzgibbon was 29 years of age the day he was killed, and prior to his receiving his commission as Lieutenant in the Fusiliers on volunteering, was a law student. He left recently with his division, and before his departure was gazetted captain. He was only a week at the Dardanelles when he was killed.

Westmeath Independent, March, 1915. Promotion of Lieutenant Fitzgibbon. His many friends will be pleased to learn that Lieutenant Michael J Fitzgibbon, 7th Battalion, Royal Dublin Fusiliers, has been promoted to the rank of first Lieutenant. The new appointment was gazetted a few days ago. Lieutenant Fitzgibbon is a son of Mr John Fitzgibbon, M. P., Castlerea, the popular and esteemed representative of South Mayo. He volunteered for active service shortly after the outbreak of the war, and was in training at the Curragh up till a few weeks ago, when the battalion was transferred to the Royal Barracks, Dublin, where they are at present quartered.

Freeman's Journal. The Ballinrobe District Council have adopted a resolution of sympathy with Mr John Fitzgibbon, M. P., on the death of his son, Captain M Fitzgibbon, who was killed in action. The chaplain attached to the Division has written Mr Fitzgibbon, M. P., stating that on the morning of the 15th August, Captain Fitzgibbon received Holy Communion, and rendered splendid services in the collection and arrangement of the troops for the recap[tion of the Blessed Sacrament. This intimation has brought the greatest consolation to Mr and Mrs Fitzgibbon and family.

Kilkenny Journal. September, 1915. The Late Captain Fitzgibbon. The Ballinrobe District Council have adopted a resolution of sympathy with Mt John Fitzgibbon, M. P., on the death of his son, Captain M. Fitzgibbon, who was killed in action. The chaplain attached to the Division has written Mr Fitzgibbon, M. P., stating that on the morning of the 15th August Captain Fitzgibbon received Holy Communion, and rendered splendid services in the collection and arrangement of the troops for the reception of the Blessed Sacrament. This intimation had brought the greatest consolation to Mr and Mrs Fitzgibbon and family.

Grave or Memorial Reference; Panel 190 to 196. Cemetery: Helles memorial in Turkey.

Fitzgibbon, William. Rank; Private. Regiment or Service: Australian Infantry A. I. F. Unit; 11th Battalion. Service Number; 3789. Date of death; 20/05/1917. Age at death;36. Born; Innesuig, Kilkenny, Ireland. Died of wounds received in action at the 6th General Hospital, Rouen, France. Occupation on enlistment, motorman. Age on enlistment; 29 years 2 months. Address on enlistment, Car Barn, East Perth. Next of kin details; (mother) Mrs Margaret O'Neill, Innesuig, Stoneyford, Kilkenny. Later changed to (wife) Mrs Josephene Fitzgerald, 9 Blackmill Street, Kilkenny, Ireland. Declaration of Marriage certificate produced. Place and date of enlistment, 23-August-1915. Blackboy Hill, Perth Western Australia. Weight, 142 lbs. Height, 5 feet, 8 ½ inches. Complexion, fair. Eyes, blue. Hair, brown. Wounded in action on 29-July-1916 (Shell Shock and a gunshot wound to the arm), treated in a Rouen Hospital and transferred to Craglingwell War Hospital, Chichester, England. Returned to France after treatment, 25-January-1917. Wounded in action (gunshot to the knee) on 05-May-1917 and died two weeks later. Grave or Memorial Reference; P II M 7A. Cemetery: St Sever Cemetery Extension, Rouen in France.

Fitzpatrick, Matthew. Rank; Private. Regiment or Service: Royal Irish Regiment. Unit; B Company, 2nd Battalion. Service Number; 10123. Date of death; 21/03/1918. Age at death; 49. Born; Slieverue, County Kilkenny. Enlisted; Waterford. Killed in action. Son of Patrick and Margaret Fitzpatrick, of Ferrybank, Waterford. Grave or Memorial Reference; I B 30. Cemetery: Templeux-Le-Guerard British Cemetery in France.

Fitzpatrick, Michael. Rank; Private. Regiment or Service: Worcestershire Regiment. Unit; 10th Battalion. Service Number; 17207. Date of death; 05/10/1916. Born; Piltown, County Kilkenny. Enlisted; Tonyrefail, Glamorganshire. Residence; Piltown, County Kilkenny. Killed in action. Grave or Memorial Reference; Pier and Face 5 A and 6 C. Cemetery: Thiepval Memorial in France.

Fitzpatrick, Stephen. Rank; Private. Regiment or Service: Royal Inniskilling Fusiliers. Unit; 2nd Battalion. Service Number; 40596. Date of death; 05/04/1917. Born; St Patrick's, Kilkenny. Enlisted; Kilkenny. Killed in action. Notes; Formerly he was with the Hussars of the Line where his number was 31707. Grave or Memorial Reference; I N 20. Cemetery: Savy British Cemetery in France.

Fitzpatrick, Thomas. Rank; Private. Regiment or Service: Royal Irish Regiment. Unit; 2nd Battalion. Service Number; 1163. Date of death; 14/07/1916. Age at death;35. Born; St Canice's, Kilkenny. Enlisted; Kilkenny. Killed in action. Husband of Maria Fitzpatrick of 16 Butts Green, Kilkenny. Grave or Memorial Reference; Pier and Face 3 A. Cemetery: Thiepval Memorial in France.

Fitzpatrick, William. Rank; Private. Regiment or Service: Royal Irish Regiment. Unit; 1st Battalion. Service Number; 9971. Date of death; 23/02/1915. Born; St Canice's, Kilkenny. Enlisted; Kilkenny. Killed in action. After his death, his effects and property were received by;- Mrs Jane O'Brien, Greens Hill, Kilkenny, Ireland. Grave or Memorial Reference; A 22. Cemetery: Dickiebusch New Military Cemetery in Belgium.

Fleming, Michael. Rank; Private. Regiment or Service: Royal Irish Regiment. Unit; 2nd Battalion. Service Number; 4134. Date of death; 26/05/1915. Born; Callan, County Kilkenny. Enlisted; Kilkenny. Died of wounds. Grave or Memorial Reference; VIII A 48. Cemetery: Boulogne Eastern Cemetery in France.

Fleming, Patrick. Rank; Gunner. Regiment or Service: Royal Garrison Artillery. Unit; 113th Siege Battery. Service Number; 163662. Date of death; 09/12/1917. Age at death; 25. Born; Danesfort, County Kilkenny. Enlisted; Carlow. Residence; Danesfort. Killed in action. (served under the alias Morrissey/Morressey). Son of Philip and Mary Fleming, of Graigue, Upper Danesfort, Co. Kilkenny. Grave or Memorial Reference; I D 40. Cemetery: Potijze Chateau Grounds Cemetery in Belgium.

Private Fleming, courtesy of Gerard Fleming, (grandnephew), Dundalk.

Fleming, Thomas. Rank; Private. Regiment or Service: Royal Irish Regiment. Unit; 1st Battalion. Service Number; 9777. Date of death; 07/05/1915. Age at death;24. Born; St John's, Kilkenny. Enlisted; Carlow. Killed in action. Son of William and Alice Fleming, of Railway Cottage, Carlow.

Born in 1891 in Maudlin Street on 07-December-1891, son of William (from Ballyhale) and Alice (from John's Well) Fleming. The Flemings have been traced back to 1766 to Newtown, Neworchard in St Johns Parish. William Fleming - his father was a railway ganger and milesman on the railways in Kilkenny city. Moved to Railway Cottage, They moved to Railway Cottage, Carlow on Friday 2nd of January 1903 where William took over the railway cottage, Carlow and length of railway between milepost 53 to 56. William Fleming kept a notebook on his son's wartime adventures and other bits of information on the 1st world war. Enlisted in the 3rd Battalion (Reserve Force) of the Royal Dublin Fusiliers in Carlow and proceeded for training to Naas on Saturday 25th of July 1908. His number at that time was 4840. Sailed for India on Saturday 19th November 1910 on board the SS Dongola. Transferred at a later time to the Royal

Irish Regiment where his number changed to no 9777. His address in India was: 9777 Pte Thomas Fleming, 1st RIR, Numich, India or Agra, Newmich, India. Thomas Fleming entered into active service in August 1914. At some point he was in England again - his address was 9777, A company, 2nd Royal Irish Regiment, Blackdown, Hants, England. Thomas was killed in action at Hooge, near Ypres on 7th May 1915. His father was notified by the war office on the 10th of June 1915. Grave or Memorial Reference; Panel 33. Cemetery: Ypres (Menin Gate) Memorial in Belgium.

Flood, Myles. Rank; Private. Regiment or Service: Royal Dublin Fusiliers. Unit; 9th Battalion. Service Number; 17402. Date of death; 09/09/1916. Age at death; 30. Born; Carlow. Enlisted; Naas. Residence; Borris, County Carlow. Killed in action. Son of William Flood; husband of Mary Power (formerly Flood), of Burnchurch, Cuffe's Grange, Co. Kilkenny. The Nationalist and Leinster Times, November, 1916. Two Brothers Killed in Action. The death in action has occurred in France of Myles and Patrick Flood (brothers). Aughmaleer (?), County Carlow. The former was killed about three weeks ago, and the latter a week back. Both were serving in the R. I. R (sic)., and their repose was prayed for at Graiguenamanagh Mass on Sunday last. Grave or Memorial Reference; Pier and Face 16 C. Cemetery: Thiepval Memorial in France.

Flood, Patrick. Rank; Private. Regiment or Service: Royal Dublin Fusiliers. Unit; 2nd Battalion. Service Number; 23746. Date of death; 15/10/1916. Born; Graiguenamanagh, County Kilkenny. Enlisted; Carlow. Residence; Borris, County Carlow. Killed in action. In his Will, 06-July-1916, his effects and property were received by;- (Sister) Mary Flood, Balllytiglea, Borris, County Carlow, Ireland. Grave or Memorial Reference; Pier and face 16 C. Cemetery: Thiepval Memorial in France

Flood, Thomas. Rank; Private. Regiment or Service: Royal Irish Regiment. Unit; 6th Battalion. Service Number; 2089. Date of death; 05/04/1917. Age at death; 25. Born; St Mary's, Kilkenny. Enlisted; Kilkenny. Killed in action. Son of John and Mary Flood, of Walkin St., Kilkenny. In his Will, dated 22-December-1915, his effects and property were received by;- (Mother) Mrs Mary Flood, Friary St, Kilkenny, Ireland. Grave or Memorial Reference; I A 23. Cemetery: La Laiterie Military Cemetery in Belgium.

Flowers, Jonathon George. Rank; Gunner. Regiment or Service: Royal Field Artillery. Unit; A Battery, 1st Reserve Brigade. Service Number; 88607. Date of death; 02/06/1918. Age at death;64. Born; Poplar, E. Enlisted; Kilkenny. Died at home. Husband of Mary Flowers, of Barrack St., Kilkenny. Grave or Memorial Reference; In the South West part. Cemetery: Kilkenny (St John) Catholic Churchyard, Kilkenny.

Flynn, John. Rank; Private. Regiment or Service: Royal Irish Regiment. Unit; 2nd Battalion. Service Number; 8786. Date of death; 02/06/1916. Born; St John's, Carrick-on-Suir. Enlisted; Carrick-on-Suir. Died of wounds at home. Grave or Memorial Reference; Near the South East boundary. Cemetery: Owning Cemetery, near Piltown Co Kilkenny.

Fogarty, Thomas. Rank; Private. Regiment or Service: Leinster Regiment. Unit; 2nd Battalion. Service Number; 6073. Date of death; 15/11/1914. Born; Kilkenny. Enlisted; Kilkenny. Died of wounds. Grave or Memorial Reference; IX B 74. Cemetery: Cite Bonjean Military Cemetery, Armentaires in France.

Foley, James. Rank; Driver. Regiment or Service: Royal Army Service Corps. Unit; Horse Transport Depot (Orleans). Service Number; T/34147. Date of death; 02/05/1915. Age at death; 31. Born; Kilkenny. Enlisted; Swansea. Residence; Rotherham. Died. Son of Edward and Elizabeth Foley, of 9, Beever St., Goldthorpe, Nr. Rotherham, Yorks. Grave or Memorial Reference; Panel 30 and 31. Cemetery: Pozieres Memorial in France.

Foley, James. Rank; Private. Regiment or Service: Royal Irish Regiment. Unit; 7th Battalion. Service Number; 5749. Date of death; 21/03/1918. Born; Kilkenny. Enlisted; Scunthorpe, Lincs. Residence; Kilkenny. Killed in action. Grave or Memorial Reference; Div. 19. C. 2. Cemetery: Ste. Marie Cemetery, Le Havre in France.

Foley, Patrick. Rank; Private. Regiment or Service: Royal Irish Regiment. Unit; 2nd Battalion. Service Number; 4136. Date of death; 24/04/1915. Age at death; 25. Born; Lisdowney. County Kilkenny. Enlisted; Kilkenny. Residence; Vallyconra, County Kilkenny. Killed in action. Son of Patrick and Kate Foley (nee Crosby), of Freshford, Co. Kilkenny. After his death his effects and property were received by;- (Wife) Mrs Kate Foley, Freshford, County Kilkenny,. Grave or Memorial Reference; Panel 4. Cemetery: Ploegsteert Memorial in Belgium.

Franklin, Thomas. Rank; Sergeant. Regiment or Service: Royal Dublin Fusiliers. Unit; 10th Battalion. Service Number; 9313. Date of death; 15/04/1917. Born; Kilkenny. Enlisted; Kilkenny. Residence; Dublin. Killed in action. Irish Times. Franklin-reported wounded and missing April 15, 1917, now reported to be killed in action on or about the same date, Sergeant T J Franklin, Royal Dublin Fusiliers, husband of Mary Franklin, 16 Gulliston Place, Rathmines, Dublin. Grave or Memorial Reference; Bay 9. Cemetery: Arras Memorial in France.

G

Gardiner, Joseph. Rank; Private. Regiment or Service: Royal Irish Regiment. Unit; 2nd Battalion. Service Number; 1076/10765. Date of death; 24/08/1914. Age at death; 18. Born; Castlecomer, County Kilkenny. Enlisted; Carlow. Residence; Castlecomer. Killed in action at Mons. Son of Joseph and Sarah Gardiner, of Chatsworth St., Castlecomer, Co. Kilkenny. In his Will, dated 07-August-1914, his effects and property were received by;- Mrs J Gardiner, Chasworth St, Castlecomer, County Kilkenny, Ireland. Kilkenny People, April, 1915. Private Joseph Gardiner, Castlecomer. I am sorry to have to say that Mr Joseph Gardiner, father of Private Joseph Gardiner, of the Royal Irish Regiment, received a communication from Headquarters, Cork, in which it is said Private Gardiner was "unofficially reported killed in action at Mons. At present it is impossible to obtain official confirmation, but it is feared that it is probably true." This news will be very much regretted by all who knew young Joe Gardiner, who was in the Post Office service and while at home in Castlecomer, was a universal favourite with everyone with whom he came into contact. We hope that the report may not be correct and that Joe will be back again, although the parents, have not had any word of him or from him until this communication, for over four months. Notes; Number listed as 1076 (CWGC) 10765 (SDGW). Grave or Memorial Reference; II B 12. Cemetery: St Symphorien Military Cemetery in Belgium.

Gaule, John. Rank; Private. Regiment or Service: Machine Gun Corps. Unit; Infantry. Service Number; 29019. Date of death; 04/07/1918. Age at death; 21. Born; Glenmore, County Kilkenny. Enlisted; Waterford. Residence; Glenmore, County Kilkenny. Died in hospital. Son of Richard Gaule, of Haggard, Glenmore. In his Will, dated 02-June1916, his effects and property were received by;- (Father) Richard Gaule, Haggard, Glenmore, County Kilkenny, Ireland. Notes; Formerly he was with the Royal Irish Rifles where his number was 5343. Died in Belton Park Military Hospital, Grantham. Grave or Memorial Reference; On the South East boundary. Cemetery: Glenmore (St James) Catholic Churchyard, County Kilkenny.

Geoghegan/Geohegan, Martin. Rank; Private. Regiment or Service: Royal Irish Regiment. Unit; 6th Battalion. Service Number; 5312. Date of death; 05/08/1917. Age at death; 24. Born; Graigue, Kilkenny. Enlisted; Kilkenny. Died of wounds at home. Husband of Johannah Geoghegan, of Graiguenamanagh, Co. Kilkenny. Notes; Name listed as Geoghegan (CWGC) Geohegan (SDGW). Grave or Memorial Reference; East of ruins. Cemetery: Tinnahinch (St Michael's) Cemetery in Carlow.

Gethin, Percy Francis. Rank; Second Lieutenant. Regiment or Service: Devonshire Regiment. Unit; 3ed Battalion attached to the 8th Battalion. Date of death; 28/06/1916. Age at death; 42. Killed in action. Son of Capt. George Gethin (late 20th Regiment) and Mabel Gethin. An artist. As Second Lieutenant Gethin is commemorated on the Connellan Memorial Window in St Canice's Church, Kilkenny, I include him for your reference… To the Glory of God and in loving memory of four brave soldiers. Grandsons of the late Peter Connellan of Coolmore in this county. Who after distinguished service laid down their lives for King and Country…. Percy Francis Gethin. Sec'd. Lieut. Devonshire Regt. Second son of Capt. Gethin. Killed near Mametz. June xxviii,

MCMXVI. Aged xlii years. Non Sibi sed Patriae. Grave or Memorial Reference; B 4. Cemetery: Devonshire Cemetery, Mametz, Somme, France.

Gleeson, Cornelius. Rank; Lance Corporal. Regiment or Service: Royal Irish Regiment. Unit; 1st Battalion. Service Number; 2927. Date of death; 13/03/1915. Age at death; 35. Born; St Canice's, Kilkenny. Enlisted; Kilkenny. Killed in action. Son of James and Bridget Gleeson, of 26, Upper Walkin St., Kilkenny; husband of Kate Gleeson. Served in the South African Campaign. Kilkenny People, April, 1915. Kilkenny Soldier Killed in Action, Mrs Gleeson, wife of Lance Corporal Gleeson, 4th Battalion, Royal Irish Regiment, has received an announcement from the War Office of the death in action of her gallant husband. Deceased went through all the South African War, had the South African Medals, Long Service and Good Conduct Medals. He was two years and eight months in South Africa. He joined the colours at the mobilisation on the outbreak of the present war, and served at Queenstown until seven weeks ago, when he was sent to the front. He fell in action at St Eloi. He leaves five children. Lord Kitchener has communicated with the widow expressing his own sympathy and that of the King. Kilkenny Journal, April, 1915. Kilkenny Soldier Killed in Action. Saturday's casualty list contained the name of Lance-Corporal Gleeson, of the 4th Battalion Royal Irish Regiment, who fell in action at St Eloi. Deceased, who was a native of Walkin Street, Kikenny, went through all the South African War, and had the South African Medals as well as long service and goods conduct medals. He joined the colours on the mobilisation at the outbreak of the present war, and served at Queenstown until about eight weeks ago, when he was sent to the front. Grave or Memorial Reference; Panel 33. Cemetery: Ypres (Menin Gate) Memorial in Belgium.

Gleeson, John. Rank; Private. Regiment or Service: Royal Munster Fusiliers. Unit; Depot. Service Number; 18398. Date of death; 29/05/1918. Born; Paulstown, County Kilkenny. Enlisted; Kilkenny. Residence; Whitehall, County Kilkenny. Died of wounds in the Military Hospital Hackney. Son of James Gleeson, of Ballinballey, Whitehall, Co. Kilkenny. In his Will, dated 02-September-1917, his effects and property were received by;- (Father) James Gleeson, Ballinabbey Whitehall, County Kilkenny. Notes; Formerly he was with the Royal Dublin Fusiliers where his number was 30209. Grave or Memorial Reference; XII C 13 B. Cemetery: Brookwood Military Cemetery, UK.

Gleeson, Kieran/Kiernan. Rank; Sapper. Regiment or Service: Royal Engineers. Unit; 9th Field Company. Service Number; 23026. Date of death; 21/12/1916. Age at death; 22. Born; Slieverue, County Kilkenny. Enlisted; Waterford. Died of wounds. Son of James and Annie Gleeson, of Ballyvalla, Ferrybank, Waterford. Grave or Memorial Reference; II D 23. Cemetery: Peronne Road Cemetery, Maricourt in France.

Gleeson, Richard. Rank; Private. Regiment or Service: Royal Dublin Fusiliers. Unit; 1st Battalion. Service Number; 11481. Date of death; 04/09/1918. Born; Paulstown, County Kilkenny. Enlisted; Carlow. Residence; Paulstown. Killed in action. He won the Military Medal and is listed in the London Gazette. In his Will, dated 14-January-1915, his effects and property were received by;- (father) James Gleeson, Ballinvalley, Paulstown, County Kilkenny, Ireland. Grave or Memorial Reference; II M 7. Cemetery: Trois Arbres Cemetery, Steenerck in France.

Glennon, Jeremiah. Rank; Private. Regiment or Service: Royal Irish Regiment. Unit; 6th Battalion. Service Number; 5344. Date of death; 09/09/1916. Born; Castlecomer, County Kilkenny. Enlisted; Kilkenny. Residence; Castlecomer. Killed in action. After his death his effects and property were received by;- (Cousin) Miss Bridget Sally (Matron), Fever Hospital, Castle Comer, County Kilkenny, Ireland. Grave or Memorial Reference; Pier and Face 3 A. Cemetery: Thiepval Memorial in France.

Glennon, William. Rank; Sergeant. Regiment or Service: Royal Dublin Fusiliers. Unit; 2nd Battalion. Service Number; 43016. Date of death; 12/10/1916. Age at death;27. Born; Rospercon, County Kilkenny. Enlisted; Dublin. Residence; Kilkenny. Killed in action. Son of John and Jane Glennon (nee Waldron), of 8, Ballybought St., Kilkenny. Volunteered from R. I. Constabulary. Notes; Formerly he was with the Royal Irish Regiment where his number was 9808. Grave or Memorial Reference; Pier and Face 16 C. Cemetery: Thiepval Memorial in France.

Gorman, John. Rank; Private. Regiment or Service: Royal Irish Regiment. Unit; 2nd Battalion. Service Number; 6323. Date of death; 03/12/1914. Born; St John's, Kilkenny. Died of wounds. Grave or Memorial Reference; V C 10. Cemetery: Belgrade Cemetery in Belgium.

Goulding, William Patrick. Rank; Second Officer. Regiment or Service: Mercantile Marine. Unit; S. S."War Song" (London). Service Number; 6517 17/18. Date of death; 15/01/1918. Age at death;52. Son of Richard and Mary Goulding of St. Kevins Rd., South Circular Rd., Dublin Ireland; husband of Mary Goulding, of The Butts Gardens, Kilkenny, Ireland. Irish Independent; Goulding-January 15, 1918, Captain W P Goulding, M. M. S., drowned (ship sunk by gunfire), son of the lare Richard Goulding, 19 St Kevin's Road, S. C/Road. R. I. P. Irish Independent; Goulding-January 15, 1918, Captain W P Goulding, M. M. S., drowned (ship sunk by gunfire), dearly loved brother of Mrs Howard, 3 Eagle Terrace, Terenure. R. I. P. Grave or Memorial Reference; Collective Grave. Cemetery: L'Isle De-Sein New Communal Cemetery, Finistere, France.

Grace, James. Rank; Private. Regiment or Service: Irish Guards. Unit; 1st Battalion. Service Number; 4794. Date of death; 10/07/1917. Born; Dunnamaggan, County Kilkenny. Enlisted; Kilkenny. Died. Brother of Miss Mary Grace, of Maxtown, Callan, Co. Kilkenny. Grave or Memorial Reference; VIII C 7. Cemetery: St Pierre Cemetery, Amiens in France.

Grace, John. Rank; Private. Regiment or Service: Household Cavalry and Cavalry of the line including the Yeomanry and Imperial Camel Corps. Unit; City of London Yeomanry (Rough Riders). Service Number; 2889. Date of death; 26/02/1915. Age at death;24. Enlisted; Putney. Residence; Kilkenny. Died at home. Cemetery: Unknown

Grace, Thomas Joseph. Rank; Sergeant Major. Regiment or Service: South African Army. Unit; 5th Mounted Rifles (Imperial Light Horse), E Squadron. Service Number; 207. Date of death; 25/11/1914. Age at death; 41. Born; Pleberstown, Thomastown. Died of wounds. Husband of Jacoba Johanna Robbertse (formerly Grace, nee Theron), of Klipkop, Hoewal, Transvaal. Kilkenny Journal, March, 1915. Thomastown Man's Death in South Africa. The death is announced of Mr Thomas Grace, which occurred in South Africa as the result of wounds received in action. Mr Grace, who was a native of Pleberstown, Thomastown, joined the South African Police Force at the termination of the Boer War, previous to which he was a member of a Cavalry regiment. He attained to the rank of Head Constable in the police force, from which he retired a few years ago. At the outbreak of the present war he volunteered for active service and joined the South African defence Force. He was sent with his regiment to German South West Africa where he was severely wounded, from the effects of which he died. Mr Grace was about forty years of age and settled in South Africa after retiring from the police force. Notes; Born 1875. Cemetery: Rooidan Farm Cemetery, Upington, Northern Cape, South Africa.

Grace, William. Rank; Corporal. Regiment or Service: Royal Irish Regiment. Unit; 2nd Battalion. Service Number; 3990. Date of death; 19/10/1914. Age at death;20. Born; St Patrick's, Kilkenny. Enlisted; Kilkenny. Killed in action. Son of James and Ellen Grace, of Jail Street, Kilkenny. Grave or Memorial Reference; Panel 11 and 12. Cemetery: Le Touret Memorial in France.

Grady, John. Rank; Private. Regiment or Service: Royal Irish Fusiliers. Unit; 5th Battalion. Service Number; 12702. Date of death; 07/12/1915. Born; Castlecomer, County Kilkenny. Enlisted; Larkhill, Lanarkshire. Residence; Castlecomer. Killed in action in Salonika. Cemetery: Doiran Memorial in Greece.

Graham, George. Rank; Corporal. Regiment or Service: Seaforth Highlanders. Unit; 7th Battalion. Service Number; S/40378. Date of death; 11/04/1918. Born; Long Easter, Kilderry, Kilkenny. Enlisted; Fort George, Inverness-Shire. Killed in action. Son of Mrs. Jessie Graham, of 10, Murray St., Tain, Ross-shire. Grave or Memorial Reference; Panels 132 to 135 and 162A. Cemetery: Tyne Cot Memorial in Belgium.

Grant, Edmund. Rank; Private. Regiment or Service: Leinster Regiment. Unit; 1st Battalion. Service Number; 7328. Date of death; 30/12/1917. Born; Kilkenny. Enlisted; Cardiff, Glamorganshire. Drowned in the loss of H T "Aragon". In his Will, 20-June-1915, his effects and property were received by;- Mrs William Coughlan Kilmacow, Waterford, Ireland. Cemetery: Chatby Memorial in Egypt.

Grant, Patrick. Rank; Private. Regiment or Service: Royal Irish Regiment. Unit; 4th Battalion. Service Number; 4807. Date of death; 25/04/1915. Born; Glenmore, County Kilkenny. Enlisted; Waterford. Residence; Glenmore, County Kilkenny. Died at home. Son of Mrs. M. Grant, of Glenmore, Co. Kilkenny. Grave or Memorial Reference; B 13 26. Cemetery: Cobh Old Church Cemetery, County Cork.

Green, Michael. Rank; Private. Regiment or Service: Royal Irish Regiment. Unit; 2nd Battalion. Service Number; 3100. Date of death; 16/08/1918. Age at death; 36. Enlisted; The Curragh, County Kildare. Residence; Piltown, County Kilkenny. Killed in action. Son of James and Mary Green. Grave or Memorial Reference; Pier and Face 3 A. Cemetery: Thiepval Memorial in France.

Greene, Godfrey Robert. Rank; Second Lieutenant. Regiment or Service: Machine Gun Corps. Unit; Infantry, 116th Company. Date of death; 03/09/1916. Age at death;20. Killed in action. Son of the Rev. Canon Godfrey George and Florence Anna Greene, of Borris-in-Ossory, Queen's Co. Grave or Memorial Reference; Pier and Face 5 C and 12 C. Cemetery: Thiepval Memorial in France

Gregory, Godfrey Levinge. Rank; Captain. Regiment or Service: Durham Light Infantry. Unit; 6th Battalion. Date of death; 05/01/1918. Age at death; 43. Son of Henry Charles and Charlotte Ann Gregory, of West Court, Callan, Co. Kilkenny. Served in the South African Campaign. Grave or Memorial Reference; Special Plot 5. Cemetery: Wokingham (St Sebastian) Churchyard, Berkshire, UK.

Gregory, Harry William. Rank; Lieutenant Commander. Regiment or Service: Royal Navy. Unit; H. M. S."Hoverfly.". Date of death; 10/09/1917. Age at death;31. Son of Mrs. A. F. Gregory, of "Kia Ora," Montpellier Park, Llandrindod Wells, and the late H. Charles Gregory. Native of Callan, Co. Kilkenny. The Weekly Irish Times. Ireland's Roll of Honour. October 13, 1917. Lieutenant Commander Harry William Gregory, R. N., who died on 10th September at the british General Hospital, Basra, of pneumonia, was the son of Mr and Mrs Henry Charles Gregory, West Court, Callan, County Kilkenny. He was 31 years of age. The Weekly Irish Times. Ireland's Roll of Honour. September 22, 1917. Lieutenant Commander Harry William Gregory, R. N., who died of pneumonia at Basra on 10th September, aged 32, was the son of Mr Henry Charles Gregory and Mrs Gregory, of West Court, Callan, County Kilkenny. Weekly Irish Times. September 22, 1917. Gregory-September 10, at British General Hospital,

Rouen, of pneumonia, Harry William Gregory, Lieutenant Commander, R. N., son of Henry Charles Gregory and Mrs Gregory, West Court, Callan, County Kilkenny. Grave or Memorial Reference; I C 14. Cemetery: Basra War Cemetery in Iraq. He is also commemorated on the Great War Memorial in St Canice's Cathedral, Kilkenny…'To the Glory of God and in loving memory of the following members of the Diocese of Ossory who gave their lives for their country in the Great War 1914-1918'.

Griffin, John. Rank; Boy Telegraphist. Regiment or Service: Royal Australian Navy. Unit; H. M. A. S."Melbourne.". Service Number; J/36937. Date of death; 10/04/1917. Age at death; 18. Son of Patrick and Annie Griffin. Native of Callan, Kilkenny, Ireland. Grave or Memorial Reference; General L. 2. 0. Cemetery: Ford Park Cemetery (Formerly Plymouth Old Cemetery) (Pennycomequick) UK.

Griffin/Griffen, John. Rank; Private. Regiment or Service: Devonshire Regiment. Unit; 9th Battalion. Service Number; 14441. Date of death; 30/09/1915. Age at death;34. Born; Kilkenny, Ireland. Enlisted; Penrhiwceiber, Wales. Killed in action. Griffin (CWGC) Griffen (SDGW, IMR), Son of Thomas and Catherine Griffin, of Upper Patrick Street, Kilkenny. Grave or Memorial Reference; Panel 35 to 37. Cemetery: Loos Memorial in France.

Hackett, Jeremiah. Rank; Bombardier. Regiment or Service: Royal Garrison Artillery. Unit; 253rd Battery. Service Number; 42228. Date of death; 20/04/1918. Born; Dublin. Enlisted; Liverpool. Died of wounds. Kilkenny People, May-1918;-Sympmathy. —The Slievardagh Rural District Cpuncil (Mr J. L. Norton presiding), on the motion of Mr John Holden, seconded by Mr John Kelly, tendered sincere sympathy to their respected county Surveyor, Mr E. A. Hackett in his recent bereavement occasioned by the death of his son at the front. Grave or Memorial Reference; XB 28. Cemetery: Mendingham Military Cemetery in Belgium.

Hackett, Thomas. Rank; Private. Regiment or Service: Royal Dublin Fusiliers. Unit; C Company, 2nd Battalion. Service Number; 18034. Date of death; 07/07/1915. Age at death;19. Born; The Butts, Kilkenny. Enlisted; Kilkenny. Killed in action. Son of Mary Hackett, of Canice''s Well Street, Kilkenny. Grave or Memorial Reference; Collective Grave I C 2. Cemetery: Bard Cottage Cemetery in Belgium.

Hall, Frederick William. Rank; Company Sergeant Major. Regiment or Service: Canadian Infantry (Manitoba Regiment). Unit; 8th Battalion. Service Number; 1539. Date of death; 25/04/1915. Age at death; 28. Killed in action. Son of Mary Hall, of 43, Union Rd., Leytonstone, London, and the late Bmdr. F. Hall. Next of kin listed as (mother), Mrs M Hall, 260 Young Street, Winnipeg. Place of birth, Kilkenny, Ireland. Date of birth, 21-February-1885. Occupation on enlistment, Clerk. Belonged to the 106th Light Infantry prior to enlistment and previous military experience of 12 years, four months with the 1st Cameronians. Place and date of enlistment, Valcartier, 26-September-1914. Address on enlistment,. Height, 5 feet, 8 inches. Complexion, ruddy. Eyes, brown. Hair, auburn. The London Gazette, No. 29202. Dated 23rd June;-"On 24th April, 1915, in the neighbourhood of Ypres, when a wounded man who was lying some 15 yards from the trench called for help, Company Serjeant-Major Hall endeavoured to reach him in the face of a very heavy enfilade fire which was being poured in by the enemy. The first attempt failed, and a non-commissioned officer and private soldier who were attempting to give assistance were both wounded. Company Serjeant-Major Hall then made a second most gallant attempt, and was in the act of lifting up the wounded man to bring him in when he fell mortally wounded in the head.". Grave or Memorial Reference; Panel 24 - 26 - 28 –. Cemetery: Ypres (Menin Gate) Memorial in Belgium.

Hall, Samuel George. Rank; Private. Regiment or Service: Inniskilling Fusiliers. Service Number; 2707. Date of death; 22/11/1919. Age at death;39. Enlisted; Kilkenny City. Died of illness contracted on active service. Son of the Richard and Isabella Caroline Hall, brother of Isabella Caroline Hall. Listed in the 1901 Census in Greensbridge Street, Kilkenny. Weekly Irish Times. November 29, 1919. Roll of Honour. Hall-November 22, 1919, at the residence of his brother, Winchester, of illness contracted on active service, Samuel G, late Inniskilling Fusiliers, youngest son of the late Richard and Isabella Hall, Kilkenny. Cemetery: Unknown

Hanley, John. Rank; Private. Regiment or Service: Royal Marine Light Infantry. Unit; Plymouth Battalion. R. N. Division. Service Number; PLY/16284. Date of death; 07/10/1914. Age at death; 22. Born; Castlecomer, County Kilkenny. Killed or died as a direct result of enemy action. Son of Timothy and Ellen Hanley, of Skehana Castlecomer, Co. Kilkenny. Notes; D. O. B. 29/08/1890. Grave or Memorial Reference; Plot II A. Cemetery: Schoonselhof Cemetery, Antwerp, Belgium.

Hanlon, Patrick. Rank; Private. Regiment or Service: Leinster Regiment. Unit; 2nd Battalion. Service Number; 5488. Date of death; 05/03/1917. Born; Limerick. Enlisted; Kilkenny. Killed in action. After his death, his effects and property were received by;- (Mother) Mrs Mary Hanlon, 32 Wolfe Tone St, Kilkenny, Ireland. Limerick Chronicle, August, 1915. Letter from Wounded Limerick Soldier. Our Glin correspondent writes;- -The following is a copy of a letter received my Mr John Conway, Clerk of the Glin District School, from Lance Corporal Hanlon, 2nd Leinster regiment;--"Dear Sir—Just a few lines to let you know how I am getting on. I would havce written before now, but my hand was very painful, and is still very painful, as some pf the wrist and part of the palm are blown away. There is a terrible hole. I expect at one time to have the hand cut off, but the doctors are trying to save it. I am quite satisfied witrh having escaped with these wounds, for I have seen men's heads knocked off. I thank God for having my life saved for my wife and little children. I always prayed for that. I have had many narrow escapes. I expect to be here at the base hospital for the next three weeks, and after that I hope, if all goes well, to go home. I have a few souvenirs which will interest you. I hope all is well. Tell all the boys I have been asking for them. I have lost a lot of blood, and am weak, but I understand I am to go under an operation when fit. I am glad to have the use of my right hand, so that I can write you this.". Notes; Formerly he was with the Royal Irish Regiment where his number was 5488. Grave or Memorial Reference; II D 10. Cemetery: Bois-De-Noulette British Cemetery, Aiz-Noulette in France.

Hannon, William. Rank: Signal Boy. Regiment or Service: Royal Naval Reserve. Unit; H.M.S. Vivid. Date of Death:13/09/1915. Age at Death,15. Service No:2219SB. Born in nKilorglin, County Kerry. Died from disease. Supplementary information; Son of William Hannon, Mullinavat,County Kilkenny. Grave or Memorial Reference: General L 14 23. Cemetery: Plymouth (Ford Park) Cemetery.

Hanrahan, Matthew. Rank; Private. Regiment or Service: Irish Guards. Unit; 1st Battalion. Service Number; 4664. Date of death; 19/05/1915. Born; Stoneyford, County Kilkenny. Enlisted; Thomastown. Died of wounds. Grave or Memorial Reference; I B 15. Cemetery: Aire Communal Cemetery in France.

Harris, Albert. Rank; Private. Regiment or Service: Royal Irish Regiment. Unit; 2nd Battalion. Service Number; 7752. Date of death; 05/07/1916. Age at death;22. Born; St Anthony's Forest gate, Middlesex. Enlisted; Kilkenny. Residence; Kilkenny. Killed in action. Grave or Memorial Reference; Pier and Face 3 A. Cemetery: Thiepval Memorial, France.

Hart/Harte, Patrick. Rank; Private. Regiment or Service: Army Service Corps. Unit; Horse Transport. Service Number; T/39364. Date of death; 12/04/1918. Age at death; 26. Born; Cleara, Kilkenny. Enlisted; Tipperary. Residence; Kilkenny. Died. Hart (SDGW) Harte (CWGC). Son of William and Annie Harte, of Maudlin St., Kilkenny. In his Will, dated 18-June-1916, his effects and property were received by;- (Mother) Mrs Hannah Harte, Maudlin Street, Kilkenny, Ireland. (An article about his brother William, who survived the war) ;-Kilkenny Journal, May-1915;-Kilkenny Soldier's Thrilling Experience. Twice Captured by the Huns and Escaped. Private William Harte, of Patrick Street, has arrived in this city, on leave, having had a most thrilling experience at the front. Private Harte, who is son of the late Mr William Harte, of Patrick Street, is attached to the Connaught Rangers, and at the outbreak of the war, left with his regiment for the front. At the historic retreat from Mons, he was taken prisoner by the Huns, and brought to Brussels, from where he escaped, but unfortunately was re-captured. From Brussels he was conveyed to Germany and placed in a detention camp there. His captors, no doubt, thought that once he was in their own country, escape was impossible. But such was not the case. Not to be deterred Private Harte set to work to devise some means of regaining his freedom, and, with the connivance of two Frenchmen, a plan of escape was decided upon. Their idea was to "silence" the sentry—and silenced he was, How harte and the Frenchmen escaped would read like a story of the Wild West, but suffice to say they made their way to Holland, and from thence Private Harte set sail for dear old Ireland and arrived in his native city last week. Notes; Formerly he was with the 4th Royal Irish Regiment (Special reserve) where his number was 413570 (CWGC) 4/3570 (SDGW). Grave or Memorial Reference; II B 29. Cemetery: Bac-Du-Sud British Cemetery, Bailleulval in France

Lieutenant Colonel Hart McHarg, from 'Bond of Sacrifice'.

Hart-McHarg, William Frederick Richard. Rank; Lieutenant Colonel. Regiment or Service: Canadian Infantry. Unit; 7th Battalion, British Columbia Regiment. Date of death; 24/04/1915. Age at death;46. Only son of Maj. W. Hart-McHarg (Essex Regt.) and Jane Scott Hart-McHarg, of 18, Cambridge Gardens, Hastings, England. Bond of Sacrifice, Volume 2. . was one of the first senior overseas officers to fall in the war. He was the only son of the late Major W. Hart-McHarg, Essex (44th) Regiment, and of Mrs Hart-McHarg, now residing at 113, Clifton Hill, St John's Wood, London, and formerly of Bruges, Belgium. He was born at Kilkenny on the 16th February, 1869, and was educated at Bruges. Colonel Hart-McHarg had lived in Canada for the last thirty years, and was a barrister-at-law and solicitor of the Supreme Court of British Columbia, practising at Vancouver as a partner in the firm of Messrs Abbott, Hart-McHarg and Duncan. He had served for twenty years in the Canadian Militia, passing through all ranks from Private to Commanding Officer. He took part in the South African War with the first contingent of the Royal Canadian Regiment, and was present at Paardeberg, Driefontein, Johannesburg, and in the Cape Colony, receiving the Queen's medal with four clasps inscribed with the above names. He was one of the Canadian contingent sent over to represent the Colony at the Coronation of H. M. King George V. He was a well-known rifle shot, and won the match at Camp Perry, Ohio, in 1913, becoming the individual champion of the world by making a total of 220 out of a possible 225 at the 800, 900, and 1, 000 yards ranges. In the year he won the Governor-General's Gold Medal at the Dominion Rifle Association's meeting, and was a member of the Canadian Bisley team on several occasions. It was in keeping with his character that on the outbreak of the war with Germany, Lieutenant-Colonel Hart-McHarg, was among the first Canadians to respond to the Empire's call. Almost at once he became a Lieutenant-Colonel in Command of the 7th Battalion, which he fitted and hardened at Valcartier, and then took for a post-graduate course to Salisbury Plain. He was wounded on the 23rd April, and died the next day, near Ypres. He was mentioned in Sir John French's Despatch of 31st May, 1915. From De Ruvigny's Roll of Honour. Only son of the late Hon. Major William Hart-McHarg, 44th (Essex) regiment, by his wife, Jane Scott (10, Netherhall Gardens, N. W.) Daughter of the late Captain Thomsett, 44th Regiment. Born in Kilkenny, 16-February-1869. Educated at Brughes; went to Canada about 1885 and was a Barrister-at-Law and Solicitor of the Supreme Court of British Columbia, practicing at Vancouver, where he was a partner in the firm of Abbott, Hart-McHarg & Duncan. He joined the Canadian Militia about 1895 as a private and rose to the command of the 7th (Vancouver) Regiment, receiving the medal for 20 years service. He served in the South African War, 1900-2, with the first contingent (Royal Canadian Regiment) and obtained the Queen's medal with four clasps (Paardeberg, Driefontein, Johannesburg and Cape Colony) and in 1911 was one of the Canadian cintingent present at the Coronation of King George V. On the outbreak of the European War, Lieut-Colonel Hart-McHarg was given command of the 7th Regiment, and came over with the first contingent and went to Fraqnce in February-1915. At the Second Battle of Ypres, the 7th formed part of the 3rd Brigade, and on Friday-23-April, occupied a position on the forward crest of a ridge, with its left flank near St Julien. This position was severely shelled by the Germans during that day, and about 4. 30, Colonel Hart-McHarg, major (now Lieut-Colonel Commanding) Oldum and Lieutenant Mathewson of the Canadian Engineers, went out to reconnoitre the ground. The exact location of the German forces opposed to them was not known, and they moved down the slope to the ruined village of Keerselacre—a distance of about 300 yards—in broad daylight without drawing a shot, but when they reached there they saw the Germans not 100 yards away, and they accordingly turned and began to retire. They were followed by a burst of rapid fire the moment they cleared the shelter of the ruins. Colonel Hart-McHarg and Major Odlum managed to get into a shell-hole near by, but not before the former had been severely wounded. When Major Odlum discovered this, he raced up the hill under heavy fire in search of surgical aid. He found Captain G. Gibson, Medical Officer, 7th Battalion, who, accompanied by Sergeant J Dryden, went down to the shell-hole immediately. They managed to move the Colonel into a ditch and there dressed his wound and remained with him till after dark, when he was carried back to Battalion Headquarters. He died the following day, 24-April-1915, in hospital at Poperinghe, and was buried there in the New Cemetery with Colonel Boyle, who fell the same day. He was mentioned in Despatches (London Gazette, 22-June-1915) for gallant and distinguished conduct in the field. Colonel Hart-McHarg was well known as a fine rifle shot. In 1908 he gained the Gold Medal of Canada after a close contest with three redoubtable antagonists, from Toronto and Ottawa. He had shot several times in Canada's national teams, and had distinguished himself in the matches for the Palma International Trophy against the selected teams of the United States, Great Britain, Australia and other countries. He held the record individual score in the match, being in this respect a world's champion. He had also shot for Canada in the Empire Trophy match, founded by the Australians as an inter-Empire competition. He was a member of the Canadian team at Bisley in 1907, 1910, and 1914, and was spoken of as the next commandant of the Canadian team for Bisley. He shot for the Dominion here in both the Mackinnon and Kolapore Imperial matches, and in 1910 he tied for the Prince of Wales's Prize with the British Army champion, the famous Captain Wallingford, who is now with the New Zealand Force. Each scored 85, the highest possible, with 17 bull's-eyes at 300 and 600 yards. Colonel Hart-McHarg lost on shooting off the tic, but he won the Bronze Cross of the Bisley Grand Aggregate. In August-1913, he won the Governor-General's prize for the second time—the Blue Riband—at the Dominion of Canada rifle meeting at Ottowa and the Long Range Championship of the World with army rifle at the International matches, Camp Perry, Ohio. Grave or Memorial Reference; II M 3. Cemetery: Poperinghe Old Military Cemetery, Poperinge, West-Vlaanderen, Belgium.

Hayden, Edward. Rank; Private. Regiment or Service: Royal Irish Regiment. Unit; 6th Battalion. Service Number; 5274. Date of death; 09/09/1916. Born; Slieverue, County Kilkenny. Enlisted; New Ross, County Wexford. Killed in action. In his Will, dated 04-July-1916, his effects and property were received by;- (Uncle) Mr Pierce, Fleming, Kilbui, Stoneyford, County Kilkenny, Ireland. Grave or Memorial Reference; Pier and Face 3 A. Cemetery: Thiepval Memorial in France.

Hayden, George. Rank; Private. Regiment or Service: Royal Inniskilling Fusiliers. Unit; 7th Battalion. Service Number; 27712. Date of death; 22/04/1916. Age at death;21. Born; Johnstown, County Kilkenny. Enlisted; Clonmel, County Tipperary. Died of wounds. Son of Patrick and Catherine Hayden, of Urlingford, Co. Kilkenny. Notes; Formerly he was with the Royal Irish Regiment where his number was 3/9073. Grave or Memorial Reference; Plot D. Row 2. Grave 10. Cemetery: Calais Southern Cemetery in France.

Hayes, Denis Alphonsus. Rank; Private. Regiment or Service: Leinster Regiment. Unit; 7th Battalion. Service Number; 3502. Date of death; 09/07/1916. Age at death; 29. Born; Parteen, County Clare. Enlisted; Camberley, London. Residence; Kilmallock, County Limerick. Died of wounds. Son of Thomas and Mary Hayes, of Bulgaden, Kilmallock, Co. Limerick. Professor in St. Kieran's College, Kilkenny. Limerick Leader,

July, 1916. Bulgaden Man's Death. From Wounds Received in Action. The intelligence has been received of the death at the front, from wounds, of Mr Denis Hayes, of the Leinsters (writes our Kilmallock correspondent). Much sympathy is felt for his parents, Mr and Mrs Thomas Hayes, Bulgaden, and the other members of the family in their bereavement. Grave or Memorial Reference; II C 33. Cemetery: Longuenesse (St Omer) Souvenir Cemetery in France.

Hayes, Michael. Rank; Private. Regiment or Service: Royal Dublin Fusiliers. Unit; 1st Battalion. Service Number; 9749. Date of death; 30/04/1915. Age at death;28. Born; Kilkenny. Enlisted; Carlow. Killed in Action in Gallipoli. Grave or Memorial Reference; Special Memorial, A, 75. Cemetery: V Beach Cemetery in Turkey.

Hayes, Patrick. Rank; Private. Regiment or Service: South Lancashire Regiment. Unit; 2nd Battalion. Service Number; 7663. Date of death; 24/10/1914. Age at death; 28. Born; Kilkenny. Enlisted; Kilkenny. Killed in action. Husband of Mrs. M. Kavanagh (formerly Hayes), of Green's Hill, Kilkenny. Grave or Memorial Reference; Panel 23. Cemetery: Le Touret Memorial In France.

Healy, John. Rank; Private. Regiment or Service: Royal Irish Regiment. Unit; 1st Battalion. Service Number; 9367. Date of death; 16/02/1915. Born; Thomastown, County Kilkenny. Enlisted; Clonmel, County Tipperary. Residence; Enniscorthy, County Wexford. Died of wounds. In his Will, 13-January-1915, his effects and property were received by Mrs Mary Coleman, Rathnure, Enniscourty, County Wexford. Notes; Died of wounds at 81st F A Hospital, RAMC. Grave or Memorial Reference; Panel 33. Cemetery: Ypres (Menin Gate) Memorial in Belgium.

Heffernan, James. Rank; Private. Regiment or Service: Royal Irish Regiment. Unit; 2nd Battalion. Service Number; 4488. Date of death; 22/10/1914. Age at death; 22. Born; Drumgoole, County Kilkenny. Enlisted; Kilkenny. Residence; Drumgoole, Castlecomer, County Kilkenny. Died. Son of Mark and Bridget Heffernan, of Drumgoole, Castlecomer, Co. Kilkenny. Grave or Memorial Reference; I G 22. Cemetery: Rue-Petillon Military Cemetery, Fleurbaix, Pas-De-Calais, France.

Heffernan, Patrick. Rank; Private. Regiment or Service: Irish Guards. Unit; 1st Battalion. Service Number; 11743. Date of death; 09/10/1917. Age at death;17. Born; Windgap, Kilkenny. Enlisted; Carrick-on-Suir. Killed in action. Son of Michael and Mary Heffernan, of Cussane Lodge, Carrick-on-Suir, Co. Tipperary. Munster Express, January, 1918. Missing. Private Patrick Heffernan, Irish Guards, who belongs to Cussane, has been missing since October 9th. Any reader who may be in a position to give information regarding him would greatly alleviate the worries of his mother by communicating with her. Grave or Memorial Reference; Panel 10 to 11. Cemetery: Tyne Cot Memorial in Belgium.

Heffernan, Robert. Rank; Lance Corporal. Regiment or Service: Royal Dublin Fusiliers. Unit; 8th Battalion. Service Number; 18841. Date of death; 30/04/1916. Born; Freshford, County Kilkenny. Enlisted; Kilkenny. Died of wounds. Grave or Memorial Reference; A 20 15. Cemetery: St Sever Cemetery, Rouen in France.

Hennebry, Maurice. Rank; Donkeyman. Regiment or Service: Mercantile Marine. Unit; S. S."Formby" (Glasgow). Date of death; 16/12/1917. Age at death;52. Son of the late Patrick and Ellen Hennebry; husband of Bridget Hennebry, of Slieverue, Kilmurry, Co. Kilkenny. Born at Roachestown. Cemetery: Tower Hill Memorial UK.

Hennebry, Michael. Rank; Lance Corporal. Regiment or Service: Leinster Regiment. Unit; 7th Battalion. Service Number; 4946. Date of death; 08/03/1917. Age at death; 23. Born; Fiddown, County Kilkenny. Enlisted; Carrick-on-Suir. Residence; Fiddown. Killed in action. Son of Philip and Johanna Hennebry, of Clonmore, Piltown, Co. Kilkenny. In his Will, written at Victoria, Barracks, Cork, dated 23-October-1916, his effects and property were received by;- (Mother) Mrs P Hennebry, Clonmore, Piltown, County Kilkenny, Ireland. Grave or Memorial Reference; K 6. Cemetery: Pond Farm Cemetery in Belgium.

Hennebry, Walter. Rank; Fireman. Regiment or Service: Mercantile Marine. Unit; S. S."Formby" (Glasgow). Date of death; 16/12/1917. Age at death;28. Son of Bridget Hennebry, of Slieverue, Kilmurry, Co. Kilkenny, and the late Maurice Hennebry. Born at Rathpatrick. Cemetery: Tower Hill Memorial UK.

Hennessey/Hennessy, Patrick. Rank; Private. Regiment or Service: Royal Irish Regiment. Unit; 2nd Battalion. Service Number; 365. Date of death; 17/02/1917. Age at death; 42. Born; Kilmacow, County Kilkenny. Enlisted; Cork. Residence; Ballyduff, County Waterford. Died. Son of James and Margaret Hennessy, of Co. Kilkenny; husband of Bridget Hennessy, of Ballyduff S. O, Co. Waterford. Grave or Memorial Reference; XXI G 12. Cemetery: Etaples Military Cemetery in France.

Sergeant Henry, from De Ruvigny's Roll of Honour.

Henry, Arhtur Bagnall. Rank; Sergeant. Regiment or Service: Royal Irish Rifles. Unit; 7th Battalion. Service Number; 6142. Date of death; 16/08/1918. Age at death;36. Born; Aghanagh, County Sligo. Enlisted; Boyle. Residence; Benchfield, County Kilkenny. Killed in action. Son of William Henry, of Aghanagh, Ballinafad, Boyle, Co. Roscommon; husband of Lilian E. Rumball (formerly Henry), of Ashley House, Glastonbury, Somerset. After his death his effects and property were received by;- (Wife) Mrs Lillian Henry, Sandfield Cottage, Mallow, County Cork. De Ruvigny's Roll of Honour…. son of the late William Henry, Framer, by his wife, Charlotte (Ballinafad, County Roscommon), daughter of John Bagnall. Born Ballinafad aforesaid, 17-July-1886. Educated at the National School there. Was a Shop Assistant. Enlisted 27-April-1915. Served with the Expeditionary Force in France and Flanders from the following December, and was killed in action at Ypres, 17-August-1917. He married at the Thomastown Parish Church, County Kilkenny, 30-November-1916, Lillian, daughter of William Lecky, of Mallow, Count Cork. Grave or Memorial Reference; Panels 138 to 140 and 162 to 162A and 163A. Cemetery: Tyne Cot Memorial in Belgium.

Heppenstal, George. Rank; Private. Regiment or Service: Yorkshire Hussars Yeomanry. Unit; 2nd/1st Battalion. Service Number; 60817. Date of death; 26/09/1919. Age at death; 22. His death certificate shows he died in the District Hospital in Castlecomer and he was a bachelor. Died from shock due to burns after 1 ½ days in hospital. Grave or Memorial Reference; In the North Part. Cemetery: Castlecomer (St Mary) Church of Ireland Churchyard, Kilkenny.

Higgins, John. Rank; Private. Regiment or Service: Royal Irish Fusiliers. Unit; 1st Battalion. Service Number; 17093. Date of death; 21/03/1918. Born; Kilkenny. Enlisted; Dublin. Residence; Plasmarl, Glamorganshire. Killed in action. Grave or Memorial Reference; II G 12. Cemetery: Grand-Seraucourt British Cemetery in France.

Higgins, Patrick. Rank; Private. Regiment or Service: Royal Irish Regiment. Unit; 2nd Battalion. Service Number; 4158. Date of death; 19/10/1914. Age at death; 23. Born; St Mary's, Kilkenny. Enlisted; Kilkenny. Killed in action. Son of Thomas and Mary Higgins, of Upper Walker Street, Kilkenny. Grave or Memorial Reference; Panel 11 and 12. Cemetery: Le Touret Memorial In France.

Hill, Michael. Rank; Private. Regiment or Service: Royal Irish Regiment. Unit; 2nd Battalion. Service Number; 5665. Date of death; 08/06/1917. Age at death;30. Born; St John's, Kilkenny. Enlisted; Kilkenny. Died of wounds. Son of Kate Hill, of Michael St., Kilkenny. After his death, his effects and property were received by;- (Mother) Mrs Kate Hill, Michael Street, Kilkenny, Ireland. Notes; Died of wounds at the 4th General Hospital, Canniers. Grave or Memorial Reference; XXV H 5. Cemetery: Etaples Military Cemetery in France.

Hoban, Gregory. Rank; Private. Regiment or Service: Irish Guards. Unit; 2nd Battalion. Service Number; 11671. Date of death; 13/09/1917. Born; Gowran, County Kilkenny. Enlisted; Kilkenny. Killed in action. Grave or Memorial Reference; Panel 11 and 12. Cemetery: Tyne Cot Memorial in Belgium.

Hoban, Michael. Rank; Private. Regiment or Service: Irish Guards. Unit; 1st Battalion. Service Number; 11881/11882. Date of death; 01/12/1917. Age at death;21. Enlisted; Carlow. Residence; Desert. County Kilkenny. Died of wounds. Son of William and Ellen Hoban, of Cuffs Grange, Desort, Co. Kilkenny. In his Will, dated 07-November-1917, his effects and property were received by;- Mrs W Hoban, Desart, Cuffesgrange, County Kilkenny, Ireland. Notes; Number listed as 11881 (CWGC) 11882 (SDGW). Died of wounds at the 21st Casualty Clearing Station, France. Grave or Memorial Reference; IV A 28. Cemetery: Rocquigny-Equancourt Road British Cemetery, Manancourt in France.

Hogan, James. Rank; Lance Sergeant. Regiment or Service: East Lancashire Regiment. Unit; 7th Battalion. Service Number; 6059/6959. Date of death; 10/07/1916. Age at death; 41. Born; Callan, County Kilkenny. Enlisted; Manchester. Residence; Andover, Hampshire. Killed in action. His Last Will and Testament (where he is listed Hogan, John, 6959, 9th Battalion,; effects and property were received by;- (Friend) Miss Emyaungman, The Vicarge, Andover. Kilkenny Journal, October, 1915. Five Sons With the Colours. Mr John Bergin, Callan, has already given five sons to the fighting line. One son, John, was killed in France last March; William, Michael and Patrick have been to the front already, and James, who was drill instructor to the Inistioge I. N. V., has lately volunteered. Mr Bergin has also a son-in-law, James Hogan in the trenches. Notes; Number listed as 6059 (SDGW) 6959 (CWGC). Grave or Memorial Reference; VI E 28. Cemetery: Tincourt New British Cemetery in France.

Hogan, Martin. Rank; Private. Regiment or Service: Household Cavalry and Cavalry of the line including the Yeomanry and Imperial Camel Corps. Unit; South Irish Horse. Service Number; 1473. Date of death; 25/10/1917. Age at death;28. Born; Little Bray, Dublin. Enlisted; Dublin. Residence; Collen. Killed in action. Brother of M. Hogan, of Flag Lane, Callan, Kilkenny. Grave or Memorial Reference; III E 28. Cemetery: Canada Farm Cemetery in Belgium.

Hogan, William. Rank; Trooper. Regiment or Service: Household Cavalry and Cavalry of the line including the Yeomanry and Imperial Camel Corps. Unit; Household Battalion. Service Number; 2608. Date of death; 22/12/1917. Born; Kilkenny. Enlisted; London. Residence; London. Died of wounds. Husband of L. Hogan, of 5, Herbert Gardens, Kensal Rise, London. Grave or Memorial Reference; V D 51. Cemetery: Duisans British Cemetery, Etrun in France. Also listed under Leighlinbridge/Old Leighlin on the Great War Memorial, Milford Street, Leighlinbridge, County Carlow.

·Image courtesy of Jim Byrne, Callan.

Holden, Patrick. Rank; Private. Regiment or Service: Machine Gun Corps. Unit; Infantry, 152nd Battalion. Service Number; 8264. Date of death; 08/12/1916. Age at death;28. Born; Callan, County Kilkenny. Enlisted; Callan. Killed in action. Son of James and Bridget Holden, of Bridge St., Callan, Co. Kilkenny. Kilkenny People, February, 1917. From the Prison Camp. I have just read a letter from our old friend, Jack Dormer, who is a prisoner of was for the past two and a half years in Germany. Jack appears to be, as ever, full of liveliness of spirits and cheer. He says in his letter that he recently saw Paddy Phelan and Paddy Holden, and they both were in good health. We are all glad of that, and we hope it will be true of them until the end of the war. When Jack comes home it is he who will tell us real stories of the "Hun" ways. Jack is an artist both in speech and action and we will be expecting great things from him. We all hope that he and the other Comer and district boys will come home "safe and sound. Grave or Memorial Reference; IV B 22. Cemetery: Regina Trench Cemetery, Grandcourt in France.

Holland, Joseph. Rank; Sapper. Regiment or Service: Corps of Royal Engineers. Unit; 429th Field Company. Service Number; 440390/440396. Date of death; 02/07/1918. Born; Butts, County Kilkenny. Enlisted; Manchester. Killed in action. Notes; Number listed as 440390 (SDGW) 440396 (CWGC). Grave or Memorial Reference; Plot 2. Row E. Grave 8. Cemetery: Bertrancourt Military Cemetery in France.

Holmes, Charles James. Rank; Major. Regiment or Service: Royal Army Medical Corps. Date of death; 05/04/1916. Born; Clare. Residence; Had a medical practice in Kilkenny. Died. Limerick Chronicle, April, 1916. The Late Colonel Charles J Holmes, R. A. M. C. The funeral took place at Lancaster Cemetery on Saturday, with full military honours, of the late Colonel Charles James Holmes, R. A. M. C, Clare, aged fifty nine, who had 34 years military service, being in all the great campaigns, and for the last three years had been in charge of the Military Hospital at Lancaster. The mourners were—Dr Holmes (of Dublin) and Mr John Holmes (of Limerick), nephews, and Mr R Clark. A firing party of fifty, under the command of Captain Mitchell, of the King's Own depot, headed the funeral procession, and there were present, besides a representative gathering of medical gentlemen of the district; Colonel W H Duffin, Commanding the 4th regimental District; Major Churchill, Major Paton, DSO; Captain de la Rue Cox, Lieutenant Maine, R. A. M. C, Lancaster; Colonel Goggin, and Major Berryman, R. A. M. C, Kendal, Alderman Preston, the Military representative, was present. The band of the King's Own Regiment, under the depot Bandmaster, Mr Richardson, was present. The officiating clergy were Rev Father Dobson, and Rev Fr Rogerson. Grave or Memorial Reference; B RC 47. Cemetery: Lancaster Cemetery, Lancashire, UK.

Holmes, Michael K. Rank; Private. Regiment or Service: U. S. Army. Unit; 165th Infantry, 42nd Division. Date of death; 27/10/1918. Age at death; 26. Born; Kilkenny. Enlisted; New Jersey, U. S. A. Son of William and Margaret, Holmes of Baunmore, Kilkenny. Brother of Anastasia, John, Elizabeth, Kate, Ellen, William and Laurence. Holmes. Notes; Born 27/10/1892. Grave or Memorial Reference; Tablets of the Missing at Meuse Argonne American Cemetery. Cemetery: Meuse Argonne, American Cemetery, Romagne, France.

Holmes, William J. Rank; Lance Corporal. Regiment or Service: Irish Guards. Unit; 1st Battalion. Service Number; 5816. Date of death; 31/12/1915. Age at death;21. Born; Killaloe, County Clare. Enlisted; Kilkenny. Killed in action. Son of Abel and Rebecca Holmes, of Great Oak, Callan, Kilkenny. Grave or Memorial Reference; I E 15. Cemetery: Rue-Du-Bacquerot No 1 Military Cemetery, Laventie in France. He is also commemorated on the Great War Memorial in St Canice's Cathedral, Kilkenny… 'To the Glory of God and in loving memory of the following members of the Diocese of Ossory who gave their lives for their country in the Great War 1914-1918'.

Holohan, Patrick. Rank; Private. Regiment or Service: Royal Irish Regiment. Unit; 1st Battalion. Service Number; 3130. Date of death; 16/03/1915. Born; St Mary's, Kilkenny. Enlisted; Tipperary. Residence; Kilkenny. Killed in action. Grave or Memorial Reference; Panel 33. Cemetery: Ypres (Menin Gate) Memorial in Belgium.

Holohan, Patrick. Rank; Corporal/Lance Sergeant. Regiment or Service: Royal Irish Regiment. Unit; 2nd Battalion. Service Number; 9877. Date of death; 26/03/1918. Born; St Canice's, Kilkenny. Enlisted; Kilkenny. Died of wounds. There are conflicting dates and years of death on this POW who died, more research is needed. Waterford News. August, 1915. Pathetic Letter from Waterford Soldier. Mrs Owens, Heathburn Hall, River Street, County Cork, sends us a pathetic letter which she has had from a soldier, prisoner of war, who is in her husband's regiment, the 2nd Royal Irish.

The letter shows that, notwithstanding the gifts which the Irish prisoners receive to alleviate their physical discomforts, they are often subject to severe mental anxiety, such as that experienced by the writer of the letter. The moral to this is, send as many comforts to them as possible, to ensure mens sana in corpore sano. (Copy) No. 9877, Pte Patrick Holohan, C Company, 2nd Battalion, Royal Irish Regiment. Limburg (Lahan), Germany. 1st July, 1915. Dear Madam—Just a line to let you know that I am a prisoner over here in Germany, and as I have no one belonging to me, and I believe you to be doing something for the Irish Prisoners, I would be thankful if you would do something for me as I am nine months a prisoner and have got nothing so far. Even to the underclothes that came for the Royal Irish I received but one pair of socks. I would be very thankful to you if you wrote to the "Waterford News" Office and ask them to put my name in the papers as I have got a sister, and I have written to her but got no reply and think she may think I am dead or wounded. I hope you won't forget me, and I will be very thankful to you, as I have been under your husband as a Sergeant in the Royal Irish Regiment in India. I have no more to say at present. Hoping if your husband is at the front he may return home with good luck---I remain your respectful servant. Notes; Date of death listed as 26/03/1918 (SDGW) 16/03/1918 (CWGC) There are conflicting dates and years of death on this POW who died. There was only ever one British soldier buried at Zossen – Pte Patrick Holohan No 9877. He may even be the Patrick Holohan above (No 3130) more research is needed. He may even have been in Casements Brigade. Grave or Memorial Reference; Zassen Cem. Mem. Cemetery: Berlin South-Western Cemetery in Germany.

Holohan, Richard. Rank; Sergeant. Regiment or Service: Royal Irish Regiment. Unit; 2nd Battalion. Service Number; 9923. Date of death; 26/03/1918. Age at death; 26. Born; St Canice's, Kilkenny. Enlisted; Kilkenny. Residence; Knocktoplin, County Kilkenny. Died of wounds. Son of William and Mary Holohan, of Co. Kilkenny; husband of Elizabeth Holohan, of 5, St. Anne's Terrace, Birkenhead. Grave or Memorial Reference; V B 10. Cemetery: Le Cateau Military Cemetery in France.

Holohan, Thomas. Rank; Rifleman. Regiment or Service: Royal Irish Rifles. Unit; 2nd Battalion. Service Number; 7909. Date of death; 28/09/1916. Age at death;19. Born; Graigue,County Carlow. Enlisted; New Ross, County Wexford. Killed in action in France. Son of Matthew Holohan, of Coolroe, Graiguenamanagh, Co. Kilkenny. After his death, his effects and property were received by;- (Father) Mr Matthew Holohan, Coolroe, Graigue, County Kilkenny, Ireland. Grave or Memorial Reference; Pier and Face 15 A and 15 B A. Cemetery: Thiepval Memorial in France

Holohan, Thomas Francis. Rank; Gunner. Regiment or Service: Royal Garrison Artillery. Unit; 122nd Battery. Service Number; 16784. Date of death; 01/05/1920. Age at death; 37. Son of Michael and Annie Holohan, of JohN. S. W. ell, Kilkenny. Grave or Memorial Reference; V 3894. Cemetery: Hong Kong St Michael's Catholic Cemetery, China including Hong Kong.

Lance Corporal Horner, from De Ruvigny's Roll of Honour.

Horner, Joseph Richard. Rank; Lance Corporal. Regiment or Service: Royal Scots. Unit; 1st Battalion. Service Number; 18320. Date of death; 17/04/1915. Age at death;39. Born; Belfast. Enlisted; Drogheda. Residence; Kilkenny. Killed in action. Son of Richard and Ruth Horner, of Belfast; husband of Mary Kate Homer, of Lower Walkin St., Kilkenny. De Ruvigny's Roll of Honour. son of Richard Horner of Hamill Street, Belfast, by his wife Ruth, daughter of William McElroy. Born in Belfast 20-January-1874. Educated at the Christian Brothers School there; was a bricklayer and Tiler. Enlisted, 23-September-1914. Went to France, 15-March-1915, and was killed in action, 17-April-1915. He married at St Mary's R. C. Cathedral, Kilkenny, 17-January-1897, mary Catherine (Lower Walkin Street, next Friary, Kilkenny), daughter of John Hogan, of Kilkenny, Merchant Tailor, and had two children; Francis Joseph, born 02-August01911 and Ruth Josephene, born 27-February-1905. Kilkenny People, August, 1915. The Street of the Seven Widows. Famous in the History of War. Johannesburg Paper on Walkin Street. Under the heading "Wonderful Irish record," the "Johannesburg Star" publishes the following paragraph;--As showing how closely identified the Irish people are with the prosecution of the war, a correspondent writes to say that he has just received a letter from a friend in Kilkenny, in which the latter stated that on a certain Monday morning in May the post brought news to the wives of no fewer than seven Irish soldiers at the front conveying the sad intelligence of their death in battle, and these women were all resident in the same street (Walkin Street) in Kilkenny—famous in the history of war in the bygone days. This is perhaps the most remarkable record of its kind since the war commenced. It is certainly eloquent testimony of the fighting qualities of the Irish as a race. Grave or Memorial Reference; Panel 11. Cemetery: Ypres (Menin Gate) Memorial in Belgium.

Houlihan, James. Rank; Private. Regiment or Service: Royal Marine Labour Corps. Service Number; Deal/148004 (S). Date of death; 14/11/1918. Age at death; 49. Born; Kilkenny. Died of disease. Daughter. Margaret. 38, Cook Street, Dublin. Grave or Memorial Reference; XI A 27. Cemetery: Terlincthun British Cemetery, Wimille, France.

Captain Hughes, from 'Our Heroes.'

Hughes, Christopher James. Rank; Captain. Regiment or Service: Connaught Rangers. Unit; 4th Battalion. Date of death; 13/05/1916. Age at death;33. Died. Son of Christopher and Nannie Hughes, of Graiguenamanah, Co. Kilkenny. Educated at Clongowes Wood College, Ireland. Gazetted to the 3rd Battalion. Connaught Rangers in 1901. Served in the South African Campaign with 3rd Battalion. Highland Light Inf. (1902). 'Our Heroes'. died from sunstroke on May 13th, 1916, while on active service in Mesopotamia. He was the only surviving son of the late Mr Christopher Hughes, of Graigue, County Kilkenny, and was in his 33rd year. He joined the 3rd Connaught Rangers in 1901 and served through the South African War with the 3rd Highland Light Infantry, and was awarded the medal and clasps. He was subsequently transferred as Captain to the 4th Battalion. Kilkenny People, July 1916. Captain C. J. Hughes, the Connaught Rangers, who died from sunstroke on May 13th-1916, while on active service was the only surviving son of the late Christopher Hughes of Graigue, County Kilkenny, and was 33 years of age. He joined the Connaught Rangers at Gravesend in 19-- as Second Lieutenant and served with the Highland Light Infantry during the South African War, returning home about October 19—and received medal and clasps. He joined the 3rd Connaught Rangers and served with them till that battalion was disbanded on the formation of the Special Reserve, when he was transferred as Captain on June 20th 1908 to the 4th Battalion Connaught Rangers. He was with them on mobilisation in August 1914, and served with them until he was ordered to join another Battalion in Mesopotamia. His late Colonel writes;--"his loss is mourned by all ranks of his Battalion. Cheery and good tempered he was always ready to help everyone, and his unselfishness and devotion to duty was an example to all ranks. He was an efficient, trustful, and energetic officer, and was loved by his brother officers and by the men under his command." Captain Hughes was the author of a valuable handbook on drill which was intended for the use of the National Volunteers. Irish Independent; Hughes-In most loving memory of Captain Christopher James Hughes, the Connaught Rangers, who died at Basra, May 13, 1918. R. I. P. The Irish Times, May 13, 1924. Roll of Honour. (1914-1918). In Memoriam. Hughes-In most loving memory of Captain Christopher James Hughes, the Connaught Rangers, who died at Basra, on May 13th, 1916. R. I. P. Grave or Memorial Reference; V S 15. Cemetery: Basra War Cemetery in Iraq.

Hughes, John. Rank; Private. Regiment or Service: Royal Dublin Fusiliers. Unit; 8th Battalion. Service Number; 16239. Date of death; 28/10/1916. Born; Bagenalstown, County Carlow. Enlisted; Kilkenny. Residence; Goresbridge, County Kilkenny. Died. Grave or Memorial Reference; III A 244. Cemetery: Bailleul Communal Cemetery Extension (Nord) in France.

Hughes, Patrick. Rank; Private. Regiment or Service: Royal Irish Regiment. Unit; 7th (South Irish Horse) Battalion. Service Number; 5791. Date of death; 23/03/1918. Age at death;21. Born; Freshford, County Kilkenny. Enlisted; Upper Court, Kilkenny. Residence; Freshford. Died in the Field Hospital, Elincourt, France. Son of John and Catherine Hughes, of Buncresho St., Freshford, Co. Kilkenny. In his Will, dated 23-April-1917 at Queenstown, his effects and property were received by;- (Mother) Mrs C Hughes, Freshford, County Kilkenny. Grave or Memorial Reference; II C 48. Cemetery: Honnechy British Cemetery in the little village of Honnechy 8 kilometres south-west of Le Cateau, in France.

Hunt, Leslie Maunsel. Rank; Lance Corporal. Regiment or Service: South Anfrican Infantry. Unit; 2nd Regiment. Service Number; 13164. Date of death; 21/03/1918. Age at death; 38. Born; Castlecomer, County Kilkenny. Killed in action. Son of Aubrey de Vere Hunt and Alice Hunt (nee Foote) ; husband of Aileen Vivienne Pope (formerly Hunt), of 247, Main St., Muckleneuk, Pretoria, South Africa. Irish Times. Hunt-March 21,killed in action, Lance Corporal Leslie Maunsel Hunt, South African Infantry, son of Aubrey de Vere Hunt, Esq., late of Ennistymon, County Clare. Grave or Memorial Reference; Panels 95-98. Cemetery: Pozieres Memorial

Hyde, Leslie Arthur. Rank; Second Lieutenant. Regiment or Service: Royal Horse Artillery. Date of death; 26/10/1915. Age at death;19. Died. Grave or Memorial Reference; South West of Church. Cemetery: Kilkenny (St John) Church of Ireland Churchyard, Kilkenny.

I

Ivory, William. Rank; Private. Regiment or Service: Connaught Rangers. Unit; 1st Battalion. Service Number; 7629. Date of death; 05/07/1916. Born; Kilkenny. Enlisted; Kilkenny. Residence; Kilkenny. Died in Mesopotamia. Grave or Memorial Reference; XX B 7. Cemetery: Amara War Cemetery in Iraq.

J

James, William Alfred. Rank; Private. Regiment or Service: Shropshire Light Infantry. Unit; 1st Battalion. Service Number; 9029. Date of death; 24/10/1914. Born; St John's, Kilkenny. Enlisted; Hereford. Killed in action. In his Will, 10-September-1914, his effects and property were received by;- (Mother) Mrs G James, 13 Cecil St, Lytham, Lancashire. Grave or Memorial Reference; Panel 8. Cemetery: Ploegsteert Memorial in Belgium.

Private Jeffares, from De Ruvigny's Roll of Honour.

Jeffares, Reginald Isaac. Rank; Private. Regiment or Service: Royal Dublin Fusiliers. Unit; 9th Battalion. Service Number; 26218. Date of death; 16/08/1917. Born; Rosbercon, New Ross, County Wexford. Enlisted; Waterford. Residence; Dalkey, County Dublin. Killed in action. Son of the late Sheppard French Jeffares; husband of Margaret S. Jeffares of 2, Mont Alto, Dalkey, Co. Dublin. De Ruvigny's Roll of Honour; 9th (Service) Battn. The Royal Dublin Fusiliers, eldest s. of the late Sheppard French Jeffares, Gentleman Farmer and Landowner, by his wife, Kate Elizabeth (Tinneranny, New Ross, co. Wexford) dau. Of William Clapham: b. The Rower, co. Kilkenny, 8 May, 1893; educ. John Ivory School, New Ross; was a Farmer and Landowner; joined the Cadet Corps of the 7th Battn. The Leinster Regt. In Dec. 1914, but, owing to a series accident, was unable to go to the front with the 16 Division; transferred to the Dublin Fusiliers in Feb. 1916; took part in the Dublin Rebellion in April, served with the Expeditionary Force in France and Flanders from the following Aug. ; came home in the spring of 1916, but returned to France early in June, and was killed in action at Ypres 16 Aug. following. One of his officers wrote: "He was popular with all ranks, and one on whom they could always rely on assistance, and it will be a long while before he is forgotten by the battalion." He m. at Monkstown, 9 May, 1916, Margaret Susan (2, Mont Alto, Dalkey, co. Dublin), dau. Of the late William Crawley, of Bloomfield Park, Lorrha, co. Tipperary. Notes; Formerly he was with the Leinster Regiment where his number was 1976. Grave or Memorial Reference; VI S 22. Cemetery: Railway Dugouts Burial Ground in Belgium.

Jennings, Martin. Rank; Rifleman. Regiment or Service: Royal Irish Rifles. Unit; 14th Battalion. Service Number; 14987. Date of death; 06/12/1917. Born; Kilkenny. Enlisted; Belfast. Killed in action. Grave or Memorial Reference; Panel 10. Cemetery: Cambrai Memorial, Louveral in France.

Jephson, John H. Rank; Clerk 3rd Class. Regiment or Service: Royal Air Force. Service Number; 306542. Date of death; 22/12/1918. Grave or Memorial Reference; 574. Cemetery: Waterford Catholic Cemetery, County Waterford.

Jestin, John Thompson. Rank; Private. Regiment or Service: Canadian Infantry (Manitoba Regiment). Unit; 43rd Battalion. Service Number; 424960. Date of death; 08/10/1916. Age at death;25. Born; Dublin. Date of Birth, 15-December-1891. Next of kin, Susan Jestin, Mother. Address of next of kin, Borris-in-Ossory, Queen's County. Occupation on enlistment, Farmer. Religion, COI. Location and date of enlistment, Brandon, 08-March-1915. Height, 5' 7". Complexion, Dark. Eyes, Brown. Hair, Dark Brown. Grave or Memorial Reference; I A 18. Cemetery: Regina Trench Cemetery, Grandcourt in France.

Jestin, Martin. Rank; Second Lieutenant. Regiment or Service: Royal Irish Fusiliers. Unit; 7th Battalion. Date of death; 07/06/1917. Age at death; 27. Killed in action. Son of Susan Jestin, of Sentry Lodge, Borris-in-Ossory, Queen's Co., and the late William Jestin, (a brother to John above.). Grave or Memorial Reference; Panel 42. Cemetery: Ypres (Menin Gate) Memorial in Belgium.

Johnston, Edward. Rank; Private. Regiment or Service: London Regiment (Royal Fusiliers). Unit; 1st/3rd Battalion. Service Number; 5021. Date of death; 24/07/1916. Age at death;18. Enlisted; Hyde Park. Residence; London W. Killed in action. Son of Thomas and Catherine Johnston, of Pipe St., Thomastown, Co. Kilkenny. Kilkenny People, August, 1916. Brave Thomastown Soldier Killed in Action. The parents of Private Edward Johnson, who reside at Ladywell Street, Thomastown, have been notified of his death in action in France on the night of July 24, by being hit by a fragment of a bomb and killed instantaneously. The deceased, who was only in his 18th year, held an important position in the Sacred Heart Convent, Charles Square, London, previous to joining the army. He enlisted the Royal London Fusiliers in October last, and had been in the trenches sine April 4 of the present year. The late Private Johnson was a popular and prominent member of the Thomastown Dramatic Class, and was held in the highest esteem by his fellow-members. He was brother to Mr John Johnson, who was manager of the Imperial Hotel, Wexford up to the death of the proprietress a few weeks ago, and is at present employed at Messrs. Clery and Company, Limited, Bagenalstown. The sad news of his death came as a shock to the members of his family and as a painful surprise to his old friends in Thomastown, but though the companions of his youth will know him no more, his memory will be cherished by his old friends in Thomastown. Sincere sympathy will be extended to the bereaved parents, brother and sisters in the sad bereavement that has befallen them. The following letter has been received by Mrs Johnson during the past week;--"Dear Mrs Johnson; I very much regret to inform you that your son, Private E. Johnson, was killed on the night of July 24 by a fragment of a bomb, instantaneously. It may be some consolation to you to know that your son died in the execution of his duty to his country. He was indeed a brave man, and volunteered with some others for a very difficult and trying work which required the greatest courage. I was proud to be in command of such a man, and I feel his loss deeply. I wish to offer you my most sincere sympathies in your very sad bereavement. I was present this afternoon at your sons funeral; he was buried in the cemetery. He did his duty and died a hero. Yours sincerely—Herbert C. Pearce, Second Lieutenant, 1/3 Battalion, London Regiment. Grave or Memorial Reference; I M 17. Cemetery: Foncquevillers Military Cemetery in France.

Jordan, Nicholas Joseph. Rank; Private. Regiment or Service: Irish Guards. Unit; 2nd Battalion. Service Number; 7299. Date of death; 01/02/1916. Age at death; 29. Born; Gowran, County Kilkenny. Enlisted; Dublin. Died of wounds. Son of Patrick and Bridget Jordan, of 9, Kilkenny Rd., Gowran, Co. Kilkenny. Irish Independent; Jordan-Killed in action on the Western Front, February 1, 1916, Private Nicholas Jordan, Irish Guards, late of the Staff, Portrane Asylum, aged 23, a native of Gowran, County Kilkenny; deeply regretted by his relatives, comrades, and friends. R. I. P. A Mass of requiem for the repose of his soul will be celebrated in the Asylum Chapel, Portrane, on Monday next, 14th inst, at 9 o'clock. 11/02/1916. Freeman's Journal. Jordan-Killed in action on the Western Front, February 1st, 1916, Private Nicholas Jordan, Irish Guards, late of the Staff, Portrane Asylum, a native of Gowran, County Kilkenny, aged 23 years, deeply regretted by his relatives, comrades, and friends R. I. P. A Mass of requiem for the repose of his soul will be celebrated in the Asylum Chapel, Portrane, on Monday next. 14th inst, at 9 o'clock. Grave or Memorial Reference; II M 7. Cemetery: Estaires Communal Cemetery and Extension in France.

K

Kane, Patrick Joseph. Rank; Private. Regiment or Service: Canadian Infantry. Unit; 53rd Battalion. Service Number; 440533. Date of death; 09/05/1916. Son of Anastasia Kane, of Rivanagh, Coolcullen, Bagenalstown, Co. Carlow, Ireland. Next of kin listed as (mother), Anastasia Kane, Rivanagh, Culcullen, Kilkenny, Ireland. Place of birth, County Kilkenny, Ireland. Date of birth, 16-February-1889. Occupation on enlistment, Locomotive Fireman. Place and date of enlistment, 17-September-1915, Camp Hughes, Manitoba. Height, 5 feet, 9 ½ inches. Complexion, fair. Eyes, blue. Hair, brown. Grave or Memorial Reference; A 1. Cemetery: Greyshott (St Joseph) Roman Catholic Churchyard, Hampshire, UK. Also listed under Leighlinbridge/Old Leighlin on the Great War Memorial, Milford Street, Leighlinbridge, County Carlow.

Kavanagh, Edward. Rank; Private. Regiment or Service: Royal Irish Regiment. Unit; 2nd Battalion. Service Number; 3128. Date of death; 09/05/1915. Born; St John's, Kilkenny. Enlisted; Tipperary. Residence; Kilkenny. Killed in action. Kilkenny People, May, 1915. Kilkenny Soldier Killed in Action. Four Brothers and Two Brothers-in-Law With the Colours. One Killed and One Missing Since October. Martin Kavanagh, Wolfe Tone Street, Corporation labourer, received a letter last week from his son of the same name, who is in the trenches "somewhere in France." After stating that the writer was well, the letter proceeded;--"I hope it will not knock you about to let you know that Ned got wounded on the morning of the 9th May, and died in the evening at 5 o'clock. He knew he was dying and shook hands with all his comrades and bid them all goodbye." Ned Kavanagh, whose death is thus pathetically described, is another son of old Martin Kavanagh, and, like his brother, young Martin, was in the 2nd Battalion, Royal Irish Regiment. A third son, Tomas Kavanagh, was also in the 2nd Battalion, Royal Irish Regiment. He went to the front the same time as Captain J. A. Smithwick, and has been missing since the 19th October. His name has not been returned amongst the prisoners of war, and there is unfortunately some grounds for believing that a worse fate has befallen him. A fourth son, James Kavanagh, was until recently in Queenstown with the 4th Battalion of the same Regiment. The Battalion has recently been changed to Queenstown. It will thus be seen that Martin Kavanagh had four sons with the colours. One of them has been killed in action, one is missing since the 19th October, a third is still fighting in the trenches, and the fourth will probably soon be in action. In addition to this, two of his daughters are married to soldiers, one of them, James Ryan, being at the front, while the second, William Bollard, is with Kitchener's army in Tipperary. The case of old Martin Kavanagh should engage the attention of those who are concerned in the administration of war relief funds. Very few can beat his record. Grave or Memorial Reference; VI E 10. Cemetery: New Irish Farm Cemetery in Belgium.

Kavanagh, James. Rank; Sergeant. Regiment or Service: Royal Irish Regiment. Unit; 4th Battalion. Service Number; 4295. Date of death; 13/01/1918. Age at death;32. Born; St John's, Kilkenny. Enlisted; Kilkenny. Died at home. Husband of Mary Kavanagh, of 11, Wolfe Tone St., Kilkenny. Grave or Memorial Reference; In the South East part. Cemetery: Kilkenny New Cemetery, Kilkenny.

Kavanagh, John. Rank; Lance Corporal. Regiment or Service: Leinster Regiment. Unit; 1st Battalion. Service Number; 9265. Date of death; 14/02/1915. Age at death; 38. Born; Callan, County Kilkenny. Enlisted; Maryborough. Killed in action. Son of James Kavanagh, of West St., Callan, Co. Kilkenny. Grave or Memorial Reference; 44. Cemetery: Ypres (Menin Gate) Memorial in Belgium.

Kavanagh, Thomas. Rank; Private. Regiment or Service: Royal Irish Regiment. Unit; 2nd Battalion. Service Number; 3489. Date of death; 19/10/1914. Age at death;32. Born; St John's, Kilkenny. Enlisted; Tipperary. Residence; Kilkenny. Killed in action. Son of Martin Kavanagh, of II, Wolfestone St., Kilkenny; husband of the late Catherine Kavanagh. His brothers Edward and James also fell. Grave or Memorial Reference; Panel 11 and 12. Cemetery: Le Touret Memorial In France.

Kavanagh, Thomas. Rank; Private. Regiment or Service: Royal Irish Regiment. Unit; 1st Battalion. Service Number; 7430. Date of death; 24/03/1919. Age at death; 20. Born; Kilkenny. Died in Egypt. Son of John and Ellen Kavanagh, brother of Tessie and Ellie Kavanagh. In his Will, dated 21-January-1918, his effects and property were received by;- (Grandfather) John Kavanagh, Buhecrussa St, Freshford, County Kilkenny. Grave or Memorial Reference; H 96. Cemetery: Cairo War Memorial Cemetery. Egypt.

Kavanagh, Thomas Osborne Joseph. Rank; Lieutenant. Regiment or Service: Royal Irish Fusiliers. Unit; 3rd Battalion attached to the 1st Battalion. Date of death; 24/08/1918. Killed in action. Kilkenny People, August, 1918. Kavanagh—August 24th-1918. Killed in action. Lieutenant T. O. J. Kavanagh, M. C., Royal Irish Fusiliers, aged 26 years, second son of P. J. Kavanagh, Monnacurragh House, Carlow, and Greystones, and nephew of Mr Kavanagh, Jordanstown House. Kilkenny People, August, 1918. Killed in Action. We regret the death in action of Lieutenant T. O. J. Kavanagh, M. C., Royal Irish Fusiliers, who was killed while gallantly leading his men on the 24th August last. Lieutenant Kavanagh, who was recently presented with the Military Cross for bravery in action, was apprenticed to Mr Fotterell, solicitor, Dublin, and joined the O. T. C. at its formation. His Colonel in a letter to his relatives wrote. —"I cannot tell you how much we feel his loss. He was always willing to do and work, particularly if it was dangerous work, and he was an officer it will be difficult to replace." Lieutenant Kavanagh was son of Mr P. J. Kavanagh, Monnacurragh House, Carlow, and Greystones, and nephew of Mr Kavanagh, Jordanstown House, Kilkenny. Grave or Memorial Reference; II A 2. Cemetery: Bertnacre Military Cemetery, Fletre, Nord in France.

Kay, Arthur Bagnall. Rank; Sergeant. Regiment or Service: Royal Irish Regiment. Age at death; 52. Killed in action. The only reference I can find to this man is contained in the following article from the Kilkenny People, December 1914. Military Funeral in Kilkenny. Sergeant A Kay, of the Royal Irish Regiment, who died on Monday night, aged 52 years, was buried in St John's Protestant cemetery on Thursday with military honours, the coffin being covered with the Union Jack, and 150 men of the 75th Brigade, R. F. A., ta present occupying the Kilkenny barracks, marching after the bier under Captain Mackesy, formerly of the 5th Munster Fusiliers and now attached to the Royal Irish Regiment. Sergeant Kay had 26 years service, and fought in the Egyptian and South African Wars, his distinctions including the Egyptian Medal, '84-'85, Khedive Medal, and the South African Medal with three clasps. Cemetery: Unknown

Kealy, Patrick. Rank; Private. Regiment or Service: South Lancashire Regiment. Unit; 2nd Battalion. Service Number; 10095. Date of death; 19/02/1922. Age at death;35. Residence; Kilkenny. Died after discharge. Cemetery: St Maul's Cemetery, Kilkenny.

Keane/Eane, William. Rank; Private. Regiment or Service: Middlesex Regiment. Unit; 12th Battalion. Service Number; G/41984. Date of death; 17/02/1917. Born; Piltown, County Kilkenny. Enlisted; Waterford. Residence; Piltown, County Kilkenny. Killed in action. Keane (CWGC, IMR), Eane (SDGW). Notes; Number listed as G/41984 (SDGW) 41984 (CWGC). Formerly he was with the 5th Lancers where his number was 23288. Grave or Memorial Reference; V F 13. Cemetery: Regina Trench Cemetery, Grandcourt in France.

Kearney, John Hempenstall. Rank; Private. Regiment or Service: Canadian Infantry (Quebec Regiment). Unit; 14th Battalion. Service Number; 25734. Date of death; 03/06/1916. Son of James and Frances Keamey, of West St., Callan, Co. Kilkenny, Ireland. A Clerk in the Quebec Bank at Montreal. Enlisted Aug., 1914. Born, Bangor, Ireland. ccupation on enlistment, Bank Clerk. Previous military experience; 1 year, Co Guards. Date of birth; 12-March-1892. Next of kin details; James Kearney, Callan,

County Kilkenny. Place and date of enlistment, 21-September-1914. Valcartier. Height, 5 feet, 8 ½ inches. Complexion, medium. Eyes, grey. Hair, dark. Irish Times. Kearney-June 3, killed in action, John H Kearney, Royal Montreal Regiment, Canadian Division, late of Ulster bank, Carrickmacross, and Trim, and of Bank of Quebec, Montreal, son of James Kearney, C. P. S., Collan. Grave or Memorial Reference; Panel 24 - 26 - 28 - 30. Cemetery: Ypres (Menin Gate) Memorial in Belgium. He is also commemorated on the Great War Memorial in St Canice's Cathedral, Kilkenny…'To the Glory of God and in loving memory of the following members of the Diocese of Ossory who gave their lives for their country in the Great War 1914-1918'.

Kearns, Tobias. Rank; Private. Regiment or Service: Labour Corps. Unit; 83rd Company. Service Number; 79214. Date of death; 15/09/1917. Age at death; 36. Enlisted; Ormskirk, Lancashire. Residence; Kilkenny. Died of wounds. Son of Michael Kearns and Bridget, his wife, of Kilkenny. Notes;,Formerly he was with the The King's (Liverpool Regiment) where his number was 49431. 18th Inf. Labour Coy. Grave or Memorial Reference; XIX B 14. Cemetery: Lijssenthoek Military Cemetery in Belgium.

Keating, James. Rank; Private. Regiment or Service: South Lancashire Regiment. Unit; 2nd Battalion. Service Number; 7424. Date of death; 21/10/1914. Born; Kilkenny. Enlisted; Kilkenny. Killed in action. After his death his effects and property were received by his mother. The Noncupative (or missing) Will was witnessed by;- (Sister of deceased) Mrs Mary Bryan, Goose Hill, Kilkenny. Miss Mary O'Mara, Newbuilding Lane, Kilkenny, Ireland and Mrs M Bryan, Goose Hill, Kilkenny Ireland. Michael Potter JP Kilkenny. James Breff, 78 High St, Kilkenny, JP. Grave or Memorial Reference; Panel 23. Cemetery: Le Touret Memorial in France.

Keating, John. Rank; Private. Regiment or Service: Royal Irish Regiment. Unit; 2nd Battalion. Service Number; 10519. Date of death; 14/02/1915. Born; St John's, Kilkenny. Enlisted; Waterford. Residence; Kilkenny. Killed in action. Grave or Memorial Reference; Panel 33. Cemetery: Ypres (Menin Gate) Memorial in Belgium.

Keating, Thomas. Rank; Private. Regiment or Service: Royal Irish Regiment. Unit; 1st Battalion. Service Number; 4734. Date of death; 15/05/1915. Age at death;19. Born; Ballyraggett, County Kilkenny. Enlisted; Kilkenny. Residence; Ballyraggett. Died of wounds received at Hooge. Son of Mary Keating, of Green St., Ballyragget, Co. Kilkenny. Listed in 'Kilkenny Soldier's Killed in Action. ', Kilkenny Journal, May, 1915 under M. Keating. After his death his effects and property were received by;- (Mother) Mrs M Keating, Green Street, Ballyragget, County Kilkenny, Ireland. Grave or Memorial Reference; Panel 33. Cemetery: Ypres (Menin Gate) Memorial in Belgium.

Keefe, John. Rank; Gunner. Regiment or Service: Royal Horse Artillery and Royal Field Artillery. Unit; 25th Battery. Service Number; 33236. Date of death; 02/04/1915. Age at death; 38. Born; Ballyhale, County Kilkenny. Enlisted; Waterford. Died of wounds. Husband of Lily Keefe, of 17, Glanlay St., Penrhiwceiber, Glamorganshire. Grave or Memorial Reference; III D 74. Cemetery: Boulogne Eastern Cemetery in France.

Keeffe, Edmund. Rank; Private. Regiment or Service: Welsh Regiment. Unit; 2nd Battalion. Service Number; 799. Date of death; 23/10/1914. Born; Mooncoin, County Kilkenny. Enlisted; Cardiff, Glamorganshire. Residence; Maesteg, Glamorganshire. Killed in action. Grave or Memorial Reference; Panel 37. Cemetery: Ypres (Menin Gate) Memorial in Belgium.

Keeffe, William. Rank; Private. Regiment or Service: Royal Dublin Fusiliers. Unit; 1st Battalion. Service Number; 10324. Date of death; 25/04/1915. Born; Connety, County Kilkenny. Enlisted; Naas. Residence; Connetty. Killed in Action in Gallipoli. In his Will, 23-April-1915, his effects and property were received by;- Ms Bridget Keeffe, Three Castles, County Kilkenny, Ireland. Kilkenny People, May, 1915. Killed in Action. News reached Threecastles a few days ago that Willie Keeffe had been killed in action at the Dardanelles. Private Keeffe, who was fine type of young man, enlisted about six years ago, the greater part of which he spent in India, and recently returned with his regiment the 1st Dublin Fusiliers, and paid a short visit to his home. He was most popular with all classes, being noted for his gentleness and kindly distinction and his friendly and unassuming bearing. Much sympathy is felt for his sorrowing family and relatives. Grave or Memorial Reference; B 8. Cemetery: V Beach Cemetery in Turkey.

Keeffe/O'Keeffe, John. Rank; Private. Regiment or Service: Royal Irish Regiment. Unit; 7th Battalion. Service Number; 10634. Date of death; 14/10/1918. Age at death;20. Born; Mooncoin. Enlisted; Waterford. Residence; Mooncoin. Killed in action. O'Keefe (CWGC) Keeffe (SDGW, IMR) Son of William and Hannah O'Keefe, of Dournane, Mooncoin, Co. Kilkenny. In his Will, dated 05-July-1916, his effects and property were received by;- (Aunt) Mrs E Comerford, 39 Wolfe Tone Street, Kilkenny, Ireland. Grave or Memorial Reference; II E 6. Cemetery: Zantvoorde British Cemetery in Belgium.

Keelan, John Horace. Rank; Rifleman. Regiment or Service: Royal Irish Rifles. Unit; 1st Battalion. Service Number; 14908. Date of death; 30/01/1915. Age at death; 34. Born; Mullingar. Enlisted; Dublin. Residence; Mullingar. Killed in action. Son of the late Patrick Keelan, of Greville St., Mullingar, Co. Westmeath. Westmeath Examiner, March-1915. The Roll of Honour. Mr John Keelan,Mullingar. We cannot find words adequate to expressing the sympathy which we, in common with the whole community of all classes in Mullingar, would wish to convey to Mr Patrick Keelan, J. P. —one of its most justly esteemed of our townsmen—to Mrs Keelan, and other relatives on the death of John Keelan, Royal Irish Rifles. On Monday the sad news reached Mr and Mrs Keelan that their beloved eldest son had been killed in action at a place called Kemmel, in France. The young soldier was genial and good-hearted, and was highly esteemed in Mullingar by all who knew him. Early in the p-ace, he volunteered for service, his training was quickly completed, and he went on active service. Like a true Irishman and a true soldier he fell fighting. Peace to his soul, and may God's eternal rest be his in the Land that lies far beyond the din of battle and the sound of human strife and turmoil. In conveying our deepest sympathy to his bereaved parents and other relatives, as already said, no mere words suffice, but it may be some consolation to remind them through our columns that he has followed in the track of many a noble son of Ireland, yielding his life as a pledge of his faith in a high noble cause— that of oppressed small nations and in defence of the most sacred inheritances of Christianity, human liberty, and civilisation. De Ruvigny's Roll of Honour. Keelan, John, Private, No 14908, 2nd Battalion, Royal Irish Rifles. Eldest son of Patrick Keelan, of 13, Greville Street, Mullingar, J. P., General Draper, by his wife, Annie, daughter of John Skerrin, Kilkenny. Born in Mullingar, 13-December-1882. Educated at the Christian Brothers Schools there. After the outbreak of war enlisted in the Royal Irish Rifles on or about 15-September-1914, and was killed in action near Kemmel, in France, 30-January-1915. Westmeath Examiner, March-1915. The Late Mr John Keelan, Mullingar. Eldest son of Mr Patrick Keelan, J. P., and Mrs Keelan, Mullingar, who was shot whilst in action, on the 30th Jan., at a place near Kemmel, in France, and whose demise is deeply lamented in Mullingar and throughout Westmeath. Freemans Journal, March-1915. Roll of Honour. Keelan-Killed in action near Kemmel, on January 30th, 1915, John Keelan, Royal Irish Rifles, eldest and dearly-beloved son of Patrick and Annie Keelan, 13 Greville Street, Mullingar."Requiscat in pace.". Grave or Memorial Reference; Panels 42 and 43. Cemetery: Le Touret Memorial in France.

Kelly, Denis. Rank; Private. Regiment or Service: Royal Irish Regiment. Unit; 6th Battalion. Service Number; 5385. Date of death; 03/09/1916. Born; Thomastown, County Kilkenny. Enlisted; Kilkenny. Residence; Gowran. Killed in action. Grave or Memorial Reference; VI A 4. Cemetery: Serre Road Cemetery No 2 in France.

Kelly, Edward. Rank; Private. Regiment or Service: Royal Army Ordnance Corps. Unit; 66th Service Company. Service Number; 12176. Date of death; 06/01/1919. Age at death; 63. Residence; Kilkenny. Died after discharge. Cemetery: Unknown

Kelly, Henry. Rank; Private. Regiment or Service: Royal Dublin Fusiliers. Unit; 2nd Battalion. Service Number; 5627. Date of death; 06/06/1915. Born; Kilkenny. Enlisted; Naas. Residence; Kilkenny. Died of wounds. Grave or Memorial Reference; III C 4. Cemetery: Roeselare Communal Cemetery in Belgium

Kelly, James. Rank; Private. Regiment or Service: Royal Dublin Fusiliers. Unit; 1st Battalion. Service Number; 5630. Date of death; 01/07/1916. Enlisted; Naas. Residence; Kilkenny. Killed in action. Son of Mrs. Kelly, of New Building Lane, Kilkenny. Grave or Memorial Reference; II A 3. Cemetery: Auchonvillers Military Cemetery in France

Kelly, John. Rank; Private. Regiment or Service: Royal Munster Fusiliers. Unit; 1st Battalion. Service Number; 5708. Date of death; 21/08/1915. Age at death;25. Born; Ballyhale, County Kilkenny. Enlisted; Dublin. Residence; Carrick-on-Suir, County Tipperary. Killed in Action in Gallipoli. Son of Mrs. Hanoria Kelly, of Jamestown, Piltown, Co. Kilkenny, and the late Constable J. Kelly, (Royal Irish Constabulary). Notes; Formerly he was with the Lancers of the line where his number was 16037. Grave or Memorial Reference; Panel 185 to 190. Cemetery: Helles Memorial

Kelly, John. Rank; Private. Regiment or Service: Royal Munster Fusiliers. Unit; 2nd Battalion. Service Number; 10846. Date of death; 31/03/1918. Born; The Butts, Kilkenny. Enlisted; Carlow. Residence; Kilkenny. Died of wounds. Son of Mr. J. Kelly, of 32, Upper Rutland St, Dublin. Notes; Formerly he was with the Royal Dublin Fusiliers where his number was 25980. Grave or Memorial Reference; I F 6. Cemetery: Namps-Au-Val British Cemetery, Somme, France.

Kelly, Michael. Rank; Sergeant. Regiment or Service: Royal Irish Regiment. Unit; 1st Battalion. Service Number; 3434. Date of death; 26/04/1915. Age at death;27. Born; St John's, Kilkenny. Enlisted; Tipperary. Residence; Kilkenny. Killed in action at St Julien, near Ypres. Son of the late Joseph and Mary Kelly, of Kilkenny; husband of Bridget West (formerly Kelly, nee Saunders), of Maudlin St., Kilkenny. Kilkenny People, May, 1915. Killed in Action. Sergeant Michael Kelly, Maudlin Street. The relatives of Sergeant Michael Kelly, 4th Battalion, Riyal Irish regiment, have received the news of his death. It occurred in action at St Julian, near Ypres on the 28th April last. He was a reservist and resided at Maudlin Street, Kilkenny, and at the mobilisation of last August joined his regiment. Since the early months of the war he was at the front, taking part in much of the fierce fighting up to the time of his death. Much sympathy is felt for his young widow and two children, and his father, Mr Joseph Kelly, Nore Terrace, Maudlin Street. Grave or Memorial Reference; Panel 33. Cemetery: Ypres (Menin Gate) Memorial in Belgium. CWGC notes;-Buried at the time in Zossen Communal Cemetery, Germany.

Kelly, Thomas. Rank; Private. Regiment or Service: Royal Irish Regiment. Unit; 6th Battalion. Service Number; 2055. Date of death; 09/09/1916. Age at death; 19. Born; Callan, County Kilkenny. Enlisted; Kilkenny. Residence; Callan. Killed in action. Son of Mrs. Ellen Kelly, of Bauntha, Callan, Co. Kilkenny. Grave or Memorial Reference; Pier and Face 3 A. Cemetery: Thiepval Memorial in France.

Kenealy, John William Kiernan. Rank; Second Lieutenant. Regiment or Service: Royal Irish Regiment. Unit; 4th Battalion. Date of death; 21/08/1915 (note incorrect year-1918, of death on his headstone). Age at death;18. Died. Son of Mrs. Alice M. Kenealy, of 30, Patrick St., Kilkenny. Kings County Chronicle;Great regret is felt at the death of Lieutenant J. W. Kenealy, R. I. R., son of Mrs Kenealy, proprietress of the 'Kilkenny Journal. '. Kilkenny Journal, August, 1915. Death of Lieutenant J. W. Kenealy. The death occurred on Friday evening Ist of Lieutenant J. W. Kenealy, second son of the late Mr C. J. Kenealy, and of Mrs A. M. Kenealy, proprietresss of the "Kilkenny Journal." Passing away in the springtime of life—he only having reached his eighteenth year—his death came as a severe shock, not alone to the members of his family and immediate friends, bt to the citizens generally. Like so many thousands of his fellow countrymen, the late Lieutenant Kenealy responded to the call of King and Country and was given a commission as Second Lieutenant in the of his fellow countrymen, the late Lieutenant Kenealy responded to the call of King and Country and was given a commission as Second Lieutenant in the 4th Battalion Royal Irish Regiment. The grief occasioned by his death is all the more poignant, as he had just been granted a week's holidays after completing his preliminary training at Cork, preparatory to joining his Regiment at Gosport, Hants, he having passed his examination with distinction. Those that met him on his return were impressed by his soldierly bearing, energy and vivacity; in fact, he was the embodiment of everything manly and brave. He was in the full enjoyment of health, and endeavoured to get as much pleasure as possible into his few days leave. On the day previous to the date of his return to his Regiment he contracted a chill. As his only thought was to be with his regiment, no little pressure had been brought to leave on him by the members of his family, to apply for an extension of leave. Dr. Charles E. James, Military Doctor, was consulted and he recommended him a further extension of 10 days sick leave, which should expire on the 24th inst. On the 19th inst his condition became serious, and he remained in bed, and the doctor and nursing Sisters of St John of God, were requisitioned. But despite all that the most skilled medical and nursing aid could accomplish, his condition became more and more grave, and on Friday afternoon, to the inexpressible grief of his devoted family, he passed peacefully away. If it has pleased the Almighty to spare him a soldier's death on the battlefield, and an unknown grave, he has none the less died a true soldier, and we hope that he is now reaping the reward of his bravery and courage. During the last moments he had the consolation of receiving the last rites of the Church from the Rev Father Chrysosetom, O. S. F. C., and Rev. Fr. Kearns, C. C., St Patrick's. A full report of the funeral, with names of all the mourners, followed in the same newspaper. There is also a complete report of his death and funeral in the Kilkenny People, August, 1915. Irish Independent; Regret is felt in Kilkenny at the death of Lieutenant J W Kenealy, RIR., second son of the late Mr G J Kenealy, Town Clerk, and of Mrs A M Kenealy, proprietress of the "Kilkenny Journal." Deceased obtained a commission some months ago, and was home on leave at the time of his death. Irish Independent; Kenealy, August 20, 1915, at 30 Patrick Street, Kilkenny, John William Kenealy, Second Lieutenant, 4th Royal Irish Regiment, aged 18, second son of the late Cornelius J Kenealy, Editor "Kilkenny Journal." R. I. P. Funeral to-morow (Sunday) at 2. 39 p. m. to Foulkstown. Freeman's Journal, 21/08/1915. Death of a Young Kilkenny Officer. Much regret is felt in Kilkenny at the death, which took place yesterday after a brief illness, of Lieutenant J W Kenealy, Royal Irish Regiment, second eldest son of the late Mr C J Kenealy, Town Clerk, Kilkenny, and of Mrs A M Kenealy, proprietors of the "Kilkenny Journal." He obtained a commission in the Royal Irish Regiment some months ago, and was at home on leave for the last week. He intended returning to his regiment in a few days. Grave or Memorial Reference; In the South East part. Cemetery: Foulkstown Catholic Churchyard, County Kilkenny.

Kennedy, Michael. Rank; Sergeant. Regiment or Service: Leinster Regiment. Service Number; 9201. Date of death; 05/10/1916. Born; Mountrath, Queen's County. Enlisted; Birr, King's County. Residence; Crosspatrick, County Kilkenny. Died of wounds in Salonika. Grave or Memorial Reference; I B 20. Cemetery: Lahana Military Cemetery in Greece.

Kennedy, Patrick. Rank; Sergeant. Regiment or Service: West Yorkshire Regiment. Unit; 12th Battalion. Service Number; 16488. Date of death; 26/09/1915. Born; Kilkenny. Enlisted; Leeds. Residence; Leeds. Killed in action. Grave or Memorial Reference; Panel 39 and 40. Cemetery: Loos Memorial in France

Kennedy, Robert. Rank; Lance Corporal. Regiment or Service: Royal Dublin Fusiliers. Unit; 9th Battalion. Service Number; 22815. Date of death; 23/05/1917. Born; Freshford, County Kilkenny. Enlisted; North Shields. Killed in action. Grave or Memorial Reference; J 80. Cemetery: Kemmel Chateau Military Cemetery in Belgium.

Kenny, Patrick. Rank; Private. Regiment or Service: Royal Irish Regiment. Unit; 6th Battalion. Service Number; 5505. Date of death; 12/07/1916. Age at death;18. Born; Callan, County Kilkenny. Enlisted; Kilkenny. Residence; Callan. Died of wounds. Son of Catherine Kenny, of Green St., Callan, Co. Kilkenny. In his Will, dated 14-June-1916, his effects and property were received by;- (Mother) Mrs Catherine Kenny,

West Street, Callan. Grave or Memorial Reference; V F 91. Cemetery: Bethune Town Cemetery in France

Kenny, Thomas. Rank; Private. Regiment or Service: Royal Irish Regiment. Unit; 6th Battalion. Service Number; 2555. Date of death; 16/12/1916. Born; St Canice's, Kilkenny. Enlisted; Kilkenny. Died of wounds. Grave or Memorial Reference; III A 167. Cemetery: Bailleul Communal Cemetery Extension, (Nord). France.

Keogh, William. Rank; Private. Regiment or Service: Royal Irish Regiment. Unit; 2nd Battalion. Service Number; 4120. Date of death; 19/10/1914. Age at death;20. Born; Callan, County Kilkenny. Enlisted; Callan. Killed in action. Son of Patrick and Mary Keogh, of Ahenure, Callan, Co. Kilkenny. After his death his effects and property were received by;- (Mother) Mrs Mary Keogh, Ahenure, Callan, County Kilkenny, Ireland. Grave or Memorial Reference; Panel 11 and 12. Cemetery: Le Touret Memorial In France.

Kidd, Charles Roland. Rank; Captain. Regiment or Service: Royal Army Medical Corps. Date of death; 08/07/1920. Age at death; 44. Born; Callan, County Kilkenny. Husband of Mary Kidd, of Dublin. Grave or Memorial Reference; 2034. Cemetery: Netley Military Cemetery, Hampshire, UK.

Kiely, Patrick. Rank; Lance Corporal. Regiment or Service: Irish Guards. Unit; 1st Battaliom. Service Number; 10970. Date of death; 04/09/1917. Born; Ahenny, County Kilkenny. Enlisted; Carrick-on-Suir, County Kilkenny (sic). Died of wounds. In his Will, dated 24-January-1917., his effects and property were received by;- (Mother) Mrs Mary Kiely, Ormonde Slate Quarries, Ahenny, Carrick-on-Suir, County Kilkenny, Ireland. Munster Express, September, 1917. Echoes from South Kilkenny. Death of Private Patrick Kiely, Slatequarries. The death of the above young and gallant soldier took place a couple of weeks ago "somewhere in France." He was a quiet, unassuming young man. His eldest brother Thomas is also at the front and was home last week. To his bereaved mother, sister and brothers we offer our condolences. R. I. P. Grave or Memorial Reference; IV F 12. Cemetery: Dozinghem Military Cemetery in Belgium.

King, Francis Joseph. Rank; Lance Corporal. Regiment or Service: Royal Irish Regiment. Unit; 2nd Battalion. Service Number; 4/5407. Date of death; 08/08/1917. Age at death; 23. Born; St John's, Kilkenny. Enlisted; Kilkenny. Died of wounds. Son of Charles and Mary King, of 6, Abbey View Terrace, Kilkenny. In his Will, dated 15-June-1917, Witnessed by;- J Lawlor, Belmont Huts, Queenstown, his effects and property were received by;- (Mother) Mrs Mary King, 6 Abbey View Terrace, Kilkenny, Ireland. Irish Independent; King-August 8, 1917, from wounds received in action, Frank, Royal Irish Regiment, youngest and dearly-loved son if Mary King, 6 Abbey View Terrace, Kilkenny, and the late Charles King, Regimental Warrant Officer of the same Regiment,"Gone, from our home, but not from our hearts.". Notes; Number listed as 4/5407 (CWGC) 4507 (SDGW). Grave or Memorial Reference; IV B 9. Cemetery: Mendinghem Military Cemetery in Belgium.

King, John. Rank; Private. Regiment or Service: Royal Irish Regiment. Unit; 2nd Battalion. Service Number; 4596. Date of death; 14/02/1915. Born; Ballyhale, County Kilkenny. Enlisted; Thomastown. Residence; Grange, County Kilkenny. Killed in action at St Eloi. In his Will, dated 16-December-1914, his effects and property were received by;- (Sister) Stasia King, C/o Mrs Higgins, Skeard, Kilmacow, County Kilkenny, Ireland. Grave or Memorial Reference; Panel 33. Cemetery: Ypres (Menin Gate) Memorial in Belgium.

Kinsella, John. Rank; Driver. Regiment or Service: Corps of Royal Engineers. Unit; 254th Tunnelling Company. Service Number; 33220. Date of death; 30/01/1916. Born; Graiguenamanagh, County Kilkenny. Enlisted; London. Died aboard HS "Marmora" of pneumonia. Son of Mrs. Margaret Kinsella, of High St., Graiguenamanagh, Co. Kilkenny. In his Will, dated 29-January-1916, Witnessed by;- Nicholas Moloney, RC Chaplain, his effects and property were received by;- (Mother) Mrs John Kinsella, High Street Graigne-na-Managh, County Kilkenny, Ireland. Cemetery: Chatby Memorial in Egypt.

Knox, John. Rank; Private. Regiment or Service: Leinster Regiment. Unit; 7th Battalion. Service Number; 3998. Date of death; 11/09/1917. Born; Piltown, County Kilkenny. Enlisted; Carrick-on-Suir. Residence; Tobernabrone, Piltown, County Kilkenny. Died of wounds. Buried beside Tipperary soldier Private Thomas Brien who died on the same day. In his Will, dated 05-October-1916, his effects and property were received by;- (Mother) Mrs J Knox, Toberna borne, Pilltown, County Kilkenny. Notes; Died of wounds at 20th Casualty Clearing Station, France. Grave or Memorial Reference; II B 4. Cemetery: Bacquoy Road Cemetery, Ficheux, in France. Grave or Memorial

Knox, Richard. Rank; Private. Regiment or Service: Irish Guards. Unit; 2nd Battalion. Service Number; 10735. Date of death; 28/09/1916. Age at death; 28. Born; Piltown, County Kilkenny. Enlisted; Waterford. Died of wounds. Listed in the CWGC as King and in SDGW as Corcoran. Supplementary information: (Served as Corcoran). Son of John and Margaret Knox, of Gurthrush, Piltown, Co. Kilkenny. Munster Express, 14/10/1916;-Killed in Action. At each of the Masses at Templeorum on Sunday last prayers were offered for the repose of the soul of PrivateRichard Knox, Tubbernabone, Piltown, who was killed in action on September, 28th. He was only three weeks at the front. (Richard Knox was a cousin of Stephen Knox below.). Grave or Memorial Reference; I G 35. Cemetery: Grove Town Cemetery, Meaulte, France.

Knox, Stephen. Rank; Sergeant. Regiment or Service: Royal Irish Regiment. Unit; 2nd Battalion. Service Number; 9861. Date of death; 17/09/1914. Age at death;23. Born; Mooncoin, County Kilkenny. Enlisted; Waterford. Residence; Piltown, County Kilkenny. Died of wounds. Son of James and Anastasia Knox, of Tobernabrone, Piltown, Co. Kilkenny. (Richard Knox above was a cousin of Stephen Knox. Author) In his Will, dated 06-August1914, his effects and property were received by;- (Mother) Mrs James Knox, Tobernabrone, Piltown, County Kilkenny. Notes; Mooncoin, County Kilkenny (Soldiers died in the Great War). Mooncoin, County Waterford (Irelands Memorial Records). Died of wounds received in action at Braisne, France. Cemetery: La Ferte-Sous-Jouarre Memorial in France.

L

Lake, Sidney. Rank; Private. Regiment or Service: Royal Fusiliers (City of London Regiment). Unit; 4th Battalion. Service Number; L/11107. Date of death; 24/07/1916. Born; St John's, Kilkenny. Enlisted; Hounslow. Residence; Deptford. Killed in action. Husband of Elizabeth Blakeley (formerly Lake), of 16, Athol St., Earlestown Lancs. Grave or Memorial Reference; Pier and Face 8C, 9A and 16A. Cemetery: Thiepval Memorial in France.

Landy, Nicholas. Rank; Ordinary Seaman. Regiment or Service: Royal Navy. Unit; H. M. S."Turbulent.". Service Number; J/51142. Date of death; 01/06/1916. Age at death;25. Son of John and Alice Landy, of Garryricken, Windgap, Co. Kilkenny. Cemetery: Stavern Churchyard, Norway.

Langrishe, Hercules Ralph. Rank; Lieutenant. Regiment or Service: and Royal Flying Corps. Date of death; 16/02/1917. Age at death; 29. Killed. Son of Sir Hercules Langrishe, 5th Bart, of Knocktopher Abbey. Kilkenny People, February, 1917. Death of Lieutenant H. R. Langrishe, R. F. C. We deeply regret to announce the death of Lieutenant Hercules Ralph Langrishe, Montgomeryshire Yeomanry, who was killed on February 16 while flying on duty. The eldest son of Sir Hercules Langrishe Bart., of Knocktopher Abbey, County Kilkenny, he got his commission in the Montgomeryshire Yeomanry in August, 1914, and went to Egypt with his regiment in March-1916. he was signalling officer and qualified wireless instructor. He returned to England in August and joined the R. F. C. The Officer commanding the squadron to which he was attached writes—"Of all the young officers I have had to train, I never had a more promising one." The remains of the late Lieutenant Langrishe arrived at Ballyhale station on Monday, 19th inst., accompanied by his father, Commander Sir Hercules Langrishe, Bart., R. N. V. R., and his brother, Lieutenant Terence Langrishe, Irish Guards, and were accorded a full military funeral by the 2nd King Edward Horse, who are stationed in Kilkenny. A large concourse of all classes and creeds attended the funeral, and there were a number of beautiful wreaths. For Sir Hercules and Lady Langrishe the greatest sympathy is felt in the loss of their gallant son. The Weekly Irish Times. Ireland's Roll of Honour. February 24, 1917. Lieutenant H R Langrishe, Montgomeryshire Yeomanry, was accidentally killed in a flying expedition on 16th inst. He was the eldest son of Sir H langrishe, of Knocktopher Abbey, County Kilkenny. The Weekly Irish Times. Ireland's Roll of Honour. March 10, 1917. Lieutenant Hercules Ralph Langrishe, Montgomeryshire Yeomanry (attached Royal Flying Corps), who was killed while flying on duty on 16th February, was the eldest son of Sir Hercules Langrishe, Bart., and Lady Langrishe, of Knocktopher Abbey, County Kilkenny. Lieutenant Langrishe was 29 years of age. Grave or Memorial Reference; Panel 3 (Screen Wall). Cemetery: Grangegorman Memorial in Dublin. He is also commemorated on the Great War Memorial in St Canice's Cathedral, Kilkenny…'To the Glory of God and in loving memory of the following members of the Diocese of Ossory who gave their lives for their country in the Great War 1914-1918'.

Langton, Patrick Francis. Rank; Private. Regiment or Service: Australian Infantry, A. I. F. Unit; 1st Battalion. Service Number; 1237. Date of death; 16/09/1917. Age at death;38. Son of Patrick and Mary Langton, of 197, Belmont St., Alexandria, Sydney, New South Wales. Native of Ireland. Born, St John's, Kikenny, Ireland. Occupation on enlistment, Carter. Age on enlistment; 36 years 11 months. Address on enlistment, 'Bathurst' Avoca Street, Randwick, Sydney. Next of kin details; (wife) Mary. Clarabella. Langton, Torquay Forest Road, Arncliffe, N. S. W. Place and date of enlistment, 22-May-1916. R. A. S. Grounds, N. S. W. Weight, 140 lbs. Height, 5 feet, 10 inches. Complexion, fresh. Eyes, blue. Hair, brown. Killed in action. High Explosive shell wound in body while marching up to the line during enemy barrage. Grave or Memorial Reference; II A1 25. Cemetery: Menin Road South Military Cemetery in Belgium.

Lanigan, James. Rank; Private. Regiment or Service: Royal Irish Regiment. Unit; 2nd Battalion. Service Number; 6690. Date of death; 24/08/1914. Born; Butts, County Kilkenny. Enlisted; Kilkenny. Killed in action. Cemetery: La Ferte-Sous-Jouarre Memorial in France.

Lannon, James. Rank; Private. Regiment or Service: King's Liverpool Regiment. Unit; 3rd Battalion. Service Number; 11060. Date of death; 08/10/1915. Born; Callan, County Kilkenny. Enlisted; Liverpool. Residence; Liverpool. Died at home. Grave or Memorial Reference; Screen Wall (AD. 11. 61). Cemetery: Liverpool (Ford) Roman Catholic Cemetery in Liverpool, UK.

Lannon, Patrick. Rank; Private. Regiment or Service: Royal Irish Regiment. Unit; 3rd Battalion. Service Number; 215711. Date of death; 26/03/1916. Age at death; 46. Killed in action. Grave or Memorial Reference; In the North East part. Cemetery: Clara Old Graveyard, County Kilkenny

Lawless, Michael. Rank; Private. Regiment or Service: Irish Guards. Unit; 4th Company, 1st Battalion. Service Number; 4112. Date of death; 15/09/1916. Age at death;28. Born; Kilkenny. Enlisted; Clonmel, County Tipperary. Killed in action. After his death his effects and property were received by;- (Cousin) Robert Connell, Garranroe, Thurles, County Tipperary, Ireland. Tipperary Star, September, 1916. Thurles Guardsman Killed. Private Michael Lawless. Mrs Michael Connell, Garranroe, Thurles, received from the Secretary for War, this week, the sad intelligence of the death in action, on the 15th inst., of her nephew, Private Michael Lawless, No 4112, 1st Battalion Irish Guards. Mrs Connell is heart-broken over her loss. She reared the boy, and a better boy she says never lived. Far away in a distant land, Suddenly struck by death's strong hand, A nephew so dear, a hero brave, Lies beneath a soldier's grave. Could I have raised your dying head, Or heard your last farewell, The blow would not have been so hard, To her you loved so well. Grave or Memorial Reference; Pier and Face 7 D. Cemetery: Thiepval Memorial in France.

Lawless, Patrick. Rank; Private. Regiment or Service: Connaught Rangers. Unit; 6th Battalion, attached to the 8th Battalion. Service Number; 3/6628. Date of death; 18/07/1916. Age at death; 35. Born; Conahy, County Kilkenny. Enlisted; Manchester. Residence; Manchester. Died of wounds. Son of John and Elizabeth Lawless. In his Will, dated 18-June-1915, his effects and property were received by;- (Mother) Mrs Eliza Lawless, Newtown, Castlecomer, County Kilkenny, Ireland. Notes; Number listed as 6028 (SDGW) 3/6628 (CWGC). Grave or Memorial Reference; IV G 3. Cemetery: Vermelles British Cemetery in France.

Lawlor, Michael. Rank; Private. Regiment or Service: Royal Irish Regiment. Unit; 1st Battalion. Service Number; 9450. Date of death; 03/05/1915. Born; Muckalee, County Kilkenny. Enlisted; Waterford. Residence; Muckalee. Killed in action. After his death, his effects and property were received by;- Ellie Bryan, 69 High St, Kilkenny. Noncupative (or missing) Will was witnessed by;- Bridget Kelay, St John St, Kilkenny. May Purtill, St John St, Kilkenny. Thomas Cantwell JP, Kilkenny. Grave or Memorial Reference; Panel 33. Cemetery: Ypres (Menin Gate) Memorial in Belgium.

Lawlor, William. Rank; Private. Regiment or Service: Household Cavalry and Cavalry of the line including the Yeomanry and Imperial Camel Corps. Unit; 8th (King's Royal Irish) Hussars. Service Number; H/3904. Date of death; 30/08/1915. Born; Kilkenny. Enlisted; Dublin. Residence; Dublin. Died of wounds. In his Will, dated 07-December1914, his effects and property were received by;- Mrs Alice Dunne, Lincoln Lodge, CidiN. S. W. ater Avenue, Southsea, England. Notes; Number listed as 3904 (SDGW) H/3904 (CGWC). Grave or Memorial Reference; I G 32. Cemetery: Peronne Road Cemetery, Maricourt in France.

Leahy, Edward James. Rank; Private. Regiment or Service: Royal Dublin Fusiliers. Unit; 2nd Battalion. Service Number; 7711. Date of death; 18/12/1914. Age at death;34. Born; Kilkenny. Enlisted; Carlow. Residence; Kilkenny. Died of wounds. Son of James and Mary Leahy, of Leggettsrath, Kilkenny. Kilkenny Journal, January, 1915. Death of Private Edward Leahy, Kilkenny. Mr James Leahy, Leggetsrath, Dublin Road, Kilkenny, has received the sad intelligence of the death of his eldest son, Edward Leahy, from wounds received in action on 20th November, '14. Deep sympathy and regret are expressed by all creeds and classes to the poor father, who is a most popular working man, in his deep sorrow. The following expression of sympathy has been addresses to Mr James Leahy;-The King commands me to assure you of the true sympathy of His majesty and the Queen in your sorrow. KITCHENER. Mr Leahy has still two sons, Joseph and John, serving at the front. Kilkenny People, January 1915. Killed in Action. On Wednesday morning Mr James Leahy, Leggatstown, Dublin Road, received a notification from the war office that his son Patrick (sic), of the Dublin Fusiliers, had died from wounds received on the 20th November. Accompanying the notification was an expression of regret from the King and Lord Kitchener. From an article in an unknown Irish regional newspaper, December, 1914;-"Died in Hospital."How the Fallen heroes are laid to Rest. December20. For have they not died for country and kin? This morning they were laid to rest, brave fellows, in God's acre on the summit of the hill rising near the cathedral—a white-sepulchred pinnacle in the centre of an amphitheatre of rolling hills, with a segment of sea stretching away beyond. The sun shining bright—the first time for many days—in a radiantly blue sky, lighted on a melancholy scene. No gun-carriage here, with Union Jack o'erlaid, and the measured tread of martial mourners following the bier to the graveside. Just two coffins side by side in a deep trench awaiting the burial place, a small bunch of hite flowers resting on one side. One is a private of the Dublin Fusiliers, the other corporal of the 2nd Essex. A Catholic chaplain comes, his robes revealing as he walks the khaki beneath. Follows a firing party, who form up on each side of the trench, rifles reversed, heads down. Quietly sobbing, there is the corporals young widow, with her a motherly woman who has lost a soldier son. Behind stand reverently the grave-diggers, two or three French people, and the writer. Sonorously in the clear air rings out the priest's appeal to the Almighty. He finishes, and the soldiers present arms. At once his place is taken by a Church of England priest, not the Chief Caplain, Dr Gwynn, Bishop of Kartum, for he has just left for the front. Never have the beautiful simple words of the burial service sounded more impressive, more poignantly in the writer's ears,"The Lord gave and the Lord hath taken away." Once more the poor widow was shaken with sobs, for these last rites were for her beloved husband. A pause—and then the melancholy-sweet calenza of the "Last Post" trumpeting the triumph of these fallen warriors gone to their Valhalla. The men in khaki again present arms, about turn, and depart. No salvo. It is out of place here. An orderly stifles the lugubrious howling of someone's little dog. The clergyman goes to comfort the weeping women. The clouds fell. Day by day has this sad scene been enacted, sometimes 30 burials at a time. Over a thousand British soldiers brought back from the field to die in the base hospitals are interred here. One day, a tall obelisk will be erected giving the names of these victims. Twenty seven officers leave teir graves here, including a colonel of the 1st Middlesex, There are just small wooden crosses with numbers as an indication at present. Crude temporary crosses with names, have been put up in memory of two captains and a lieutenant. Here and there are a few wreaths of immortelles. In the officers section lies a nurse of the Red Cross, named Ethel Fearney. She also was given the soldiers funeral described above. Fifty yards away may be seen a small forest of little wooden crosses-only a small patch of ground—the Germans sepulchre. Thirty-three of them have died in the hospitals, including a captain and three lieutenants, and they were given the same honours and rites as our own men. In a day or two there will be a new grave in the British officers section—a young lieutenant who passed away yesterday before his mother could reach him. He died as a soldier would. Was it not Carlyle who asked,"What better could a man than die in the service of his country." (With a bit of detective work it was possible to identify these two solders and the cemetery as they had died relatively early in the war, buried in a cemetery that had a section for officers and was also the resting place of a nurse named Ethel Fearnley who died in 1914 (the article lists her as Fearney) The Corporal was Herbert Jones of Barking in Essex who also died of wounds the day after Private Leahy. Author. Grave or Memorial Reference; III B 66. Cemetery: Boulogne Eastern Cemetery in France.

Leahy, John. Rank; Private. Regiment or Service: Lancashire Fusiliers. Unit; 2nd Battalion. Service Number; 367. Date of death; 27/10/1914. Age at death; 35. Born; Kilkenny. Enlisted; Manchester. Died of wounds at home. Son of James and Kate Leahy, of Kilkenny. Grave or Memorial Reference; St. Anthony's Sect. 1842. Cemetery: Moston (St Joseph's) Roman Catholic Cemetery, UK.

Leahy, Joseph William. Rank; Private. Regiment or Service: Australian Infantry, A. I. F. Unit; 11th Battalion. Service Number; 1051. Date of death; 09/04/1917. Age at death;27. Killed in action. Son of Timothy and Margaret Leahy. Native of Kilkenny, Ireland. Born, Dublin, Ireland. Occupation on enlistment, teamster. Age on enlistment; 24 years 9 months. Next of kin details; (brother) M. J. Leahy. Place and date of enlistment, 07-September-1914. Blackboy Hill. In various places in his records he is listed as William Joseph instead of Joseph William although in correspondence between his brother and the authorities he is referred to as William Joseph. Weight, 157 lbs. Height, 5 feet, 11 ½ inches. Complexion, ruddy. Eyes, blue. Hair, dark brown. Grave or Memorial Reference; B 12. Cemetery: Morchies Australian Cemetery, Morchies, Pas De Calais, France.

Leahy, Richard. Rank; Driver. Regiment or Service: Royal Field Artillery. Unit; C Battery, 162nd Brigade. Service Number; 101648/101642. Date of death; 22/09/1917. Age at death; 20. Born; Kilkenny. Enlisted; Kilkenny. Killed in action. Son of James and Margaret Buggy Leahy, of Dublin Rd., Kilkenny. Notes; Number listed as 101648 (CWGC) 101642 (SDGW). Grave or Memorial Reference; IV D 6. Cemetery: Reninghelst New Military Cemetery, Poperinge, West-Vlaanderen, Belgium.

Leahy, Richard. Rank; Private. Regiment or Service: Australian Infantry, A. I. F. Unit; 43rd Battalion. Service Number; 2845. Date of death; 08/08/1918. Killed in action. Son of Mrs. Kate Leahy, of Glendine, Kilkenny, Ireland. Born, Kilkenny, Ireland. Occupation on enlistment, SAR porter. Age on enlistment; 24 years 9 months. Next of kin details; (mother) Mrs Kate Leahy, Glendine, Kilkenny, Ireland. Place and date of enlistment, 26-September-1916. Adelaide, South Australia. Weight, 140 lbs. Height, 5 feet, 7 inches. Complexion, fresh. Eyes, blue. Hair, brown. Initially buried in an isolated grave (Cerisy Road) ¾ mile west of Cerisy Sailly, 4 ¾ miles east of Corbie.
Will;- I give unto devise and bequeath unto my mother Kate Leahy of Glendine, Kilkenny, Ireland absolutely all my property both real and personal whatsoever and wheresoever and in the event of my said mother predeceasing me than I give evise and bequeath unto my father William Leahy of Glendine, Kilkenny, Ireland all my aid property absolutely. In witness whereof I the said Richard Leahy have to this my past Will and Testament set my hand the ninth day of December in the year of our Lord one thousand nine hundred and sixteen. Signed;- Richard Leahy. –The above will of Richard Leahy late of Murray Bridge but formerly of Mitcham in the State of South Australian Expeditionary Force deceased who died in France on the eighth of August 1918 was proved in the Supreme Court of South Australia on the second day of December 1918 by William Joseph McEvoy of Gawler in the said State of Catholice Clergyman Uncle of the said deceased the sole executor therein named.
Grave or Memorial Reference; I E 1. Cemetery: Villers-Bretonneux Military Cemetery in France.

Leakes/Leekes, Joseph. Rank; Private. Regiment or Service: Royal Irish Regiment. Unit; 1st Battalion. Service Number; 10185. Date of death; 10/05/1915. Age at death; 24. Born; Bagenalstown, County Carlow. Enlisted; Kilkenny. Residence; Shankill, County Kilkenny. Killed in action. Son of James and Maria Leakes, of Shankill, Whitehall, Co. Kilkenny. Grave or Memorial Reference; Panel 33. Cemetery: Ypres (Menin Gate) Memorial in Belgium.

Leary, Martin. Rank; Private. Regiment or Service: Duke of Cornwalls Light Infantry. Unit; 9th Battalion. Service Number; 3 6258. Date of death; 06/05/1916. Born; St James. Dublin. Enlisted; Dublin. Residence; Kilkenny. Died at home. Grave or Memorial Reference; BB 16. Cemetery: Wareham Cemetery, Dorset, UK.

Ledger, Edward Henry. Rank; Private. Regiment or Service: Royal Fusiliers (City of London Regiment). Unit; 9th Battalion. Service Number; L/13234. Date of death; 07/07/1916. Age at death; 26. Born; Kilkenny. Enlisted; Hounslow. Residence; Hornsey. Killed in action. Son of Edward and Rose Elizabeth Ledger, of 20, Park Hill Road, Ilfracombe, Devon. Grave or Memorial Reference; Pier and Face 8C, 9A and. Cemetery: Thiepval Memorial in France.

Lee, Arthur James. Rank; Private. Regiment or Service: Middlesex Regiment. Unit; 3rd BattalionL. Service Number; L/10862. Date of death; 10/02/1915. Age at death;24. Born; Kilkenny. Enlisted; Mill Hill, Middlesez. Killed in action. Son of Captain and Mrs. James Lee, of "Francesca," Parkland Grove, Ashford, Middlesex. Notes; Number listed as L/10862 (SDGW) 10862 (CWGC). Grave or Memorial Reference; B 18. Cemetery: Ramparts Cemetery, Lille Gate, Ieper in Belgium.

Lord, Frank. Rank; Corporal. Regiment or Service: Yorkshire Regiment. Service Number; 60833. Date of death; 27/09/1919. Age at death; 20. Son of Henry and Sarah Annie Lord, of Bury, Lancs. Grave or Memorial Reference; In the North part. Cemetery: Castlecomer (St Mary) Church of Ireland Churchyard, Kilkenny.

Loughman, William. Rank; Private. Regiment or Service: Leinster Regiment. Unit; 2nd Battalion. Service Number; 6143. Date of death; 20/10/1914. Born; Kilkenny. Enlisted; Kilkenny. Killed in action. Grave or Memorial Reference; Panel 10. Cemetery: Ploegsteert Memorial in Belgium.

Loughren, Matthew. Rank; Private. Regiment or Service: Labour Corps. Service Number; 553054. Date of death; 20/03/1919. Notes; Formerly he was with the Royal Garrison Artillery where his number was 18816. Grave or Memorial Reference; In the South West part. Cemetery: Kilkenny (St John) Catholic Churchyard, Kilkenny.

Loughrey, Daniel. Rank; Gunner. Regiment or Service: Royal Field Artillery. Service Number; 19663. Date of death; 21/06/1917. Died after discharge. Daniel in his Will and David on his medal index card. Died after discharge. In his Will, dated 21-July-1916, his effects and property were received by;- (Wife) Mrs Alice Loughrey, Lower Miltown, Kilmacow, County Kilkenny, Ireland. Cemetery: Unknown

Lowrie, John. Rank; Private. Regiment or Service: Australian Infantry, A. I. F. Unit; 9th Battalion. Service Number; 5419. Date of death; 03/09/1916. Age at death; 38. Born; Kilkenny. Died of wounds. Son of James and Maria Lowrie, of Mooloalah, Queensland. Native of Urlingford, Co. Kilkenny, Ireland. France. Occupation on enlistment, labourer. Age on enlistment; 36 years 7 months. Next of kin details; (father) Mr J Lowrie, Woydene, Via Beenleigh, Queensland. Place and date of enlistment, 10-January-1916. Brisbane, Queensland. His mother Maria, Laurie (sic) Mooloolah was granted a pension of £2 per fortnight from 15-November-1916. Weight, 140 lbs. Height, 5 feet, 5 1/8 inches. Complexion, fresh. Eyes, blue. Hair, brown. Notes; Died of wounds (gunshot to the thigh) at the 26th General Hospital, Etaples,. Grave or Memorial Reference; X B 7 A. Cemetery: Etaples Military Cemetery in France.

Lucas, Daniel. Rank; Private. Regiment or Service: Royal Irish Regiment. Unit; 2nd Battalion. Service Number; 5948. Date of death; 12/04/1918. Born; Ferrybank, County Waterford. Enlisted; Waterford. Killed in action. Notes; Born Ferrybank, County Kilkenny (SDGW). Ferrybank, County Waterford (Irelands Memorial Records). Grave or Memorial Reference; I B 37. Cemetery: Le Cateau Military Cemetery in France.

Lynch, Bartholomew Patrick. Rank; Lieutenant. Regiment or Service: Rifle Brigade. Unit; Attached to the 9th Brigade. Date of death; 15/09/1916. Age at death; 34. Born; Castlecomer, County Kilkenny. Killed in action. Listed in the 1901 Census living in Oxmanstown Road, Dublin. Son of Michael and Mary Anne Lynch, brother of Martha, Agnes, Kate, Cornelius, John and David Lynch. Irish Times. Lynch-September 15, killed in action, Lieutenant and Adjutant B P Lynch, Rifle Brigade, son of the late Michael and Mary Anne Lynch, 73 Clonliffe Road. Grave or Memorial Reference; Pier and Face 16B and. Cemetery: Thiepval Memorial in France.

Lynch, James. Rank; Private. Regiment or Service: Royal Irish Regiment. Unit; 2nd (Home Service) Garrison Battalion. Service Number; 2G/2780. Date of death; 23/05/1918. Born; Kilkenny. Enlisted; Carlow. Residence; Kilkenny. Died in hospital. In his Will, dated 24-October-1916, his effects and property were received by;- (Sister) Miss Bee Lynch, Freary Street, Kilkenny, Ireland. Notes; Number listed as 2G/2780 (CWGC) 2780 (SDGW). Formerly he was with the Leinster Regiment where his number was 3765. Died in hospital in Dublin. Grave or Memorial Reference; In the North East part. Cemetery: Kilkenny (St John) Catholic Churchyard, Kilkenny. Also listed under Leighlinbridge/Old Leighlin on the Great War Memorial, Milford Street, Leighlinbridge, County Carlow.

M

MacFadden/McFadden, George Loftus. Rank; Private. Regiment or Service: Irish Guards. Unit; 1st Battalion. Service Number; 4834. Date of death; 03/06/1915. Age at death; 18. Born; Kilmanagh, County Kilkenny. Enlisted; Dublin. Residence; Arklow, County Wixklow. Died of wounds at home. McFadden (SDGW) Macfaddin (CWGC), Son of the late Rev. T. H. MacFaddin and Ellen MacFaddin, of Kilmanagh, Co. Kilkenny. Irish Times. McFadden-June 3, 1915, of wounds received in action in France, George Loftus, 1st Battalion, Irish Guards, aged 18 years, fourth son of the late Rev. T W MacFadden. Canadian papers please copy. Grave or Memorial Reference; O 280. Cemetery: Shorncliffe Military Cemetery, UK.

Madden, Stephen. Rank; Private. Regiment or Service: Royal Inniskilling Fusiliers. Unit; 8th Battalion. Service Number; 43159. Date of death; 16/08/1917. Age at death;29. Born; Kilkenny. Enlisted; Liverpool. Killed in action. Son of Mary Madden, of 27, Hatfield St., Liverpool. Notes; Formerly he was with the Connaught Rangers where his number was 1499. Grave or Memorial Reference; II F 19. Cemetery: Potijze Chateau Grounds Cemetery in Belgium.

Maher, John. Rank; Corporal. Regiment or Service: Leinster Regiment. Unit; 1st Battalion. Service Number; 7622. Date of death; 09/05/1917. Age at death; 35. Born; Callan, County Kilkenny. Enlisted; Kilkenny. Died of wounds at Ypres. Won the D C M and Bar and Order of St. George 4th Class (Russia). Son of Mrs. Elizabeth Maher, of James St., Kilkenny. In his Will, dated 09-April-1915, effects and property ;- £5 To Mary Donavan, 14 Model Cottages, Cork, Ireland. Remaining to (Mother) Mrs Elizabeth Maher, James Street, Kilkenny, Ireland. Kilkenny People, May, 1915. Another Distinction for Kilkenny Hero. A few weeks ago we had pleasure in announcing that lance Corporal John Maher, of the 2nd Battalion, Leinster Regiment, had been awarded the D. C. M. for conspicuous gallantry in the field. Since then this plucky soldier has been transferred to the 1st Battalion of his Regiment, and promoted to the rank of Sergeant. He has further distinguished himself by his bravery and has received the following from Major General J. D. O'Snow, commanding 27th Division—"7622, Sergeant J. Maher, 1st Battalion, Leinster Regiment—Your commanding officer and brigade Commander have informed me that you have again distinguished yourself by your conduct in the field. I have read their report with much pleasure and have brought it to the notice of higher authority." Sergeant Maher is a well known Kilkennyman, and was on a visit to his mother at James's Street some few months ago, having been wounded "somewhere in France." Since his return he has won the D. C. M., and is now recommended for a further distinction. We heartily congratulate our courageous fellow-townsman. Kilkenny People, June, 1915. Honour for Dear Kilkenny Hero. The "Gazette" of Tuesday night contained the following;- "The under-mentioned non-commissioned officer has been awarded a clasp to his Distinguished Conduct Medal, which was granted to him for gallantry during the present campaign, published in the "Gazette" on the 1st April;-"Sergeant John Maher, 1st Leinster Regiment, for conspicuous gallantry, marked ability and coolness at St Eloi, on the 15tn March, 1915, when he took command of the trench after his officer had been killed and repulsed the attack of a very superior force inflicting great losses to the enemy."Sergeant

Maher is a Kilkennyman, the news of whose death officially appeared as "Died of wounds" in the casualty lists published on Thursday last. It is sad to think that he never lived to enjoy the distinctions which he won by his conspicuous bravery. Kilkenny People, May, 1915. Death of Sergeant J. Maher. Leinster Regiment. We sincerely regret to announce the death of the above named gallant soldier, notification of the sad fact being received by his mother on Thursday last. It will be remembered from paragraphs which appeared in these columns that the deceased was on a visit late last year to his mother, and subsequently on his return to the firing line he distinguished himself so highly that he was promoted to the rank of Sergeant and was awarded the Distinguished Conduct Medal. He was subsequently recommended for further honours and congratulated by his Commanding Officers. The sad news of his death has been received with feelings of keen regret in the city, where this gallant Kilkennyman was well-known and deservedly respected. To his sorrowing mother and the other members of his family we offer our respectful sympathy. Kilkenny Journal, May, 1915. Kilkenny Hero's Death. Sergeant John Maher. Killed in Action. Mrs E. Maher, James's Street, Kilkenny, has received the following letter from a Sergeant-Major of the 1st Leinster Regiment;-"Ypres, 9th May, 1915." " Dear Mrs Maher—I am extremely sorry to inform you of the death of your son, Sergeant J Maher, who was killed in action today, 9th inst. He was an admirable N. C. O. in every way; always cool and collected no matter what the emergency, and was extremely well liked by all ranks. It was touching to witness the marks of respect paid by the men when we buried him. I can imagine your motherly grief at the loss of such a fine fellow. I offer you my deepest sympathy, and can assure you the regiment can ill-afford to lose such a man in every sense these trying times."The sad intelligence of the death of Sergeant Maher was received in this city with feelings of deep regret. Sergeant Maher was attached to the Leinster regiment and shortly after the outbreak of war left for the front. He took part in many fierce battles, and by his indomitable courage nobly upheld the traditions of the fighting race. His conspicuous bravery attracted the attention if his commanding officers, who frequently congratulated him. At Armentiers he again distinguished himself, and by his acts of valour won for himself the coveted Distinguished Service Medal. Here a machine gun was trained upon him and he was wounded in five places. His wounds having healed, he left for the front again about two months ago, and the manner in which he behaved may be gathered from the fact that he was recommended for further honours. Now, when Kilkenny was keenly interested in the brave deeds of this gallant soldier, comes the news that he has died a soldier's death. Kilkenny Journal, September, 1915. A Kilkenny Hero. The Late Sergeant John Maher. D. C. M. Mrs. E. Maher, James's Street, Kilkenny has received the following letter;-War Office, London, S. W., 13th September, 1915. Madam—I am directed to inform you that his Imperial Majesty the Emperor of Russia has been graciously pleased to confer, with the approval of His Majesty the King, the Cross of the Order of St George, 4th Class, on your son, the late No. 7622, Acting Sergeant John Maher, 1st Battalion the Leinster Regiment, in recognition of his gallant conduct in the field. I am accordingly to forward herewith, to be retained as a memorial of the deceased non-commissioner officer's distinguished service, and to request that you will be so good as to acknowledge its receipt. —I am, Madam, your obedient servant, R. O. Montgomery, Inspector-General. The late Sergeant Maher, who was a young man of fine physique, and aged about 28 years, was educated at the Christian Brothers Schools, James's Street, where he held the position of teacher for some years. When about nineteen years of age he enlisted and joined the Leinster regiment. At the outbreak of war he proceeded with his regiment to the front, and took part in all the earlier—now historic—engagements. For his conspicuous bravery he was promoted on the field to the rank of sergeant, and, in addition, his bravery won for him the Distinguished Conduct Medal. Always to the fore where fighting was to be done, the gallant sergeant was made the target of a German machine gun, receiving five wounds. After having been in hospital for some time, he returned to his home in Kilkenny quite recently. He was the object of much interest in his native city, but, being possessed of a retiring and unostentatious disposition, the only account of his experience was summed up in the words,"Not too bad." After having stayed a short time in this city he rejoined his regiment, and ti was then, and then only, that the people of Kilkenny realised what a hero he had proved himself, as shortly after having rejoined his regiment, came the news of his having obtained the Distinguished Conduct Medal for conspicuous bravery. After having, practically, completely recovered from the effects of his wounds, he again left for the front, and a short time afterwards came the news that his bravery had been again rewarded, this time by the conferring on his of a clasp, in addition to the D. C. M. But "the paths of glory lead but to the grave," and while the people of Kilkenny were watching with pride the distinguished career of their fellow-citizen, the news came that he had died a soldier's death, he having been shot through the head at Ypres on the 9th of May. ow did he meet his death?—like a true son of Erin. The monotony of trench life proved too much for the indomitable sergeant, and—as related by another Kilkennyman who saw him die—he crawled over the parapet of his trench on the fatal day, and sniped for some time at the Germans in the opposite trench. The rest is soon told. A German bullet hit him in the forehead, killing him instantaneously. His death came as a severe blow to his comrades, by whom the late Sergeant Maher was know as the espirit de corps of the regiment. He was buried by his comrades amidst every manifestation of regret that such a boon companion, and one who had shed much lustre on the regiment, should be taken forever from amongst them. Grave or Memorial Reference; Panel 44. Cemetery: Ypres (Menin Gate) Memorial in Belgium.

Maher, Michael. Rank; Private. Regiment or Service: Royal Irish Regiment. Unit; 2nd Battalion. Service Number; 6497. Date of death; 24/05/1915. Age at death;43. Born; Callan, County Kilkenny. Enlisted; Manchester. Killed in action. Son of Michael Maher and Bridget Camfell, his wife; husband of Mary Maher, of 15, Appleton St., Collyhurst Road, Manchester. Grave or Memorial Reference; Panel 33. Cemetery: Ypres (Menin Gate) Memorial in Belgium

Maher, Michael. Rank; Private. Regiment or Service: Royal Irish Regiment. Unit; 2nd Battalion. Service Number; 7598. Date of death; 24/05/1915. Age at death; 41. Born; Urlingford. Enlisted; Liverpool. Residence; Urlingford, County Kilkenny. Killed in action. Son of Matthew and Margaret Maher; husband of Elizabeth Mary Maher, of 172, Conover St, Brooklyn, New York, U. S. A. Grave or Memorial Reference; II B 12. Cemetery: White House Cemetery, St Jean-Les-Ypres in Belgium.

Maher, Patrick. Rank; Private. Regiment or Service: South Wales Borderers. Unit; 2nd Battalion. Service Number; 25837. Date of death; 06/04/1916. Age at death;35. Born; County Klkenny. Enlisted; Cardiff, Glamorganshire. Killed in action. Listed in SDGW as Walsh, Patrick. (Served as Walsh), Son of James and Mary Maher (nee

Walsh), of Lower Conahy, Jenkinstown, Co. Kilkenny. Kilkenny People, April, 1916. Killed in Action. News has just reached Conahy notifying the death in action of Private Patrick Maher which occurred on April 6th. Deceased, who had 12 years service, was a son of Mrs James Maher, Lower Conahy, and had gone through some severe engagements. Mr James Burke, of Conahy, has also received news of the death of his nephew, private Michael Burke, who was killed on March 27th. He had been in France since the start of the war, and was a signaller in the Royal Engineers. He worked with Mr Maher, and was a prominent member of the National Volunteers and instructor of the Lower Conahy branch. Much sympathy is felt for the relatives of deceased men, who were deservedly popular in the locality. Grave or Memorial Reference; Pier and Face 4 A. Cemetery: Thiepval Memorial in France.

Maher, Peter. Rank; Corporal. Regiment or Service: U. S. Army. Unit; 308th Infantry Regiment, 77th Division. Date of death; 29/09/1918. Killed in action. Kilkenny People, November, 1918. Kilkennyman Killed Fighting with Americans. Early last week the sad news was received, at Springmount from Washington, D. C., of the death of Mr Peter Maher, third son of Mr Daniel Maher, who was killed in action while fighting with the American forces at the battle of Metz. A younger brother, John, was seriously wounded at the battle of Cambrai, but is making good progress towards convalescence. Quiet, gentle and unassuming, a real warm-hearted fellow, peter was deservedly a general favourite amongst the public, and his memory will be gratefully cherished by those who knew him sufficiently in life to regret him sincerely in death. On Wednesday an Office and High Mass were celebrated in the Windgap Church for the repose of his soul. A large number of relatives and friends attended the ceremonies. Much sympathy is felt for Mr Daniel Maher, and family in their bereavement. Grave or Memorial Reference; Plot G Row 34 Grave 5. Cemetery: Meuse-Argonne American cemetery, Romagne, France.

Mahon, Patrick. Rank; Company Sergeant Major. Regiment or Service: Leinster Regiment. Unit; 1st Battalion. Service Number; 6219. Date of death; 01/01/1918. Born; Clough, County Kilkenny. Enlisted; Aldershot, Hants. Died of wounds. Won the D. C. M. In his Will, dated 03-December1915, his effects and property were received by;- (Wife) Mrs A Mahon, C/o J F Reeves Esq, Kathgodam, United Provinces, India. Kilkenny People, February, 1918. The Military Medal for Castlecomer Soldier. The Military Medal has been gained by Colour-Sergeant-Major P. Mahon, Leinster Regiment of Castlecomer, County Kilkenny, for conspicuous gallantry and devotion to duty. Although wounded he went forward and rejoined his platoon, which was being attacked, and continued to direct it and to use his rifle until the attack was beaten off. He set a splendid example of pluck and fearlessness, and has on all occasions rendered exceptionally good an continuous service since the commencement of the war. Grave or Memorial Reference; G 27. Cemetery: Ramleh War Cemetery in Israel.

Mahoney, Edward. Rank; Private. Regiment or Service: Royal Irish Regiment. Unit; 5th Battalion. Service Number; 1570. Date of death; 28/03/1919. Age at death; 44. Grave or Memorial Reference; Near the North boundary. Cemetery: St Patrick's Graveyard, County Kilkenny.

Mahoney, John. Rank; Rifleman. Regiment or Service: Royal Irish Rifles. Unit; 1st Battalion. Service Number; 10178. Date of death; 07/09/1918. Born; Kilmacow, County Kilkenny. Enlisted; Waterford. Killed in action. Grave or Memorial Reference; Panel 9. Cemetery: Ploegsteert Memorial in Belgium.

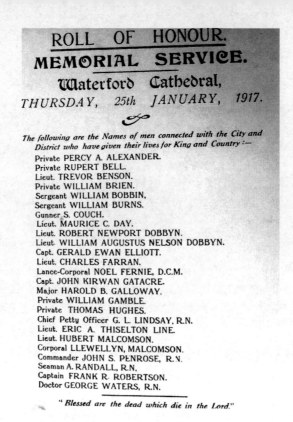

ROLL OF HONOUR.
MEMORIAL SERVICE.
Waterford Cathedral,
THURSDAY, 25th JANUARY, 1917.

The following are the Names of men connected with the City and District who have given their lives for King and Country :—

Private PERCY A. ALEXANDER.
Private RUPERT BELL.
Lieut. TREVOR BENSON.
Private WILLIAM BRIEN.
Sergeant WILLIAM BOBBIN,
Sergeant WILLIAM BURNS.
Gunner S. COUCH.
Lieut. MAURICE C. DAY.
Lieut. ROBERT NEWPORT DOBBYN.
Lieut. WILLIAM AUGUSTUS NELSON DOBBYN.
Capt. GERALD EWAN ELLIOTT.
Lieut. CHARLES FARRAN.
Lance-Corporal NOEL FERNIE, D.C.M.
Capt. JOHN KIRWAN GATACRE.
Major HAROLD B. GALLOWAY.
Private WILLIAM GAMBLE.
Private THOMAS HUGHES.
Chief Petty Officer G. L. LINDSAY, R.N.
Lieut. ERIC A. THISELTON LINE.
Lieut. HUBERT MALCOMSON.
Corporal LLEWELLYN, MALCOMSON.
Commander JOHN S. PENROSE, R.N.
Seaman A. RANDALL, R.N.
Captain FRANK R. ROBERTSON.
Doctor GEORGE WATERS, R.N.

" Blessed are the dead which die in the Lord."

Lieutenant Malcomson, courtesy of Eddie Sullivan, Waterford.

Malcomson, Hubert. Rank; Temporary Lieutenant and Adjutant. Regiment or Service: Royal Irish Regiment. Unit; 6th Battalion. Date of death; 16/09/1916. Died of wounds. The Waterford News, September 1916. LOCAL WAR ITEMS. County Waterford Officers Wounded. Lieut. H. Malcomson, Royal Irish Regiment, wounded, was born at Portlaw, Co. Waterford, being son of Mr. W. Malcomson, J. P. He graduated in 1912 at Cambridge with honours in mechnical sciences. He had been with Scott's Shipbuilding Company, Greenock, until the outbreak of war. He captained Pembroke College R. F. C. in 1911, and played for Greenock Wanderers. Captain H. G. Newport, Leinster Regiment, younger son of Mr. G. B. Newport, J. P., of Ballygallon, Inistioge, Co. Kilkenny, has been seriously wounded. Second Lieutenant N. L. Bor, Connaught Rangers, wounded was born at Tramore, County Waterford, 22 years ago. He is a son of Mr. E. N. C. Bor, Maryborough, a cousin of the late General J. N. Bor, of Lieutenant-Colonel Hobbs. and brother of Lieutenant T. H. Bor, R. N. R. He was a medical student at Trinity before entering the army. He played for the Wanderers, Dublin University Rugby Football Club, Clontarf Cricket Club, and Dublin University Swimming Club. Munster Express. Death of Co. Waterford Officer. Among Thursdays list of casualties the name of Second Lieutenant Malcomson, Royal Irish regiment appeared, who died of wounds received in action. This young officer was born in Portlaw, and was the son of Mr W Malcomson, J. P. He was wounded in the attack on the Somme by the Irish Division, and his name appeared on the casualty list for September 16th. He graduated from Cambridge in 1912. In the previous year he captained the Pembroke College Rugby Club. Waterford News. October, 1916. Death of an Officer. Amongst this week's list of casualties we regret to find the name of Second

Lieutenant Malcomson, Royal Irish Regiment, who died of wounds receivd in action. This gallant young officer was born at Portlaw, and was the son of Mr W. Malcomson, J. P. He was wounded in the attack at the Somme by the irish Division, and his name appeared in the casualty list for September 16th. He graduated at Cambridge in 1912. In the previous year he captained the Pembroke College Rugby Club. 23/09/1916. Freeman's Journal. County Waterford Officer's Funeral. The remains of Lieutenant H Malcomson, 18th Royal Irish Regiment, were brought to Clonmel by rail and have bee interred tin the Friends Burial Ground with military honours. Deceased was son of the late Mr William Malcolmson, Mayfield, Portlaw, and was severely wounded leading his men in the great action at Ginchy. He died of his wounds in a Manchester Hospital. Colonel Cooke, Commandant, 18th Royal Irish Depot, and staff officers of the R. F. A., and a large party of the 18th Royal Irish Regiment from the Depot, attended the funeral in addition to the public. The chief mourners were Miss Pim, Waterford, Miss Morley, Waterford; Misses Malcomson, Clonmel; Mrs H J Clibborn, Clonmel; Mrs R Malcomson, Clonmel, Mr Pim, Dublin (cousins). Listed in ODGW as Malcomson and CWGC as Malcolmson. Grave or Memorial Reference; In the South West corner. Cemetery: Clonmel Friends Burial Ground

Malone, James. Rank; Private. Regiment or Service: Royal Munster Fusiliers. Unit; 6th Battalion. Service Number; 353. Date of death; 15/08/1915. Age at death;43. Born; Kilkenny. Enlisted; St Helen's, Lancashire. Killed in Action in Gallipoli. Son of John and Mary Malone, of Inistioge, Co. Kilkenny. Grave or Memorial Reference; Panel 185 to 190. Cemetery: Helles Memorial in Turkey

Maloney, Andrew. Rank; Lance Corporal. Regiment or Service: Royal Munster Fusiliers. Unit; 1st Battalion. Service Number; 6882. Date of death; 12/04/1917. Born; Ballyhale, County Kilkenny. Enlisted; Waterford. Residence; Waterford. Died of wounds. Grave or Memorial Reference; I C 37. Cemetery: Fosse No. 10 Communal Cemetery Extension, Sains-En-Gohelle in France.

Manning, Christopher. Rank; Private. Regiment or Service: Welsh Regiment. Unit; C Company, 1st/6th Battalion. Service Number; 1663. Date of death; 01/10/1915. Age at death;36. Born; Kilkenny. Enlisted; Clydach, Glamorganshire. Killed in action. Son of Mrs. Johanna Ryan, of Ballincur, Mooncoin. Waterford. After his death, his effects and property were received by;- (Mother or Grandmother) Mrs Johanna Ryan, Ballincure, Mooncoin, County Kilkenny, Ireland. Grave or Memorial Reference; 77 and 78. Cemetery: Loos Memorial in France.

Manning, George Frederick. Rank; Lieutenant. Regiment or Service: Africal Imperial Forces. Date of death; Unknown. Killed in action. This officer is not in ny of the databases. Cemetery: Great War Memorial in St Canice's Cathedral, Kilkenny. 'To the Glory of God and in loving memory of the following members of the Diocese of Ossory who gave their lives for their country in the Great War 1914-1918'.

Marescaux, Gerald Charles Adolphe. Rank; Vice Admiral. Regiment or Service: Royal Navy. Date of death; 03/09/1920. Age at death;60. Awarded C B, C M G, 4 times Mentioned in Despatches. Commander of the Legion of Honour. Born in London. Son of Laurence and Grace Marescaux; husband of Kathleen Marescaux (nee Dennis) of Inchihholohan, Kilkenny. Entered R. N. 1873; Commander 1896; Captain 1903; Rear Admiral 1913; Vice Admiral (retired) 1915. Retired from the army with the rank of Colonel. Colonel Commandant of Dunkirk, 1916-1918; O. C. Troops, Paris, during Armistice. Grave or Memorial Reference; Naval 8 427. Cemetery: Gillingham (Woodlands) Cemetery, UK. He is also commemorated on the Great War Memorial in St Canice's Cathedral, Kilkenny…'To the Glory of God and in loving memory of the following members of the Diocese of Ossory who gave their lives for their country in the Great War 1914-1918'.

Marnell, Walter. Rank; Private. Regiment or Service: Irish Guards. Unit; 1st Battalion. Service Number; 6414. Date of death; 01/07/1916. Age at death; 22. Born; Dunamaggin, County Kilkenny. Enlisted; Kilkenny. Died of wounds in Belgium. Son of John Marnell and Kate Marnell, of Dunamaggan, Callan, Co. Kilkenny. Volunteered after outbreak of war. In his Will, dated 02-June-1916, effects and property were received by;- (Mother) Mrs John Marnell, Dunnamaggan, Callan, County Kilkenny, Ireland. Grave or Memorial Reference; VIII B 34A. Cemetery: Lijssenthoek Military Cemetery in Belgium.

Marsh, Gilbert Howe Maxwell. Rank; Captain. Regiment or Service: Indian Army. Unit; 41st Dogras. Date of death; 01/11/1914. Son of the late Col. Jeremy Taylor-Marsh (Royal Engineers) and Mrs. Marsh. Grave or Memorial Reference; I A 9. Cemetery: Bethune Town Cemetery, Pas-de-Calais, France.

Marsh, Harry Frances Freke. Rank; Captain. Regiment or Service: Indian Army. Unit; 2nd King Edward's Own Gurkha Rifles (The Sirmoor Rifles). Date of death; 02/02/1917. Son of Henry Marsh, C. I. E., of Springmount, Mountrath, Queen's Co., and the late Helen E. Marsh. Grave or Memorial Reference; XXI J 11. Cemetery: Amara War Cemetery in Iraq.

Martin, Laurence Henry. Rank; Lieutenant. Regiment or Service: Royal Irish Fusiliers. Unit; 9th Battalion (North Irish Horse). Date of death; 23/11/1917. Killed in action. Son of the Rev. Richard D'Olier Martin and Mrs. Catharine Mary Martin, of The Rectory, Killeshandra, Co. Cavan. De Ruvigny's Roll of Honour;-…. 2nd son of the Reverend Richard D'Olier Martin, M. A., incumbent of Killeshandra, County Cavan, by his wife, Catherine Mary, daughter of Richard Clifford, I. C. S. Born at Duncannon, County Wexford, 07-August-1897. Educated at Monkstown College O. T. C. 01-August-1916. Gazetted 2nd lieutenant, Royal Irish Fusiliers, 25 April-1917. Served with the Expeditionary Force in France and Flanders from July, and was killed in action at Moeuvres, near Cambrai, 27-November-1917. Buried between Moeuvres and the Canal du Nort. An officer wrote; " A gallant Irish gentleman," and one of his men; " We all loved him; there wasn't a man in his platoon but would have died for him." He was unmarried. Grave or Memorial Reference; II A 9. Cemetery: Moeuvres Communal Cemetery Extension, Nord, France.

Martin, Michael. Rank; Private. Regiment or Service: Irish Guards. Unit; 2st Battalion. Service Number; 6314. Date of death; 15/09/1916. Age at death; 22. Born; Gouran, County Kilkenny. Enlisted; Carlow. Killed in action. Son of John and Mary Martin, of High St., Gowran, Co. Kilkenny. Grave. Grave or Memorial Reference; Pier and Face & D. Cemetery: Thiepval Memorial in France.

Matthews, Thomas. Rank; Private. Regiment or Service: Labour Corps. Unit; 4th Battalion. Service Number; 174810. Date of death; 15/06/1920. Notes; Formerly he was with the 4th Battalion, Royal Irish Regiment where his number was 11534. Grave or Memorial Reference; In the West part. Cemetery: Columbkille Old Graveyard, County Kilkenny.

McCarthy, James. Rank; Private. Regiment or Service: Irish Guards. Unit; 1st Battalion. Service Number; 4640. Date of death; 10/10/1917. Age at death; 26. Born; Gowran, County Kilkenny. Enlisted; Kilkenny. Killed in action. Son of Thomas McCarthy, of Brickana, Gowran, Co. Kilkenny. Grave or Memorial Reference; Panel 10 to 11. Cemetery: Tyne Cot Memorial in Belgium.

McCarthy, John. Rank; Private. Regiment or Service: Household Cavalry and Cavalry of the line including the Yeomanry and Imperial Camel Corps. Unit; 4th (Queen's Own) Hussars. Service Number; 9581. Date of death; 03/05/1915. Age at death;22. Born;

Danesfort, County Kilkenny. Enlisted; Kilkenny. Residence; Kilkenny. Died of wounds. Son of John and Johanna McCarthy, of Cuffe's Grange, Co. Kilkenny. After his death, his effects and property were received by;- (Mother) Mrs J McCarthy, Cuffes Grange, County Kilkenny, Ireland. Grave or Memorial Reference; Panel 5. Cemetery: Ypres (Menin Gate) Memorial in Belgium

McClean, John Willoughby. Rank; Private. Regiment or Service: Canadian Infantry (Alberta Regiment). Unit; 10th Battalion. Service Number; 20795. Date of death; 23/04/1915. Born; Valcartier. Next of kin listed as William McClean, 32 Madison Ave, Cave Hill Road, Belfast. Place of birth, Newry, County Down. Date of birth, 1886. Occupation on enlistment, Clerk. Height, 5 feet, 7 inches. Complexion, dark. Eyes, grey. Hair, black. Notes; Born 25/09/1914. Grave or Memorial Reference; II M 32. Cemetery: Poperinghe Old Military Cemetery in Belgium. This man is also listed on the War Memorial in Portlaoise.

McCombie, Robert Hercules Brideoake. Rank; Private (Rev). Regiment or Service: New Zealand Medical Corps. Service Number; 3 3507. Date of death; 09/11/1918. Age at death;23. Born; Kyle, Kilkenny. Died of wounds. Son of Thomas Gerald Fitzgibbon McCombie and Louisa Frances Gordon McCombie (nee Wilkie) of Laurel Bank, Monkstown, County Dublin. Rector of St Peters, Granity, New Zealand. Notes; Born 16-November-1890, Kyle, Kilkenny. Wounded in action at the battle of Le Quesnoyon 04-November-1918 and died of wounds 09-November-1918. Grave or Memorial Reference; IV D 31. Cemetery: Caudry British Cemetery, Nord in France.

McConville, Edward. Rank; Acting Sergeant. Regiment or Service: Lancashire Regiment. Unit; 7th Battalion. Service Number; 6741. Date of death; 05/07/1916. Born; Kilkenny. Enlisted; Burnley, Lancashire. Killed in action. Grave or Memorial Reference; VI I 5. Cemetery: Gordon Dump Cemetery, Ovilliers-La-Boiselle in France.

McCreery, Mona James Nathaniel. Rank; Captain. Regiment or Service: Royal Dublin Fusiliers. Unit; 3rd Battalion. Date of death; 21/10/1918. Age at death;26. Died. Grave or Memorial Reference; Close to North entrance of Cathedral. Cemetery: Kilkenny (St Canice) Church of Ireland Cathedral, Kilkenny. He is also commemorated on the Great War Memorial in St Canice's Cathedral, Kilkenny…'To the Glory of God and in loving memory of the following members of the Diocese of Ossory who gave their lives for their country in the Great War 1914-1918'.

McDonald, James. Rank; Private. Regiment or Service: Royal Irish Regiment. Unit; 2nd Battalion. Service Number; 8189. Date of death; 25/05/1915. Age at death; 35. Born; Kilrush, County Clare. Enlisted; Wexford. Residence; Ferrybank, County Kilkenny. Died of from the effects of gas poisoning. Husband of Mary Anne McDonald of Glasshouse, Ferrybank, Waterford. After his death, his effects and property were received by;- (Wife) Maryanna MacDonald, Rahcullene Lodge, Ferry Bank, County Kilkenny. Notes; Born Kilrush, County Wexford (CWGC) Born in Kilrush, Co Wexford. Irelands Memorial Records states that he was born in Kilrush, County Clare. Grave or Memorial Reference; I F 75. Cemetery: Bailleul Communal Cemetery Extension (Nord) in France.

McDonald, Kenneth William. Rank; Lieutenant. Regiment or Service: Corps of Royal Engineers Territorials and Royal Flying Corps. Unit; Lowland Field Company. Date of death; 04/09/1917. Age at death;21. Died of wounds in German hands. Son of Joseph McDonald, of Kilkenny. The Weekly Irish Times. Ireland's Roll of Honour. December 8, 1917. Lieutenant K W McDonald, R. E., and R. F. C., died of wounds on September 4th last while a prisoner of war. He was wounded on September 3rd, and was the younger son of Mr Joseph McDonald, J. P., Glendine Cottage, Kilkenny. The Weekly Irish Times. Ireland's Roll of Honour. October 13, 1917. Mr Joseph McDonald, Glendine Cottage, Kilkenny, has been officially informed that his younger son is reported wounded and a prisoner in Germany. Lieutenant McDonald, who was an apprecntice engineer with Messrs Yarrow, Glasgow, at the beginning of the war, joined the Royal Engineers as a sapper, and was afterwards granted a commission with his company, and thereafter promoted Lieutenant. He became attached to the Royal Flying Corps, and after qualifying as pilot had been employed in France, where he was brought down wounded behind the German lines. His elder brother is Surgeon Charles McDonald, M. B., R. N., on active service. Grave or Memorial Reference; XIII C 5. Cemetery: Harlebeke New British Cemetery in Belgium. He is also commemorated on the Great War Memorial in St Canice's Cathedral, Kilkenny…'To the Glory of God and in loving memory of the following members of the Diocese of Ossory who gave their lives for their country in the Great War 1914-1918'. Listed on the memorial as attached to the Royal Flying Corps.

McDonald/Macdonald, Archibald. Rank; Lance Sergeant/Band Sergeant. Regiment or Service: Yorkshire Light Infantry. Unit; 2nd Battalion. Service Number; 6923. Date of death; 28/10/1914. Age at death; 33. Born; Kilkenny. Enlisted; Ashton-under-Lyne. Killed in action. Won the DCM in the South African War and the Clasp to the DCM in 1914. Mentioned in Despatches: (South African War). Medaille Militaire (France). Son of Mrs. Eliza Macdonald, of 10, Napoleon Rd., St. Margaret's, Twickenham. McDONALD (SDGW, IMR) Macdonald (CWGC),. Notes; McDonald (SDGW) MacDonald (ODGW). Grave or Memorial Reference; Panel 31. Cemetery: Le Touret Memorial in France.

McDonnell, John. Rank; Corporal. Regiment or Service: Royal Irish Regiment. Unit; 6th Battalion. Service Number; 4113. Date of death; 09/05/1916. Born; Cuff's Green. County Kilkenny. Enlisted; Callan. Killed in action. After his death, his effects and property were received by;- (Wife) Mrs McDonald, Green Street, Callan, County Kilkenny, Ireland. (In his Will he is named McDonald, John.). Grave or Memorial Reference; I G 4. Cemetery: Dud Corner Cemetery, Loos in France.

McEvoy, James. Rank; Guardsman. Regiment or Service: Irish Guards. Unit; 1st Battalion. Service Number; 274. Date of death; 22/05/1920. Age at death; 38. Died in hospital. Son of Denis and Ellen McEvoy. Native of Kilkenny, Ireland. In his Will, dated 02-April-1914, effects and property were received by;- Patrick Brennan, Birchfield, County Kilkenny. Notes; Died in Queen Alexandra Military Hospital, Millbank, London. Grave or Memorial Reference; XII A 7A. Cemetery: Brookwood Military Cemetery, UK.

McGee, Patrick. Rank; Private. Regiment or Service: Cameronians (Scottish Rifles). Unit; 9th Battalion. Service Number; 7876. Date of death; 25/09/1915. Age at death;31. Born; Dungannon, County Tyrone. Enlisted; Glasgow. Killed in action. Son of John and Mary McGee, of 47, Churchill Street, Belfast; husband of Margaret Mary McGee, of 58, High Street, Kilkenny. Grave or Memorial Reference; Panel 57 to 59. Cemetery: Loos Memorial in France.

McGee, Patrick. Rank; Private. Regiment or Service: Royal Inniskilling Fusiliers. Unit; 8th Battalion. Service Number; 26157. Date of death; 27/04/1916. Age at death; 27. Born; Kilkenny. Enlisted; Kilkenny. Killed in action. Son of Dennis McGee, of Upper Walkin Street, Kilkenny. Notes; Formerly he was with the Royal Irish Regiment where his number was 1804. Grave or Memorial Reference; Panel 60. Cemetery: Loos Memorial in France.

McGee, Paul. Rank; Private. Regiment or Service: Royal Irish Regiment. Unit; 6th Battalion. Service Number; 1802. Date of death; 06/06/1916. Age at death;26. Born; St Canice's, Kilkenny. Enlisted; Kilkenny. Killed in action. Son of Margaret McGee, of 8, Upper Walkin Street, Kilkenny. Grave. Grave or Memorial Reference; VII D 6. Cemetery: St Mary's A. D. S. Cemetery, Haisnes in France.

McGrath, John Robert. Rank; Stoker 1st Class. Regiment or Service: Royal Navy. Unit; H. M. S. Conquest. Service Number; SS103926. Date of death; 28/03/1916. Age at death; 28. Born; Kilkenny. Killed or died by means other than disease, accident or enemy action. Son of Annie McGrath of 6, Ludlow Street, Belfast, and the late Thomas McGrath. Next of kin listed as Mother. Annie. 95, New Lodge Rd., Belfast, Ireland. Notes; D. O. B. 05/12/1887. Cemetery: Walton-on-the-Naze (or Walton-le-Soken) (All Saints) Churchyard Extension, Essex, UK.

McGrath, Michael. Rank; Rifleman. Regiment or Service: Royal Irish Rifles. Unit; 2nd Battalion. Service Number; 8012. Date of death; 17/11/1916. Age at death;18. Born; Roscrea, County Tipperary. Enlisted; Waterford. Killed in action. Son of Mrs. Elizabeth McGrath, of 4, Pound St, Nenagh, Co. Tipperary. His will gives his mothers address as 13 Peters Street, Waterford. The only Irish McGrath that died around this time is Michael listed above, I include the articles below for your reference. Munster Express, 23-December-1916. Private McGrath, Rogerstown, Kilmoganny, son of Mr Thomas McGrath, has been killed in action at the front. Much sympathy is felt for the young man's parents and family in the district. Waterford News. August, 1916. Waterford Men in the Casualty List. In the casualty lists published to-day appear the names of the following Waterford soldiers who have been wounded;- Private T. Croke, Royal Irish Regiment, (5233), Waterford; Private J. Keane, (8018), do. ; Private M. McGrath (8012),do. ; Private J. Sullivan, (5227), do. ; Private S. Thompson, (8866), do. Grave or Memorial Reference; I J 5. Cemetery: Berks Cemetery Extension in Belgium.

McGrath, Patrick. Rank; Corporal/Lance Sergeant. Regiment or Service: Royal Irish Regiment. Unit; 1st Battalion. Service Number; 4038. Date of death; 22/09/1915. Born; Ballyraggett, County Kilkenny. Enlisted; Kilkenny. Residence; Ballyraggett. Died of wounds. After his death his effects and property were received by;- Mrs M Annie McGrath, High St, Ballyragget, County Killkenny, Ireland. Grave or Memorial Reference; Plot 1. Row A. Grave 32. Cemetery: Corbie Communal Cemetery in France.

McGrath, Richard. Rank; Driver. Regiment or Service: Australian Field Artillery. Unit; 13th Brigade. Service Number; 1903. Date of death; 12/12/1917. Age at death;33. Born; Kilkenny. Killed in action in the field. Son of Patrick and Margaret McGrath, of Raff St., Toowoomba, Queensland. Occupation on enlistment, engine driver. Age on enlistment; 31 years 7 months. Next of kin details; (mother) Margaret McGrath, C/o Mrs Rooks,"Cowra", Hill Street, Toowoomba, in 1920 this was changed to Raff Street, Toowoomba. His widowed mother received a pension of £2/3/-per fortnight from 04-March-1918. Place and date of enlistment, 20-August-1915. Toowoomba. Weight, 145 lbs. Height, 5 feet, 11 inches. Complexion, ruddy. Eyes, grey. Hair, auburn. Grave or Memorial Reference; II D 7. Cemetery: Westhof Farm Cemetery, Heuvelland, West-Vlaanderen, Belgium.

McGuire, Philip. Rank; Private. Regiment or Service: Royal Irish Regiment. Unit; 6th Battalion. Service Number; 1975. Date of death; 25/01/1916. Born; Mooncoin, County Kilkenny. Enlisted; Merthyr, Glamorganshire. Killed in action. Grave or Memorial Reference; I. B. 4. Cemetery: Philosophe British Cemetery, Mazingarbe in France.

McKenna, Harry. Rank; Private. Regiment or Service: Australian Infantry, A. I. F. Unit; 34th Battalion. Service Number; 2931. Date of death; 20/03/1919. Born; Kilkenny. Enlisted; Sydney, N. S. W. Died. Occupation on enlistment, labourer, barber. Age on enlistment; 44 years 2 months. Previous military experience; 3rd Hussars, 12 years. Horneycroft Mounted Infantry (Boer War), 3 years. Natal Field Artillery, 5 months. Next of kin details; (wife) Agnes McKenna, 1 Military Road, North Sydney, N. S. W. Weight, 168 lbs. Height, 5 feet, 9 ½ inches. Complexion, fair. Eyes, brown. Hair, brown. On 25-August-1916 he was 'discharged medically unfit not due to misconduct. ' 'Permanently unfit for General Service but fit for Home Service. ' Due to Bunions/ deformed feet. Re-enlisted in November-1916. He was passed b the medical team for home service as he could gain employment in civilian life due to bunions. Information of Witness severally taken and acknowledged on behalf of our sovereign Lord and King touching the death of Harry McKenna at No 10 East Street in the Parish of Nelcombe Regis in the County of Dorset the 22nd day of March 1919 before Gustavus Phelps Symes B. C. L one of his majesty's Coroners for the said County of Dorset on view of the body of the said person then and there lying dead. Henry George Rugg. On oath states;-Licence Fountain Hotel, King Street, Weymouth. On Thursday 20th March 1919 about 5. 55. p. m. went out to the lavatory at the back of my hotel. I had locked up the lavatory at 2. 30. I noticed a bad smell. I tried to open the closet door out and found it closed. Saw a man sitting on the seat fully dressed. I thought he was asleep and tried to rouse him. Found he was unconscious. Sent for Police. P. C. Scriven came. We sent for Dr Lane—he came. Said man was dead. Took him out. Taken to Mortuary. Did not know the man…William James Gordon. On oath states;-Captain A. I. F. I have seen the body at the Weymouth Mortuary as seen by the Coroner. It is that of Harry McKenna, 34th Batt., A. I. F/ Stationed at Camp Littlemore. Native of No 1. Military Road, North Sydney, N. S. W. Single man (in his military records there are a few references to his wife being 'unmarried' Author). Been at Littlemore since 24th/5/16. No complaint of any illness. Received information Thursday evening of finding of body…Doctor Lane. On oath states;--Duly registered Medical Practitioner. On Thursday evening called to Fountain. Found deceased there dead. Removed to Mortuary. No evidence of cause of death. No struggle. Nothing wrong of any sort. Made P. M. by coroners Order—I found that a piece of artificial tooth plate had become broken off and got into wind pipe and death was due to asphyxia caused by this obstruction…. Notes; Enlisted 10-May-1916. Found dead in Weymouth. Cause of death ;-'suffocation caused by breaking artificial teeth. '.

From his records;-Dear Madam. With reference to the report of the regrettable loss of your husband, the late No 2931, Private H McKenna, 34th Battalion, I am now in receipt of advice which shows that he died on 20th March, 1919, at Weymouth, England, from suffocation, caused by breaking artificial teeth, and was buried on the 24th idem in Melcombe Regis Cemetery, Weymouth. Separate single grave in Virgin Soil, Consecrated Ground, Chaplain the Rev. Father Halpin officiating. The deceased soldier was buried with full military honors, the coffin (elm with brass mounts) draped with the Australian flag being borne to the graveside on a gun-carriage preceded by a Friting Party from No 2 Australian Command Depot, Weymouth. Six Australians supported the Pall. The "Last Post" was sounded and volleys fired over the grave. A large number of Non-Commissioned Officers and Men followed the remains and were present at the graveside ceremony. Headquarters A.I.F. Depots in United Kingdom were represented at the funeral.

Grave or Memorial Reference; II C 3034. Cemetery: Melcombe Regis Cemetery, Dorset, UK.

McKenna, Michael. Rank; Private. Regiment or Service: Royal Irish Regiment. Unit; 2nd/3rd Battalion. Service Number; 3083. Date of death; 26/05/1915. Born; St Canice's, Kilkenny. Enlisted; Tipperary. Residence; Kilkenny. Died of wounds. In his Will, dated 06-May-1915, effects and property were received by;- (Father) Mr Michael McKenna, Bishops Hill, Kilkenny. Kilkenny People, June, 1915. Kilkenny Soldier Killed by Gas. Private Michael McKenna, 4th Royal Irish, son of Mr Michael McKenna, Bishop's Hill, Kilkenny, is the first victim of Germany's new "technical weapon"— poisonous gas. Father Edward Stilton, the Catholic Chaplain, writing to the father of the dead soldier on the 26th May, states;--"Private McKenna came to the hospital in a bad state through the effects of gas. He lingered for some time, but he has laid down his life for this great cause, and I am so sorry to send this news, but pray that God, Our Father, will help you through this great sorrow. I thought you would like know although the news is so sad and painful to you. God's Benediction upon you." Private McKenna joined the 4th Battalion several years ago. At the outbreak of the war in August, being on the reserve, he was called up, and in the course of a few months went to the front. There he took part in many desperate engagements, escaping unscathed. Eventually while in the trenches he got frost-bitten, and under heavy shell fire was wounded by shrapnel in the wrist and shoulder. After remaining several weeks in hospital, he spent a fortnight on furlough in Kilkenny. Being a young man of robust constitution he rapidly recovered and having reported himself fit was sent to the front again, being actually under fire four days after the termination of his visit to Kilkenny. He had many hair-breath escapes, but succumbed to the poisonous gases, which are now such a formidable weapon in the hands of the Huns. Much sympathy is felt with the relatives of Private Kenny. Notes; Battalion listed as 2nd Battalion (SDGW) 3rd Battalion (CWGC). Grave or Memorial Reference; II B 16. Cemetery: Hazebrouck Communal Cemetery, Nord, in France.

McKenna, Patrick. Rank; Driver. Regiment or Service: Royal Field Artillery. Unit; D Battry, 121st Brigade. Service Number; 77374. Date of death; 19/08/1917. Age at death;34. Enlisted; Cork. Residence; Bishop's Hill, Kilkenny. Killed in action in Belgium. Son of Michael McKenna, of Kilkenny. In his Will, dated 20-August-1916, effects and property were received by;- (Sister) Miss Nora McKenna, Bishop's Hill St, Kilkenny. Grave or Memorial Reference; IV D 14. Cemetery: Bard Cottage Cemetery in Belgium.

Sergeant McKeone, from De Ruvigny's Roll of Honour.

McKeon/McKeone, John Henry. Rank; Sergeant. Regiment or Service: Cheshire Regiment. Unit; 16th Battalion. Service Number; W/405. Date of death; 22/04/1917. Age at death; 35. Born; Waterford. Enlisted; Port Sunlight, Cheshire. Residence; Rock Ferry, Cheshire. Killed in action. McKeon (SDGW), McKeone (CWGC), Son of William and Eleanor McKeone, of Waterford; husband of Annie McKeone, of 31, BruN. S. W. ick St, Roch Ferry, Cheshire. De Ruvigny's Roll of Honour. 13th (Service) Battalion (Wirrall), The Cheshire Regiment. Son of William McKeone, of Waterford, Groom, by his wife, Elenor, daughter of William Thorpe; and stepfather to Private R. Thompson (q. v). Born Kilfane, Tomastown, County Kilkenny, 11-November-1882. Educated at the Model School, Waterford. Was a Labourer. Served in the South African War, 1899-1902 (Queen's and king's medals). Volunteered for foreign service after the outbreak of the European War, and joined the Wirrall Battalion of the Cheshire Regiment, 04-September-1914. Served with the Expeditionary Force in France and Flanders from September-1915, until 26-April-1916, when he was wounded and sent to England. Returned to France, 08-March-1917, and was killed in action at St Quentin, 27-April following. Buried there. He married at Dublin, 08-August-1908, Annie (31, Brunswick Street, Rock Ferry, Co. Chester), widow of James George Thompson and daughter of William Weatherup of Dublin. Grave or Memorial Reference; III E 13. Cemetery: Chapelle British Cemetery, Holnon, in France.

McLean, Henry Abraham. Rank; Trooper. Regiment or Service: Australian Light Horse. Unit; 2nd, attached to the Railway Section, Anzac. Service Number; 1105. Date of death; 03/12/1915. Age at death;33. Born; Rathielty, County Kilkenny. Enlisted; Beaufort, Queensland. Died of dysentery. Son of Edmond and Margaret McLean. Native of Rathelty, County Kilkenny, Ireland. Born, Freshford, County Kilkenny, Ireland. Occupation on enlistment, labourer. Age on enlistment; 26 years - months. Next of kin details; (aunt) Louisa Daniels, Rathmole, Kilkenny Ireland. Weight, 12st 9 lbs. Height, 5 feet, 11 ¾ inches. Complexion, fair. Eyes, grey. Hair, dark brown. Notes; Enlisted 06-February-1915. Died of dysentery in Gallipoli and buried at sea from the Hospital Ship 'Glenart Castle'. Grave or Memorial Reference; 2. Cemetery: Lone Pine Memorial in Turkey. He is also commemorated on the Great War Memorial in St Canice's Cathedral, Kilkenny…'To the Glory of God and in loving memory of the following members of the Diocese of Ossory who gave their lives for their country in the Great War 1914-1918'.

McNamee, Peter. Rank; Private. Regiment or Service: Suffolk Regiment. Unit; 2nd Battalion. Service Number; 3 9316. Date of death; 18/06/1915. Born; Kilkenny. Enlisted; Ipswitch. Killed in action. Grave or Memorial Reference; I D 17. Cemetery: Voormezeele Enclosures No1 and No2 in Belgium.

Meagher/Maher, Edward/Edmond. Rank; Private. Regiment or Service: Irish Guards. Service Number; 11872. Date of death; 06/06/1917. Age at death;30. Born; Kilkenny. Died. Son of John and Mary Maher. Eldest brother of Margaret, Thomas, William, Daniel and Patrick Maher, Tullaghanbrogue, Kilkenny. Notes; Name listed as Edward (CWGC) Edmond (Census) Meagher (CWGC) Maher (Census). Cemetery: Brookwood (United Kingdom) Memorial, Surrey.

Mealy, Stephen. Rank; Private. Regiment or Service: Leinster Regiment. Unit; 1st Battalion. Service Number; 3774. Date of death; 12/05/1915. Born; Clough, County Kilkenny. Enlisted; Athy, County Kildare. Residence; Wolfhill, Athy, County Kildare. Killed in action. Grave or Memorial Reference; Panel 44. Cemetery: Ypres (Menin Gate) Memorial in Belgium.

Meara, Patrick. Rank; Gunner. Regiment or Service: Royal Garrison Artillery. Unit; 154th Siege Battery. Service Number; 3153. Date of death; 23/06/1919. Born; Rosservarn, Callan, County Kilkenny. Died in the War Hospital, Belfast. Son of James and Mary Meara, of Kilmoganny, Co. Kilkenny. Grave or Memorial Reference; Screen Wall N E 26. Cemetery: Belfast (Milltown) Roman Catholic Cemetery.

Meeham/Meehan, Michael. Rank; Private. Regiment or Service: Royal Munster Fusiliers. Unit; 1st Battalion. Service Number; 4294. Date of death; 08/12/1917. Age at death; 20. Born; Butts, County Kilkenny. Enlisted; Clonmel, County Tipperary. Residence; Kilkenny. Died. Meeham (CWGC), Meehan (SDGW, IMR), Son of Mrs. Bridget Meeham, of Lower Greens Hill, Kilkenny. Notes; Formerly he was with the Royal Irish Regiment where his number was 1867. Grave or Memorial Reference; IV B 12. Cemetery: Tincourt New British Cemetery in France

Meehan, Cornels. Rank; Sergeant/Drummer. Regiment or Service: Royal Dublin Fusiliers. Unit; 3rd Battalion. Service Number; 7900. Date of death; 20/12/1918. Age at death;36. Killed in action. Husband of Julia Lawlor (formerly Meehan), of 29, St. Finbarr's Place, Cork. Grave or Memorial Reference; Near the North boundary. Cemetery: Kilkenny (St Maul's) Graveyard, Kilkenny.

Meehan, Kieran. Rank; Private. Regiment or Service: Royal Munster Fusiliers. Unit; 6th Battalion. Service Number; 5165. Date of death; 21/08/1915. Age at death; 24. Born; St Mary's, Kilkenny. Enlisted; Kilkenny. Residence; Kilkenny. Killed in Action in Gallipoli. Son of Kieran and Bridget Meehan, of 4, Garden Row, Kilkenny. Kilkenny People, June 1916. Kilkenny Soldier's Letter. (Passed by Censor). Balkan States, 12-04-1916. Dear Mr Keane—I take the liberty of writing to you to let you know if you would be so kind as to spare a space in your valuable paper for this letter. Being an old reader of the "Kilkenny People" I will try and let the readers at home know, through you, of the doings of the "People's" readers abroad. I have been through the landing on the 6th August, 1915, at Suvla Bay, where, I am sorry to say, we lost a few Kilkenny boys. From there we found ourselves on the Serbian frontier facing the Germans, Bulgars, Austrians and Turks. We, however gave them to understand that they were "up against" Irishmen, much to their surprise; but they came on in overwhelming numbers. Still there was no Kilkennyman coming down from the mountains wounded, but unfortunately the frost and snow proved too masterful for a couple of Kilkenny lads, who had got frost-bitten, but they proved themselves men and passed on with a smilw on their lips to hospital, and as they passed you could hear their "pass-word"— "Up the Black and Amber!" To mention the names of these brave lads—I only think it will serve to gather them some praise, which they highly deserve. Their names are;-- John Sheridan,"Dido" Kenny, as we used to call him, from Walkin Street Upper, and the renowned "Cock" Byrne's brother James, who got wounded through the thigh. All belong to the Connaught Rangers. Well, the "Kilkenny People" has been a great welcome to us, Kilkenny boys, both in Gallipoli and in the Balkans, and every post that comes the cry is."Did you get the 'People'?" Our division is the 10th Irish Division, which bore the brunt at the landing and saved the day in Serbia, and which all the papers gave praise to on that memorable retreat. We are now nine months on active service, and don't expect to get leave before we finish the Huns up out here. I may mention that the boys from the city and county have been very lucky out here, thank God. I also may mention the names of the heroes who fell at Svla Bay, viz., Sergeant Michael O'Keeffe, late of Greensbridge and Privates K. Meehan, of Garden Row, and W. O'Connell, from Maudlin Street. Their memory is still fresh with us, and I trust that the people at home offer up a prayer for their happy repose. The English papers may boast of the deeds of valour performed by the Australian forces, but let them compare them with the magnificent dash of the Irish regiments and see who comes first. I think I will draw this letter to a close by saying that all the boys from city and county are "in the pink," and all hope to be back again soon, with the help of God. I enclose a few verses I composed by the help of Private J. Hogan, 3909, of the 4th Battalion., on thinking of the landing at Suvla Bay. I conclude by sending my best wishes for the success of your valuable paper. —I am, sir, yours sincerely. No 78, Corporal P. Staunton. A Company, 5th Royal Irish regiment, 10th Division, Salonika Field Force. The Landing at Suvla Bay. 'Twas on the 6th of August, on a bright and sunny day. We landed at the Dardanelles, some thousands of miles away. We knew not what before us lay, but we hear the shot and shell. And many an Irish soldier there that day now lives no more to tell. It was a bright and glorious day which we will never forget. When the Connaughts and the 5th Royal Irish went through that Vale of Death. It was death by fire, and water going through the Suvla tide. But those gallant sons of Erin their enemy defied! I will raise a glass, filled to the brim, of Smithwick's sparkling ale, and drink to the health of the boys that live who fought and did no quail. And whenever I hear the sound of guns and the clamour of war and din. I never will forget Gallipoli and the struggle I there was in. Notes; Formerly he was with the Royal Dublin FusiLiers where his number was 19400. Grave or Memorial Reference; Helles Memorial in Turkey. Cemetery: Helles Memorial in Turkey

Melea, Michael. Rank; Private. Regiment or Service: Royal Munster Fusiliers. Unit; 1st Battalion. Service Number; 4230. Date of death; 16/08/1917. Age at death;27. Born; Kilmoganny, County Kilkenny. Enlisted; Kilkenny. Residence; Kells, County Kilkenny. Killed in action. Son of the late John Melea. Notes; Formerly he was with the Royal Irish Regiment where his number was 2724. Grave or Memorial Reference; Panel 23. Cemetery: Le Touret Memorial In France.

Miller, James Charles. Rank; Corporal. Regiment or Service: Royal Engineers. Unit; Motor Cyclist Section and 'L' Company, Royal Engineers. Service Number; 30247. Date of death; 07/01/1915. Age at death; 23. Born; Bennettsbridge, County Kilkenny. Enlisted; Dublin. Residence; Kilkenny. Died. Son of Catherine Miller of 96, North Main St, Wexford and the late Robert Miller. The Waterford News, January 1915. Kilkenny Man's Death at the Front. News has been received in Kilkenny that Mr Charles Millar, who was engaged in the motor cycle service at the front, has died from the result of an accident received in the discharge of his military duties. Mr Millar was a member of a respected Kilkenny family. Grave or Memorial Reference; Div. 14. J. I. Cemetery: Ste. Marie Cemetery, Le Havre in France. He is also commemorated on the Great War Memorial in St Canice's Cathedral, Kilkenny…'To the Glory of God and in loving memory of the following members of the Diocese of Ossory who gave their lives for their country in the Great War 1914-1918'.

Mines, Michael. Rank; Private. Regiment or Service: South Wales Borderers. Unit; Depot. Service Number; 15446. Date of death; 14/02/1915. Born; Hugginstown, County Kilkenny. Enlisted; Brynawr. Died at home. Grave or Memorial Reference; 24. Cemetery: Brecon Cemetery, Brecknockshire, UK.

Minogue, Patrick. Rank; Private. Regiment or Service: Royal Irish Regiment. Unit; 4th Battalion. Service Number; 3134. Date of death; 11/03/1915. Born; Thomastown, County Kilkenny. Enlisted; Tipperary. Residence; Thomastown, County Kilkenny. Died of Pneumonia. After his death his effects and property were received by;- (Wife) Mrs M Minogue, Jerpoint West, Thomastown, County Kilkenny. Notes; Died at Queenstown Military Hospital (Pneumonia). Grave or Memorial Reference; In the North East Corner. Cemetery: Columbkille Old Graveyard, County Kilkenny.

Molloy, Michael. Rank; Private. Regiment or Service: Royal Irish Regiment. Unit; 6th Battalion. Service Number; 2060. Date of death; 08/05/1916. Age at death;36. Born; Callan, County Kilkenny. Enlisted; Kilkenny. Residence; Callan. Killed in action. Son of John and Johanna Molloy, of Callan, Co. Kilkenny; husband of Margaret Mary Molloy, of Freshford, Co. Kilkenny. Grave or Memorial Reference; II F 15. Cemetery: Dud Corner Cemetery, Loos in France.

Moore, James. Rank; Private. Regiment or Service: Royal Dublin Fusiliers. Unit; C Company, 9th Battalion. Service Number; 12962. Date of death; 21/10/1916. Age at death; 37. Born; Killcasey, County Kilkenny. Enlisted; St Helen's, Lancashire. Residence; Hugginstown, County Kiikenny. Died. Son of Edward and Mary Moore, of Kilkeasey, Hugginstown, Thomastown, Co. Kilkenny. Grave or Memorial Reference; Y 28. Cemetery: Kemmel Chateau Military Cemetery in Belgium.

Morahan, Maurice Joseph. Rank; Private. Regiment or Service: Cheshire Regiment. Unit; A Company 1st/4th Battalion. Service Number; 50311. Date of death; 07/10/1918. Age at death;32. Enlisted; Chester. Residence; Piltown, County Kilkenny. Killed in action. Son of William and Nora Morahan, of Clonmore, Piltown, Co. Kilkenny. Grave or Memorial Reference; I D 20. Cemetery: Zantvoorde British Cemetery in Belgium.

Moran, Edward. Rank; Private. Regiment or Service: Royal Irish Regiment. Unit; C Company, 2nd Battalion. Service Number; 7345. Date of death; 25/05/1915. Age at death; 31. Born; Kilmoganny, County Kilkenny. Enlisted; Carrick-on-Suir, County Tipperary. Residence; Kilmoganny. Died of gas poisoning. Son of Patrick and Bridget Moran, of Kilmoganny; husband of Lizzie Moran, of Kilmoganny, Co. Kilkenny. Munster Express, June, 1915. Killed in Action. Great sympathy is felt in Kilmoganny and the surrounding district for Mr Patrick Moran, whose son, Private Edward Moran, was shot in France. The sad news reached his afflicted parents on Monday evening. He was a member of the Kilmoganny Temperence Society and of the Irish National Volunteers before volunteering for the front, and a member of the Kilmoganny Fife and Drum Band. Grave or Memorial Reference; I F 102. Cemetery: Bailleul Communal Cemetery Extension (Nord) in France.

Moran, John. Rank; Private. Regiment or Service: Irish Guards. Unit; 1st Battalion. Service Number; 3498. Date of death; 06/11/1914. Born; Johnstown, County Kilkenny. Enlisted; Kilkenny. Residence; Portarlington. Killed in action. (Sister) Mrs Mary Mc Cormack, Maryborough. Grave or Memorial Reference; Panel 11. Cemetery: Ypres (Menin Gate) Memorial in Belgium.

Moran, James. Rank; Private. Regiment or Service: Royal Irish Regiment. Unit; 2nd Battalion. Service Number; 6486. Date of death; 19/10/1914. Age at death; 34. Born; Dungarvan, County Waterford. Enlisted; Kilkenny. Killed in action. COMERFORD (Alias, true family name is MORAN), JAMES Son of the late Mr. and Mrs. Moran, of King's St., Kilkenny; husband of Mrs. Moran. of New Building Lane, Kilkenny. Notes; Alias Comerford. Grave or Memorial Reference; Panel 11 and 12. Cemetery: Le Touret Memorial in France.

Morley, Patrick. Rank; Private. Regiment or Service: Royal Irish Regiment. Unit; 2nd Battalion. Service Number; 4337. Date of death; 24/04/1915. Age at death; 40. Born; Callan, County Kilkenny. Enlisted; Kilkenny. Killed in action. Husband of Kathleen Morley, of 351, Hackney Road. London. Grave or Memorial Reference; Panel 4. Cemetery: Ploegsteert Memorial in Belgium.

Moroney, Edward Francis. Rank; Stoker 1st Class. Regiment or Service: Royal Navy. Unit; (RFR/PO/B/3965). H. M. S."Good Hope. Service Number; SS/102026. Date of death; 01/11/1914. Age at death;35. Born; Carrick, County Tipperary. Son of Mr. and Mrs. Edward Moroney, of 5, Munday's Court, Portsea, Portsmouth; husband of Mary Phelan (formerly Moroney), of Rogerstown, Kilmoganny, Co. Kilkenny. De Ruvigny's Roll of Honour;-Stoker, 1st Class (R. F. R., B, 3965), S. S. 102026, H. M. S. Good Hope. Lost in action off Coronel, on the coast of Chili, 01-November-1914. Grave or Memorial Reference; 4. Cemetery: Portsmouth Naval Memorial, UK.

Morris, John. Rank; Private. Regiment or Service: Royao Marine Artillery. Unit; H. Q. Eastney. Service Number; RMA/1818. Date of death; 19/10/1916. Age at death; 52. Born; Kilkenny. Husband of Mary Jane Morris, Father of Gwendoline and Majorie Morris. 43 Bristol Road, Southsea, Hampshire. Grave or Memorial Reference; J 28 24. Cemetery: Portsmouth (Highland Road) Cemetery, Hampshire.

Private Morris, from De Ruvigny's Roll of Honour.

Morris, Michael F S. Rank; Private. Regiment or Service: Leinster Regiment. Unit; 7th Battalion. Service Number; 5356. Date of death; 11/05/1916. Age at death;36. Born; Kilkenny. Enlisted; Clonmel, County Tipperary. Residence; Clonmel. Killed in action. Son of Mr. and Mrs. Samuel Morris, of Newrath House, Waterford. In his Will, dated 22-April-1916, his effects and property were received by;- (Father) Mr Samuel Morris, New Rath House, Waterford, Ireland. De Ruvignys Roll of Honour. Son of Samuel Morris, Merchant and Ship Owner, Nationalist M. P. for South Kilkenny 1894-1900, J. P., by his wife, Catherine, Younger daughter of the late James Feehan, County Kilkenny. Born in Airmount Clonmel, educated at Clongowes Wood College, subsequently became Gentleman Farmer. Enlisted after the outbreak of war and served with the Expeditionary Force in France and Flanders and was killed in action at Loos 11 May-1916, by an aerial grenade while on sentry duty. His Commanding Officer wrote; "I knew him quite well as a fine soldier and a brave fellow, who promised great things, and it was with deep regret that I learned of his death.". Kilkenny People, June 1916. Well Known Kilkennyman Killed in Action. Deep sympathy will be felt with Mr Samuel Morris, Newrath, County Kilkenny, who has just received word of the death of his son, Mr Michael F. S. Morris, Leinster Regment, who was killed in action in France on May 11. The deceased, who was a brother of Mr George J. Morris, Secretary County Council, Kilkenny; was educated at Clongowes, where he gained many academic successes. He afterwards entered his fathers business at Waterford, and was engaged in commercial life until shortly after the outbreak of the war, when, in January-1915, he joined the Connaught Rangers. About three months ago he was transferred to the Leinster Regiment, and was ordered to France. Deceased had a great many friends in Waterford, where he was extremely popular, and his death is sincerely regretted. Munster Express. Waterford Gentleman killed in action. Sincere sympathy is felt with Mr Samuel Morris, J. P., Newrath House, on having heard the sad news that his son, Mr Michael F. Morris, has lost his life on the battle front in France. The deceased, who was only 30 years of age, was a private in the 7th Leinster's, and he was not a month in France when he was killed on the 11th of May. He was a splendid type of manhood, standing six feet, and he was a great favourite in Waterford. Mr Morris has two other sons serving in the Army, one of them a Lieutenant in the Leinster's. The blow is a heavy one on our respected townsman, coming so soon after his recent bereavement. Office and High Mass for the repose of the soul of the deceased took place to-day (Friday) at 11 o'clock at the Chapel of Ease, Ferrybank, at which a large number of priests attended. Notes; Formerly he was with the Connaught Rangers where his number was 3819. Grave or Memorial Reference; I B 4. Cemetery: Philosophe British Cemetery, Mazingarbe in France.

Morris, Michael J. Rank; Private. Regiment or Service: King's Liverpool Regiment. Unit; 14th Battalion. Service Number; 19801. Date of death; 27/04/1917. Born; Callean, County Kilkenny. Enlisted; Southport, Lancashire. Residence; London. Died of wounds in Salonika. Brother of Mr. M. Morris, of 3, Sydney Road, Tilbury, Essex. Grave or Memorial Reference; A 55. Cemetery: Sarigol Military Cemetery, Kriston in the Town of Sarigol in Turkey.

Morris, William Joseph. Rank; Private. Regiment or Service: Honorable Artillery Company. Unit; Infantry. Service Number; 7201. Date of death; 08/02/1917. Enlisted; Armoury House. Residence; Hartlands, County Kilkenny. Died of wounds. Grave or Memorial Reference; H 73. Cemetery: Varennes Military Cemetery, Somme, France.

Morris, William Richard. Rank; Lieutenant. Regiment or Service: Royal Army Medical Corps. Date of death; 11/09/1921. Age at death; 56. Born; Kilkenny. Died after discharge. Cemetery: Clonmore, Piltown, County Kilkenny.

Morrison, John. Rank; Private. Regiment or Service: Labour Corps. Service Number; 669811. Date of death; 29/03/1920. Age at death;32. Killed in action. Notes; Formerly he was with the 3rd Battalion, Royal Inniskilling Fusiliers where his number was 40657. Grave or Memorial Reference; North of North-East door. Cemetery: Kilkenny (St Mary) Church of Ireland Churchyard, Kilkenny.

Morrissey, Robert. Rank; Private. Regiment or Service: Royal Irish Regiment. Unit; F Company, 2nd Battalion. Service Number; 6388. Date of death; 13/09/1914. Age at death;38. Born; Pitt, County Kilkenny. Enlisted; Kilkenny. Residence; Dunbell, County Kilkenny. Killed in action. Son of Thomas and Anastasia Morrissey, of Freshford, Co. Kilkenny. Served in the South African War. In his Will, dated 08-September-1914, his effects and property were received by;- (Brother) Thomas Morrissey, Freshford, County Kilkenny, Ireland. Notes; Date of death between 19-October-1914 and 21-October-1914 (CWGC), 13/09/1914 (SDGW). Grave or Memorial Reference; VII L 7. Cemetery: Cabaret-Rouge British Cemetery, Souchez in France.

Morrissey, Thomas. Rank; Private. Regiment or Service: Royal Irish Regiment. Unit; 6th Battalion. Service Number; 4/3125. Date of death; 15/03/1918. Age at death; 29. Born; Slieverue, County Kilkenny. Enlisted; Waterford. Died. Son of Ellen Morrissey, of Waterford, Ireland. Notes; Number listed as 4/3125 (Commonwealth War Graves Commission), 3125 (Soldiers died in the Great War). Grave or Memorial Reference; III G 25. Cemetery: Abbeville Communal Cemetery Extension in France.

Morrissy, John. Rank; Sergeant. Regiment or Service: Royal Inniskilling Fusiliers. Unit; 11th Battalion. Service Number; 24215. Date of death; 27/03/1918. Born; Gowran, County Kilkenny. Enlisted; Enniskillen. Residence; Gowran. Died of wounds. After his death his effects and property were received by;- Miss S Jones, Dunereggan, Portrush, County Antrim, Ireland. Grave or Memorial Reference; IV. B. 22. Cemetery: Regina Trench Cemetery, Grandcourt in France.

Morton, William. Rank; Private. Regiment or Service: Royal Dublin Fusiliers. Unit; 6th Battalion. Service Number; 630931. Date of death; 08/10/1918. Born; Kilkenny. Enlisted; Carlow. Killed in action. Information from his last will and testament dated 30-June-1915. Effects and property received; (Wife) Mrs Margaret Morton, 1 Charlotte Street, Carlow. Notes; Number listed as 30931 (SDGW) 630931 (CWGC). Formerly he was with the Army Service Corps where his number was S/4/094698. Grave or Memorial Reference; G 7. Cemetery: Beaurevoir British Cemetery in France.

Moynan, Alfred. Rank; Private. Regiment or Service: Irish Guards. Unit; 2nd Battalion. Service Number; 8057. Date of death; 05/05/1916. Born; Rathdowney, Queen's County. Enlisted; Donaghmore, Queen's County. Killed in action. Grave or Memorial Reference; I H 10. Cemetery: White House Vemetery, St Jean-Les-Ypres in Belgium. He is also commemorated on the Great War Memorial in St Canice's Cathedral, Kilkenny…'To the Glory of God and in loving memory of the following members of the Diocese of Ossory who gave their lives for their country in the Great War 1914-1918'. Listed on the memorial under Guardsman Albert Moynan.

Moynes, Thomas. Rank; Private. Regiment or Service: Connaught Rangers. Unit; 2nd Battalion. Service Number; 10574. Date of death; 13/09/1914. Born; Kilkenny. Enlisted; Dublin. Killed in action. Cemetery: La Ferte-Sous-Jouarre-Memorial in France.

Mulhall, Daniel. Rank; Private. Regiment or Service: Royal Dublin Fusiliers. Unit; 1st Battalion. Service Number; 10714. Date of death; 26/04/1915. Born; Kilkenny. Enlisted; Carlow. Residence; Kilkenny. Killed in Action in Gallipoli. Grave or Memorial Reference; Special memorial B 60. Cemetery: V Beach Cemetery in Turkey.

Mulhall, Edward. Rank; Stoker 1st Class. Regiment or Service: Royal Navy. Unit; HMS Bulwark. Service Number; SS/110177. Date of death; 26/11/1914. Age at death; 22. Born; Kilkenny. Killed or died by means other than disease, accident or enemy action. Brother of Anastasia, Patrick Street, Durrow and Rebecca, 15 Synge Street, Dublin. Limerick Chronicle, October, 1918. The Leinster Crime. More of The Victims. Mr Arthur Adshead, Midland Railway Co, General Traffic Agent for Ireland, was among those lost on the Leinster, and his body has since been recovered. He was well known in railway service and was 61. Prior to entering the Midland service he was with the shipping firm of James Little and Co, Barrow. Notes; D. O. B. 05/04/1892. Grave or Memorial Reference; G."C." 834. Cemetery: Leicester (Welford Road) Cemetery, Leicestershire.

Mulroney, William Benedict. Rank; Trooper. Regiment or Service: Australian Light Horse. Unit; 6th. Service Number; 3364. Date of death; 06/08/1918. Born; Kilkenny. Enlisted; Sydney, N. S. W. Died of disease. Native of Carrigan, Ireland. Son of Patrick and Mary Mulroney, of Broadview, Manly, New South Wales. Occupation on enlistment, carter. Age on enlistment; 37 years 9 months. Next of kin details; (mother) Mary Mulroney, Broadview, P. O. Manly, Sydney. Father deceased. Weight, 120 lbs. Height, 5 feet, 4 ½ inches. Complexion, medium. Eyes, blue. Hair, brown. Previous military experience; 20th Battalion, A. I. F. 1914, discharged as medically unfit due to a fall from a horse. The incident occurred at Glenreagh, North Coast, N. S. W. in October-1916. He was confined to bed for six weeks with an injured back and foot. At the end of this time the ligaments in his foot were permanently stretched. This is the last Will and Testament of me, William Benedict Mulroney, Of Manly, Pittwater Road in the County of Cumberland, New South Wales, Australia. I hereby revoke all Wills by me at any time heretofore made, and declare this to be my last Will and Testament. I appoint Patrick Francis Marun of Eddystone Corunna Avenue, Waverly, N. S. Wales to be executer of this my will, and direct that all my just Debts and Funeral and Testamentary Expenses shall be paid as soon as conveniently may be after my decease. I give and bequeath to Mrs Mary Mulroney where so ever and what so ever W. B. M. Military or otherwise and in the event of her death to go to my sister Mrs Mary French at present residing at 146 Paddington Street, Paddington, half to my two sisters in the Mercy Convent Parramatta. Mrs C Mulroney and Mrs P Mulroney at Mrs French's death the estate to g to the propagation of the Catholic Church and the poor…William Benedict Mulroney. Dated this Seventeenth day of July in the year of our Lord One Thousand Nine Hundred and Seventeen. Two letters were sent from his mother and saved in his records;-28-August-1919. Dear Sir. Received yours thanking for information re last resting place my son late William Benedict Mulroney No 3367 6th Light Horse. I will be thankful for photograph grave and any belongings of his left at the hospital where he passed away on the 6th August-18. I cabled him £3-0-0 for his birthday, which was on the 15th June, have not heard if he received it. Grateful and thankful for the news I have received and in anticipation receiving more mementos of his. I am dear sir. Respectfully yours. Mary Mulroney. 31-May-1921. Dear Sir. In reply to youre No 3367 late W. B. Mulroney 6th Light Horse Regiment the soldiers father Patrick Mulroney passed away August 1889 at our residence--------Cottage, Mandy and his remains interred in the Mandy Cemetery. First off the years after his arrival in this country was on the gold fields a good many years. He laboured in New Zealand on the Thames Gold Fields. He was interested in gold mining to the last. Under the Doctors advice he was confined to the bed over three months. I am Dear Sir. Respectfully yours. Mary Mulroney. Notes; Place and date of enlistment, First time, 05-April-1916, R. A. S. Grounds. Second time;-04-April-1917. Sydney, N. S. W. Died of disease, pneumonia and pleurisy at the 26th Casualty Clearing Station in Egypt. Grave or Memorial Reference; AA 36. Cemetery: Ramleh War Cemetery in Israel.

Mulrooney, Patrick. Rank; Private. Regiment or Service: Connaught Rangers. Unit; 1st Battalion. Service Number; 9657. Date of death; 21/01/1916. Born; Kilkenny. Enlisted; Kilkenny. Residence; Kilkenny. Killed in action in Mesopotamia. After his death his effects and property were received by;- (Sister) Mrs Ellen O Mahoney, Lord Edward St, Kilkenny. Noncupative (or missing) Will was witnessed by;- (Brother in law) Thomas Mahoney. (Brother) Richard Mullrooney, Bennettstown, County Kilkenny. Grave or Memorial Reference; Panel 40 and 64. Cemetery: Basra memorial in Iraq.

Murphy, Alexander. Rank; Private. Regiment or Service: Royal Scots Fusiliers. Unit; 6th/7th Battalion. Service Number; 19211. Date of death; 05/04/1917. Born; Bennettsbridge, County Kilkenny. Enlisted; Ardrossan in Ayrshire. Residence; Sailcoats, Ayrshire. Killed in action. Son of John and Ellen Murphy of Broadway, Co. Wexford. Grave or Memorial Reference; Bay 5. Cemetery: Arras Memorial in France.

Murphy, Andrew. Rank; Private. Regiment or Service: Royal Inniskilling Fusiliers. Unit; 7th Battalion. Service Number; 27546. Date of death; 06/04/1916. Age at death; 26. Born; Clough, County Kilkenny. Enlisted; Maryborough. Residence; Castlecomer. Killed in action. Son of Andrew and Mary T. Murphy. Notes; Formerly he was with the Leinster Regiment where his number was 908. Grave or Memorial Reference; I C 25. Cemetery: Philosophe British Cemetery, Mazingarbe in France.

Murphy, Daniel. Rank; Gunner. Regiment or Service: Royal Garrison Artillery. Unit; 1st/104th Howitzer Battery. Service Number; 26129. Date of death; 09/05/1916. Age at death;27. Enlisted; Templemore. Residence; Templetouhy. Killed in action. Son of Thomas and Ellen Fogarty, of Shamrock St, Urlingford, Co. Kilkenny. Grave or Memorial Reference; VII F 3. Cemetery: Amara War Cemetery in Iraq.

Murphy, Denis. Rank; Private. Regiment or Service: Leinster Regiment. Unit; 1st Battalion. Service Number; 4004/4094. Date of death; 25/06/1915. Born; Gowran, County Kilkenny. Enlisted; Carlow. Killed in action. Notes; Number listed as 4004 (SDGW) 4094 (CWGC). Grave or Memorial Reference; X K 6. Cemetery: Strand Military Cemetery, Ploegsteert near Ypres, Belgium.

Murphy, James. Rank; Private. Regiment or Service: Royal Irish Regiment. Unit; 1st Battalion. Service Number; 3255. Date of death; 17/03/1915. Born; Kilfane, County Kilkenny. Enlisted; Tipperary. Residence; Thomastown, County Kilkenny. Died of wounds. After his death his effects and property were received by;- (Sister) Miss J Murphy, Ryalnds Cuffs Grange, Kilkenny. Kilkenny People, April, 1915. Thomastown Soldier Killed in Action. Notification has been received from the War Office of the death at the front of private James Murphy, Royal Irish Regiment, as the results of wounds received at the battle of Neuve Chapelle on the 17th March. The deceased soldier, who was a native of Thomastown, was about 35 years of age and unmarried. Grave or Memorial Reference; J 30. Cemetery: Bailleul Communal Cemetery (Nord) in France.

Murphy, James. Rank; Private. Regiment or Service: Royal Dublin Fusiliers. Unit; 1st Battalion. Service Number; 21383. Date of death; 24/09/1915. Born; Callan, County Kilkenny. Enlisted; Kilkennt. Killed in Action in Gallipoli. Buried beside Wickow soldier, Pte Michael Gorman from the same unit who died five days after him. Grave or Memorial Reference; I E 9. Cemetery: Azmak Cemetery, Suvla in Turkey.

Murphy, James. Rank; Private. Regiment or Service: King's Liverpool Regiment. Unit; Labour Companies. Service Number; 63126. Date of death; 17/02/1917. Born; Kilkenny. Enlisted; Merthyr, Glamorganshire. Died at home. Grave or Memorial Reference; N R C 330. Cemetery: Oswestry General Cemetery in Shropshire, UK.

Murphy, James. Rank; Private. Regiment or Service: Connaught Rangers. Unit; 5th Battalion. Service Number; 5626. Date of death; 03/08/1918. Born; Kilkenny. Enlisted; Kilkenny. Died at sea. In his Will, dated 08-August-1918, his effects and property were received by;- (Mother) Mrs James Murphy, 43 Up Walkin Street, Killkenny, Ireland. Cemetery: Hollybrook Memorial, Southampton, UK

Murphy, James. Rank; Private. Regiment or Service: Connaught Rangers. Unit; 5th Battalion. Service Number; 5624. Date of death; 08/10/1918. Born; Kilkenny. Enlisted; Kilkenny. Killed in action. Son of Mrs. K. Murphy, of 88, Upper Walkin Street, Kilkenny. Grave or Memorial Reference; A 27. Cemetery: Serain Communal Cemetery Extension in France.

Murphy, John. Rank; Rifleman. Regiment or Service: Royal Dublin Fusiliers. Unit; 6th Battalion. Service Number; 18445. Date of death; 16/08/1915. Born; Rosbercon, County Kilkenny. Enlisted; Seaforth. Residence; Bootle. Killed in Action in Gallipoli. Enniscorthy Guardian; Private John Murphy, of Rosbercon, New Ross, was killed at the Dardanelles on 16th of August last. He was 31 years of age, and volunteered at Brikinhead where he had a good position with a ship building firm. Sixteen others of the same firm volunteered along with him. He joined the Dublin Fusiliers in February last. He served his time with his uncle Mr Shanahan, ship builder, Rosbercon, before going to England where he married a Wexford lady about four years ago. He was very popular and held in high esteem by the owners of the firm in which he worked. He wrote several letters to his wife and his parents and sisters, and in the last ones he he wrote before going into action he related how he prepared by going to confession and holy Communion, and was not afraid to die. He has a brother in Hants, London, a member of the Army Service Corps. Grave or Memorial Reference; Panel 190 to 196. Cemetery: Helles Memorial in Turkey.

Murphy, John. Rank; Acting Corporal. Regiment or Service: Devonshire Regiment. Unit; 10th (Service) Battalion. Service Number; 13896. Date of death; 25/04/1917. Born; Kilkenny. Enlisted; Ferndale, Glamorganshire. Residence; Kilkenny. Killed in action in Salonika. Cemetery: Doiran Memorial in Greece.

Murphy, Martin. Rank; Private. Regiment or Service: Australian Infantry, A. I. F. Unit; 4th Battalion. Service Number; 1233. Date of death; 14/04/1918. Born; Castlecomer, County Kilkenny. Enlisted; Roseberry Park Camp, N. S. W. Killed in action. Served in Alexandria, Gallipoli, Egypt, Malta and England. Wounded in action in Gallipoli with a gunshot wound to the thigh in August-1915. Sent to Malta and England for treatment. Sent to France October-1916. Occupation on enlistment, Labourer. Age on enlistment; 36 years - months. Previous military experience; Royal Irish Regiment, 12 years, resigned. Next of kin details; relations unknown (sic). His own address at Berabong Street, Golgandra, N. S. W. in is this section instead of NOK details. Weight, 11st 12 lbs. Height, 5 feet, 7 inches. Complexion, fair. Eyes, grey. Hair, fair. Pte Murphy did not give his next of kin details so when he died the military authorities applied for his pre ww1 records for any clues. This is the reply they received;-1233 Private M. Murphy, 4th Battalion, A. I. F. -Deceased-I have to advise that certain effects of the above-named, viz;--Army discharge, note-book and one devotional book, obtained from a kit bag held in his name at the A. I. F. Kit Store, were sent to you for disposal in parcel No. D/S. 50814 in basket No. 2662 per the S. S."Cooee" on the 9th instant. The late soldier on enlistment in the Australian Imperial Force regietsred "no next-of-kin" and advertisements inserted in the press in the United Kingdom have elicited no information in this regard. An Army discharge certificate included in the effects held here indicates that he enlisted in the Royal Irish regiment at Waterford on the 16th September-1897 and was discharged at Agra, India on the 23rd November-1909, Rank, Private, regimental Number, No 6135, the matter was therefore referred to the Imperial Authorities and I append hereto a copy of a reply received to my communication from the Assistant Secretary, The Royal Hospital, Chelsea, S. W. 3."With reference to your letter of the 12th July, 1919, No;Qk. 395/6/2 relative to the case of No;1233 Private M. Murphy, 4th Battalion, Australian Imperial Force. I am directed by the Lords and others, Commissioners of this Hospital, to inform you that according to the Discharge Documents deposited in this Office, Private Murphy gave no next-of-kin on enlistment into the Royal Irish Regiment."Private Murphy's address on enlistment in the Australian Imperial Force is registered as Berabong Street, Gilgandra, New South Wales. After his death his grave could not be located and his name was added to the Villers-Bretonneux Memorial. A request from a friend of his from his Battalion applied for his burial details. As his next-of-kin was 'untraceable' his medals could not be issued. Notes; Place and date of enlistment, 17-September-1917. Roseberry Park Camp, N. S. W. Cemetery: Villers-Bretonneux Memorial in France.

Murphy, Michael. Rank; Private. Regiment or Service: Connaught Rangers. Unit; 1st Battalion. Service Number; 5671. Date of death; 27/04/1916. Age at death;45. Born; Nova Scotia. Enlisted; Kilkenny. Residence; Kilkenny. Died in Mesopotamia. Son of Michael and Mary Murphy, of Kilkenny. Grave or Memorial Reference; XX B 13. Cemetery: Amara War Cemetery in Iraq.

Murphy, Patrick. Rank; Company Sergeant Major. Regiment or Service: Connaught Rangers. Unit; C Company, 6th Battalion. Service Number; 6912. Date of death; 20/11/1917. Age at death; 35. Born; Kilkenny. Enlisted; Kilkenny. Residence; Kilkenny. Killed in action. Son of Michael and Mary Murphy, of Kilkenny. His Last Will and Testament written at Kinsale was witnessed by;- (Brother) John Murphy,. Grave or Memorial Reference; I C 12. Cemetery: Croisilles Railway Cemetery in France.

Murphy, Peter. Rank; Private. Regiment or Service: Northumberland Fusiliers. Unit; 1/6th Battalion (Territorial). Service Number; 36533. Date of death; 11/04/1918. Age at death;32. Born; Kilkenny. Enlisted; Halifax, Yorkshire. Killed in action. Son of Michael and Ciceley Murphy, of Salmonford, Kilkelly, Co. Mayo; husband of Annie Murphy, of 26, Town Gate, Marsden, Huddersfield. Notes; Born Kilkenny, County Mayo (sic). Grave or Memorial Reference; Panel 2. Cemetery: Ploegsteert Memorial in Belgium.

Murphy, Richard Victor. Rank; Acting Sergeant. Regiment or Service: Royal Dublin Fusiliers. Unit; 7th Battalion. Service Number; 14200. Date of death; 29/03/1918. Age at death; 32. Born; Ballinrea, County Carlow. Enlisted; Dublin. Residence; Gowran. Killed in action. Son of the late William Alexander and Sarah Murphy; husband of Alice Mary Murphy. A Civil Servant (Registry of Titles, Dublin). De Ruvigny's Roll of Honour. . son of the late William Alexander Murphy, by his wife, Sarah (--) (Gouran, County Kilkenny). Born in Ballinree, Borris, County Carlow, 28-February-1886. Educated at Kilkenny College Collegiate School, Portarlington, and Mountjoy School, Dublin. Wasd a Civil Servant, Land Registry of Ireland. Enlisted on 14-September-1914. Served with the Mediterranean Expeditionary Force at Gallipoli from August-1915, and subsequently with the Serbian Army. Wa sinvalided home in July-1916. On recovery proceeded to France, and was killed in action at Morlincourt 26-March-1918. He married at the Parish Church, Gouran, Alice Mary, daughter of the Reverend Henry hare, of Dublin. The Irish Times, March 26, 1921. Roll of Honour. In Memoriam. Murphy-In fond and loving memory of Sergeant R V Murphy, 7th Royal Dublin Fusiliers, killed, in France, 26th March, 1918."At rest."—Elam (?). Murphy-In proud and loving meoory of R V Murphy, Sergeant, Pals Battalion, Royal Dublin Fusiliers, second son of Mrs W A (N?) Murphy, Gowran, County Kilkenny, killed in action, near Morlancourt, March 25th, 1918. Irish Times. Murphy-March 26, killed in action, Sergeant Richard Victor Murphy, Royal Dublin Fusiliers, son of the late W A Murphy, Borris, County Carlow, and of Mrs Murphy, Gowran, County Kilkenny. Grave or Memorial Reference; Panel 79 and 80. Cemetery: Pozieres Memorial in France. He is also commemorated on the Great War Memorial in St Canice's Cathedral, Kilkenny…'To the Glory of God and in loving memory of the following members of the Diocese of Ossory who gave their lives for their country in the Great War 1914-1918'.

Murphy, William. Rank; Private. Regiment or Service: Royal Dublin Fusiliers. Unit; 4th Battalion. Service Number; 26079. Date of death; 22/05/1916. Age at death;36. Born; Clough, County Kilkenny. Enlisted; Athy, County Kildare. Residence; Crettyard, County Carlow. Died at home. Husband of Alice Murphy, of Crossard, Wolfhill, Athy. Grave or Memorial Reference; C 3. Cemetery: Ballyglass Cemetery, County Westmeath.

Murray, James. Rank; Private. Regiment or Service: Irish Guards. Unit; 1st Battalion. Service Number; 2924. Date of death; 29/10/1914. Born; Kilkenny. Residence; Kilkenny. Killed in action. Grave or Memorial Reference; Panel 11. Cemetery: Ypres (Menin Gate) Memorial in Belgium.

Murray, Peter. Rank; Private. Regiment or Service: Northumberland Fusiliers. Unit; 9th Battalion. Service Number; 34712. Date of death; 29/04/1917. Born; Kilkenny. Enlisted; Kilkenny. Died. Notes; Formerly he was with the K. O. Y. L. I. where his number was 41181. Grave or Memorial Reference; Bay 2 and 3. Cemetery: Arras Memorial in France

Mynes, James. Rank; Sergeant. Regiment or Service: Connaught Rangers. Unit; 1st Battalion. Service Number; 7433. Date of death; 26/04/1916. Born; Kilkenny. Enlisted; Kilkenny. Killed in action. After his death his effects and property were received by;- (Sister) Mrs Mary Moynes, 15 Hatch Street, Dublin, Ireland. In his will he is named Moynes, James. Grave or Memorial Reference; Panel 42. Cemetery: Ypres (Menin Gate) Memorial in Belgium.

N

Naylor, Benjamin. Rank; Sergeant. Regiment or Service: Norfolk Regiment. Unit; 7th Battalion. Service Number; 7474. Date of death; 13/10/1915. Age at death;28. Born; St Denis's, Kilkenny. Enlisted; Colchester, Essex. Killed in action. Son of James and Annie Naylor; husband of Sarah A. Naylor, of Park Rd., Blockley, Worcs. Grave or Memorial Reference; Panel 30 and 31. Cemetery: Loos Memorial in France.

Nealon, Cedric Dunnill. Rank; Lieutenant. Regiment or Service: Royal Irish Regiment. Unit; 4th Battalion attached to the Royal Inniskilling Fusiliers. Date of death; 19/08/1918. Age at death; 18. Born; Dublin. Killed in action. Son of William M. Nealon and Sarah his wife, of Stanley Ville, Ramsey, Isle of Man. The Weekly Irish Times. Ireland's Roll of Honour. September 1, 1917. Second Lieutenant C D Nealon, Royal Irish Regiment, who was killed in action on 16th inst, was the second son of Mr William M Nealon, Manager Munster and Leinster Bank, Skibbereen. He was educated at Midleton College, and got his commission in January, 1917. Irish Times. Nealon-August 16, killed in action, Cedric Dunnill Nealon, Second Lieutenant Royal Irish regiment, son of William M Nealon, Manager Munster and Leinster Bank Ltd, Skibbereen. Grave or Memorial Reference; Panel 51 to 52. Cemetery: Tyne Cot Memorial in Belgium.

Captain Neville, from Bond of Sacrifice.

Neville, Thomas Villiers Tuthill Thacker. Rank; Captain. Regiment or Service: Household Cavalry and Cavalry of the line including the Yeomanry and Imperial Camel Corps. Unit; 3rd Dragoon Guards (Prince of Wales Own). Date of death; 13/05/1915. Age at death;34. Killed in action. Son of Joseph William Thacker and Anne Bene Thacker. Bond of Sacrifice, Volume 2. . was the eldest son of the late Joseph William Thacker and Anne, only daughter of the late Thomas Neville, of Borrismore, County Kilkenny, whose surname he assumed in 1914. Captain Neville was born on the 12th August, 1880, at Borrismore, and was educated at St Columba's College and at Trinity College, Dublin. He entered the Army in May, 1900, when he was gazetted 2nd Lieutenant in the 3rd Dragoon Guards, becoming Lieutenant in February, 1901.

He was on active service in the South African War, taking part in the operations in the Transvaal, the Orange River Colony, and Cape colony. For his services he received the Queen's medal with five clasps. Afterwards he served with his regiment in Egypt. ; Captain Neville, whose promotion to that rank dated from September, 1909, became an Adjutant in the Territorial Force in the same month, and appointment which terminated in September, 1912. He went to France with his regiment for active service in the war with Germany, and was killed in action on the 13th May, 1915, near Ypres, while in command of his squadron in the trenches. His Major sent the following report to Brigade Headquarters under recommendation for gallantry for the period ending 15th May, 1915; "Captain T. V. T. Neville for conspicuous bravery and good work while in command of his squadron during the 13th May until his death. His squadron, though heavily bombarded and attacked both in front and rear, held its ground. He had shown similar gallantry in a severe action in November last." Captain Neville was a keen sportsman and a fearless rider. In 1906 he won the 3rd Dragoon Guards "Subaltern's Cup," and in 1907 the cup was presented by the Earl of Aberdeen for the Welter-weight Race at the Army Point-to-point races. In 1908 he also won the 14 st race at the Kildare Hunt Sportsmen's Races. Kilkenny Journal, June, 1915. Captain T. V. T. Neville, 3rd Dragoon Guards, who has died from the effects of wounds, had been recommended for conspicuous bravery in command of his squadron on 13th ult, and also in November. Deceased officer was the son of Mr J. W. Thacker, late of Upper Fitzwilliam Street, Dublin, and of Borrismore, Kilkenny, and grandson of the late Mr T. Neville, D. L., Borrismore, whose surname he recently assumed. A very fine young officer in the South African war, he served in that campaign with distinction, gaining the Queen's medal with five clasps. He was a keen polo player and a hard rider to hounds. Carlow Sentinel, May, 1915. Captain T. V. T. Neville, 3rd Dragoon Guards, who was killed in action on May 13th, was the eldest son of the late Joseph William Thacker, of 40 Upper Fitzwiliam Street, Dublin. He was grandson of the late Thomas Neville, or Borrismore, County Kilkenny, whose name he took only last year. He was gazetted on May 23rd, 1900, and served in the South African War. He obtained his captaincy in 1909. He was in his 35th year. 'Our Heroes'. was the eldest son of the late Mr Joseph William Thacker, of 40 Upper Fitzwilliam Street, Dublin, and a grandson of the late Mr Thomas Neville, of Borrismore, County Kilkenny, whose surname he took last year. He reached the rank of Captain in 1909, was Adjutant of the Yorkshire Dragoons, after which he rejoined his regiment and proceeded to Egypt. At the outbreak of the present war his regiment was ordered to the front. He was killed fighting in the trenches near Ypres on may 13th, 1915, in a very severe engagement, in which his squadron, though heavily bombarded and attacked both in front and rear, held its ground. The Weekly Irish Times. Ireland's Roll of Honour. May 29, 1915. Captain T V Thacker Neville. Captain T V T Neville, 3rd Dragoon Guards, who was killed in action on may 13th, was the eldest son of the late Joseph William Thacker, of 40 Upper Fitzwilliam Street, Dublin. He was grandson of the late Thomas Neville, of Borrismore, County Kilkenny, whose name he took only last year. He was Gazetted on May 23rd, 1900, and served in the South African War. He obtained his captaincy in 1909. He was in his 35th year. The Weekly Irish Times. Ireland's Roll of Honour. June 12, 1915. Captain T V Neville. The following report was sent into Brigade Headquarters, under recommendation for gallantry, for period ending 15th May;--"Captain T V T T Neville, for conspicuous bravery and good work whilst in command of his squadron during 13th May until his death. His squadron though heavily bombarded and attacked, both in front and rear, held its ground. He had shown similar gallantry in a severe action in November last." Captain Thomas Villiers Tuthill Neville, 3rd Dragoon Guards, was the son of Mr Joseph William Thacker, late of Upper Fitzwilliam Street, Dublin, and of Borrismore, County Kilkenny. At the outbreak of the present war his regiment was ordered to the front. He was a keen polo player, and a hard rider to hounds, having inherited his sporting tastes from his grandfather, Thomas Neville, D. L., of County Kilkenny, a noted sportsman of his time, one of his famous greyhounds having won the much coveted Waterloo Cup. Grave or Memorial Reference; 4 XII L 24. Cemetery: Bedford House Cemetery. Ypres, Belgium.

Nevin, Thomas. Rank; Private. Regiment or Service: Royal Dublin Fusiliers. Unit; 9th Battalion. Service Number; 5562. Date of death; 19/06/1916. Age at death; 36. Born; Kilkenny. Enlisted; Carlow. Residence; Kilkenny. Died of wounds. Son of Edward Nevin, of Abbey St., Kilkenny, and the late Mary Nevin. Served 12 years with Royal Irish Fusiliers (9 years and 8 months in India). Grave or Memorial Reference; V E 49. Cemetery: Bethune Town Cemetery in France.

Newman, William. Rank; Sergeant. Regiment or Service: Royal Irish Regiment. Unit; 8th (South Irish Horse) Battalion. Service Number; 25653. Age at death;29. Born; Queen's County. Enlisted; Dublin. Killed in action. Son of the late Robert and Anne Newman, of Rathsaran, Rathdowney, Queen's Co, After his death his effects and property were received by;- Mrs Newman, Rathsasan, Grogan, Ballybrothy, Queens County, Ireland. Notes; Formerly 1896, South Irish Horse. Born Dublin (SDGW) Queen's County (Census). Grave or Memorial Reference; II A 12. Cemetery: Croisilles British Cemetery in France.

Lieutenant Nixon, from De Ruvigny's Roll of Honour.

Nixon, Gerard Ferrers. Rank; Lieutenant. Regiment or Service: Royal Horse Artillery and Royal Field Artillery. Unit; 129th Battery. Date of death; 24/10/1914. Killed in action. Son of Major. General. A. I. Nixon and Mrs. M. L. Nixon, of "The Gables," Fife Road, East Sheen, Surrey. De Ruvigny's Roll of Honour. Youngest son of Major-General Arundel James Nixon, of Clone, Ballyragget, County Kilkenny, D. L., late R. A., by his wife, Maria Lucy, daughter of the late John Laurence, D. L. Born in

Stoke, Devonport, 25-January-1891. Educated at Cheltenham College ad Royal Military Academy, Woolwich. Gazetted 2nd Lieutenant, R. F. A., 23-December-1910 and promoted Lieutenant, 23-December-1913. Left for France, August-1914, and was killed in action near Neuve Chapelle, 24-October following. Buried at Fauquissart, in an orchard in the Rue de Bacquerot. The Officer commanding his battery wrote; "It is a very great sorrow indeed to us all that we have lost him. Officers and men were devoted to him. He was a gallant little fellow and a first-class officer." He was mentioned in Sir John (now Lord) French's Despatch of 14-January-1915, for gallant and distinguished conduct in the field. He was a keen sportsman; rode very well and was very good at all games. 'Our Heroes'. was the son of Major-General Nixon, D. L., of Clone, Ballyregget, County Kilkenny. He joined the Artillery in decemebr-1910, and was 23 years of age at the time of his death. He was a keen sportsman and well known with the Kilkenny hounds. Bond of Sacrifice, Volume 1. was the youngest son of Major-General Nixon, D. L., late R. A., and Mrs Nixon, of Clone, Ballyragget, County Kilkenny. He was born on the 25th January, 1891, and educated at Cheltenham College and the R. M. A., Woolwich, from which he entered the R. A. in December, 1910, becoming Lieutenant in December, 1913. He was a good all-round sportsman, and rode well. He went out with the first Expeditionary Force to France for the Great War, and was acting as Observation Officer in an advanced position when he was killed in a sudden night attack by the enemy in France. He was mentioned in Sir John French's despatch of the 14th January, 1915. Irish Independent; Lieutenant G F Nixon, RFA, youngest son of Major-General Nixon, D. L., of Clone, Ballyragget, was killed on 25th October. He was a member of the Artllery for four years. Grave or Memorial Reference; III I 16. Cemetery: Royal Irish Rifles Graveyard, Laventie, France.

Nolan, John. Rank; Private. Regiment or Service: Royal Irish Regiment. Unit; 2nd Battalion. Service Number; 4747. Date of death; 24/05/1915. Age at death;20. Born; Castlecomer, County Kilkenny. Enlisted; Carlow. Residence; Castlecomer. Died. Son of the late John Nolan and of Anne McGrath (formerly Nolan), of Love Lane, Castlecomer, Co. Kilkenny. Kilkenny People, June, 1915. Kilkenny and the War. Further Deaths Reported from France and Germany. Another Death in the German Prison. Our Castlecomer correspondent writes;--I regret very much to have again to record another death amongst the Castlecomer young men who are prisoners of war in Germany, the sad case this time being young John Nolan, eldest son of Mrs John Nolan, Love Lane, Castlecomer, and who was a Private in the Royal Irish Regiment. Mrs Nolan received the following letter from Rev. R. Warren, C. C., Chaplain;-Limburg, Lahn, 24th May, 1915. Dear Mrs Nolan, --I sincerely regret to have to announce to you the death of your son, John Nolan, which took place here after a brief illness. His death is due to consumption, which crept rapidly into the poor boy's constitution. His death is greatly regretted amongst his poor companions, who long for the day soon to come when they may see Ireland once more. Your son received all the consolations which Our Holy Mother the Church gives to her children, before he left this world. I sympathise with you in your sad bereavement. —Very truly yours. R. Warren. This is the second death in this prison, and moreover they are the death of two men (D. Deevy and J. Nolan) whose constitutions and general physique were always of the best when in Castlecomer. Oh! The Germans will have a lot to aN. S. W. er for on the accounting day, for one can only draw the one conclusion from such events, and that is that starvation diet is very nearly the rule of the German prisons. May his soul rest in peace. Notes; Formerly he was with the Royal Dublin Fusiliers where his number was 5441. Grave or Memorial Reference; III K 7. Cemetery: Niederzwehren Cemetery in Germany.

Nolan, Michael. Rank; Sergeant. Regiment or Service: Royal Irish Regiment. Unit; 6th Battalion. Service Number; 11063. Date of death; 18/12/1916. Age at death; 20. Born; Castlecomer, County Kilkenny. Enlisted; Carlow. Residence; Castlecomer. Killed in action. Son of Anne McGrath (formerly Nolan), of Love Lane, Castlecomer, Co. Kilkenny, and the late John Nolan. Grave or Memorial Reference; G 9. Cemetery: Pond Farm Cemetery in Belgium.

Nolan, Michael. Rank; Private. Regiment or Service: Royal Irish Regiment. Unit; 2nd Battalion. Service Number; 4890. Date of death; 21/03/1918. Enlisted; Carlow. Residence; Graiguenamanagh, County ilkenny. Killed in action. (Wife) Mrs Ellen Nolan, Graiguenamanagh, County Kilkenny. Grave or Memorial Reference; Panels 30 and 31. Cemetery: Pozieres Memorial in France.

Nolan, Thomas. Rank; Private. Regiment or Service: Royal Irish Regiment. Unit; 1st Battalion. Service Number; 4300. Date of death; 04/05/1915. Age at death; 20. Born; Castlecomer, County Kilkenny. Enlisted; Carlow. Residence; Castlecomer. Died of wounds. Eldest son of Michael and Ellen Nolan, of Donaguile, Castlecomer, Co. Kilkenny. In his Will, dated 06-February-1915, his effects and property were received by;- (Mother) Mrs Ellen Nolan, Douaguile, Castle Comer, County Kilkenny, Ireland. Kilkenny People, June, 1915. Castlecomer Man wounded in Action. Mrs Michael Nolan, Donaguile, has received word that her son Thomas Nolan, a Private in the Royal Irish Regiment, was wounded in action at St Julian on the 3rd May. I am glad it is only wounded he has been, for a report was circulated that the poor fellow (who was the best of a son) was killed. I hope he will shortly be able to write to his parents and tell them when he may be able to come home to see them. Notes; Died of wounds at the 84th Field Ambulance. Grave or Memorial Reference; Panel 33. Cemetery: Ypres (Menin Gate) Memorial in Belgium.

Nolan, William. Rank; Private. Regiment or Service: Royal Irish Regiment. Unit; 2nd Battalion. Service Number; 7222. Date of death; 03/09/1916. Born; St Patrick's, Kilkenny. Enlisted; Kilkenny. Killed in action. Grave or Memorial Reference; XXI E 8. Cemetery: Delville Wood Cemetery, Longueval in France.

Michael Noonan's death plaques, courtesy of Eddie Sullivan, Waterford.

Noonan, Michael. Rank; Private. Regiment or Service: Royal Irish Regiment. Unit; 2nd Garrison Battalion. Service Number; 1605. Date of death; 11/12/1917. Age at death; 32. Enlisted; Liverpool. Residence; Waterford. Died at home. Husband of Mary Noonan, of 140, Barrack St, Waterford. Michael Moran has two entries in 'Soldiers Died in the Great War', with the result that he one of the few men ever to have been awarded two death plaques. He was stationed at the Depot Barracks in Clonmel. The image attached are his two death plaques. Notes; Company listed as 2nd Garrison Battalion (SDGW) Depot (CWGC) Previously he was with the Royal Irish Fusiliers where his number was G/1287. Grave or Memorial Reference; Near the South Boundary. Cemetery: Regina Caeli Cemetery, Mooncoin, County Kilkenny.

Norris, Thomas. Rank; Private. Regiment or Service: Irish Guards. Unit; 1st Battalion. Service Number; 3647. Date of death; 06/12/1914. Age at death;23. Born; Newtownbarry, County Wexford. Enlisted; Dublin. Residence; Dublin. Killed in action. Son of William and Anne Norris of Kilbranish, Newtownbarry, Co Wexford. Grave or Memorial Reference; Panel 11. Cemetery: Ypres (Menin Gate) Memorial in Belgium.

North, John. Rank; Rifleman. Regiment or Service: London Regiment. Unit; 8th (City of London) Battalion) Battalion (Post Office Rifles). Service Number; 4986. Date of death; 15/09/1916. Age at death; 25. Born; Kilkenny. Enlisted; Killenaule, County Tipperary. Residence; Killenaule, County Tipperary. Killed in action. Son of Honorah North, of Causeway View Lane, Portrush, Co. Antrim, and the late William Charles North. Notes; Born Callal (SDGW) Kilkenny (1901 Census). Grave or Memorial Reference; Pier and Face 9 C and 9. Cemetery: Theipval Memorial in France.

Noyes, Herbert Hahnemann. Rank; Private. Regiment or Service: Canadian Infantry (Saskatchewan Regiment). Unit; 5th Battalion. Service Number; 81675. Date of death; 09/09/1916. Age at death;30. Born; Johnstown, County Kilkenny. Killed in action. Son of the Rev. Robert J. Noyes (formerly Rector of Sevington, Ashford, Kent, England), and Mary Noyes, of Lloydminster, Saskatchewan. Native of Johnstown, Co. Kilkenny, Ireland. Born, Kilkenny, Ireland. Occupation on enlistment, farmer. Date of birth;11-March-1886. Next of kin details; Rev R. J. Moyes, Limavaddy, Derry. Date of enlistment, 18-December-1914. Height, 5 feet, 10 inches. Complexion, fair. Eyes, hazel. Hair, straw color. Grave or Memorial Reference; IV M 20. Cemetery: Pozieres British Cemetery, Ovillers-La Boisselle in France.

O'Brien, Daniel. Rank; Stoker. Regiment or Service: Royal Naval Reserve. Unit; H. M. S. Drake. Service Number; 400. V. (Dev). Date of death; 26/10/1916. Age at death; 48. Born; Tipperary. Died from disease. Next of kin listed as Widow:- Bridget. 43 Ballybricken Waterford, Ireland. Notes; D. O. B. 09/10/1867. Grave or Memorial Reference; Right of path between entrance and Church. Cemetery: Slievrue Catholic Churchyard Slievrue Co. Kilkenny.

O'Brien, James. Rank; Private. Regiment or Service: Royal Irish Regiment. Unit; 2nd Battalion. Service Number; 10672. Date of death; 29/11/1918. Born; Mooncoin, County Kilkenny. Enlisted; Waterford. Residence; Mooncoin. Died of wounds. In his Will, dated 15-September-1918, his effects and property were received by;- (Uncle) John Carney, Mooncain, County Kilkenny, Ireland. Grave or Memorial Reference; III A 73. Cemetery: Cambrai East Military cemetery, Nord, France.

O'Brien, John. Rank; Private. Regiment or Service: Royal Irish Regiment. Unit; 2nd Battalion. Service Number; 8087. Date of death; 03/09/1916. Age at death; 17. Born; Ballyraggett, County Kilkenny. Enlisted; Freshford. Residence; Ballyraggett. Killed in action. Son of John and Johanna O'Brien, of Oldtown, Ballyragget, Co. Kilkenny. In his Will, dated 14-June-1915, his effects and property were received by;- (Uncle) (Mother) Mrs J O'Brien, Oldtown, Ballyragget, County Kilkenny, Ireland. Grave or Memorial Reference; Pier and Face 3 A. Cemetery: Thiepval Memorial in France.

O'Connell, Donal/Donald Charles. Rank; Second Lieutenant. Regiment or Service: Connaught Rangers. Unit; 4th Battalion attached to the 8th Battalion, Royal Inniskilling Fusiliers. Date of death; 09/09/1916. Age at death;21. Born; Athlone, County Westmeath. Son of James John O'Connell, of "Arona", Clonskea, County Dublin. Brother of Maurice James, O'Connell who also died in the Great War. Limerick Chronicle, September, 1916. Second Lieutenant D C O;Connell. The death in action is officially announced of Second Lieutenant Donal Charles O'Connell,

Connaught Rangers. He was only 21 years of age and was the second son of Mr and Mrs James P O'Connell, Arona, Clonskeagh, Dublin. Notes; Name listed as Donal Charles (CWGC+Limerick Chronicle) Donald Charles (MIC) Born Roscommon (1911 Census) Thurles, County Tipperary (1901 Census) Birth registered in Athlone, County Westmeath. Grave or Memorial Reference; Pier and Face 15 A. Cemetery: Thiepval Memorial in France and listed under Borris/Ballyellin on the Great War Memorial, Milford Street, Leighlinbridge, County Carlow.

O'Connor, Arthur. Rank; Sergeant. Regiment or Service: Leinster Regiment. Unit; 2nd Battalion. Service Number; 9367. Date of death; 31/08/1916. Age at death; 23. Born; Ballyraggett, County Kilkenny. Enlisted; Cork. Killed in action. Son of, John O'Connor and Katherine O'Connor (nee Lyne), of 4, Sunview Terrace, South Douglas Rd., Cork. In his Will, dated 21-August1914, his effects and property were received by;- (Father) John O' Connor, 4 Sunview Terrace, South Douglas Road, Cork, Ireland. Grave or Memorial Reference; XXXV J 8. Cemetery: Serre Road Cemetery No 2 in France.

O'Connor, James Charles. Rank; Lance Corporal. Regiment or Service: Irish Guards. Unit; 2nd Battalion. Service Number; 10164. Date of death; 27/11/1917. Age at death;22. Born; Durrow, Queen's County. Enlisted; Dublin. Residence; Castlecolumn, County Kilkenny. Killed in action. Son of Terence and Catherine O'Connor, of Castlecolumb, Knocktopher, Co. Kilkenny. His brother Thomas also died on service and is buried in Co. Kilkenny, Republic of Ireland. Grave or Memorial Reference; Panel 2 and 3. Cemetery: Cambrai Memorial in Louveral in France.

O'Connor, Thomas James. Rank; Staff Sergeant. Regiment or Service: Royal Garrison Artillery. Service Number; 45973/65973. Date of death; 23/02/1919. Age at death; 28. Born; Union House, Thomastown, County Kilkenny. Son of Mrs. Catherine O'Connor, of Castlecolumb, Knocktopher. His brother James also died on service and is commemorated on the Cambrai Memorial, France. Notes; Number listed as 45973 (CWGC) 65973 (IMR). Grave or Memorial Reference; About 10 yards North of ruins. Cemetery: Knocktopher (Old Abbey) Graveyard, Kilkenny.

O'Dea, Laurence (Very Rev). Rank; Chaplain 4th Class. Regiment or Service: Army Chaplains Department. Date of death; 04/11/1917. Age at death;66. Died. Son of Kyran and Mary O'Dea, of William Street, Kilkenny. O. S. F. C. Irish Times. O'Dea-At the Military Hospital, London, Very Rev. Laurence O'Dea, O. S. F. C., late Chaplain to Invalid Forces at Eastbourne. Cemetery: Crawley Monastery Burial Ground, Sussex.

O'Gorman, Michael. Rank; Private. Regiment or Service: Royal Irish Regiment. Unit; 1st Garrison Battalion. Service Number; 1758. Date of death; 08/12/1915. Born; St John's, Kilkenny. Enlisted; Waterford. Died in hospital. Waterford News. March, 1916. Death of Waterford Soldier. To the Editor "Waterford News."1st Garrison Battalion, R. I. Regiment. 25th February, 1916. Dear Sir- I would feel very thankful to you if you if you would spare me space in your paper to express the sympathy of the 1st Garrison Battalion, Royal Irish Regiment, touching on the death of Corporal Gorman, late of the G. P. O., Waterford, also of Private J Brennan, of Clonmel. No words of mine could express, or give even a faint idea of how popular they were, and how cheerful and inspiring they had always been. It is certainly no exaggeration to say that they were esteemed by avery officer, N. C. O., and man in the Battalion. We all owe them a deep and lasting debt of gratitude as long as we are in the land of the living out here. One of them is asleep in the sands of Egypt and the other in Mudros. May they rest in peace. —Yours sincerely. Pte P. Condon. 1st Garrison Battalion, R. I. R. Notes; Died at the 15th Stationary Hospital, Mudros. Grave or Memorial Reference; III D 124. Cemetery: East Mudros Military Cemetery in Greece.

Lieutenant O'Hara, from 'Our Heroes.'

O'Hara, Henry Desmond. Rank; Lieutenant. Regiment or Service: Royal Dublin Fusiliers. Unit; 1st Battalion. Date of death; 29/08/1915. Age at death;23. Died of wounds. Son of William T. O'Hara, of Cheney Longville, Craven Arms, Salop. Born 021-May-1892 in Ballyduff, Thomastown. Also commemorated on the Connellan Memorial Window in St Canice's Church, Kilkenny;- To the Glory of God and in loving memory of four brave soldiers. Grandsons of the late Peter Connellan of Coolmore in this county. Who after distinguished service laid down their lives for King and Country…. Henry Desmond O'Hara, D. S. O., Captain, Royal Dublin Fusiliers. Only son of W. J. O'Hara, R. M. Died of wounds received in the Gallipoli Peninsula, August xxix, MCMXV, aged xxiii years. Non Sibi sed Patriae. De Ruvigny's Roll of Honour. son of William James O'Hara, of Oriel House, Ballincollig, Cork, Resident Magistrate, by his wife, Cecilia, 7th and youngest daughter of the late Peter Connellan, of Coolmore, County Kilkenny, J. P., D. L., and grandson of the late Rev. James Dunn O'Hara, of O'Hara

Brook and The Castle, Portstewart, County Antrim. Born in Ballyduff, Thomastown, County Kilkenny, 21-May-1892. Educated at Dunschurch Hall, Rugby, Charterhouse and the Royal Military College, Sandhurst. Gazetted 2nd lieutenant, Royal Dublin Fusiliers, 04-September-1912. promoted Lieutenant 29-April-1914. Went to the Dardanelles 17-March-1915. Took part in the heavy fighting following the landing there, and died on the hospital ship 'Arcadian, ' 29-August-1915, of wounds received in action on the 12th. Buried in the military cemetery, Gibraltar."On 25 April, 1915, at Sedd-el-Bahr, he took command of his Battalion when all other officers had been killed or wounded. At night, when the enemy broke through the line, he displayed great initiative and resource in organising a successful counter-attack, restoring the line and causing great loss to the enemy." For this he was awarded the D. S. O. (London Gazette, 3 June, 1915). Lieutenant O'Hara was also mentioned in Sir Ian Hamilton's Despatch of 20 May (London Gazette, 5 August), 1915, for his conduct during and after the landing of the 29th Division on 25 April. Irish at the Front. Page 67; Altogether more than 1,000 men had left the River Clyde by 1 1 o'clock in the morning. Two-thirds of them had been shot dead, drowned, or wounded. The landing was then discontinued. It was resumed under the shelter of darkness, when, strange to say,' the 1,000 men remaining on the River Clyde got ashore without a single casualty. In fact not a shot was fired against them. But before they were landed a night attack was made by the Turks on the remnants of the Dublins and Munsters crouching on the beach under the protection of the bank. Lieutenant Henry Desmond O'Hara, of the Dublins, took command, all the senior officers having been killed and wounded. He was awarded the Distinguished Service Order and promoted to be captain for his initiative and resource in restoring the line when it had been broken by the Turks, and organising a successful counter-attack which caused great loss to the enemy. Captain O'Hara died soon afterwards of wounds received in action. He was the only son of Mr. W. J. O'Hara, resident magistrate, Ballincollig, Co. Cork, and am nephew of Dr. O'Hara, Bishop of Cashel. 'The Distinguished Service Order, 1886-1915. '...was born at Ballyduff, Thoamstown, County Kilkenny, 21-May-1892, son of W. J. O'Hara, resident Magistrate, Ballincollig, County Cork, and Cecilia, seventh and youngest daughter of the late Peter Connellan, od Coolmore, County Kilkenny, J. P., and D. L. ; and grandson pf the late reverend James Dunn O'Hara, of O'Hara Brook and the Castle, Portstewart, County Antrim. He was educated at Dunchurch Hall; Rugby' Charterhouse, and the Royal Military College, Sandhurst, and was gazetted to the Royal Dublin Fusiliers, 04-September-1912, becoming Lieutenant, 29-April-1914. He went to the Dardanelles, 07-March-1915. Took part in the heavy fighting following the landing there, and died on the Hospital Ship 'Arcadian' 29-August-1915, of wounds received in action on the 12th. He was buried in the Military Cemetery at Gibralter. Lieutenant O'Hara was mentioned in Sir Ian Hamilton's Despatch of 20-May (London Gazette, 05-August-1915), for his conduct during and after the landing of the 29th Division on 25-April. He was created a Companion of the Distinguished Service Order for gallantry and resource on the 25th April at Sedd-el-bahr, where he took command of his battalion when all other officers had been killed or wounded. At night when the enemy broke through the line he displayed great initiative and resource in organising a successful counter-attack, restoring the line and causing great loss to the enemy (London Gazette, 3-June-1915) ; "Henry Desmond O'Hara, Lieutenant, 1st Battalion. The Royal Dublin Fusiliers. For gallantry and devotion to duty in connection with the operations at the dardanelles.". 'Our Heroes'. who will be remembered for the part he took in the memorable landing at Sedd-el-Bahr on April 25th last, when, though the junior officer, he took command of the remnant of his battalion, all the officers of which, with the exception of Captain (then Lieutenant) O'Hara, having been either killed or wounded, on which occasion his initiative and resource and the coolness and gallantry he displayed earned for him the D. S. O and special mention in despatches, was wounded in action on August 12th last at the dardanelles and died on the hospital ship 'Arcadian' near Gibraltar on the 29th. The gallant young soldier was laid to rest in the cemetery at Gibraltar with full military honours. He was the only son of Mr W. J. O'Hara, R. M., Oriel House, Ballincollig, County Cork. London Gazette, 23-June-1915;-"War Office, 23-June-1915. His Majesty, The King, has been graciously pleased to approve of the under-mentioned Honours and rewards, for distinguished service in the field, with effect from 03-June-1915, inclusive. To be Companions of the Distinguished service Order.". Kilkenny Journal, September, 1915. The Roll of Honour. Captain H. D. O'Hara, R. D. F., who was wounded on the 11th ult., and whose death has been announced, was the only son of W. J. O'Hara, R. M., and Cecilia, youngest daughter of the late Peter Connellan, Esq., D. L., Coolmore, Thomastown. The many friends of Lieutenant S. C. Webb, R. M. F., whose name appears amongst the wounded, will be glad to learn that he is making speedy progress towards recovery, he was wounded during the landing and advance of the Irish Division under General Mahon on the shores of the Gallipoli Peninsula. Waterford News;- We regret to learn that Captain H. D. O'Hara, D. S. O., whose gallantry in leading the Royal Dublin Fusiliers on their landing at Gallipoli was recently recorded, and who was shot through the lungs on the 11th ult, has died of his wounds. Captain O'Hara was only 22 years of age. He was the only son of W. J. O'Hara, R. M. and Cecilia, youngest daughter of the late Peter Connellan, Esq., D. L., Coolmore, Thomastown, County Kilkenny, and the nephew of the Right rev. Dr O'Hara, Protestant Bishop of Cashel. Kilkenny Journal, June, 1915. The Roll of Honour. Lieutenant H. D. O'Hara, who has been appointed Companion of the Distinguished Service Order for gallantry and devotion to duty in connection with the operations at the Dardanelles, is son of W. O'Hara, Esq, D. I., R. I. C., who married a sister of Major J. H. Connellan, D. L., J. P., of Coolmore. He was with his Battalion, the 1st Battalion Royal Dublin Fusiliers, when they suffered so terribly in the recent landing pf the Mediterranean Expeditionary Force in Galipoli. When all his senior officers had been rendered hors de combat he commanded what was left of his Battalion in the advance against the Turkish position. Kilkenny Journal, September, 1915. Sympathy With Major J. H. Connellan, D. L. Much sympathy is felt for Major J. H. Connellan, D. L., Coolmore House, Thomastown, on the death of his nephew—Captain O'Hara, R. M. —who died from wounds received in action at the Dardanelles. Deceased officer was only in his 22nd year. Grave or Memorial Reference; C 3065. Cemetery: Gibraltar (North Front) Cemetery.

O'Keefe, Patrick. Rank; Private. Regiment or Service: Royal Irish Regiment. Unit; 6th Battalion. Service Number; 2110. Date of death; 01/09/1916. Age at death; 22. Born; Clare, King's County. Enlisted; Kilkenny. Residence; Clifton, County Kilkenny. Killed in action. Son of John and Mary O'Keefe, of Ballysalla, Kilderry, Co. Kilkenny. Born Clifden, Co. Kilkenny. Grave or Memorial Reference; III M 4. Cemetery: Quarry Cemetery, Montauban in France.

O'Keeffe, Henry. Rank; Lance Corporal/Private. Regiment or Service: Royal Irish Regiment. Unit; 2nd Battalion. Service Number; 11605. Date of death; 03/09/1916. Born; St John's, Kilkenny. Enlisted; Maryborough. Residence; Kilkenny. Killed in action. Notes; Formerly he was with the Leinster Regiment where his number was 10308. Grave or Memorial Reference; Pier and Face 3 A. Cemetery: Thiepval Memorial in France.

O'Keeffe, Michael. Rank; Private. Regiment or Service: Royal Irish Regiment. Unit; 1st Battalion. Service Number; 4573. Date of death; 04/04/1915. Age at death; 19. Born; Thomastown, County Kilkenny. Enlisted; Thomastown. Died of wounds. Son of John and Alice O'Keeffe, of Moonteen, Thomastown, Co. Kilkenny. In his Will, dated 05-March-1915, his effects and property were received by;- (Mother) Mrs Alice O'Keeffe, Moonteen, Thomastown, County Kilkenny. Kilkenny People, April, 1915. Thomastown Soldier Killed in Action. Notification has been received from the War Office of the death at the front of private James Murphy, Royal Irish Regiment, as the results of wounds received at the battle of Neuve Chapelle on the 17th March. The deceased soldier, who was a native of Thomastown, was about 35 years of age and unmarried. Notes; Date of death listed as 04/04/1915 Irelands Memorial Records gives his date of death as 08/09/1915. Died of wounds at Hooge, Ypres. Grave or Memorial Reference; I F 8. Cemetery: Ypres Town Cemetery Extension in Belgium.

O'Keeffe/O'Keefle, Michael. Rank; Lance Sergeant. Regiment or Service: Royal Dublin Fusiliers. Unit; 6th Battalion. Service Number; 13496. Date of death; 09/09/1915. Born; Kilkenny. Enlisted; Cork. Residence; Buttevany, County Cork. Killed in Action in Gallipoli. O'Keeffe (CWGC, IMR), O'Keefle (SDGW),. Kilkenny People, June 1916. Kilkenny Soldier's Letter. (Passed by Censor). Balkan States, 12-04-1916. Dear Mr Keane—I take the liberty of writing to you to let you know if you would be so kind as to spare a space in your valuable paper for this letter. Being an old reader of the "Kilkenny People" I will try and let the readers at home know, through you, of the doings of the "People's" readers abroad. I have been through the landing on the 6th August, 1915, at Suvla Bay, where, I am sorry to say, we lost a few Kilkenny boys. From there we found ourselves on the Serbian frontier facing the Germans, Bulgars, Austrians and Turks. We, however gave them to understand that they were "up against" Irishmen, much to their surprise; but they came on in overwhelming numbers. Still there was no Kilkennyman coming down from the mountains wounded, but unfortunately the frost and snow proved too masterful for a couple of Kilkenny lads, who had got frost-bitten, but they proved themselves men and passed on with a smilw on their lips to hospital, and as they passed you could hear their "pass-word"—"Up the Black and Amber!" To mention the names of these brave lads—I only think it will serve to gather them some praise, which they highly deserve. Their names are;-- John Sheridan,"Dido" Kenny, as we used to call him, from Walkin Street Upper, and the renowned "Cock" Byrne's brother James, who got wounded through the thigh. All belong to the Connaught Rangers. Well, the "Kilkenny People" has been a great welcome to us, Kilkenny boys, both in Gallipoli and in the Balkans, and every post that comes the cry is."Did you get the 'People'?" Our division is the 10th Irish Division, which bore the brunt at the landing and saved the day in Serbia, and which all the papers gave praise to on that memorable retreat. We are now nine months on active service, and don't expect to get leave before we finish the Huns up out here. I may mention that the boys from the city and county have been very lucky out here, thank God. I also may mention the names of the heroes who fell at Svla Bay, viz., Sergeant Michael O'Keeffe, late of Greensbridge and Privates K. Meehan, of Garden Row, and W. O'Connell, from Maudlin Street. Their memory is still fresh with us, and I trust that the people at home offer up a prayer for their happy repose. The English papers may boast of the deeds of valour performed by the Australian forces, but let them compare them with the magnificent dash of the Irish regiments and see who comes first. I think I will draw this letter to a close by saying that all the boys from city and county are "in the pink," and all hope to be back again soon, with the help of God. I enclose a few verses I composed by the help of Private J. Hogan, 3909, of the 4th Battalion., on thinking of the landing at Suvla Bay. I conclude by sending my best wishes for the success of your valuable paper. —I am, sir, yours sincerely. No 78, Corporal P. Staunton. A Company, 5th Royal Irish regiment, 10th Division, Salonika Field Force. The Landing at Suvla Bay. 'Twas on the 6th of August, on a bright and sunny day. We landed at the Dardanelles, some thousands of miles away. We knew not what before us lay, but we hear the shot and shell. And many an Irish soldier there that day now lives no more to tell. It was a bright and glorious day which we will never forget. When the Connaughts and the 5th Royal Irish went through that Vale of Death. It was death by fire, and water going through the Suvla tide. But those gallant sons of Erin their enemy defied! I will raise a glass, filled to the brim, of Smithwick's sparkling ale, and drink to the health of the boys that live who fought and did no quail. And whenever I hear the sound of guns and the clamour of war and din. I never will forget Gallipoli and the struggle I there was in. Grave or Memorial Reference; Special Memorial G 2. Cemetery: Green Hill Cemetery in Turkey.

Omara, Patrick. Rank; Sergeant. Regiment or Service: Royal Scots, Lothian Regiment. Unit; 11th Battalion. Service Number; 13268. Date of death; 27/09/1915. Born; Kildare. Enlisted; Kildare. Residence; Castlecomer. Killed in action. Grave or Memorial Reference; Panel 10 to 13. Cemetery: Loos Memorial in France.

O'Neil/O'Neill, Thomas. Rank; Private. Regiment or Service: Royal Irish Fusiliers. Unit; 1st Battalion. Service Number; 10135. Date of death; 22/04/1918. Age at death;30. Born; Thomastown, County Kilkenny. Enlisted; Dublin. Residence; Thomastown, County Kilkenny. Died of wounds. Son of Thos. and Catherine O'Neil, of Barretstown, Co. Kilkenny. Served 42 years in India. Grave or Memorial Reference; XXIX M 4 A. Cemetery: Etaples Military Cemetery in France.

O'Neill, Andrew. Rank; Sergeant. Regiment or Service: Northumberland Fusiliers. Unit; 26th Battalion (Tyneside Irish). Service Number; 26/521. Date of death; 28/04/1917. Born; Kilkenny. Enlisted; Newcastle-on-Tyne. Killed in action. After his death his effects and property were received by;- (Wife) Mrs Margaret O'Neill, 14 Atkinson Buildings, Birtley, County Durham, England. Grave or Memorial Reference; III A 21. Cemetery: Brown's Copse Cemetery, Roeux in France.

O'Neill, Daniel. Rank; Private. Regiment or Service: Royal Inniskilling Fusiliers. Unit; 7/8th Battalion. Service Number; 29608. Date of death; 21/03/1918. Born; Castlecomer, County Kilkenny. Enlisted; Omagh. Residence; Castlecomer. Killed in action. In his Will, dated 14-December-1917, his effects and property were received by;- (Mother) Mrs Bridget O'Neill, Barrack St, Castlecower, County Kilkenny. Grave or Memorial Reference; Panel 38 to 40. Cemetery: Pozieres Memorial in France.

O'Neill, Edward. Rank; Private. Regiment or Service: Connaught Rangers. Unit; 5th Battalion. Service Number; 5474. Date of death; 07/12/1915. Born; Liverpool. Enlisted; Liverpool. Residence; Liverpool. Killed in action in Salonika. Son of John and Mary O'Neill, of Co. Kilkenny; husband of Rose O'Neill, of 8, Flint St., Bootle, Liverpool. Cemetery: Doiran Memorial in Greece.

O'Neill, James. Rank; Sergeant. Regiment or Service: Durham Light Infantry. Unit; 11th Battalion. Service Number; 25774. Date of death; 21/10/1917. Born; Kilkenny. Enlisted; Gateshead. Residence; Kilkenny. Died at home. Notes; Number listed as 25774 (SDGW, IMR), TR5/11757 (CWGC). Grave or Memorial Reference; Special Memorial. Cemetery: Birtley (St Joseph) Roman Catholic Cemetery, Durham, U. K.

O'Neill, John. Rank; Private. Regiment or Service: Royal Irish Regiment. Unit; 2nd Battalion. Service Number; 5664. Date of death; 23/08/1917. Born; Ballyhale, County Kilkenny. Enlisted; Kilkenny. Residence; Knocktopher, County Kilkenny. Died. In his Will, written at Queenstown, dated 24-November-1916, his effects and property were received by;- (Mother) Mrs Mary O'Neill, Knocktopher, County Kilkenny. Grave or Memorial Reference; XXX N 9. Cemetery: Etaples Military Cemetery in France

O'Neill, Joseph Francis. Rank; Private. Regiment or Service: Northumberland Fusiliers. Unit; 26th Battalion (Tyneside Irish). Service Number; 24/85. Date of death; 01/07/1916. Born; Kilkenny. Enlisted; Newcastle-on-Tyne. Killed in action. Grave or Memorial Reference; Pier and Face 10B, 11B and. Cemetery: Theipval Memorial in France.

O'Neill, Lawrence. Rank; Private. Regiment or Service: Somerset Light Infantry. Unit; 8th Battalion. Service Number; 11399. Date of death; 27/01/1916. Born; Ferrybank, County Kilkenny. Enlisted; Merthyr, Glamorganshire. Residence; Ferrybank, County Kilkenny. Died of wounds. Grave or Memorial Reference; II C 91. Cemetery: Bailleul Communal Cemetery Extension (Nord) in France.

O'Neill, Michael. Rank; Private. Regiment or Service: Royal Irish Regiment. Unit; 4th Battalion. Service Number; 5384. Date of death; 19/03/1916. Age at death;21. Born; Paulstown, County Kilkenny. Enlisted; Kilkenny. Residence; Clifton, County Kilkenny. Died at home. Son of Mrs. Kate O'Neill, of Talbot's Hill, Clifden, Co. Kilkenny. Grave or Memorial Reference; Panel 5 (Screen Wall). Cemetery: Grangegorman Memorial in Dublin.

O'Neill, Richard. Rank; Lance Corporal. Regiment or Service: Connaught Rangers. Unit; 6th Battalion. Service Number; 5612. Date of death; 03/08/1917. Age at death; 21. Born; Kilkenny. Enlisted; Kilkenny. Residence; Kilkenny. Killed in action. Son of Richard and Mary O'Neill, of Walkin St., Kilkenny. In his Will, dated 01-July-1916, his effects and property were received by;- (Mother) Mrs Mary O'Neill, Walkin St, Kilkenny. Grave or Memorial Reference; Panel 42. Cemetery: Ypres (Menin Gate) Memorial in Belgium.

O'Neill, Thomas. Rank; Private. Regiment or Service: Royal Irish Regiment. Unit; 2nd Battalion. Service Number; 8121. Date of death; 19/10/1914. Born; Kilmanagh, County Kilkenny. Enlisted; Kilkenny. Residence; Kilmanagh. Killed in action. Grave or Memorial Reference; A 7. Cemetery: Caudry Old Communal Cemetery, Nord in France.

O'Roie, Clarence. Rank; Private. Regiment or Service: Australian Infantry. Unit; Base Depot. Service Number; 2228. Date of death; 02/11/1915. Age at death; 32. Born; Kilkenny. Enlisted; Melbourne, Victoria. Occupation on enlistment, bricklayer. Age on enlistment; 32 years 6 months. Next of kin details; (wife) Eleanor O'Roie, 64 Charles Street Northcote. Weight, 12st 2 lbs. Height, 5 feet, 4 ½ inches. Complexion, fresh. Eyes, blue. Hair, dark brown. Supplementary information; Husband of Mrs. E. O'Roie, of North Coburg. Died in Base Hospital 02-November-1915 supposed to have been run over by a motor car in St Kilda Road, Melbourne.
A letter in his records;- Re the late Pte C O'Roie, of the Permanent Force. I have this day forwarded on the BVase Records the attestation papers duly signed and my report on the late Private O'Roie. I am informed that the above man Private C O'Roie was found unconscious, near Government House…on 02/11/1915. That he was taken to No 5, A.G.H. and died the same night and the body was removed to the Morgue for the Coroners inquest. The aforesaid Private O'Roie was on duty at the Domain Camp on Piquet from 6 p.m to 8 p.m., 02/11/1915, he was relieved from duty at 8 p.m. and shortly afterwards by the Orderly Corporal and apparently was never seen alive by any of the Guard afterwards. I am informed that while on duty at the Barracks the previous day he had left his overcoat in the Guard Room and it is suggested that he was proceeding to the Guard Room for the purpose of getting his overcoat (as he was to have gone on duty again at 12 hrs…..ght) when he apparently met with the supposed accident which is alleged to have caused his death. Private O'Roie was one of the most capable and reliable soldiers under my command.

His daughters Kathleen and Sheila of 64 Charles Street Northcote were awarded a pension of £13 each per annum and his wife Eleanor of the same address received £52 per annum. Notes; Place and date of enlistment, 20-July-1915. Melbourne, Victoria. Grave or Memorial Reference; R C E 222. Cemetery: Pine Ridge Memorial Park, Australia.

O'Rourke, James. Rank; Private. Regiment or Service: Irish Guards. Unit; 1st Battalion. Service Number; 2820. Date of death; 06/11/1914. Born; Kilkenny. Enlisted; Kilkenny. Killed in action. Grave or Memorial Reference; Panel 11. Cemetery: Ypres (Menin Gate) Memorial in Belgium.

O'Rourke, James. Rank; Private. Regiment or Service: Royal Irish Regiment. Unit; 6th Battalion. Service Number; 7788. Date of death; 05/04/1917. Age at death; 22. Born; Kildare. Enlisted; Kilkenny. Killed in action. Son of John and Mary O'Rourke (nee Hegarty), of Maudlin Street, Kilkenny. Previously wounded. Grave or Memorial Reference; Panel 33. Cemetery: Ypres (Menin Gate) Memorial in Belgium.

O'Shea, John. Rank; Private. Regiment or Service: Royal Irish Regiment. Unit; 2nd Battalion. Service Number; 4775. Date of death; 05/07/1916. Age at death;36. Born; Callan, County Kilkenny. Enlisted; Cashel. Residence; Thurles. Died of wounds. Son of John and Bridget Osborne O' Shea, of Friar Street, Thurles, Co. Tipperary. Native of Callan, Co. Kilkenny. In his Will, dated 12-July-1915, his effects and property were received by;- (Father) Mr John O'Shea, Friar Street, Thurles, County Tipperary, Ireland. Grave or Memorial Reference; Plot 1. Row B. Grave 43. Cemetery: Corbie Communal Cemetery Extension in France.

O'Shea, Patrick. Rank; Private. Regiment or Service: Irish Guards. Unit; 2nd Battalion. Service Number; 3501. Date of death; 14/11/1917. Born; Kilkenny. Enlisted; Limerick. Died. Son of Patrick and Mary O'shea, of Dromkeen Station, Co. Limerick. Grave or Memorial Reference; On the West boundary. Cemetery: Ostreville Churchyard, Pas De Calais, France.

O'Shea, Thomas. Rank; 2nd Corporal. Regiment or Service: Royal Engineers. Unit; 12th Field Company. Service Number; 19185. Date of death; 09/08/1915. Age at death;29. Born; Inishtioge, County Kilkenny. Enlisted; Naas. Residence; Inishtioge, County Kilkenny. Killed in action. Son of Richard and Maria O'shea, of Kilmacshane, Inistioge, Co. Kilkenny. Grave or Memorial Reference; Panel 9. Cemetery: Ypres (Menin Gate) Memorial in Belgium

O'Sullivan, John. Rank; Corporal. Regiment or Service: Leinster Regiment. Unit; 2nd Battalion. Service Number; 7944. Date of death; 10/09/1915. Born; Secundrabad, India. Enlisted; Cork. Killed in action. Kilkenny People, September, 1915. Killed in Action. Barrack Warden O'Sullivan, Kilkenny Military Barracks, has received a letter from the Rev. J. P. Moloney, Chaplain to the 2nd Leinsters, announcing that his son, Corporal O'Sullivan, was killed in action on the night of September 10. Father Moloney states that the gallant soldier was present at Holy Mass and received Holy Communion on the morning of the day he was killed, and before death he received Extreme Unction and the Last Blessing. Grave or Memorial Reference; F 4. Cemetery: La Brique Military Cemetery, No 1 in Belgium.

O'Toole, William. Rank; Private. Regiment or Service: Royal Irish Regiment. Unit; 2nd Battalion. Service Number; 4797. Date of death; 05/07/1916. Born; Ballyraggett, County Kilkenny. Enlisted; Kilkenny. Residence; Ballyraggett. Killed in action. Son of the late James O'Toole, of Ballyragget, Co. Kilkenny. After his death his effects and property were received by;- (Sister) Mrs M Stanton, Bridge St, Ballyragget, County Kilkenny. Grave or Memorial Reference; Pier and Face 3 A. Cemetery: Thiepval Memorial in France.

Owens, Denis Patrick. Rank; Second Engineer. Regiment or Service: Mercantile Marine. Unit; S. S. Brodholme. Date of death; 10/06/1918. Age at death; 30. Son of John and Sarah Owens. of Castlecomer, Co. Kilkenny; husband of Maud Owens, of 32, Hamstel Rd., Southchurch. Southend-on-Sea. Kilkenny People February-1915. A Castlecomer Man. At the sinking of the Emden. Mrs Sarah Owens, Castlecomer, has just received the following letter from her son, Mr Denis Owens, Fourth Engineer, S. S. Arawa, dated the 4th inst;- "My Dear Mother—Just a few lines to ask you how you are. I hope you are very well. I was over in Belfast for two days at Xmas, Annie and Dick are both very well. We are leaving about Tuesday for Australia and new Zealand, and expect to be away five months. Last trip lasted seven months, out we were kept in New Zealand till the troops were ready, and then too 1,400 of them to Alexandria (Egypt). They are now fighting the Turks at the Suez Canal. There were 30,000 in all, 20,000 from Australia and 10,000 from New Zealand. We were 38 transports and 4 battleships. One of the battleships (the Ibuki) is a Japanese. We all joined up at Albany, and on our way to Colombo we sank the German battleship Emden. Our convoy was the Minotaur, Melbourne, Sydney, and Ibuki, The Arawa for the call for help from the cocos Islands, where the fight took place, and we sent it to the Melbourne (acting flagship) as the Minotaur had left the day previous. The Melbourne sent the Sydney for the Islands, where she made very short work of sinking the Emden. The Sydney fired 120 shells and never missed a single shot. She simply smashed the German up, killed 200 of her crew, and wounded all the others with the exception of about 100 which she took as prisoners. We had 3o of the prisoners on board from Colombo to Suez, where we transferred them to the Hampshire, which was then acting as convoy, all the other battleships having left us. The prisoners were under the impression that the Germans had captured Paris and London, and were greatly surprised when they heard it was not so. The Arawa was the only ship of the lot to hear the call from the Cocos Islands, so we were very pleased with ourselves. Passing through the Canal we found it lined with Indian troops and home territorials, and at Port Said end of the Canal we passed a lot of French battleships. The Frenchmen gave us a great reception. It was the biggest convoy of ships and the biggest in regard to distance though not of men that has even been. We landed all the troops at Alexandria, and then the Arawa came to London as we had some cargo and gifts from New Zealand to Belfast. We have been here just over a week, having a month in London. I've heard there has been a lot of soldiers from the County Kilkenny killed at the front. They were part of the Royal Irish regiment, and right well they fought. The war will probably last a long time, but Great Britain with her allies will win. Drop me a line and tell me how you are, and now I will close with best love, Your affectionate son,"Denis" Mr Owens, the writer of the above served his apprenticeship as an engineer to a firm in Wexford, and passed his examinations in the Engineers with distinction. He is brother of Miss Owens, of the Union Hotel, Belfast. (Second Engineer Denis Patrick Owens died NE of Syracuse, with 4 others when the Steam Ship Brodholme was torpedoed and beached in June 1918). Grave or Memorial Reference; H 2 103. Cemetery: Syracuse Communal Cemetery, Sicily.

P

Parker, Elizabeth Kelly. Rank; Matron. Regiment or Service: Queen Alexandra's Imperial Military Nursing Service. Service Number; 2/P/193. Born in Castlecomer 31/12/1878. Date of death; 16/10/1916. Age at death 37. Educated at Victoria High School Londonderry. Trained at Warneford Hospital, Leamington Spa, from 1901 to 1904. Appointed Staff Nurse in 1907. Her sisters were also nurses, Letitia Anna Parker (QAIMNS), and Emily Alice Mary (QAIMNSR). Daughter of Joseph Donaldson Parker, J. P.,(died 1927 and buried in St Marys, Ardra, Castlecomer), and Elizabeth Dobbs Parker (died 1931), of Castlecomer, Co. Kilkenny. Limerick Chronicle, October, 1916. Parker—October 16, 1916, at Alexandria, Egypt, Elizabeth Kelly, (Elsie), Matron, Queen Alexandra's Imperial Military Nursing Service, the dearly-loved daughter of Joseph Donal laon (sic) and Elizabeth Dobbs Parker, Castlecomer."Thy will be done.". Grave or Memorial Reference; B 4. Cemetery: Alexandria (Hadra) War memorial Cemetery in Egypt. Elizabeth is also commemorated on the Great War Memorial in St Canice's Cathedral, Kilkenny…'To the Glory of God and in loving memory of the following members of the Diocese of Ossory who gave their lives for their country in the Great War 1914-1918'.

Payne, Frederick. Rank; Sergeant. Regiment or Service: Royal Field Artillery. Unit; Guards Divisional Artillery Headquarters. Service Number; 95557. Date of death; 10/03/1918. Age at death; 40. Born; Potters Bar, Middlesex. Enlisted; Lewes, Sussex. Died. Son of Peter and Mary Payne, of Potter's Bar, Middx; husband of Bridget Payne, of 4, Lower John Street, Kilkenny. Grave or Memorial Reference; II B 23. Cemetery: Bac-Du-Sud British Cemetery, Bailleulval in France

Pender, James. Rank; Private. Regiment or Service: Royal Irish Regiment. Unit; 2nd Battalion. Service Number; 6413. Date of death; 24/05/1915. Age at death;21. Born; Abbeyside, County Waterford. Enlisted; Dungarvan, County Waterford. Residence; Abbeyside. Killed in action. Grave or Memorial Reference; Panel 33. Cemetery: Ypres (Menin Gate) Memorial in Belgium.

Pender, James. Rank; Rifleman. Regiment or Service: Royal Irish Rifles. Unit; 1st Battalion. Service Number; 16130. Date of death; 02/07/1916. Age at death; 21. Born; Kilkenny. Enlisted; Tonypandy, Glamorganshire. Residence; Ystrad, Glamorganshire. Died of wounds near Hooge. Son of Michael and Bridget Pender, of Gauls Mills, Ferrybank, Waterford. Born at Kilmacow, Waterford. His brother Patrick also fell. Information from his Will;- (Father) Mr Michael Pender, Gaules Mills, Ferry Bank, Waterford, Ireland. If his father is dead, all property and effects are to go to his brother. Notes; Born Kilkenny (SDGW) Kilmacow, County Waterford (CWGC). Grave or Memorial Reference; Special Memorial. Cemetery: Sanctuary Wood Cemetery, Ypres, Belgium.

Pender, Patrick. Rank; Private. Regiment or Service: Royal Munster Fusiliers. Unit; 9th Battalion. Service Number; 3464. Date of death; 01/05/1916. Age at death;26. Born; Waterford. Enlisted; Tonpentre, South Wales. Residence; Tonpentre. Died of wounds at home. Son of Michael and Bridget Pender, of Gaul's Mills, Ferry Bank, Waterford. Native of Kilmacow, Co. Kilkenny. Grave or Memorial Reference; E V II. Cemetery: Dover (St James) Cemetery.

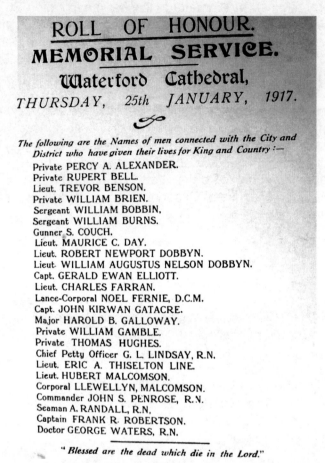

ROLL OF HONOUR.
MEMORIAL SERVICE.
Waterford Cathedral,
THURSDAY, 25th JANUARY, 1917.

The following are the Names of men connected with the City and District who have given their lives for King and Country :—

Private PERCY A. ALEXANDER.
Private RUPERT BELL.
Lieut. TREVOR BENSON.
Private WILLIAM BRIEN.
Sergeant WILLIAM BOBBIN,
Sergeant WILLIAM BURNS.
Gunner S. COUCH.
Lieut. MAURICE C. DAY.
Lieut. ROBERT NEWPORT DOBBYN.
Lieut. WILLIAM AUGUSTUS NELSON DOBBYN.
Capt. GERALD EWAN ELLIOTT.
Lieut. CHARLES FARRAN.
Lance-Corporal NOEL FERNIE, D.C.M.
Capt. JOHN KIRWAN GATACRE.
Major HAROLD B. GALLOWAY.
Private WILLIAM GAMBLE.
Private THOMAS HUGHES.
Chief Petty Officer G. L. LINDSAY, R.N.
Lieut. ERIC A. THISELTON LINE.
Lieut. HUBERT MALCOMSON.
Corporal LLEWELLYN, MALCOMSON.
Commander JOHN S. PENROSE, R.N.
Seaman A. RANDALL, R.N.
Captain FRANK R. ROBERTSON.
Doctor GEORGE WATERS, R.N.

" Blessed are the dead which die in the Lord."

Lieutenant Malcomson, courtesy of Eddie Sullivan, Waterford.

Penrose, John Samuel Sandford. Rank; Lieutenant Commander. Regiment or Service: Royal Navy. Unit; H. M. S. Bulwark. Date of death; 26/11/1914. Age at death; 35. Son of Frances Alice Penrose and the late Robert W. H. Penrose; husband of Irene Hester Penrose. He is listed on the Waterford and District Roll of Honour. Located in Christ Church Cathedral (Church of Ireland), Henrietta Street, Waterford. Gazetted, January 3, 1902. Munster Express. November, 1914. The Late Lieutenant Commander Penrose. The Waterford Battalion of the Volunteers have passed a resolution of sympathy with Mr E. W. Penrose, a member of the Volunteers, on the death of his brother, Lieutenant Commander J. S. Penrose, who was lost on H. M. S. Bulwark, which went down in Sheerness on Thursday week. Kilkenny People, December 1914. Lieutenant Commander F. R. Penrose, reported lost of the Bulwark, was a brother of Captain W. Penrose, J. P., Belline, Piltown, County Kilkenny, agent for the Earl of Bessborough. Grave or Memorial Reference; 1. Cemetery: Portsmouth Naval Memorial, U. K. He is also commemorated on the Great War Memorial in St Canice's Cathedral, Kilkenny…'To the Glory of God and in loving memory of the following members of the Diocese of Ossory who gave their lives for their country in the Great War 1914-1918'.

Perrin, George. Rank; Lance Corporal. Regiment or Service: Grenadier Guards. Unit; 3rd Battalion. Service Number; 20957. Date of death; 15/09/1916. Born; Kilkenny. Enlisted; Cardiff, Glamorganshire. Killed in action. Grave or Memorial Reference; Pier and Face 8 D. Cemetery: Thiepval Memorial in France.

Phelan, James. Rank; Private. Regiment or Service: Royal Irish Regiment. Unit; 1st Battalion. Service Number; 3180. Date of death; 26/04/1915. Born; St Patrick's, Kilkenny. Enlisted; Tipperary. Residence; Kilkenny. Died of wounds. After his death his effects and property were received by;- (Wife) Mrs E Phelan, Maddoxtown, County Kilkenny. Kilkenny People, May, 1915. Another Kilkenny Soldier Killed at the Front. Mrs Ellen Phelan, Upper Walkin Street, Kilkenny, has received official intimation that her husband, James Phelan, 4th Battalion, Royal Irish Regiment, died on the 26th April of wounds received in action. He was 41 years of age, and had seen service in the South African War, where he was wounded. He volunteered at the outbreak of the present war, and was over three months in France when he met his death. He was blacksmith by trade, and had been working with Messrs. W. Lewis and Son, John Street. In addition to his widow, he leaves three young children to mourn his loss. Grave or Memorial Reference; Panel 33. Cemetery: Ypres (Menin Gate) Memorial in Belgium.

Phelan, John. Rank; Corporal. Regiment or Service: Leinster Regiment. Unit; 2nd Battalion. Service Number; 6239. Date of death; 20/10/1914. Born; Gowran, County kilkenny. Enlisted; Aldershot, Hampshire. Killed in action. Grave or Memorial Reference; Panel 10. Cemetery: Ploegsteert Memorial in Belgium.

Phelan, Kieran/Kiernan. Rank; Private. Regiment or Service: Royal Irish Regiment. Unit; 2nd Battalion. Service Number; 4368. Date of death; 27/05/1915. Born; St Patrick's, Kilkenny. Enlisted; Kilkenny. Died of wounds. Grave or Memorial Reference; II A 12. Cemetery: Hazebrouck Communal Cemetery in

Phelan, Patrick. Rank; Private. Regiment or Service: Royal Irish Regiment. Unit; 2nd Battalion. Service Number; 6635. Date of death; 14/05/1915. Born; St Patrick's, Kilkenny. Enlisted; Kilkenny. Killed in action. Kilkenny People, June, 1915. Kilkenny and the War. Further Deaths Reported from France and Germany. Son Buries His Father. Notification has been officially received from the War Office of the death in action at Ypres of Private Pat Phelan, of the 2nd Battalion, Royal Irish Regiment, who was a native of the city. He was killed whilst having a smoke in the trenches, and a very pathetic feature in connection with the matter is that the deceased who left for the front with the first batch of the Royal Irish, was buried by his own son. Here is the very touching manner in which the matter describes the sad event from "somewhere in France";--My Dear---Just a few lines hoping to find you in good health. This leaves me in trouble, and I have very bad news for you this time. Y father was killed on Saturday

morning by a bullet. I was only five yards away from hi m at the time. He was smoking and he got struck in the head. What will I do now? My heart will break. I was never known before to have a father and son in the one trench. Well, all I have to do is suffer on. I suppose---will go mad. May God look down on ye now and bring me back to look after you all. I buried my father and I put a cross over his grave. May he rest in peace.".
Kilkenny Journal, June, 1915. Private Kieran Phelan, Walkin Street, Kilkenny, who is attached to the 2nd Battalion, Royal Irish regiment, writing from the trenches in Ypres to his sister, states;--"I have sad news for you; my father has been killed. I was in the same trench with him—about five yards away from him. He stood up in a trench to light his pipe when he was shot—the bullet passing through his head. I buried him and put a little cross over his grave. I believe it was never known before of a father and son fighting in the same trench side by side."Private K. Phelan is a young man of 21 years of age, he belonged to the 4th Battalion, R. I. R., but on leaving for the front, about eight months ago was attached t the 2nd battalion. His father, Private Patrick, who had also been in the 4th Battalion, R. I. R., rejoined his regiment at the outbreak of the war, and, being attached to the 2nd Battalion., left for the front with his son, Kieran. Father and son fought side by side in every engagement in which the Battalion took part—sixteen in all—and came unscathed through all the recent fierce encounters, including Neuve Chapelle, St Eloi, and "Hill 60." The late Private Phelan was a man of fine physique—a typical specimen of an Irishman—and was much respected by all with whom he was acquainted. Grave or Memorial Reference; Panel 33. Cemetery: Ypres (Menin Gate) Memorial in Belgium.

Pittman, William. Rank; Private. Regiment or Service: Leinster Regiment. Unit; 7th Battalion. Service Number; 3453. Date of death; 02/09/1916. Age at death; 17. Born; Thomastown, County Kilkenny. Enlisted; Cork. Residence; Thomastown, County Kilkenny. Killed in action. Son of William and Mary Ellen Pittman, of Parochial Hall, Wood Quay, Galway. Grave or Memorial Reference; Pier and Face 16 C. Cemetery: Thiepval memorial in France. He is also commemorated on the Great War Memorial in St Canice's Cathedral, Kilkenny…'To the Glory of God and in loving memory of the following members of the Diocese of Ossory who gave their lives for their country in the Great War 1914-1918'. Listed on the memorial under William P. Pittman.

Major Ponsonby, from De Ruvigny's Roll of Honour.

Ponsonby, Cyril Myles Brabazon (The Hon). Rank; Major. Regiment or Service: Grenadier Guards. Unit; 3rd Battalion attached to the 2nd Battalion. Date of death; 27/09/1915. Killed in action. Second son of 8th Earl of Bessborough and the Countess of Bessborough; husband of Rita Narcissa Ponsonby (now Mrs. Cyril Flower, of Codicote Mill, Welwyn, Herts). Carlow Sentinel, October, 1915. Capt. Hon. C. M. B. Ponsonby. 2nd Grenadier Guards, who has been killed in France, was the second son of Earl and Countess of Bessborough, of Garryhill, Bagenalstown. He had been at the front for some time, and was reported wounded in November last. De Ruvigny's Roll of Honour. 2nd son of Edward, 8th Earl of Bessborough, K. P., C. V. O., C. B., by his wife, Blanche Vere, youngest daughter of the late Sir John Guest, 1st Bart., M. P. Born in London, 06-November-1881. Educated at harrow, and at the Royal Military College, Sandhurst. Gazetted 2nd Lieutenant, Grenadier Guards, 11-August-1900, and promoted Lieutenant, 12-April-1904. Captain, 03-June-1908, and major, May-1915. Was A. D. C to Governor and Commander-in-Chief, Ceylon, 27-November-1903 to 30-September-1905; to the Inspector-General of the Forces, etc., 01-July-1906, to 20-December-1907, and to the F. M. Commanding-in-Chief (H. R. H. the Duke of Connaught) 31-December-1907, to 31-July-1909. Served (1) in the South African War 1902, taking part in the operations in Cape Colony February to 31-May-1902; and (2) with the Expeditionary Force in France and Flanders from September-1914, and was killed in action 28-September-1915, while leading the 4th Battalion of his Regiment to retake Hill 70. He was at the time temporarily in command, owing to the Commanding Officer having been gassed. He received the Victorian Order (Fourth Class) 1909, and was a knight of the Order of the Sword of Sweden, and of the Order of Isabella the catholic of Spain. He married at St George's, Hanover Square, W., 20-July-1911, Rita Narcissa (44, Gloucester Square, W.), eldest daughter of Lieutenant-Colonel Mountifort John Courtenay Longfield of Castle Mary, County Cork, J. P., D. L., and had a son, Arthur Mountifort Longfield (for whom H. R. H. the Duke of Connaught was a sponsor), born 11-December-1912. 'Our Heroes'. who was killed in France on September 28th, was the second son of the Earl and Countess of Bessborough. Born in 1881, he was educated at harrow and Sandhurst, and joined the Grenadier Guards in 1900. he served in the South African War, 1902, taking part in the later operations in Cape Colony, and was A. D. C. to the Duke of Connaught from 1907 to 1909. He received his last promotion in May of this year. Major Ponsonby, who lived at 44 Gloucester Square, married, in 1911, Rita Narcissa, eldest daughter of lieutenant-Colonel M. P. C. Longfield, of Castle Mary, County Cork and leaves one son, born in 1912, Arthur M. L. Ponsonby. Grave or Memorial Reference; Panel 5 to 7. Cemetery: Loos Memorial Pas de Calais, France. He is also commemorated on the Great War Memorial in St Canice's Cathedral, Kilkenny…'To the Glory of God and in loving memory of the following members of the Diocese of Ossory who gave their lives for their country in the Great War 1914-1918'. Listed on the memorial under Major The Hon. Myles. B. Ponsonby.

Popkin, Thomas Joseph. Rank; Private. Regiment or Service: Northumberland Fusiliers. Unit; 1st Battalion. Service Number; 271. Date of death; 08/11/1914. Born; Kilkenny. Enlisted; Winberg, Cape Colony. Killed in action. Grave or Memorial Reference; Panel 8 to 12. Cemetery: Ypres (Menin Gate) Memorial in Belgium.

Power, Edward. Rank; Private. Regiment or Service: Royal Irish Regiment. Unit; 2nd Battalion. Service Number; 3028. Date of death; 17/05/1915. Born; Slieverue, County Kilkenny. Enlisted; Tipperary. Residence; Waterford. Died of wounds at home. Son of Michael and Margaret Power, of 29, Peter St, Waterford. Grave or Memorial Reference; D 2477. Cemetery: Cambridge City Cemetery, UK.

Power, James. Rank; Private. Regiment or Service: Royal Marine Light Infantry. Unit; Plymouth Battalion Royal Naval Division. Service Number; Ply. /240 (S). Date of death; 04/03/1915. Age at death; 23. Born; Mullinavat, County Kilkenny. Killed or died as a direct result of enemy action. Son of Thomas Power, of Ballintlea, Mullinavat, Waterford. Next of kin listed as Father. Thomas; Ballintlea, Mullunavat, Kilkenny. Notes; D. O. B. 05/09/1893. His records gives his place of burial as Kum Kale, Asia Minor. Grave or Memorial Reference; Panel 2 to 7. Cemetery: Helles Memorial, Turkey.

Power, James Francis. Rank; Company Quartermaster Sergeant. Regiment or Service: Royal Inniskilling Fusiliers. Unit; C Company, 2nd Battalion. Service Number; 6291. Date of death; 13/07/1917. Age at death;36. Born; Fleetwood, Lancashire. Enlisted; Omagh. Died of wounds. Son of P. F. Power (late Colour Sergeant, 2nd Battalion. Royal Inniskilling Fusiliers) and Anastasia Mary Power, of 1 and 2, St. George's Circus, Southwark, London. Of Kilkenny. Grave or Memorial Reference; I E 12. Cemetery: Coxyde Military Cemetery in Belgium.

Power, Jeremiah. Rank; Private. Regiment or Service: Royal Irish Regiment. Unit; C Company, 2nd Battalion. Service Number; 6954. Date of death; 07/05/1915. Age at death; 38. Born; Callan, County Kilkenny. Enlisted; Dublin. Residence; Callan. Died of wounds. Son of Thomas and Ellen Power, of Bridge St., Callan; husband of Catherine Power, of Green St., Callan, Co. Kilkenny. Grave or Memorial Reference; I A 105. Cemetery: Bailleul Communal Cemetery Extension (Nord) in France.

Power, John. Rank; Private. Regiment or Service: Royal Irish Fusiliers. Unit; 7th Battalion. Service Number; 19807. Date of death; 22/04/1916. Age at death;21. Born; Gowran, County Kilkenny. Enlisted; Kilkenny. Died of wounds. Son of Peter and Johanna Power, of Granges Road, Kilkenny. Grave or Memorial Reference; III H 19. Cemetery: Bethune Town Cemetery in France.

Power, Kathleen. Rank; Nursing Sister. Regiment or Service: Australian Army Nursing Service. Date of death; 13/08/1916. Age at death; 28. Daughter of Michael and Johanna Power, of Garrygauge, Piltown, Co. Kilkenny, Republic of Ireland. Died of Cholera at Family Hospital, Colaba, Bombay, India. Born, Templeorum, Kilkenny. Occupation on enlistment, Nurse. Trained at Dr Steevens Hospital, Dublin, 4 ½ years and at Dr Steevens Private Nursing Home. Sister and night Superintendent, 2 ½ years. Age on enlistment; 27 years - months. Previous experience; A. A. R. S. from 24th-August-1915. Q. A. A. N. R. for 4 ½ years. Next of kin details; (father) Michael Power, Garnygauge, Piltown, County Kilkenny, Ireland. Place and date of enlistment, 09-March-1916. No 4 Military Hispital, Heliopolis, Cairo, Egypt. Although she enlisted in March-1916 her records show that she embarked at Melbourne aboard the H. M. A. T."More" on 24-August-1915. Weight, 133 lbs. Height, 5 feet, 4 inches. Complexion, fair. Hair, brown. Sewree Cemetery, Bombay, Plot No 10, Line V, Grave No 16. Grave or Memorial Reference; Plot No 10, Line V, Grave No 16. Cemetery: Sewree Cemetery, Bombay

Power, Nicholas John. Rank; Private. Regiment or Service: Royal Munster Fusiliers. Unit; 2nd Battalion. Service Number; 6567. Date of death; 27/08/1916. Age at death;21. Born; Cardiff, Wales. Enlisted; Cardiff, Glamorganshire. Residence; Cardiff, Wales. Died of wounds. Son of John and Ellen Power, of 25, Sanquhar St., Cardiff, Glam. Native of Piltown, Co. Kilkenny (CWGC). Grave or Memorial Reference; III E 45. Cemetery: Puchevillers British Cemetery in France.

Power, Thomas. Rank; Private. Regiment or Service: Middlesex Regiment. Unit; 13th Battalion. Service Number; G/41953. Date of death; 27/08/1917. Age at death; 17. Born; Bennettsbridge, County Kilkenny. Enlisted; Dublin. Residence; Kilkenny. Died of wounds. Son of Thomas and Mary Power, of Baronsland, Bennettsbridge, Co. Kilkenny. Grave or Memorial Reference; Panel 113 to 115. Cemetery: Tyne Cot Memorial in Belgium.

Lieutenant Prior-Wandesforde, from De Ruvigny's Roll of Honour.

Prior-Wandesforde, Christopher Butler. Rank; Lieutenant. Regiment or Service: Yorkshire Regiment. Unit; 4th Battalion. Date of death; 27/06/1917. Age at death;20. Died of wounds. Son of Capt. R. H. and Mrs. Prior-Wandesforde, of Castlecomer House, Castlecomer, Co. Kilkenny. Lieutenant Christopher Prior-Wandesford also had a brother, Captain F. C. R. Prior-Wandesford who served with the R. F. A during ww1. He won the D. S. O and survived the war. De Ruvigny's Roll of Honour. eldest son of Richard Henry Prior-Wandesforde, of castlecomer House, Kilkenny, and Kirkington Hall, and Hipswell Lodge, Co. York, J. P., D. L., by his wife, Florence, daughter of the late Reverend W. F. Pryor. Born at Castlecomer, 15-December-1896. Educated at Mourne Grange, County Down, and Rugby, where he was for two years in the Rugby Shooting Eight, including the 1912, when the school won the "Ashburton Shield" at Bisley. He passed into Trinity College, Cambrige, in March-1915, but instead of entering the University volunteered for active service, and obtained a commission on the 31st of that month. Served with the Expeditionary Force in France and Flanders. Was wounded slightly in September-1916, and died at No 49 Casualty Clearing Station 27-June-1917 from the effects of gas poisoning. After having been himself gassed in a dug out, he persisted in rescuing others, and this extra exertion caused the gas to penetrate his system, and resulted in his death the same day. Buried at Achiet-le-Grand near Bapaume. His Colonel wrote; "He was such a food keen officer, and so popular with us all and with his men, that I cannot tell you how sorry we are for you" and his major; "We were all so fond of your son, and our loss is indeed great". His Captain also wrote; "His was one of the sunniest natures I have ever met, and no danger or difficulty seemed to damp his spirits for more than a few minutes. And he was the very embodiment of charity. I never once heard him say an evil or unkind word of anybody behind that man's back. He was wonderful company. After he was gassed he spent the greater part of two hours looking after his men and getting them safely out of danger. Kilkenny People, April, 1915. Commission For Castlecomer Gentleman. Mr Christopher Prior-Wandesforde, eldest son of Mr R. H. Prior-Wandesforde, D. L., Castlecomer House, Castlecomer, has obtained a Commission as 2nd Lieutenant in Alexandra Princess of Wales Own (Yorkshire Regiment), 4th Battalion, and left Castlecomer on Tuesday, 30th March, to join his regiment at Northallerton, Yorkshire. Kilkenny Journal, April, 1915. Commission in the Army. Mr Christopher B. Prior-Wandesforde, eldest son of R. H. Prior-Wandesforde,

Esq, J. P., D. L, Co. C, Castlecomer, has obtained a commission as 2nd Lieutenant in the 4th Battalion of Alexandra, Princess of Wales's Own (Yorkshire) Regiment. He left Castlecomer on Tuesday to join his regiment at Northallerton, Yorkshire. We congratulate the gallant Lieutenant on being called to the colours, and have no hesitation in predicting for him a distinguished career and, we trust, a safe return with the tokens of victory and the laurels that a brave soldier can obtain. Kilkenny Journal, September, 1915. With the Colours. The following was received from Mrs Florence Prior-Wandesforde, Castlecomer House;--"Dear Sir-Captain Prior-Wandesforde will not be able to attend the quarterly meeting of the County Council on September 20th, as he is in France with his regiment, and will not be able to attend any meetings until he returns after the war, please God.". Kilkenny Journal, September, 1915. Captain R. H. Prior-Wandesforde. At the Castlecomer Petty Sessions, the following resolution was, on the motion of Mr Denis O'Carroll, seconded by Mr James Muhall (presiding), unanimously passed—"That we, the magistrates at Castlecomer Petty Sessions, have learned with pleasure of the promotion of lieutenant R. H. Prior-Wandesforde, J. P., D. L., Co. C., Royal Field Artillery, the senior magistrate of Castlecomer Petty Sessions, to Captaincy, in his regiment, with which he is now on active service in France. That we wish him from our hearts continued success in his military career and a speedy homecoming to his family and Castlecomer, crowned with laurels which the victory of the Allies will give him on the termination of the war, and that a copy of this resolution be sent to Mrs Wandesforde for transmission to Captain Prior-Wandesforde.". Irish Times. Prior-Wandesforde-June 27, died on active service from poison gas, Lieutenant C B Prior-Wandesforde, Yorlshire Regiment, son of R H Prior-Wandesforde. J. P., D. L.,m Temporary Captain RFA., and Mrs Prior-Wandesforde, of Castlecomer House, Castlecomer, County Kilkenny. The Weekly Irish Times. Ireland's Roll of Honour. July 7, 1917. The death is announced from poison gas, on June 27th, of Liuetenant C B Prior-Wandesforde, Yorkshire Regiment. He was the eldest son of Mr R B Prior-Wandesforde, J. P., D. L., (temporary Captain, R. F. A.), of Castlecomer House, Castlecomer, County Kilkenny, and was 20 years of age. His brother, wrongly listed are died during the war;-King's County Chronicle. The D. S. O. Second Lieutenant (now Captain) Ferdinand Charles Richard Prior-Wandesford, Royal Field Artillery, Special Reserve, has been awarded the Distinguished Service Order,"for conspicuous gallantry and devotion to duty." When his battery was in action under heavy enemy shell fire a bomb stoke close to one of the guns exploded, killing the battery commander and causing other casualties. Seeing that the gun and its detachment were in great danger, he rushed to the bomb store and extinguished the fire at great personal risk. He then assumed command of the battery and kept it in action under very difficult conditions. On several previous occasions he behaved with great gallantry and set a magnificent example to his men…. Prior-Wandesforde-On Wednesday, June 29, 1917, died on active service from poison gas, Lieutenant C B Prior-Wandesforde, Yorkshire Regiment, eldest and dearly loved son of R H Prior-Wandesforde, J. P., D. L., Temporary Captain R. F. A., and Mrs Prior-Wandesforde, of Castlecomer House, County Kilkenny, aged 20 years. Unknown regional newspaper. Prior-Wandesford-On Wednesday, June 29, 1917, died on active service from poison gas, Lieutenant C B Prior-Wandesford, Yorkshire Regiment, eldest and dearly-loved son of R H Prior-Wandesford, J. P., D. L., Temporary Captain R F A., and Mrs Prior-Wandesford, of Castlecomer House, County Kilkenny, aged 20 years. Grave or Memorial Reference; I K 8. Cemetery: Achiet-Le-Grand Communal Cemetery Extension in France.

Prout, William. Rank; Private. Regiment or Service: Royal Irish Regiment. Unit; 2nd Battalion. Service Number; 7826. Date of death; 30/01/1917. Born; St Patrick's, Kilkenny. Enlisted; Kilkenny. Died. Grave or Memorial Reference; II A 93. Cemetery: Bailleul Communal Cemetery Extension (Nord) in France.

Pulham, William. Rank; Private. Regiment or Service: King Edwardr's Horse. Unit; 2nd Battalion. Service Number; 2284. Date of death; 17/11/1918. Killed in action. Grave or Memorial Reference; In the West part. Cemetery: Kilkenny (St John) Church of Ireland Churchyard, Kilkenny.

Purcell, Christopher. Rank; Private. Regiment or Service: Connaught Rangers. Unit; 4th Battalion. Service Number; 5735. Date of death; 16/11/1915. Born; Kilkenny. Enlisted; Kilkenny. Residence; Kilkenny. Died of wounds at home. Son of Mrs. K. Purcell, of 22, Ossory Park, Habron Road, Kilkenny. Grave or Memorial Reference; About the middle of the North boundary. Cemetery: Ballinakilla Churchyard, County Cork.

Purcell, James. Rank; Gunner. Regiment or Service: Royal Horse Artillery. Unit; T Battery, 14th Brigade. Service Number; 42657. Date of death; 27/09/1916. Age at death;32. Born; Kilkenny. Enlisted; Kilkenny. Died of wounds. Son of James and Anastatia Purcell, of Upper Maudlin St., Kilkenny. After his death his effects and property were received by;- (Mother) Mrs Annastatia Purcell, Maudlin Street, Kilkenny, Ireland. Grave or Memorial Reference; I A 3. Cemetery: Bronfay Farm Military Cemetery, Bray-Sur-Somme in France.

Purcell, James. Rank; Private. Regiment or Service: Durham Light Infantry. Unit; 1/8th Battalion. Service Number; 91383. Date of death; 27/05/1918. Born; Kilmanagh, County Kilkenny. Enlisted; Kilkenny. Killed in action. Notes; Formerly he was with the Royal Irish Regiment where his number was 5816. Cemetery: Soissons memorial in France.

James Purcell's original grave marker.

Purcell, James Patrick. Rank; Private. Regiment or Service: Australian Light Trench Mortar Battery. Unit; 3rd. Service Number; 3926. Date of death; 03/07/1916. Born; Paulstown, County Kilkenny. Enlisted; Blackboy Hill. Killed in action. Occupation on enlistment, butcher. Age on enlistment; 32 years 1 months. Next of kin details; (sister) Alice Cummins, County Carlow, Ireland. Later changed to (wife) Mrs Loretta Bella Purcell, 1 Beaufort Street, Perth. After the war Loretta Purcell applied for a pension and later withdrew the application. No pension was paid out. Weight, 145 lbs. Height, 5 feet, 6 inches. Complexion, dark. Eyes, blue. Hair, dark brown. Notes; Place and date of enlistment, 09-August-1915. Blackboy Hill. Grave or Memorial Reference; I J 31. Cemetery: Rue-Petillon Military Cemetery, Fleurbaix in France.

Purcell, Jeremiah. Rank; Private. Regiment or Service: Royal Dublin Fusiliers. Unit; 7th Battalion. Service Number; 24871. Date of death; 31/10/1916. Age at death; 16. Born; Kilkenny. Enlisted; Kilkenny. Killed in action in the Balkans. Son of Patrick and Norah Purcell, of Archer Street, Kilkenny. In his Will, dated 11-September-1916, his effects and property were received by;- (Sister) B Purcell, Archer Street, Kilkenny, Ireland. Grave or Memorial Reference; II C 4. Cemetery: Struma Military Cemetery in Greece.

Private Purcell, courtesy of Donal Croghan.

Purcell, John. Rank; Private. Regiment or Service: Royal Dublin Fusiliers. Unit; 1st Battalion. Service Number; 43129. Date of death; 20/04/1918. Age at death;22. Born; Gowran, County Kilkenny. Enlisted; Kilkenny. Died of Lobar Pneumonia at 7th Canadian Field Hospital. Son of John and Kate Purcell, of Highrath, Maddoxtown, Kilkenny. In his Will, dated 12-December-1916, his effects and property were received by;- (Mother) Mrs J Purcell, Highrath, Maddoxtown, County Kilkenny, Ireland. Notes; Formerly he was with the Royal Irish Regiment where his number was 9701. Grave or Memorial Reference; V A 65. Cemetery: Longuenesse (St Omer) Souvenir Cemetery. Pas de Calais, France.

Purcell, Michael. Rank; Private. Regiment or Service: Loyal North Lancashire Regiment. Unit; 1st Battalion. Service Number; 26714. Date of death; 10/07/1917. Age at death; 23. Born; Liverpool. Enlisted; Liverpool. Killed in action. Son of Pierce and Joanna Purcell, of Urard, Urlingford. Notes; Formerly he was with the Liverpool Regiment where his number was 5593. Cemetery: Nieuport Memorial, Nieuwpoort, West-Vlaanderen, Belgium

Purcell, Richard. Rank; Private. Regiment or Service: Royal Irish Regiment. Unit; 2nd Battalion. Service Number; 5206. Date of death; 23/06/1918. Born; Urlingford. Enlisted; Kilkenny. Died in Germany. After his death his effects and property were received by;- (Wife) Mrs Mary Purcell, King St, Kilkenny. Grave or Memorial Reference; III F 4. Cemetery: Hamburg Cemetery in Germany.

Purcell, Robert. Rank; Private. Regiment or Service: Royal Dublin Fusiliers. Unit; 1st Battalion. Service Number; 43138. Date of death; 28/02/1917. Born; Kilmanagh, County Kilkenny. Enlisted; Kilkenny. Killed in action. Notes; Formerly he was with the Royal Irish Regiment where his number was 8891. Grave or Memorial Reference; Pier and Face 16C and 13C. Cemetery: Thiepval Memorial in France.

Purcell, Philip. Rank; Private. Regiment or Service: Royal Irish Regiment. Unit; 2nd Battalion. Service Number; 7615. Date of death; 14/07/1916. Age at death;30. Born; Ballingarry, County Tipperary. Enlisted; Ballingarry, County Tipperary. Residence; Thurles, County Tipperary. Killed in action. Brother of Edmond Purcell, of 6, Grange Urlingford, Co. Kilkenny. Grave or Memorial Reference; Pier and Face 3 A. Cemetery: Theipval Memorial in France.

Pye, William. Rank; Private. Regiment or Service: Royal Army Medical Corps. Unit; Attached to the Desert Mounted Corps, H. Q. Service Number; 7208. Date of death; 15/10/1918. Age at death; 27. Born; Kilkenny. Enlisted; Cork. Died in Palestine. Son of James and Isabella Pye, of Dublin. In his Will, dated 17-April-1916, his effects and property were received by;- (Aunt) Mrs Baldwin, 20 Alexander Rd, Hendon, London. Grave or Memorial Reference; B 86. Cemetery: Damascus Commonwealth War Cemetery in Syria.

Q

Quinlan, Arthur. Rank; Private. Regiment or Service: Royal Dublin Fusiliers. Unit; 1st Battalion. Service Number; 7734. Date of death; 27/11/1915. Born; Kilkenny. Enlisted; Kilkenny. Died in Gallipoli. This man has only recently been added to the Commonwealth War Graves Commission Database. Grave or Memorial Reference; Addenda Panel. Cemetery: Helles Memorial in Turkey.

R

Raftis, James. Rank; Private. Regiment or Service: Royal Dublin Fusiliers. Unit; 2nd Battalion. Service Number; 28007. Date of death; 16/08/1917. Age at death; 19. Born; Thomastown, County Kilkenny. Enlisted; Thomastown. Killed in action. Son of Michael and Nora Raftis, of Mill Street, Thomastown, Co. Kilkenny. Grave or Memorial Reference; Panel 144 to 145. Cemetery: Tyne Cot Memorial in Belgium.

Reddy, John. Rank; Private. Regiment or Service: South Wales Borderers. Unit; 1st Battalion. Service Number; 18773. Date of death; 09/09/1916. Born; Mooncoin, County Kilkenny. Enlisted; Waterford. Killed in action. Grave or Memorial Reference; Pier and Face 4 A. Cemetery: Thiepval Memorial in France.

Reddy, Joseph Francis. Rank; Lance Sergeant. Regiment or Service: Irish Guards. Unit; 2nd Battalion. Service Number; 8091. Date of death; 31/07/1917. Born; Kilkenny. Enlisted; Liverpool. Residence; Chelmsford, Middlesex. Killed in action. Grave or Memorial Reference; Panel 11. Cemetery: Ypres (Menin Gate) Memorial in Belgium.

Redman, William Stephen. Rank; Bandsman. Regiment or Service: East Kent Regiment. Unit; 2nd Battalion. Service Number; L/9251. Date of death; 03/05/1915. Age at death;19. Born; Kilkenny. Enlisted; Hong Kong, China. Residence; Bethnal Green, Middlesex. Killed in action. Son of William Henry and Julia Redman, of 39, Algar Buildings, Webber Row, Waterloo Road, London. Grave or Memorial Reference; Panel 12 and 14. Cemetery: Ypres (Menin Gate) Memorial in Belgium.

Redmond, Patrick. Rank; Sapper. Regiment or Service: Corps of Royal Engineers. Unit; 61st Field Company. Service Number; 40056. Date of death; 30/07/1915. Born; Kilkenny. Enlisted; Kilkenny. Killed in action. In his Will, dated 08-June-1915, his effects and property were received by;- (Wife) Mrs M M Redmond, Abbey Street, Kilkenny, Ireland. Kilkenny People, August, 1915. Kilkennyman Killed in Action. Much sympathy is felt for Mrs P. Redmond, Abbey Street, Kilkenny, whose husband has fallen at the front. The late Mr Redmond was eldest son of mr Patrick Redmond, King Street a respected citizen and valued city official. The deceased served in South Africa during the Boer War, taking part in many engagements, including the Siege of Ladysmith. His term of service in the Army expired in July, 1914, just a week before the outbreak of the present war, and immediately there was a call for volunteers to the colours he rejoined his old Regiment, the Royal Engineers. He went to the front in April, and till early in July escaped unscathed. He was then only slightly wounded, and was able to return to the danger zone in a few weeks. Within a few days, however, of his return he was mortally wounded. His wife has received the following sad message;-- "Dear Mrs Redmond—I am extremely sorry to have to write and tell you the sad news that your husband was killed I action on July 30th by a bullet wound in the head. He was killed instantly. Please accept the deepest sympathy from all the officers, N. C. O. 's and men of the Company in your great sorrow. Your husband was much respected by everyone and his loss is deeply regretted.""S. M. Bates, C. S. M., Royal Engineers, 61st Field Company."Deceased was a plumber by trade, and had worked with Messrs Power and Son and Messrs Kelly and Son, of this city, and was much respected by his employers and fellow tradesmen. Kilkenny Journal, August, 1915. Kilkenny Soldier Killed in Action. News has been received in Kilkenny of the death in action of Private Patrick Redmond. Private Redmond, who belonged to the Royal Engineers, was eldest son of Mr Patrick Redmond, S. S. O., King Street, Kilkenny, and has been serving with his regiment since the outbreak of war. Private Redmond had been serving with his regiment in the South African War, through which campaign he escaped unscathed. At the weekly meeting of St Mary's Confraternity—of which deceased was a member—the rosary was offered up for the repose of his soul. Grave or Memorial Reference; Panel 9. Cemetery: Ypres (Menin Gate) Memorial in Belgium.

Major Reeves, from 'Our Heroes.'

Reeves, Victor Charles Methuen. Rank; Major. Regiment or Service: Household Cavalry and Cavalry of the line including the Yeomanry and Imperial Camel Corps. Unit; Dorset Yeomanry. Date of death; 26/02/1916. Age at death;29. Killed in action 'while leading his squadron against the Senussi tribe at the Battle of Agagia on the Western frontier of Egypt. '. Son of Edward and Kate Reeves; husband of Cherry Georgina Reeves, of Castle Kevin, Mallow, Co. Cork. Mentioned in despatches by Sir John Maxwell in the London Gazette of 21 Jun 16 for "gallant and distinguished service in the field." On 19 Jun 12 at Christ Church, Rushbrook, Queenstown, he married Cherry Georgina, youngest daughter of James Carnegie Shee of Ballyreddin, Co. Kilkenny. De Ruvigny's Roll of Honour. youngest son of the late Edward Hoare

Reeves, by his wife, Kate (Castle Kevin, Mallow, County Cork), daughter of the late Willian Wrixton Leycester, of Ennismore, County Cork. Born in Ennismore, County Cork, 30-November-1886. Educated at Cheam, Cheltenham College, and Cambridge University. Gazetted 2nd Lieutenant, Dorset Yeomanry, 01-April-1906, Lieutenant 1907, and Captain 04-October-1913; whilst at Cambridge he was first in the foils and sabre contests against Oxford. Went to Egypt with his regiment in April-1915. Killed in action 26-February-1916, whilst leading his squadron against the Senussi tribe at the battle of Agagin, on the Western frontier of Egypt. Buried on the battlefield. He was mentioned in General Sir John Maxwell's Despatch (London Gazette, 21-June-1916), for "gallant and distinguished service in the field." His Colonel wrote; "He was my right-hand man throughout that hard-fought day; always cool and collected always in the right place, and always inspiring his men. He was perfectly splendid. In the charge he led his men magnificently, and the blow his squadron struck their section of the line was due to his leading. Throughout the day his absolutely perfect handling of his men was worthy of all praise, and he had worked them up to a high pitch of excellence." He married at Christ Church, Rushbrook, Queenstown, 19-June-1912, Cherry Georgina (Leitrim House, Kilworth, County Cork), youngest daughter of the late James Carnegie Shee, of Ballyreddin, County Kilkenny. Grave or Memorial Reference; G 36. Cemetery: Alexandria (Chatby) Military and War Memorial Cemetery in Egypt.

Reilly, David. Rank; Private. Regiment or Service: Royal Irish Regiment. Unit; 2nd Battalion. Service Number; 10869. Date of death; 27/09/1918. Born; Callan, County Kilkenny. Enlisted; Clonmel, County Tipperary. Residence; Callan. Killed in action. He won the Military Medal and is listed in the London Gazette. In his Will, dated 06-August-1914, his effects and property were received by;- Mrs Kate Whelan, 4 Cottage Green Street, Callan, County Kilkenny, Ireland. Grave or Memorial Reference; Panel 5. Cemetery: Vis-En-Artois memorial in France.

Rice, Jerome. Rank; Private. Regiment or Service: Canadian Infantry (Quebec Regiment). Unit; 13th Battalion. Service Number; 46075. Date of death; 03/09/1916. Age at death;38. Born; Callan, County Kilkenny. Enlisted; Valcartier. Son of John and Catherine Rice (nee Nolan), of Callan, Kilkenny, Ireland. Occupation on enlistment, Clerk. Age on enlistment; 35 years 3 months. Previous military experience; 12 years with the 12th Dragoon Guards. Date of birth;12-July-1878. Next of kin details; (father) John Rice, Kilkenny, Ireland. Height, 5 feet, 8 inches. Complexion, medium brown. Eyes, grey. Hair, medium brown. Notes; Place and date of enlistment, 02-October-1914. Valcartier. Cemetery: Vimy Memorial in France.

Richardson, Henry. Rank; Private. Regiment or Service: Royal Dublin Fusiliers. Unit; 10th Battalion. Service Number; 24701. Date of death; 13/11/1916. Born; Kilkenny. Enlisted; Dublin. Killed in action. Grave or Memorial Reference; Pier and Face 16 C. Cemetery: Thiepval Memorial in France.

Rielly, Edmond. Rank; Private. Regiment or Service: Connaught Rangers. Unit; 1st Battalion. Service Number; 5945. Date of death; 15/04/1915. Born; Callan, County Kilkenny. Enlisted; Templemore. Residence; Callan. Died. Grave or Memorial Reference; Panel 43. Cemetery: Le Touret Memorial in France.

Rielly, Edward. Rank; Private. Regiment or Service: Royal Irish Regiment. Unit; A Company 2nd Battalion. Service Number; 7412. Date of death; 19/10/1914. Age at death; 24. Born; Thomastown, County Kilkenny. Enlisted; Waterford. Killed in action. Husband of Margaret Fanning (formerly Rielly), of Moonteen, Thomastown, Co. Kilkenny. Grave or Memorial Reference; A 7. Cemetery: Caudry Old Communal Cemetery, Nord, France.

Rielly, Patrick. Rank; Lance Corporal. Regiment or Service: Royal Irish Regiment. Unit; 6th Battalion. Service Number; 7742. Date of death; 13/12/1916. Age at death;20. Born; Johnstown, County Kilkenny. Enlisted; Templemore. Residence; Johnstown. Died of wounds. Son of Michael and Bridget Rielly, of Cronpatrick, Johnstown, Co. Kilkenny. Grave or Memorial Reference; III A 171. Cemetery: Bailleul Communal Cemetery Extension (Nord) in France.

Roache, Patrick. Rank; Private. Regiment or Service: Labour Corps. Service Number; 412977. Date of death; 02/10/1918. Age at death; 39. Born; Callan, County Kilkenny. Enlisted; Tipperary. Residence; Callan. Died at home. Husband of Bridget Roache, of 11, Cottage, Green Street, Callan, Co. Kilkenny. Notes; Formerly he was with the 4th Battalion, Royal Irish Regiment where his number was 3345. Grave or Memorial Reference; In the South East part. Cemetery: Mallardstown (Whitechurch) Cemetery, County Kilkenny.

Roberts, Alan Michael. Rank; Private. Regiment or Service: Australian Infantry, A. I. F. Unit; 20th Battalion. Service Number; 979. Date of death; 20/09/1917. Age at death;21. Born; Kilkenny. Enlisted; Liverpool, N. S. W. Son of Frank and Mary Hope Roberts, of 12, Randolph Gardens, Maida Vale, London, England. Native of Kilkenny, Ireland. Occupation on enlistment, farmhand. Age on enlistment; 18 years 7 months. Next of kin details; (father) Frank Augustus Roberts, 57 Bridge Street, Andover, Hants, England. Address later changed to 'Birdge House' Buttevant, County Cork, Ireland. Served in Abbasia, Gallipoli, Egypt, Mudros, Ghezireh, Heliopolis, Alexandria, Marseilles, Moascar, Rouen and England. Wounded in action in November-1916 with gunshot wounds to the chest and left side. Treated in Rouen and Englnad and returned to battlefields three months later. Weight, 154 lbs. Height, 5 feet, 9 ¾ inches. Complexion, light. Eyes, good blue. Hair, light brown. Notes; Enlisted Place and date of enlistment, 25-March-1915. Liverpool, N. S. W. Grave or Memorial Reference; IV D 3. Cemetery: Hooge Crater Cemetery Zillebeke, Belgium.

Roberts, Llewellyn. Rank; Private. Regiment or Service: South Staffordshire Regiment. Unit; 2nd Battalion. Service Number; 8768. Date of death; 15/05/1915. Born; Kilkenny. Enlisted; Stoke-on-Trent, Stafforshire. Residence; Newcastle, Staffordshire. Killed in action. Grave or Memorial Reference; Panel 21 and 22. Cemetery: Le Touret Memorial in France.

Lafayette. · MISS ROBINETTE,
Who has been awarded the Royal Red
Cross, and who was on the " Britannic "
when it was torpedoed last November.

Staff Nurse Robinette, from 'The British Journal of Nursing'June 22-1916;-
Nursing and the War

Robinette, Caroline Amelia. Rank; Staff Nurse. Regiment or Service: Queen Alexandra's Imperial Military Nursing Service. Unit; 2/Reserve. Service Number; R/741. Date of death; 30/03/1917. Age at death;41. Born; Kilkenny. Awarded the Red Cross Medal 2nd Class in 1916 and is listed in the London Gazette June 3-1916. Among others Nurse Robinette served in the Norfolk War Hospital, Norwich and on the Hospital Ship 'Brittanic' when it was torpedoed. Died of influenza/pleurisy at Herne Bay Hospital. Listed in the UK 1911 Census living in Paddington, London and in the 1911 Irish Census as a Church of Ireland boarder in the Hospital in Upper Baggot Street, Dublin. She is also listed in Officers Died in the Great War. Two snippets and the image above from 'The British Journal of Nursing'June 22-1916;-Nursing and the War. The Royal Red Cross. At the Investiture held by the King at Buckingham Palace on July 11th, the Royal Red Cross (second class) was conferred by His Majesty on Miss Florence Price, Miss Jessie Burns, and Miss Caroline Robinette. By the courtesy of the Editor of 'The Gentlewoman' we publish the accompanying portrait of Miss Robinette, one of the nursing staff aboard the Britannic—a hospital shi bound for Mudros—when it was sunk by an enemy submarine. It will be remembered that an R. A. M. C. officer subsequently stated;--"I know that women can be brave, but I never dreamed they could rise to such heights of cool, unflinching courage as those nurses did when under Miss Dowse, the Matron, they lined up on deck like so many soldiers and unconcernedly and calmly waited their turn to enter the boats. We men are proud of them, and we can only hope England will hear of their courage. They were magnificent.". Notes; Born 1882. Grave or Memorial Reference; T 114. Cemetery: Herne Bay Cemetery, Canterbury, Kent, U. K.

Roche, Thomas. Rank; Private. Regiment or Service: Royal Irish Regiment. Unit; G Company, 2nd Battalion. Service Number; 10929. Date of death; 07/06/1917. Born; Callan, County Kilkenny. Enlisted; Tipperary. Residence; Callan. Died at home. Son of John and Hannah Roche, of 6, Cottage Green View, Callan, Co. Kilkenny. Notes; Formerly he was with the Royal Irish Regiment where his number was 3345. Grave or Memorial Reference; Panel 33. Cemetery: Ypres (Menin Gate) Memorial in Belgium.

Private Roe, from 'Our Heroes.'

Roe, Sidney George. Rank; Private. Regiment or Service: Royal Irish Regiment. Unit; 7th (South Irish Horse) Battalion. Service Number; 25742. Date of death; 01/12/1917. Age at death;29. Born; Rathdowney, Queen's County. Enlisted; Roscrea. Residence; Ballybrophy, Queen's County. Died of wounds. Son of Kingsley and Alicia Roe, of "Clonmore", Errill, Ballybrophy, Queen's Co. The Leinster Express;-January, 1918. Roll of Honour. Roe-December 1, 1917, died of wounds received in action. Private Sidney George Roe, Irish Horse (attached to the Royal Irish Regiment), dearly –loved and loving son of Kingsley and Alicia Roe, Clondrive, Ballybrophy, Queen's County. De Ruvigny's Roll of Honour;-Roe, Sydney George, Private, No 25742. South Irish Horse (Special Reserve). Attached to the Royal Irish regiment. Son of Kingsley Roe, of Cooldrive, Balybrophy. Farmer, by his wife, Alicia, daughter of Richard Pratt. Born at Clonmore, Queen's County on 01-May-1887. Educated at Castlefleming. Was a Farmer. Volunteered for active service on the outbreak of war, and joined the South Irish Horse in August-1914. Served with the Expeditionary Force in France and Flanders from 1915m being attached to the Royal Irish regiment, and died of wounds received in action in Tunnel Trench at Croiselles. Buried at St Leger. His Commanding Officer wrote; "I mourn his loss, for he was a gallant soldier and a good fighter, and did not now the meaning of the word fear. He was bright and cheerful, and a general favourite with both officers and men.". Notes; Formerly he was with the South Irish Horse where his number was 915. Grave or Memorial Reference; G 10. Cemetery: St Leger British Cemetery in France.

Rowe, Michael. Rank; Private. Regiment or Service: Irish Guards. Unit; 2nd Battalion. Service Number; 11050. Date of death; 27/11/1917. Born; Kilkenny. Enlisted; Kilkenny. Killed in action. Grave or Memorial Reference; Panel 2 and 3. Cemetery: Cambrai Memorial, Louveral in France.

Ryan, Edward. Rank; Corporal. Regiment or Service: Royal Irish Regiment. Unit; 2nd Battalion. Service Number; 7792. Date of death; 29/10/1918. Age at death;22. Son of Richard Francis Ryan, of 21, Upper Patrick Street, Kilkenny. In his Will, dated 10-May-1916, his effects and property were received by;- Mrs R F Ryan, Upper Patrick Street, Kilkenny. Grave or Memorial Reference; In the South West part. Cemetery: St Patricks Graveyard, Kilkenny.

Ryan, James. Rank; Private. Regiment or Service: Royal Irish Regiment. Unit; 4th Battalion. Service Number; 4485. Date of death; 20/08/1914. Born; St Mary's, Kilkenny. Enlisted; Kilkenny. Died at home. Son of James Ryan, of 31, South Richmond Street, Dublin. Limerick Chronicle. August, 1914. Killed on The Railway. A soldier guarding Fota railway bridge, says a Queenstown message, was run over in the darkness last night and killed. The police are investigating. Limerick Chronicle. August, 1914. Soldier Killed on Railway. On the Great Southern and Western Railway at Fota Bridge, not far from Queenstown, a private of the Royal Irish Regiment, names James Ryan, aged 20, a native of Kilkenny, was killed on the permanent way whilst on protection duty. An engine struck him, tearing away the back portion of his head, and knocking him close to the rails, where he died. At the inquest on Thursday a verdict of accidental death was returned, and the jury recommended the next of kin to the kind consideration of the military authorities and the railway company. Waterford News January, 1915. Soldier Killed on Railway. Case against Great Southern and Western Railway. Dismissed at Quarter sessions. At the Kilkenny Quarter Sessions last week, before his honour County Court Judge David Fitzgerald, K. C., James

Ryan, Annamult, Stoneyford, sued the G. S. and W. R. Conpany to recover the sum of £50 for—"That the defendants so negligently and unskilfully drove and managed an engine and train along a railway, their property, which James Ryan, junior (plaintiffs son), was then upon, at Fota, County Cork, that he, the said James Ryan, junior, was knocked down and killed on the 20th day of August, 1914. Mr M. J. Buggy, solicitor, appeared for the plaintiff, and Mr Kinahan, B. L. (instructed by Mr James Poe, LL. D.), appeared for the defendant Company. In opening the case, Mr Buggy said there were four men on the bridge, two on either end. The bridge was about 150 yards long, and it was the duty of the sentries to march backwards and forwards and meet in the middle. The line was divided by a trellis work, and it was on the opposite side of the line that the dead body of Private Ryan was found. His Honour—What really did the Company do wrong?Mr Baggy said on this particular night the company sent down an engine from Queenstown to take up some derailed wagons. The driver should have whistled when coming to the bridge and he also should have lights on. He was instructed that there were no lights on the engine and that the driver did not whistle. The sentries got no notice of the approach of the train, and one of the sentries who was on the trellis side of the bridge was enabled to jump in through the trellis work off the track. The unfortunate man, Ryan, had no time to get away and the train came along and killed him. He would examine two of the soldiers who were on duty with Ryan on the night in question, and they would tell his Honour that there was no light on the engine, and that there was no whistle sounded. Two policemen could say that there were no lights on the engine. There are three bridges at Fota station, and a careful man would have whistled at this station. At the request the driver of the engine said he could not say that he whistled for this bridge. He spoke to the engine drivers when he went down first and asked them to whistle when coming to these places, and they gave him to understand that it was their duty to do so. Cross-examined by Mr Kinahan—If Private Sullivan had been where Private Ryan was he would not have got any notice of the approach of the train, and he did not think that he would escape……. in aN. S. W. er to Mr Buggy, witness said the deceased gave directions that money be sent to his father. Witness sent ten shillings for Ryan to the latter's father. Private Daniel Sullivan, in reply to Mr Buggy, said he was on guard with Ryan on the occasion. He did not hear the train until it was quite on top of him. He had to jump on to the Queenstown track to get clear. When he walked back he saw Ryan lying on his back, and he called the other men. The engine had no lights only the red light on the back. There was no whistle sounded. Cross-examined by Mr Kinahan—When I looked after the engine it had got past the place where Ryan was. I would not hear the train rumbling over the iron bridges. To His Honour—The last train is at twelve o'clock at night, but this happened at about 1. 30 o'clock. We had no reason to expect a train before morning. Private Michael Corcoran gave corroborative evidence. Constable John Gregan, in reply to Mr Buggy, said he was stationed at Hartlands Island bridge on the morning of the 20th August. He saw the train passing, but he could not say whether there were lights on the engine or not. The engine did not whistle, but it whistled at the junction station. Constable Morcan corroborated, and added that there were generally three or four whistles sounded. Cornelius Spellane, in reply to Mr Knahan, said he was the driver of the light engine. He left Quenstown about one o'clock. When he left he had a white light on the front of the engine, and he was certain it was still lighting when he reached. They had no instructions as to whistling at bridges, but they had to whistle approaching stations. He might whistle 100 times a day and he could not remember any exact spot…. Jeremiah Meany, in reply to Mr Kinahan, said he was stoker on the engine by which Ryan was killed. He knew nothing about the accident until the next morning about the accident. There was a white light on the front of the engine. His Honour said he was satisfied the light was there. Mr Carroll, Station Master at Fota, said he suggested to Sergeant Lawlor that experienced en should be put at this place and the Sergeant said he had not anything to do with it. In reply to Mr Buggy, witness said the driver need not whistle at Fota station at that hour of the morning because it was a switched-off station at night. His Honour said he had to be satisfied that the company was guilty of negligence, and as he was not satisfied he dismissed the action. There is another long article in the Kilkenny People about this tragedy in August-1914 and in the Kilkenny Journal, January, 1915. Grave or Memorial Reference; B 18 18. Cemetery: Cobh Old Church Cemetery, County Cork.

Ryan, James. Rank; Private. Regiment or Service: Royal Irish Regiment. Unit; 2nd Battalion. Service Number; 3146. Date of death; 08/07/1916. Born; St Patrick's, Kilkenny. Enlisted; Tipperary. Residence; Kilkenny. Died of wounds. In his Will, dated 03-January-1916, his effects and property were received by;- (Wife) Mrs Kate Ryan, 11 Wolfe Tone Street, Kilkenny, Ireland. Notes; Died of wounds in the 13th General Hospital. Grave or Memorial Reference; VIII C 111. Cemetery: Boulogne Eastern Cemetery in France.

Ryan, James. Rank; Private. Regiment or Service: Northumberland Fusiliers. Unit; 8th Battalion. Service Number; 8 4087. Date of death; 11/10/1917. Died after discharge. Notes; Died after discharge in the District Asylum, Kilkenny. After his death his effects and property were received by;- (sister) Annie. Cemetery: Unknown

Ryan, John. Rank; Private. Regiment or Service: Royal Irish Regiment. Unit; 2nd Battalion. Service Number; 6795. Date of death; 24/04/1915. Born; Freshford, County Kilkenny. Enlisted; Kilkenny. Killed in action. Grave or Memorial Reference; Panel 4. Cemetery: Ploegsteert Memorial in Belgium.

Ryan, John. Rank; Private. Regiment or Service: Royal Munster Fusiliers. Unit; 8th Battalion. Service Number; 1854. Date of death; 09/09/1916. Born; Kilmacow, County Kilkenny. Enlisted; Waterford. Residence; Kilmacow. Killed in action. Grave or Memorial Reference; Pier and Face 16 C. Cemetery: Thiepval Memorial in France.

Ryan, John. Rank; Gunner. Regiment or Service: Royal Garrison Artillery. Unit; 336th Siege Battery. Service Number; 130898. Date of death; 14/01/1919. Age at death;23. Born; Glenmore, County Kilkenny. Son of Patrick and Margaret Ryan of Priesthaggart, County Wexford. Notes; Served under the name Sullivan. Formerly he was with the 3rd Battalion, Royal Dublin Fusiliers where his number was 17633. Grave or Memorial Reference; Panel 24 - 26 - 28 - 30. Cemetery: Ypres (Menin Gate) Memorial in Belgium. He is also commemorated on the Great War Memorial in St Canice's Cathedral, Kilkenny…'To the Glory of God and in loving memory of the following members of the Diocese of Ossory who gave their lives for their country in the Great War 1914-1918'.

Ryan, John. Rank; Sergeant. Regiment or Service: Royal Garrison Artillery. Unit; 69th Company. Service Number; 1403379. Date of death; 13/07/1921. Age at death; 43. Son of Mary Ryan, of Lady Well, Thomastown, Co. Kilkenny. Grave or Memorial Reference; Face 2. Cemetery: Kirkee 1914-1918 Memorial in India.

Ryan, John Joseph. Rank; Private. Regiment or Service: Leinster Regiment. Unit; 2nd Battalion. Service Number; 4211. Date of death; 12/11/1917. Age at death;19. Born; Johnstown, County Kilkenny. Enlisted; Upper Court, Kilkenny. Residence; Johnstown. Killed in action. Son of John and Bridget Ryan, of Bawn, Johnstown, Co. Kilkenny. Grave or Memorial Reference; Pier and Face 16 C. Cemetery: Thiepval Memorial in France.

Ryan, John Patrick. Rank; Private. Regiment or Service: Household Cavalry and Cavalry of the line including the Yeomanry and Imperial Camel Corps. Unit; Old 2nd Cavalry Regiment (2nd Dragoon Guards and 6th Dragoons). Service Number; 21275. Date of death; 08/12/1915. Enlisted; Newport, Monmouthshire. Residence; Kilkenny. Died at home. Grave or Memorial Reference; Panel 2 (Screen Wall). Cemetery: Grangegorman Memorial in Dublin.

Ryan, Joseph. Rank; Private. Regiment or Service: Irish Guards. Unit; 1st Battalion. Service Number; 5543. Date of death; 16/04/1915. Born; Urlingford. Enlisted; Dublin. Residence; Carlow. Died of wounds. Husband of Kate Ryan, of 7, Charlotte Street, Carlow. Limerick Leader, July, 1915. At the Front. Catholic Chaplain's Experiences. Impression of Fierce Fighting. Interesting Letter to Clare Doctor. Dr M. P. Garry, Tuberculosis Officer for Clare, Trinaderry, Ennis, has received an interesting letter from Father J Gwynn, S. J., one of the Catholic Chaplains at the front, who is attached to the Irish Guards, and was wounded some time ago, from which we take some extracts…"It was very good of you to write about my wound. It is nearly all right now, thank God. I had a very narrow escape, and I know it was prayers saved me. It was the day the Irish Guards took the brickstacks and trenches at Cuinchy. I knew they were going to attack, and knew there would be a number of casualties, so kept very near. Our bombardment of the German position began exactly at 2 p. m. I had a splendid view of it—it was simply appalling. Shell of every kind, shrapnel, high explosives, percussion, rained on the German position. At 2. 15 the Irish Guards went forward, and as they fixed bayonets under cover of a ridge, I could see the sun glancing and sparking off their steel. In the meantime the Germans began a heavy shelling of the rere of the Irish Guards to prevent reinforcements coming up. Several shells burst near where I was, but I was not touched. The last think I remember was seeing the Guards get to the top of a ridge, when a lurid red blase seemed to flash into my eyes with a deafening crash. I was hurled back some five yards or so, and lay unconscious for some minutes. When I came to I felt my face all streaming blood, and my leg paining me. I was suffocated too, with a thick creamy, vile gas which came from the shell. A doctor bandaged me up, and I found that I was not so bad—splinters of the shell just grazed my face, cutting it; a bit too, struck me an inch or two above the knee and lodged inside. But in an hour's time, when everything was washed and bandaged, I was able to go and give Extreme Unction to a poor Irish Guardsman who had been badly hit. Luckily that night we came out of the trenches and got a day's rest; although I was very sick and dazed for two or three days I never had to give up. I am writing this in a little cellar or cave under a graveyard. It is about 150 yards from the German lines, and 80 or so from our own. You would laugh if you saw our furniture. The main thing and the most important is a bundle of straw in the corner, where I sleep at night. Everyone here has a cellar or 'dug out,' and the Germans are continually shelling us. As I write they are sending over big shells known as 'Jack Johnson' or 'Black Marias,' One had just fallen 20 or 30 yards away. If it had fallen on my little dug out, well I'm afraid you'd never get this letter. They are firing all sorts of shells to-day, give no warning and don't do much damage unless they get a direct hit amongst the men; then, ordinary shrapnel, bursting in the air and scattering some 300 bullets over 50 or sixty square yards; high explosive shrapnel which burst, with terrific force and cover a larger area; percussion shell, from 5. 9 inch to 8 inch, which simply blow a house into the air. As I write there are big fellows screaming over my head, bursting with terrific force, 40, 50, or 60 yards away. Now, there's a treatise on artillery for you…. When in the trenches I see any wounded man immediately he's hit I give him the last Sacraments. Then I hear the confession of men in the trenches, in their posts, of 'dug outs. ' I can tell you it is easy to have contrition when the air is simply alive with bullets and shell. At any moment, if a shell dropped, it would be all over with priest an penitent. Then, a day we get a rest, and we go back a little or so from the firing line. Then I say Mass in a field for the battalion. When we arrived I got a few of the men to get poles and put them down in a field, with a rough covering on top, just sufficient to cover the altar, if it rained. We have to have Mass in a field as the Irish Guards are nearly all Catholics, and we are at present the strongest battalion in the Guards Brigade. The men then sing some hymns at Mass, and it is fine to hear nearly a thousand men singing out in the open at the top of their voices. You have no idea what a splendid battalion the Irish Guards are. You have Sergeant Mike O'Leary, V. C, with you. I often had a chat with him when he came to see me. But do you know that there are plenty of men in the Irish Guards who have don as bravely as O'Leary, and there is never a word about it…A Young officer was here in my 'dug out' the other day, as officer of the Grenadier Guards. He went out and just at the door he turned back, exclaiming, 'My God! I am shot'; and so he was. He fell and was dead in about half a minute. It is curious when men are brought vividly and really face to face with death God is all they want. Pray for me—if anything happens to me, pray for me, too. I often think they will get me! I am off now to hear the confessions of No. 3 Company of the Irish Guards—they are about 100 yards from here, and it will be dodging behind walls and risking in the open to get to them, so good bye.". In a letter a few days later Father Gwynn wrote—"Every day comes with its own strange event for me. At twelve o'clock last night I was called to a man shot through the throat. I was with him immediately. The poor fellow was perfectly conscious, but could not speak—he spoke by signs. I heard his confession, and gave him Extreme Unction. At breakfast a note has handed to me that a Coldstream Guard had been shot in the head in the Coldstream trenches. I started off at once, a Coldstream orderly with me. It was a cold, bleak, muddy morning, and when I got to the place I found the poor fellow was lying out in the open, at the back of our trenches, in a very exposed spot, the Germans were not 70 yards away. I crawled out flat to him and he was still alive, and I gave him the Sacraments. He was absolutely unconscious, and I crawled back again. The Germans had one shot at me but missed badly. Of course they were afraid to take long aim, as our men were firing all the time. I was very glad to get back. I was going down the Coldstream advanced trenches afterwards, when an Irish Guards officer, all perspiring and muddy, came after me shouting that one of our men named Ryan had been shot and wanted to see me. I went back immediately, and found that the poor fellow had been shot through the lung. I heard his confession, gave him Extreme Unction and saw him off to hospital. When I gave him Extreme Unction it was extraordinary how cheerful he got. He was very badly wounded. I hope he'll get through. I had to go off then about a mile to bury a poor Irish Guardsman named Murrin, who had been shot dead during the day. Going a mile seems very simple to you at home, but here it means dodging bullets, a shell bursting now and again. When you hear a shell coming all you have got to do is to lie flat on the ground, be it wet, muddy, or dry, and not mind your clothes, and wait until it bursts. If you get down quickly enough one escapes unless it actually falls on top of you."Wednesday. --Just finished Mass, and some hundreds of the Guards were at it. While we were at Mass a shell passed over us, and burst a short distance beyond. The men did not stir…I am sending you the brass noses of two German shells which burst quite near me. This morning I saw Ryan, the Irish Guardsman, who was shot through the lung; he has a narrow escape. He said to me "Ye can tell the Germans, your reverence, that they are not done with Joe Ryan yet!"". Grave or Memorial Reference; VIII A 1. Cemetery: Boulogne Eastern Cemetery in France.

Ryan, Martin. Rank; Sergeant and lance Sergeant. Regiment or Service: Royal Dublin Fusiliers. Unit; 2nd Battalion. Service Number; 5380. Date of death; 25/01/1915. Age at death; 21. Born; Kilkenny. Enlisted; Carlow. Residence; Kilkenny. Died of wounds. Son of Martin and Mrs. A. Ryan, of Chapel Lane, Kilkenny. After his death his effects and property were received by;- Mrs Annie Ryan, Chapel Lane, Kilkenny, Ireland. Kilkenny Journal, February, 1915. Death of Kilkenny Soldier at the Front. News has been received of the death of Sergeant Martin Ryan, Walkin Street., who was killed in action while serving with his regiment, the Dublin Fusiliers. Sergeant Ryan, who had just reached his 21st year, was possessed of every manly quality, and was very popular in the city. He was in command of a machine gun section, which was subjected to a writhing fire. Sergeant Ryan kept his gun playing upon the enemy until he was mortally wounded. Notes; Died of wounds at Ploegsteert. Grave or Memorial Reference; I. A. 18. Cemetery: London Rifle Brigade Cemetery, Comines-Warneton, Hainaut, Belgium.

Ryan, Michael. Rank; Private. Regiment or Service: Royal Irish Regiment. Unit; 2nd Battalion. Service Number; 7747. Date of death; 02/08/1916. Age at death;23. Born; St John's, Kilkenny. Enlisted; Kilkenny. Died of wounds. Eldest son of James and Bridget Ryan, of Keatingstown Cottage, Kilkenny. Grave or Memorial Reference; IX C 3A. Cemetery: Etaples Military Cemetery in France.

Ryan, Michael. Rank; Private. Regiment or Service: Royal Irish Regiment. Unit; 2nd Battalion. Service Number; 4516. Date of death; 11/09/1916. Born; St Patrick's, Kilkenny. Enlisted; Kilkenny. Died of wounds. After his death his effects and property were received by;- (Mother) Bridget Ryan, Water Barracks, Kilkenny,. Grave or Memorial Reference; IV C 56. Cemetery: Heilly Station Cemetery, Mericourt-L'Abbe in France.

Ryan, Patrick. Rank; Private. Regiment or Service: Leinster Regiment. Unit; B Company, 2nd Battalion. Service Number; 7717. Date of death; 06/06/1915. Age at death;28. Born; Ballyhale, County Kilkenny. Enlisted; Camp Ballydaniel, County Kilkenny. Killed in action. Nephew of Mrs. Statia Aylward, of Ballyhale Cottage, Knocktopher, Co. Kilkenny. Kilkenny People, July, 1915. Death of a Gallant Leinster. Mrs Statia Aylward, Ballyhale, County Kilkenny, has been informed that her nephew, Private P. Ryan, of the 2nd Leinster Regiment, has been killed in action at the front. Deceased was a brave soldier and did service in India and had been 11 months in the firing line in the thick of all the heavy fighting and never received a wound till he was killed on the 6th June, near Hill 60. Kilkenny People, August, 1915. Ballyhale Soldier's Death. Mrs Statia Aylward, Ballyhale Cottages, Ballyhale, whose nephew, Private Patrick Ryan, of the 2nd Leinsters, was killed in action on the 6th June, has received letters of sympathy from his officers. Captain Louis Daly, B Company, end Leinster Regiment, writes;--"Dear Mrs Aylward; Your nephew was the greatest loss to my Company and the regiment. He had been out since the start, never gave any trouble, was full of courage, and was in every way a wise, and excellent soldier. He was the type of a man who, given the opportunity, would earn distinction for himself and his Regiment, so it is mighty sad to have lost him. He was killed in action on June 6, at 9-30p. m., north of Ypres. A bullet got your nephew in the head, killing him instantly and painlessly, and to our great sorrow. He received Absolution with the rest of us in the evening. In any case he died for his country and doing his duty, so you need have no fear of his eternal salvation. No man can do more than to give his life for another, and he gave his for all of us. He is buried by a priest, Father Moloney, at La Brique, north of Ypres, and his grave is marked distinctly by a cross. In the course of another letter of sympathy, Lieutenant J. H. Monaghan, the officer commanding the deceased's platoon, said they all keenly felt his loss, as he,"was truly a gallant soldier who could be depended on to do his duty in an unflimching manner."Sergeant T. T. Geary, of the same regiment, on behalf of the N. C. O's and men, also extends his sympathy to Mrs Aylward, and says;--"He died like an Irishman should, with his face to the enemy. I am glad to be able to tell you he was at Holy Communion the very day he was killed. Cemetery: La-Brique Military Cemetery, Number 1. Ieper, West-Vlaanderen, Belgium

Ryan, Patrick. Rank; Private. Regiment or Service: Royal Irish Regiment. Unit; B Company, 6th Battalion. Service Number; 4418. Date of death; 03/09/1916. Age at death; 21. Born; Dunamaggin, County Kilkenny. Enlisted; Thomastown. Residence; Kells, County Meath. Killed in action. Son of Timothy and Kate Ryan, of Kells Boro, Kells, Co. Kilkenny. In his Will, dated 10-June-1916, his effects and property were received by (Mother) Mrs R Ryan, Kells, County Kilkenny. Grave or Memorial Reference; Pier and Face 3 A. Cemetery: Thiepval Memorial in France.

Ryan, Richard. Rank; Sapper. Regiment or Service: Royal Engineers. Unit; Special Signal Company. Service Number; 160891. Date of death; 06/11/1918. Born; Ballyhall, County Kilkenny. Enlisted; Kilkenny. Died at home. Husband of A. Ryan. Grave or Memorial Reference; Near the South Boundary. Cemetery: Castlegannon Catholic Churchyard, County Kilkenny

S

Sarsfield, Patrick. Rank; Private. Regiment or Service: Royal Irish Regiment. Unit; 4th Battalion. Service Number; 3157. Date of death; 24/02/1915. Age at death; 26. Born; St Patrick's, Kilkenny. Enlisted; Tipperary. Residence; Kilkenny. Died at home. Grave or Memorial Reference; C 24 66. Cemetery: Cobh Old Church I Cemetery, County Cork.

Sarsfield, Richard. Rank; Ordianry Signalman. Regiment or Service: Royal Navy. Unit; H. M. S."Defence.". Service Number; J/28661. Date of death; 31/05/1916. Age at death;18. Born; Kilkenny. Son of Michael and Katherine Sarsfield, of 86, North Porter Street, Oldham Road, Manchester. Native of Callan, Co. Kilkenny. Grave or Memorial Reference; 13. Cemetery: Plymouth Naval Memorial, UK.

Sarsfield, Thomas. Rank; Boy 1st Class. Regiment or Service: Royal Navy. Unit; H. M. S."Invincible.". Service Number; J/35785. Date of death; 31/05/1916. Born;. Kilkenny People, June 1916. Callan Man at the Great Sea Battle. First Class Gunner, William McLean, a native of bridge Street, Callan, as on board H. M. torpedo boat destroyer Naraboro, Flotilla 13, in the North Sea battle. His mother received a letter from him on Wednesday saying he was safe and that it was a grand sight to see the German Fleet flying when they sighted Sir John Jellicoe's fleet coming. His destroyer came out of the battle without a scrape. First Class Bay, Richard Sarsfield, Green Street, is missing. He was on H. M. S., Defence. He was on furlough in Callan three weeks ago. Grave or Memorial Reference; 13. Cemetery: Plymouth Naval Memorial, UK.

Scollard, David Francis. Rank; Captain. Regiment or Service: Royal Irish Rifles. Unit; 7th Battalion. Date of death; 20/04/1917. Age at death;44. Killed in action. He won the Military Medal and is listed in the London Gazette. Son of David Francis Scollard, of Kilkenny; husband of Zelia Letitia Scollard, of "Hamlot," 22, Park Road, Hanwell, London. Grave or Memorial Reference; N 25. Cemetery: Kemmel Chateau Military Cemetery in Belgium.

Scully, Lawrence. Rank; Acting Bombardier. Regiment or Service: Royal Horse Artillery and Royal Field Artillery. Unit; C Battery, 283rd Brigade. Service Number; 50791. Date of death; 10/10/1916. Born; Tullow, County Carlow. Enlisted; Kilkenny. Killed in action. In his Will, dated 30-May-1916, his effects and property were received by;- (Sister) Mrs M Sullivan, Ballon Hill, County Carlow, Ireland. Notes; Formerly he was with the Royal Irish Regiment where his number was 9767. Grave or Memorial Reference; X P 2. Cemetery: Guards Cemetery, Lesboeufs in France.

Shanahan, John. Rank; Private. Regiment or Service: Machine Gun Corps. Unit; 47th Company. Service Number; 12614. Date of death; 17/08/1917. Born; Shinrone, King's County. Enlisted; Dublin. Residence; Johnstown, County Kilkenny. Died of wounds. Grave or Memorial Reference; III F 14. Cemetery: Mendingham Military Cemetery in Belgium.

Shea, John W. Rank; Sergeant. Regiment or Service: Royal Irish Fusiliers. Unit; 7/8th Battalion. Service Number; 43015. Date of death; 21/07/1917. Born; Kilkenny. Enlisted; Kilkenny. Died of wounds. In his Will, dated 28-June-1916, his effects and property were received by ;- Mrs Margaret Shea, Chapel Lane, Kilkenny, Ireland. Notes; Formerly he was with the Royal Irish Regiment where his number was 6702. Grave or Memorial Reference; III A 115. Cemetery: Bailleul Communal Cemetery Extension (Nord) in France.

Shea, Joseph. Rank; Private. Regiment or Service: Royal Irish Regiment. Unit; 1st Battalion. Service Number; 3895. Date of death; 02/11/1917. Age at death;26. Born; St Mary's, Kilkenny. Enlisted; Kilkenny. Died of wounds in Palestine. Son of Patrick and Margaret Shea, of Kilkenny; husband of Margaret Shea, of Upper Walkin Street, Kilkenny. 3 years' service in France,. Grave or Memorial Reference; N 7. Cemetery: Beersheba War Cemetery, Israel.

Shea, Martin. Rank; Private. Regiment or Service: Royal Irish Regiment. Unit; 2nd Battalion. Service Number; 8171. Date of death; 21/03/1918. Age at death; 34. Born; Windgap, County Kilkenny. Enlisted; Kilkenny. Residence; Birchwood, County Kilkenny. Killed in action. In his Will, dated 08-February-1917, his effects and property were received by;- (Wife) Katherine Shea, Tullahaught, Pilltown, County Kilkenny. Son of Michael and Margaret Shea, of Corragawn, Piltown; husband of Katie Shea, of Birchwood, Piltown, Co. Kilkenny. Private Shea first entered the Theatre of War on the 13th of August-1914. Munster Express;News from the front. Our Windgap correspondent informs us that during the week he received a postcard and letter from Private Martin O'Shea (8171), Tullahought, who says he is yet in the land of the living, and would have written our correspondent long since but could get no paper. He is also anxious to know when the Volunteer Corps will be fit enough to go out and give them (the Regulars) a final push in exterminating the Alemands. He sends his best wishes to all his friends, and intends to drink "Slainthe" at Mr Power's with his old pals before long. Munster Express, February;-Tullahought Man Wounded at the Front. A correspondent says that the numerous friends of Private Martin O'Shea, Tullahought, will be sorry to hear that he has been wounded at the front, but will rejoice to learn that he is progressing well in hospital at Boulogne (France). Writing to Mr Denis Coughlan, he states, during his six months at the front he has received lots of experience in warfare. He enquires for all friends, and regrets the rather sudden demise of other old chums. He expects to see the Kaiser locked up before next June. Munster Express, 1915Letter from the Front. Our Windgap correspondent has received the following. Just a few lines hoping to find you all in good health, as this leaves myself in good health at present. I got your letter all right yesterday. I see there are lots of changes around the place—al the marriages. The war is the same old go all the time. There is no knowing when it will be over. I think it will hold another year, anyhow. How I wish the d--- thing was over! Themselves and the Russians have it very hard al the time. They are getting the best of the Russians all the time, but there might come a change before long. Every man in Germany is a man of brains, there is nothing smarter than them. I think it will take a long time if they fight it out to a finish, but they may settle it in some other way. Where we are at present it is all a white chalk quarry all around for miles. We have to run our trenches through it. The weather is very wet here at present. We had thunder and lightening terribly here. You would see the French working here behind the line the same as if nothing was on. They are working reapers and binders cutting down the harvest. I saw a farmer working the other day. One of the horses was killed under the machine; he did not mind; h went and got another and worked away. They take no notice of it. Tell al around there I was asking for them. I might be home soon with one leg; an old pensioner, hopping down to Delaney to hear him telling some good ones, and have an odd sup of old Dunville whiskey. I have no more to say at present. I hope they will settle the war soon. Good-bye for the present. Martin Shea. Munster Express, Letter from the Front. Private Shea, some of whose letters we have previously published, writes to an old friend in Windgap as follows;-September, 10th. Just a few lines hoping to find you all well, as this leaves myself in good health at present. I am sure you have all the hay and oats cut now. There is no sign of the war finishing at all. The lads around, tell them I was asking for them. I am sure everything is very dear. It is a terrible war-the country will be destroyed after this. How is Ned Power-does he have much drinking? Tell him I was asking for him. How are all the Barnathasna fellows? Tell Denis I was asking for him. I am going to write to Mr Farrell soon. I am sure he is back from Tramore. Do you see Thomas Connolly? Tell him there is plenty of old iron out here, but it is very risky to pick it up. How is Connors going on? Tell Delaney that I was asking for him; I am sure he is telling some good ones all the time. The weather is very fine here now, but the nights are getting very cold. I wish this d--- war was over. But the Germans have to be beaten yet. It will take some time. Well, remember me to all the old neighbours around, and tell them that I will appear some day home again when the war is over. Good-bye. P. S. -I am left my regiment. I am now in the Royal Flying Corps. Letter from the Front. Our Windgap correspondent sends us a letter which he has received from a friend of his at the front, in the course of which he says;-"We are in a hot spot at present (May 20th). Ypres and Hill 60. We got a terrible dose of the gas from the Germans. It is a d---l of a war. It is impossible to escape it all. I am with the Medical Corps now, carrying the wounded off the field to the dressing station—that is a mile behind the line. Our own doctor was killed yesterday morning, he was a very nice man. I am a stretcher-bearer and wearing a Red Cross on my sleeve. We have to dress the wounded and carry them on our back, as well as a small bottle of medicine to put on the wound. It is awful—you would see such terrible sights. I have no rifle or ammunition. You have to go through shot and shell as quick as you can, but it has to be done. It was I carried Paddy Reddy in when he was wounded' he is gone home now; so you see how friends meet. Walsh from Kilmoganny was also wounded. This is the 20th. Italy is to start to-day. I think if you saw this country—it is terrible; it is knocked to the ground. This is Belgium. I was in Mons on the 23rd of last month. Grave or Memorial Reference; Panel 30 and 31. Cemetery: Pozieres Memorial in France.

Shea, Michael. Rank; Private. Regiment or Service: Army Cyclist Corps. Unit; 27th Divion Cyclist Corps. Service Number; 5671. Date of death; 28/04/1915. Born; St John's, Kilkenny. Enlisted; Kilkenny. Killed in action. Son of Mrs. Ellen Ryan, of Callan Road, Kilkenny. Notes; Formerly he was with the Royal Irish Regiment where his number was 9815. Grave or Memorial Reference; II H 14. Cemetery: Hazebrouck Communal Cemetery, Nord, in France

Shea, Patrick Joseph. Rank; Private. Regiment or Service: Royal Dublin Fusiliers. Unit; 2nd Battalion. Service Number; 5629. Date of death; 01/09/1916. Born; Kilkenny. Enlisted; Naas. Residence; Kilkenny. Killed in action. Grave or Memorial Reference; VL L 16. Cemetery: Railway Dugouts Burial Ground in Belgium.

Shea, Richard. Rank; Private. Regiment or Service: Royal Irish Regiment. Unit; 2nd Battalion. Service Number; 10602. Date of death; 24/04/1915. Born; St Mary's, Kilkenny. Enlisted; Kilkenny. Killed in action. Grave or Memorial Reference; V R 8. Cemetery: Sanctuary Wood Cemetery, Ypres, Belgium.

Shearman, Ambrose Augustine. Rank; Captain. Regiment or Service: London Regiment. Unit; "C" Coy. 2nd/7th Battalion. Date of death; 20/04/1918. Age at death; 26. Died of wounds. Son of Johanna and the late Edward Shearman, of 84, High Street, Kilkenny. Kilkenny Journal, April, 1915. For the Front. Mr A. A. Shearman, youngest son of Mrs Shearman, High Street, Kilkenny, has volunteered for active service, and is to be attached to the Officers Training Corps for a brief period preparatory to being appointed a Lieutenant. Mr Shearman has been in the service of the National bank for some years, and held the position of Cashier in the Baltinglass Branch for a considerable time. We congratulate our young citizen on is patriotism, and sincerely hope that his future in the strenuous but nobler career he has so opportunely chosen will not be less successful than the life of comparative comfort which his professional abilities would undoubtedly secure for him in civil life. Kilkenny People, September, 1915. Lieutenant Ambrose Shearman, youngest son of Mrs Shearman, High Street, who obtained his Commission some weeks ago, is at present enjoying the luxury of a week's rest in Kilkenny. His military duties are being carried out "somewhere in England" where Zeppelins never cease from troubling and the weary know no rest. Kilkenny People, April, 1918. Shearman. —On 20th April-1918, from wounds received in action, Lieutenant (Acting Captain) Ambrose A. Shearman, London Regiment, fourth surviving son of the late Edward Shearman and Mrs Shearman, High Street, Kilkenny. R. I. P. Irish Independent; Shearman—April 20, 1918, from wounds received in action, Lieutenant (Acting Captain) Ambrose A Shearman, London Regiment, fourth surviving son of the late Edward Shearman and Mrs Shearman, High Street, Kilkenny. R. I. P. Kilkenny People, April, 1918. Death of Lieutenant Ambrose A. Shearman, London Regiment. Mrs Shearman, High Street, Kilkenny, has been officially informed of the death on 21st inst., from wounds received in action of her son, Lieutenant (Acting Captain) Ambrose A. Shearman, London Regiment. The deceased officer was educated at the Christian Schools, Kilkenny, and Rockwell College, and subsequently entered the service of the national Bank, having been stationed prior to the war at Killarney and Baltinglass. Lieutenant Shearman joined the army shortly after the outbreak of hostilities and was commissioner in the London regiment, and was at the front for more than year prior to his death. His elder brother, Captain Francis J. Shearman, is serving abroad in the Army Veterinary Corps. The death of Lieutenant Shearman at such an early age and under such tragic circumstances is deeply regretted by the large number of friends of his respected family in the city and county of Kilkenny and in many places outside. He was an extremely popular young Kilkennyman, and everyone who knew him liked him. During the few years he spent in the service of the national Bank he showed that he was possessed of exceptional ability, united with a modest and unassuming personality and urbanity of manner, and there is no doubt that a bright and successful career was before him if he had continued his official connection with the Bank. Lieutenant Shearman was in Kilkenny on short leave last March, and he spent St Patrick's Day at his mothers home. Unhappily it was the last time she had the supreme joy of seeing him. In little over a month his life was added to the stupendous toll claimed by this ruthless war, which has brought sorrow and desolation to countless households. On Sunday afternoon the melancholy tidings of his death were conveyed by wire to his brother, Mr Edward J. Shearman, who immediately solicited the kindly offices of the Rev. A. O'Keeffe, Adm., St Mary's, upon whom devolved the sad duty of breaking the news to the afflicted mother and sister of this deeply lamented young Kilkennyman. For all the members of his family the most sincere sympathy is felt in the great sorrow that has befallen them. Irish Times. Shearman-April 20, from wounds, Lieutenant (Acting Captain), Ambrose Shearman, London regiment, son of the late Edward Shearman and Mrs Shearman, High Street, Kilkenny. The Weekly Irish Times. Ireland's Roll of Honour. April 27, 1918. Lieutenant (Acting Captain) A A Shearman, London Regiment, son of Mrs Shearman, High Street, Kilkenny, died of wounds on 29th instant. The deceased officer was enucated at the Christian brothers Schools, Kilkenny, and Rockwell College, abnd subsequently entered the service of the National Bank, having been stationed prior to the wat at Killarney and Baltinglass. Lieutenant Shearman joined the Army shortly after the outbreak of hostilities, and was mentioned in the London Regiment, and was at the front for more than a year prior to his death. His elder brother, Captain Francis J Shearman, is serving in the Army Veterinary Corps. Grave or Memorial Reference; B 16. Cemetery: Picquigny British Cemetery, Somme, France.

Sheehan, Patrick. Rank; Private. Regiment or Service: Royal Army Medical Corps. Unit; 16th Field Ambulance. Service Number; 7358. Date of death; 09/08/1915. Age at death;18. Born; Rosbercan, Kilkenny. Enlisted; New Ross. Killed in action. Son of Mary Sheehan. 'People' newspaper; Official information has reached New Ross that two New Ross soldiers were killed at the front last week. One is Private Patrick Sheehan, who's parents are dead, but who has an Aunt living in Michael Street. He was about 21 (sic) years of age and was attached to the Royal Army Medical Corps. Grave or Memorial Reference; I G 15. Cemetery: Poperinghe New Military Cemetery in Belgium.

Shelly, John. Rank; Private. Regiment or Service: Royal Garrison Artillery. Unit; 71st Heavy Battery. Service Number; 5237. Date of death; 23/07/1915. Age at death; 38. Born; Callan, County Kilkenny. Enlisted; Glasgow. Killed in action. Son of Patrick and Margaret Shelly. Grave or Memorial Reference; C 26. Cemetery: Divisional Cemetery, Ieper, West-Vlaanderen, Belgium.

Shortall, Francis L. Rank; Private. Regiment or Service: R. I. C, Ex-Irish Guards. Unit; 1st Battalion. Service Number; 2585. Date of death; 07/01/1921. Born; Tipperary. Residence; Kilkenny. Died of wounds. Tipperary Star, April, 1915. Tipperary Soldiers. Prisoners of War in Germany. An Appeal to the County. The rev. T Dunne, sends us for publication, with a view to an appeal to their fellow countrymen and women for comforts for them, the undermentioned list of names of Tipperarymen who are now prisoners of war in Kriegsgefangennan Lager, Limburg, Lahn, Germany, where the Rev. T Crotty, O. P., a close personal friend of Father Dunne, is acting as chaplain.

Father Crotty writes;--"The hospitals and prisons tell a tale of woe and misery which shocks me." We shall have pleasure in acknowledging and forwarding to Father Dunne any subscriptions received at this office. Private F Shortal, Irish Guards, Clonmel; R Hayes, Cheshire regiment, do; D Shine, Royal Irish, do; M Cahill, Royal Irish, do; T Maloney, Royal Irish, do; M O'Brien, Royal Irish, do; T Flynn, Royal Irish, do; M Meling, Royal Irish, do; P Barry, Royal Irish, do; D Hackett, Royal Irish, do; C Cummins, Royal Irish, do; J Keating, Connaught Rangers, do; M Young, Leinsters, do;--Mahony, Leinsters, do;--Sweeney, Leinsters, do; J Brown, Royal Irish, do; R Fahey, Royal Irish, do; J Foley, Royal Irish, do; J Hanrahan, Royal Irish, do; R Hennessy, Royal Irish, do;--Mansfield, Royal Irish, Newcastle. The Waterford News, January 1915. Sergeant Harris, of the Guards, in the course of his letters, mentions the names of several Waterfordmen whom he met at the front. Constable Shortall, of Ferrybank, who also went out with the Irish Guards at the commencement of the war, was, he said,"The first man of ours to be wounded, he was hit on the left knee with the cap of a shell." In the course of another letter he states that he met Richard Harrison, of the Irish Guards, son of Sergeant-at-Mace Harrison, and Mr Jack Mitchell, son of Mrs Mitchell, Bath Street, who was well-known in rugby and association football circles in Waterford previous to joining the army. The latter has been given a commission as Second Lieutenant. In one of his letters, Sergeant Harris states; -- "I have seen some of the British papers, and they give a very good idea of what is going on. Thanks very much for the parcels of cigarettes and coffee, which I received all right. The coffee is the very thing I want out here, so you might send me an occasional tin when you think of it. It is very handy when you are in the trenches. Whatever chance we have of getting hot water, we have no chance of getting tea. I was speaking to Jack Mitchell yesterday. He is a Sergeant now (has since been promoted Second Lieutenant) and is in our division. We were talking for a long time all about Waterford. I suppose you read in the papers that we had a bit of a hard time. We lost a lot of men. The Germans charged us one day. They came in batches of about fifty, we cut up about twelve batches of them before we retired, and when we retired they got their artillery on us and shelled us, dropping about thirty shells a minute. It was something terrible to see the men getting killed and wounded, but I was one of the lucky birds." In another letter he states; -- "We are busy keeping those blokes on the move. We are in a position now seven days. We are opposed by about 3, 000 Germans, but we are giving them hell. The place about us is like the Park on a hot day with all the fellows lying about dead.". Cemetery: UnknownAmbushed by the I. R. A. in Cork City and died of wounds.

Shortall, Thomas. Rank; Acting Sergeant. Regiment or Service: York and Lancaster Regiment. Unit; 13th (Service) (1st Barnsley) Battalion. Service Number; 39986. Date of death; 13/09/1917. Born; Kilkenny. Enlisted; Hartley, Witney. Killed in action. Notes; Formerly he was with the West Yorkshire Regiment where his number was 19600. Grave or Memorial Reference; I H 28. Cemetery: Le Targette British Cemetery, Neuville-St, Vaast in France

Slacke, Roger Cecil. Rank; Major. Regiment or Service: The Buffs (East Kent Regiment). Unit; 3rd Battalion. Date of death; 16/05/1915. Killed in action. Grave or Memorial Reference; III V 4. Cemetery: Guards Cemetery, Lesboeufs in France.

Smitheram, William. Rank; Private. Regiment or Service: Royal Irish Regiment. Unit; 6th Battalion. Service Number; 3545. Date of death; 05/04/1917. Age at death; 30. Born; St Mary's, Kilkenny. Enlisted; Kilkenny. Killed in action. Smotheram (CWGC, SDGW) Smitheran (IMR), Son of Mary Smitheram, of Upper Walkin Street, Kilkenny; husband of Bridget Smitheram, of James Street, Kilkenny. In his Will, dated 09-December-1916 at Queenstown, his effects and property were received by;- (Mother) Mrs Mary Kavanagh, Upper Walkin Street, Kilkenny. Grave or Memorial Reference; Panel 33. Cemetery: Ypres (Menin Gate) Memorial in Belgium.

Captain Smithwick from 'Our Heroes.'

Smithwick, James Arnold. Rank; Captain. Regiment or Service: Royal Irish Regiment. Unit; 4th Battalion attached to 2nd Battalion. Date of death; 09/11/1915. Age at death;34. Died. Limerick Chronicle, November, 1914. The Royal Irish Regiment. News has been received by Major French Lloyd from his nephew, Lieutenant G Dowling, that the following officers of the Royal Irish Regiment are prisoners of war at Husarne Kaserne, Crefield, Germany;-Captain G O M Furnell, Captain J A Smithwick, Lieutenant W E Bredin, Lieutenant E Foulkes, and Lieutenant G Dowling. 'Our Heroes'. has died in London from consumption due to injuries received on October 20th, 1914, at Le Pelly whilst gallantly leading his men, when he was seriously wounded and lay for several hours unconscious until picked up by a German ambulance party. He was removed to the German internment camp at Crefield, where he was detained for nearly ten months before he was exchanged. His recovery from his wounds was very slow, and consumption directly traceable to his injuries set in which prevented any hope of his recovery. On his arrival in London he was visited in hospital by His majesty King George, who complimented him on his great gallantry. Captain Smithwick was the elder surviving son of the late Mr J. F. Smithwick, J. P., who represented the Coty of Kilkenny in Parliament from 1880 to 1885, and a member of a well-known Kilkenny family. Kilkenny People, November 1914. From the Front. Interesting Interviews. Captain James A. Smithwick Wounded. A prisoner in Germany. Mr Richard H. Smithwick, T. C., Co. C, Larchfield House, has received the following letter from his brother, Captain James A. Smithwick, J. P., who left for the front a few weeks ago in command of a detachment of the 4th Battalion, Royal Irish Regiment (Kilkenny Militia) ;-Husaren, Kaserne. Crefield, Germany, 27th October, 1914. My Dear Dick. I am here wounded and a prisoner, and am being well treated. As you have seen by the casualty list the regiment suffered very heavily. It is bad luck being here, but I am lucky to be above ground. I escaped until half an hour before the end without a scratch. Then while trying to retire with some of my men to deal with a machine gun which was enfilading us from our left rere, I was grazed twice on the shoulder and on the hand. The next got me plump on my right breast. It hit my compass, then on to a rib and through the muscles on top of my stomach and out the left side. Narrow squeak. It knocked me clean out at the time, and I am a bit stiff and sore, but it is going on well, and there is no danger. This letter is censored at both ends, so I cannot make it too long. — Your fond brother. J. A. Smithwick. The news was learned with keen satisfaction in the city and county as there were rumours that Captain Smithwick had been killed in action. King's County Chronicle, September, 1915. Captain J. A. Smithwick, 4th Batt, Royal Irish Regiment, who was severely wounded while leading his men in a bayonet charge on October, 20, 1914, was one of the exchanged wounded officers who recently arrived in England, and is now under treatment at the Pine Wood Sanitorium, Wokingham. The King spent nearly a quarter of an hour chatting with him at the hospital. Waterford News. The Late Captain J. A. Smithwick. The remains of the late Captain J. A. Smithwick, who died in a London nursing home on Tuesday last, passed through Waterford North station this morning on their way to Kilkenny for internment in the burial ground there. Captain Smithwick, who saw service in South Africa, was in command of the first detachment of the 14th Battalion, Royal Irish Regiment to leave Ireland for France. Captain Smithwick was severely wounded and taken prisoner by the Germans. Some months ago he was released in exchange, but despite the welcome change, a robust constitution was unable to bear the strain, and he died as aforementioned on Tuesday last. The Nationalist and Leinster Times October, 1915. Smithwick, and Moore (Michael and his brother Martin mentioned in this article survived the war,.) Irish Prisoners in Germany. How Comforts from Home are Appreciated. Recently Private Michael Moore, belonging to the Royal Army Medical Corps, whose mother resides at Upper Patrick Street, Kilkenny, arrived home fro Germany, where he had been a prisoner of war for about thirteen months past. Needless to say, he had some interesting experiences to relate. He was taken prisoner with a number of his comrades in the course of the fierce fighting which marked the German invasion of Belgium. While engaged with a comrade removing an officer of the Coldstream Guards, who had portion of his head and face blown away, Moore received a blow of the butt end of a rifle on the back of the neck and almost immediately a stab from a bayonet in the ribs. Shortly afterwards the large number of prisoners, of which he was one, started their long weary journey by rail to Germany; huddled together in cattle trucks, the captives were kept travelling for some two or three days, and their general discomfort and hardship were made all the more acute by the worse-than-animal like fashion in which they were treated; it is related that on of the stations at which a stop was made one of the British soldiers asked for a drink of water, and was rewarded by having a large bucketful thrown over his companions and himself in the cattle truck. This any many others no less insulting incidents were but a prelude to what was to come, and though prepared for the worst, those brave fellows could not possibly have conjectured that their subsequent treatment would be anything like what it was. For a long time during the winter months their place of confinement was not even up to the low-standard cleanliness and comfort of a pig-sty. In keeping with those surroundings was the provision made for the feeding of the prisoners, whose daily diet consisted of coffee, without sugar or milk, for breakfast; something like, but not as palatable as, cabbage-water for dinner, and a second dose of the morning's fare, with a slice of black bread thrown in for supper. This is given as an unexaggerated fact by Private Moore, who says that were it not for the kindness of their friends at home in sending them food and comforts, their plight would be one approaching the verge of starvation. He lays special emphasis on the need existing for an increased continuance of the food supply from home if the captive soldiers are to be kept in anything like a healthy condition, and assures us that parcels sent to Germany invariably arrive at their destination all right. Speaking of the harsh treatment generally meted out by the Germans to prisoners wounded and otherwise. Moore said that he could never obliterate from memory the sickening sight which he personally witnessed when wounded Russian prisoners, captured at the fall of Warsaw, were brought to Germany. The dressings, which had been hurriedly put to their wounds on the battlefield, had not been removed for weeks, and when taken off revealed a sight that none could care to witness—a sight rendered all the more objectionable by the low condition of bodily uncleanliness into which the unfortunate fellows, through want of care, were allowed to lapse. Asked as to the futile attempt of Sir Roger Casement to form an Irish Brigade from amongst the Irish soldiers at Limburg, Moore said that the reception accorded to Casement was so warm that were it not for the protection afforded him by a company of Prussian Guards his visit to the camp might possibility have eventuated in an obituary notice. For the past two or three months the prisoners have been engaged on agricultural work, and the change has been to the one for the better, both mentally and physically. Private Moore, who is looking hale and hearty after his exile, was exchanged under condition of the Haigue Convention, which provides, we understand, that soldiers engaged on red Cross work should be granted immunity from arrest, but such considerations found no place in the programme of wholesale violation practiced by the German hordes in their wild onrush through Belgium and Northern France. He states that Captain Barry George—still known in sporting circles in Kilkenny—was to be one of the last batch of exchanged wounded prisoners, but at the last moment, to his great disappointment he was ordered back, Captain Barry George, his many friends will learn with pleasure, has almost completely recovered from his wounds, but they will no less regret that his recovery entails his further detention in the enemy's hands. He expressed to private Moore the delight he felt that Captain J. A. Smithwick, J. P., had been released, and hoped that he was well on the way to recovery, and also that he himself would soon be back in the old land. Private Moore also wishes it to be known that despite the manner of their treatment, the Irish prisoners of war, especially those of them hailing from the Marble City, are in high spirits, and await with patient hope the day of their release to celebrate with their brave comrades the glorious victory of the Allies. Despite the fact of his being under orders for service at the Dardanelles, Private Moore—whose brother Martin of the Lancashire Regiment, is also a prisoner of war in Germany—is glad beyond measure to be once more a free man, though he is not without sympathy for the loyal comrades he has left behind in the land of the Hun. Kilkenny people, November-1915. Urlingford Private's Story. Private Cain, of Urlingford, who belongs to the 4th Battalion of the Royal Irish Regiment, told an interesting story of the fighting in France to an "Irish Independent" representative. He was wounded on the shoulder by shrapnel, and is now in the Mater Hospital, Dublin. Having left the troop train the advance was ordered, and after about two miles of a march the Royal Irish were in close quarters with the Germans. The bayonets work he described as awful, and the shell-fire unceasing. While the shelling and rifle firing went on, people were running away from their homes and the crops were being destroyed. His regiment marched on a village called Lascines. The enemy advanced towards the village, and he got a piece of a shell on the arm. There were 900 of the Royal Irish advancing, and afterwards when the roll was called only 55 aN. S. W. ered. The battle lasted from 10 o'clock in the morning to 10 at night. The scene was desperate. Captain Smithwick, Kilkenny, who was in charge of his company, was shot through the mouth. The Germans used both shell and rifle fire with terrible effect. His experience was that though some of the Germans might waver before the bayonet, the majority stood their ground and fought. Their rifle dire is generally accurate."We had to retire from the trenches," he continued,"owing to re shell fire. It was Sunday evening, and the people who were reciting the Rosary in the village, were disturbed by the shells, which burst over them. Some of the church was taken away. About a mile away from the village the Germans posted a battery close to a church, and the British were obliged to shell it. A remarkable circumstance in connection with the demolition of the church was that not one of the sacred images were destroyed." As to the "Jack Johnson," the name given to the German shell, he said its killing capacity extends over three hundred yards, and when it explodes the ground shakes like a moving bog. His wounded arm was bandaged by a comrade, and eventually he was taken to a hospital at the rere."The Germans," he added, are wonderful snipers, and take most accurate aim from trees. Sometimes the red Cross wagon they carry as a Maxim gun, which is twice as effective as the English Gun." (Pte Cain survived the war). There are further long articles concerning Captain Smithwick in;-- Kilkenny People, May, 1915, Kilkenny People, June, 1915, Kilkenny People, July, 1915, Kilkenny People, August, 1915, Kilkenny Journal, August, 1915, Kilkenny Journal, September, 1915, Kilkenny People, September, 1915, Kilkenny People, November, 1915. The Weekly Irish Times. Ireland's Roll of Honour. June 26, 1915. Captain D J Smithwick. Mrs J Smithwick, Kilcreene Lodge, Kilkenny, has receved the following telegram from the Secretary of the War Office;--"Regret to inform you that Captain D J Smithwick, Worcester Regiment, attached to the Royal Munster Fusiliers, has been wounded. Further news will be telegraphed when received." Captain Smithwick's wound was received in one of the engagements in the Dardanelles. He is a brother of Mr James Smithwick, Kilcreene Lodge, and a cousin of Captain J A Smithwick, Royal Irish regiment, who was wounded in France in October, and has been since a prisoner of war in Germany. Irish Times. Smithwick-November 9, 1915, at the Private Nursing Home, 19 Beaumont Street, Portland Place, London, of consumption, contracted whilst a prisoner of war at Crefield, Germany, from wounds received in action, Captain A Smithwick, 4th Battalion, Royal Irish Regiment, elder surviving son of the late John Francis Smithwick, J. P., Birchfield, Kilkenny, aged 34 years. 10/11/1915. Freeman's Journal. Smithwick-November 9, 1915, at the private Nursing Home, 19 Beaumont Street, Portland Place, London, of consumption, contracted whilst a prisoner of war at Crefeld, Germany, from wounds received in action, Captain James A Smithwick, 4th Battalion, Royal Irish Regiment, elder surviving son of the late John Francis Smithwick, J. P., Birchfield, Kilkenny, aged 34 years. R. I. P. Funeral will take place at Kilkenny at 11 o'clock to-morrow (Friday), and not in London, as previously arranged. Grave or Memorial Reference; About 9 yards South of the Church. Cemetery: Foulkstown Catholic Churchyard, County Kilkenny.

Image courtesy of Paul Molloy

Smyth, Patrick. Rank; Sergeant. Regiment or Service: Royal Irish Regiment. Unit; "B" Coy. 6th Battalion. Service Number; 1772. Date of death; 19/01/1917. Age at death; 46. Born; St John's, Kilkenny. Enlisted; Kilkenny. Killed in action. Son of Michael and Mary Smyth, of John''s Green, Kilkenny; husband of Margaret Smyth, of 3, Wolftone Street, Kilkenny. After his death his effects and property were received by;- (Wife) Margaret Smyth, 3 Walkin Street, Kilkenny, Ireland. Grave or Memorial Reference; I 17. Cemetery: Pond Farm Cemetery in Belgium.

Smyth, William. Rank; Lance Sergeant. Regiment or Service: Irish Guards. Unit; 2nd Battalion. Service Number; 7827. Date of death; 15/03/1917. Born; Kilkenny. Enlisted; Kilkenny. Killed in action. Grave or Memorial Reference; II I 10. Cemetery: Sailly-Saillisel British Cemetery in France.

Somers, John. Rank; Private. Regiment or Service: Royal Irish Fusiliers. Unit; 7th Battalion. Service Number; 16505. Date of death; 27/04/1916. Born; Kilkenny. Enlisted; Carlow. Residence; Kilkenny. Killed in action. After his death his effects and property were received by;- Susan Walsh and children. Noncupative (or missing) Will was witnessed by;- Mrs Bridget Somers, Evans Lane, Kilkenny, Ireland. Mrs A Bourke, Evans Lane, Kilkenny, Ireland. Notes; Formerly he was with the Royal Irish Regiment where his number was 1855. Grave or Memorial Reference; Panel 124. Cemetery: Loos Memorial in France.

Sparrow, Frank Edward. Rank; Lieutenant (TP). Regiment or Service: Corps of Royal Engineers. Unit; 129th Field Company. Date of death; 13/08/1918. Age at death;37. Died of wounds. Son of Edward and Annie Sparrow, of 55, Palmerston Rd., Dublin. Junior Architect, Local Govt. Board (Ireland), M. R. I. A. I. Clare Journal, August, 1916. Second Lieutenant F. E. Sparrow, killed on August 13, was a L. G. B Inspector and was the elder son of the late Mr E. Sparrow, 55 Palmerstown Road, Dublin. He was in charge of the Ennis district at the time he volunteered. De Ruvigny's Roll of Honour;-Sparrow, Frank Edward, M. R. I. A. I., Lieutenant, 129th Field Company, Royal Engineers. Elder son of the late Edward Sparrow, by his wife, Annie (55, Palmerstown Road, Dublin), daughter of William Pillar and grandson of the late Jacob Sparrow, of Cairn Hill, Foxrock, County Dublin. Born in Dublin on 09-November-1878. Educated at Newtown School, Waterford, and the Royal College of Science, Dublin; also matriculating at the Royal University, Ireland. Was engaged as Junior Architect to the Local Government Board, Ireland for several years. Subsequently was appointed temporary Poor Law Inspector. Obtained a commission 16-December-1915. Served with the Expeditionary Force in France and Flanders, and was killed in action, 13-August-1916, while inspecting new ground just taken from the enemy at the Battle of the Somme. Buried in the Military Cemetery, Dives Copse, near Corbie, Picardy. His Commanding Officer wrote; "He was a great loss to us out here.... He was one of the cheeriest and best officers I have met, and his men were very fond of him. There was a groan of dismay when I told them on parade about it. I had a very high opinion of him, and when he was attached to my company and belonged to another, I managed to arrange to get him transferred to me.... He died doing his duty.... We have lost a good officer, and a gallant gentleman, and all of us mourn his loss with you." He was a member of the St. Stephen's Green Club; was also a keen yachtsman and golfer, winning prizes at various clubs to which he belonged.". Grave or Memorial Reference; I C 6. Cemetery: Dive Copse British Cemetery, Sailly-Le-Sec in France. He is also commemorated on the Great War Memorial in St Canice's Cathedral, Kilkenny...'To the Glory of God and in loving memory of the following members of the Diocese of Ossory who gave their lives for their country in the Great War 1914-1918'.

Spillane, Patrick. Rank; Private. Regiment or Service: Royal Irish Regiment. Unit; 6th Battalion. Service Number; 7760. Date of death; 09/09/1916. Born; Thomastown, County Kilkenny. Enlisted; Kilkenny. Residence; Bennetts Bridge, County Kilkenny. Killed in action. Grave or Memorial Reference; Pier and Face 3 A. Cemetery: Thiepval memorial in France

Stackpoole/Stackpole, James. Rank; Private. Regiment or Service: Leinster Regiment. Unit; 2nd Battalion, Action. Service Number; 10729. Date of death; 31/07/1917. Age at death;19. Born; Kilkenny. Enlisted; Carlow. Killed in action. Stackpoole(SDGW, IMR) Stackpole (CWGC), Son of Thomas Albert and Mary Stackpole, of I, High Street, Kilkenny. Notes; Formerly he was with the Royal Irish Regiment where his number was 11499. Grave or Memorial Reference; LV B 3. Cemetery: Tyne Cot Cemetery in Belgium.

Stannage, Thomas. Rank; Corporal. Regiment or Service: Household Cavalry and Cavalry of the line including the Yeomanry and Imperial Camel Corps. Unit; 10th (Prince of Wales Own) Hussars. Service Number; 74010. Date of death; 09/10/1918. Age at death; 26. Born; Rathdowney. Enlisted; Dunblin. Residence; Philipstown. Killed in action. Son of the late Thomas and M. J. Stannage, of Philipstown, King's Co. Grave or Memorial Reference; Panel 5. Cemetery: Vis-En-Artois Memorial in France.

Stapleton, Edward. Rank; Private. Regiment or Service: Royal Irish Regiment. Unit; 7th Battalion (South Irish Horse). Service Number; 7101. Date of death; 22/10/1918. Born; Carrick-on-Suir, County Tipperary. Enlisted; Waterford. Residence; Kilmacow, County Kilkenny. Killed in action. Grave or Memorial Reference; V E 5. Cemetery: Tournai Communal Cemetery Allied Extension in Belgium.

Stapleton, Patrick. Rank; Private. Regiment or Service: Royal Irish Regiment. Service Number; 3837. Date of death; 08/08/1920. Age at death; 45. Born; Kilkenny. Died after discharge. Cemetery: Unknown

Stenning, Shradrach. Rank; Lance Corporal. Regiment or Service: Royal Sussex Regiment. Unit; 1st/4th Battalion. Service Number; L/7514. Date of death; 06/11/1917. Age at death;32. Born; Kirdford, Sussex. Enlisted; Chichester. Killed in action in Egypt. Son of Meshac and Annie Stenning, of Butts Common, Kirdford, Sussex; husband of Ellen Stenning, of Ballygub, Inistioge, Co. Kilkenny. Grave or Memorial Reference; G 70. Cemetery: Beersheba War Cemetery, Israel.

Lieutenant Colonel Stewart, from 'Our Heroes.'

Stewart, Hugh. Rank; Lieutenant Colonel. Regiment or Service: Royal Army Medical Corps. Unit; 94th Field Ambulance. Date of death; 12/04/1918. Age at death; 38. Killed in action. Awarded the DSO and also won the Military Medal. He is listed in the London Gazette. Killed in action. Son of Capt. and Mrs. Stewart, of Kilkenny; husband of Muriel Dalzell Stewart, of 4, Rostrevor Terrace, Rathgar, Dublin. 'Our Heroes'. son of the late Hugh Stewart, Cheshire Regiment, joined the Army Medical Service in 1905, and has since served five years in India. Since the outbreak of hostilities he has been attached to the 10th Field Ambulance (4th Division), and has been mentioned Despatches. Grave or Memorial Reference; B 1. Cemetery: Borre Churchyard, Nord, France

Stone, George. Rank; Private. Regiment or Service: Royal Irish Regiment. Unit; 2nd Battalion. Service Number; 7833. Date of death; 03/09/1916. Age at death;20. Born; Castlecomer, County Kilkenny. Enlisted; Castlecomer. Killed in action. Son of Mrs. Julia Stone, of Market Street, Castlecomer, Co. Kilkenny. Grave or Memorial Reference; XXI I 7. Cemetery: Delville Wood Cemetery, Longueval in France.

Stone, James. Rank; Lance Corporal/Private. Regiment or Service: Royal Irish Regiment. Unit; 7th Battalion (South Irish Horse). Service Number; 7861. Date of death; 21/03/1918. Born; Castlecomer, County Kilkenny. Enlisted; Castlecomer. Killed in action. After his death his effects and property were received by;- (Mother) Mrs Stone, Boherkyle, Castlecomer, County Kilkenny, Ireland. Kilkenny People, September, 1916. Home on Leave. Private James Stone, Royal Irish Regiment, son of Mr John Stone, Boherkile, Castlecomer, is home on a 14 days leave, after being 15 months at the front. Private Stone is a volunteer and before entering the army was in the postal service, Castlecomer. He has come fresh from the fighting line at Guillemont and Ginchy. He was in many sharp engagements and in over a dozen bayonet charges. He is in the bombing company. I am precluded by Censorial arrangements from describing some of the encounters in which his company took part, but suffice to say that the descriptions given in the Press of the deeds of valour of the Irish Regiment were in no way exaggerated, nor up to the reality. He looks well, and speaks—though a Protestant in religion-in the highest terms of praise of the bravery and spirit of devotion of the Catholic Chaplain to his Regiment, who in the midst of shells and machine gun fire and in face of the enemy attended to the wounded in the firing zone, ministering spiritually to them as well as attending to their wounds and for which he has been recommended for the Military Medal and for the D. S. O. Private Stone states that the German doctors captured treat all the wounded and treat them well. Grave or Memorial Reference; II D 14. Cemetery: Templeux-Le-Guerard British Cemetery in France.

Stone, Stephen. Rank; Private. Regiment or Service: Canadian Pioneers. Service Number; 862975. Date of death; 09/11/1917. Killed in action. Next of kin listed as Julia Stone, Market Square, Castlecomer, County Kilkenny. Place of birth, Kilkenny. Date of birth, March-12-1889. Occupation on enlistment, Teamster. Place and date of enlistment, Toronto, Canada, 08-March-1916. Address on enlistment, 1003, Keele Street, Toronto, Canada. Height, 5 feet, 5 ¾ inches. Complexion, fresh. Eyes, brown. Hair, auburn. Grave or Memorial Reference; M 6. Cemetery: Oxford Road Cemetery, Ieper, West-Vlaanderen, Belgium.

Strong, Albert Ernest. Rank; Lance Corporal. Regiment or Service: Royal Inniskilling Fusiliers. Unit; 7th Battalion. Service Number; 28746. Date of death; 16/08/1917. Age at death; 21. Born; Thomastown, County Kilkenny. Enlisted; Clydebank. Killed in action. Son of Edward and Marion Strong, of 46, Coldwell Street, Kingstown, Co. Dublin. Born at Thomastown, Co. Kilkenny. Limerick Chronicle, August, 1918. Deaths. Strong—August 16, 1918, wounded and missing, now reported dead, Lance Corporal Albert Ernest Strong, R Inniskilling Fusiliers, aged 21 years, youngest son of Edward and Marian Strong, late of Thomastown, County Kilkenny. Weekly Irish Times, August 24, 1918. Strong-August 16, 1917, wounded and missing, now reported dead, Lance Corporal Albert Ernest Strong, R Inniskilling Fusiliers, son of Edward and Marian Strong, late of Thomastown, County Kilkenny. Grave or Memorial Reference; Panel 70 to 72. Cemetery: Tyne Cot Memorial in Belgium.

Image courtesy of Jim Corcoran.

Sullivan, James. Rank; Private. Regiment or Service: Royal Irish Regiment. Unit; 1st Battalion. Service Number; 4583. Date of death; 27/06/1915. Age at death;20. Born; Callan, County Kilkenny. Enlisted; Kilkenny. Residence; Callan. Died of wounds. Son of James Sullivan, of Rathculbin, Kells, Co. Kilkenny. Grave or Memorial Reference; I D 55. Cemetery: Bailleul Communal Cemetery Extension (Nord) in France.

Sullivan, John. Rank; Private. Regiment or Service: Australian Infantry. Unit; 26th Battalion. Service Number; 4586. Date of death; 14/12/1916. Age at death; 32. Enlisted; Brisbane Queensland. Wounded in France on 5-8-1916. Gunshot wounds to the arms and legs. After treatment he was discharged on 13-December-1916. He died the day after. Cause of death; Fracture of skull (accident on Railway line). He felt sick during a train journey and put his head out of a window to vomit and his head struck a tunnel or bridge. His enlistment document states he was born in Tipperary, His Mother lived in Ballingarry in Tipperary and he was a 29 year old labourer when he joined up. This conflicts with information from other sources. Supplementary information; Son of John and Alice Doheny, of Callow, Co. Kilkenny, Ireland. Born at Harley Park, Callow, Co Kilkenny. Documentary evidence was produced and his name on the official records. Waterford News, December, 1915;-Kikenny Soldier's Terrible Death. While travelling by the Irish Mail train from Holyhead to London yesterday morning, Private John Sullivan, Australian Imperial Forces, put his head out of the window, and came in contact with a tunnel. He sustained severe injuries, and was conveyed to hospital at Bangor, where he died. His next of kin lives at Horley Park, Callan, County Kilkenny. Notes; Alias, true family name was Dohney. Grave or Memorial Reference; W OG 704A. Cemetery: Bangor, Flandva (Glanadda) Cemetery in Wales.

Sweeney, Charles W. Rank; Acting Lance Corporal. Regiment or Service: King's (Liverpool) Regiment. Unit; 3rd Battalion. Service Number; 16208. Date of death; 10/10/1918. Born; Kilkenny. Enlisted; Liverpool. Residence; Liverpool. Died at sea. The RMS Leinster sank on this day. and the victims are remembered on the Hollybrook Memorial,. Cemetery: Hollybrook Memorial, Southampton UK.

T

Talbot, Luke. Rank; Private. Regiment or Service: North Staffordhsire Regiment. Unit; 1st/6th Battalion. Service Number; 260037. Date of death; 14/06/1917. Age at death; 25. Born; Kilkenny. Enlisted; Glasgow. Residence; Kilkenny. Killed in action. Son of Patrick Talbot, of John's Green, Kilkenny. In his Will, dated 06-June-1917, his effects and property were received by;- Property and effects now at 12 Cumberland Street, East Glasgow in the care of Mrs Stark to (Father) Mrs P Talbot, Johns Green, Kilkenny, Ireland. Notes; Formerly he was with the Lowland Division, Royal Engineers where his number was 5125. Grave or Memorial Reference; II C 16. Cemetery: Maroc British Cemetery, Grenay in France.

Tallis, Harry. Rank; Second Officer. Regiment or Service: H M Merchant Service. Date of death; 23/10/1918. Age at death;23. Born; Kilkenny. Died in hospital. Son of William and Charlotte, brother of Frederick Tallis of High Street, Kilkenny. Notes; Died of influenza in the Royal Infirmary, Bristol. Cemetery: Great War Memorial in St Canice's Cathedral, Kilkenny. 'To the Glory of God and in loving memory of the following members of the Diocese of Ossory who gave their lives for their country in the Great War 1914-1918'.

Taylor, James. Rank; Private. Regiment or Service: Connaught Rangers. Unit; "B" Coy. 5th Battalion. Service Number; 5429. Date of death; 13/10/1918. Age at death; 23. Born; Urlingford. Enlisted; Templemore. Residence; Urlingford. Died. Son of Mrs. Kate Taylor, of Shamrock Street, Urlingford, Co. Kilkenny. Grave or Memorial Reference; Memorial 1. Cemetery: Le Quesnoy Communal Cemetery Extension, Nord, France.

Tector, Ralph S. Rank; Private. Regiment or Service: American Army. Unit; Engineers. Date of death; 11/10/1918. Died in a Military Hospital in London on 11-October-1918. Born 28-June-1898 in Philadelphia, Pennsylvania, USA. Parents Samuel and Emily Tector were Irish by birth and his grandmother lived with her brother Arthur J. Wilsdon at Lacken Lodge, Kilkenny. His family are listed as living on the Dublin Road in the 1911 Census but are not in the 1901. They returned to the USA (Chicago) aboard the S. S. Cedric departing from Liverpool on 03-December-1919. Cemetery: Great War Memorial in St Canice's Cathedral, Kilkenny…'To the Glory of God and in loving memory of the following members of the Diocese of Ossory who gave their lives for their country in the Great War 1914-1918'.

Teehan, James. Rank; Private. Regiment or Service: Royal Irish Regiment. Unit; 1st Battalion. Service Number; 9934. Date of death; 17/04/1916. Born; St Canice's, Kilkenny. Enlisted; Kilkenny. Killed in action in Salonika. Cemetery: Doiran Memorial in Greece.

Tennyson, Patrick. Rank; Private. Regiment or Service: Connaught Rangers. Unit; 1st Battalion. Service Number; 6035. Date of death; 18/10/1916. Age at death;38. Born; Kilkenny. Enlisted; Greenock. Residence; Kilkenny. Died in Mesopotamia. Son of Timothy and Mary Tennyson, of Kilkenny. Grave or Memorial Reference; XIV F 22. Cemetery: Amara War Cemetery in Iraq

Tidmarsh, John Moriarty. Rank; Lieutenant. Regiment or Service: Duke of Wellingtons West Riding Regiment. Unit; 12th Battalion attached to the Royal Flying Corps. Date of death; 03/09/1918. Kilkenny People, September-1918;-Accidental Death of Lieutenant Tidmarsh. We regret to record the accidental death of Lieutenant John Moriarty Tidmarsh, of the Aerial Force, which occurred through his machine colliding with another at a high elevation in Yorkshire. He was the son of Mr David Tidmarsh, a native of Kilkenny, and long resident in Limerick, of which he is one of the most popular citizens. He was the grandson of the late James M. Tidmarsh, mayor of Kilkenny in 1855. many of the older citizens, especially the people of St John's parish, remember the Tidmarsh family as the most benevolent and charitable which has ever occupied Sion Villa. Grave or Memorial Reference; 32096. Cemetery: Limerick (St. Lawrence's) Catholic Cemetery, Limerick.

Tierney, James. Rank; Lance Corporal/Private. Regiment or Service: Royal Irish Regiment. Unit; 6th Battalion. Service Number; 2059. Date of death; 15/04/1916. Born; Callan. Enlisted; Kilkenny. Residence; Callan. Killed in action. Grave or Memorial Reference; E 4. Cemetery: Bois-Carre Military Cemetery, Haisns in France.

Tobin, Edward James. Rank; Private. Regiment or Service: Royal Irish Regiment. Unit; 2nd Battalion. Service Number; 9186. Date of death; 21/04/1917. Age at death; 29. Born; Paulstown, County Kilkenny. Enlisted; Carlow. Residence; Paulstown. Died. Son of Thomas and Mary Tobin, of Paulstown, Co. Kilkenny; husband of Una May Queripel Ferguson (formerly Tobin), of 24, Paris Street, Guernsey. Grave or Memorial Reference; 69. Cemetery: Vevey (St Martins) Cemetery, Switzerland.

Tobin, James. Rank; Private. Regiment or Service: Royal Irish Regiment. Unit; 4th Battalion. Service Number; 2860. Date of death; 04/01/1917. Born; St Mary's, Kilkenny. Enlisted; Tipperary. Residence; Kilkenny. Died at home. Son of Mrs M Tobin of Garden Row, Kilkenny. Grave or Memorial Reference; In the North West part. Cemetery: Kilkenny New Cemetery, Kilkenny.

Tobin, Michael. Rank; Private. Regiment or Service: Royal Irish Regiment. Unit; 5th Battalion. Service Number; 8032. Date of death; 04/02/1915. Born; Ownin, County Kilkenny. Enlisted; Clonmel, County Tipperary. Residence; Castletown, County Kilkenny. Died in Salonika. Grave or Memorial Reference; 76. Cemetery: Salonika (Lembet Road) Military Cemetery in Greece.

Tombe/Toombe, George. Rank; Lance Corporal. Regiment or Service: Royal Inniskilling Fusiliers. Unit; 9th Battalion. Service Number; 25982. Date of death; 01/07/1916. Born; Rostrevor, County Down. Enlisted; Clonmel, County Tipperary. Killed in action. Tombe (CWGC) Toombe (SDGW),. Notes; Formerly he was with the Rifle Brigade where his number was 10743. Grave or Memorial Reference; Pier and Face 4D and. Cemetery: Thiepval Memorial in France.

Tone, John. Rank; Private. Regiment or Service: Royal Irish Regiment. Unit; 1st Battalion. Service Number; 4477. Date of death; 19/04/1915. Age at death; 19. Born; Urlingford, County Kilkenny. Enlisted; Templemore. Residence; Urlingford. Killed in action. Son of John and Kate Tone, of Urlingford, Co. Kilkenny. In his Will, dated 17-November1914, his effects and property were received by;- Mrs C Tone, Main St, Urlingford, Kilkenny. Grave or Memorial Reference; Panel 33. Cemetery: Ypres (Menin Gate) Memorial in Belgium

Trehy, Kiernan. Rank; Private. Regiment or Service: Royal Dublin Fusiliers. Unit; 7th Battalion. Service Number; 27031. Date of death; 31/05/1917. Born; Kilkenny. Enlisted; Dublin. Died of wounds in the Balkans. Grave or Memorial Reference; V H 11. Cemetery: Struma Military Cemetery in Greece.

Troy, Martin. Rank; Private. Regiment or Service: Royal Irish Regiment. Unit; 5th Battalion. Service Number; 42. Date of death; 14/02/1919. Age at death; 42. Born; St Patrick's, Kilkenny. Died . Cemetery: Unknown

Troy, Thomas. Rank; Lance Corporal. Regiment or Service: Royal Irish Regiment. Unit; 2nd Battalion. Service Number; 6402. Date of death; 24/08/1914. Age at death;36. Born; Kilkenny. Enlisted; Kilkenny. Killed in action. Son of John and Mary Troy, of Walkin Street, Kilkenny; husband of Sarah Ann Troy, of 18, Victor Street, Mountain Ash, Glam. Grave or Memorial Reference; Special Memorial 5. Cemetery: St Symphorien Military Cemetery in Belgium.

Tudenham, Maurice. Rank; Private. Regiment or Service: Irish Guards. Unit; 2nd Battalion. Service Number; 6898. Date of death; 30/09/1915. Born; Kilkenny. Enlisted; Deptford, Essex. Killed in action. Grave or Memorial Reference; Panel 9 and 10. Cemetery: Loos Memorial in France.

Tynan, John. Rank; Private. Regiment or Service: King's (Liverpool) Regiment. Unit; 1st Battalion. Service Number; 8138. Date of death; 10/03/1915. Age at death;40. Born; Dublin. Enlisted; The Curragh Camp. Residence; Kilkenny. Killed in action at Givenchy. Son of Ellen McCabe (formerly Tynan), of Poulgour, Co. Kilkenny, and the late Patrick Tynan. His effects and property were willed to ;- Mrs Isabella Tynan, 72 Brook Street. Miss Rose Kenny, Manor House, Didbury. Grave or Memorial Reference; IX F 16. Cemetery: Vielle-Chapelle New Military Cemetery, Lacouture, Pas-de-Calais, France.

Tynan, Patrick. Rank; Private. Regiment or Service: Royal Dublin Fusiliers. Unit; 1st Battalion. Service Number; 11210. Date of death; 04/07/1915. Born; Kilkenny. Enlisted; Carlow. Residence; Kilkenny. Killed in Action in Gallipoli. In his Will, dated 22-March-1915, his effects and property were received by;- Mr Michael Tynan, Abbey Street, Kilkenny, Ireland. Notes; Initially listed as missing, later changed to killed in Action in Gallipoli. Grave or Memorial Reference; Panel 190 to 196. Cemetery: Helles Memorial in Turkey

U-V

Vickers, Thomas Bernard. Rank; Lieutenant. Regiment or Service: Queen Victoria's Own Sappers and Miners. Unit; 2nd, attached to the 14th Field Company, Royal Engineers. Date of death; 16/07/1921. Age at death;24. Born; Mexico. Residence; Coolroe, Graiguenamanagh, County Kilkenny. Cemetery: Unknown

Vigors, Arthur Cecil. Rank; Second Lieutenant. Regiment or Service: Royal Munster Fusiliers. Unit; 9th Battalion. Attached to the 3rd Bn Royal Dublin Fusiliers. Date of death; 09/09/1916. Age at death; 21. Killed in action at Ginchy. Son of Hannah Marion Vigors, of Blessington, Co. Wicklow, and the late Charles Henry Vigors. Brother Capt. C. H. Vigors also died in service. Grave or Memorial Reference; Pier and Face 16 C. Cemetery: Theipval Memorial in France. He is also commemorated on the Great War Memorial in St Canice's Cathedral, Kilkenny…'To the Glory of God and in loving memory of the following members of the Diocese of Ossory who gave their lives for their country in the Great War 1914-1918'. He is listed under the Cheshire Regiment and also under the Royal Munster Fusiliers.

Vigors, Charles Henry. Rank; Captain (Acting Major). Regiment or Service: Cheshire Regiment. Unit; 12th Battalion. Date of death; 18/09/1918. Age at death;28. Killed in Action in the Balkans. He won the Military Cross and is listed in the London Gazette. Croix de Guerre with palms (France). Son of Hannah Marion Vigor, of Blessington, Co. Wicklow and the late Charles Henry Vigors; Husband of Kate Mary Vigors, of 33, Church St, Lenton, Nottingham. Brother 2nd Lt. A. C. Vigors also died on service. Limerick Chronicle, March, 1918. The Military Cross. Captain (the Lieutenant) C H Vigors, 12th S Battalion, Cheshire Regiment, was awarded the Military Cross in November last, for conspicuous gallantry and devotion to duty in the field, on an Eastern Front. Captain Vigors obtained his commission fro the Nottingham University, O. T. C, in December, 1914. His only brother was killed at the battle of Ginchy. He is elder son of Mr and Mrs C Vigors, Kells, County Kilkenny, formerly of Pallas, County Limerick. Notes; Cause of death listed as Killed in Action on Pip ridge in the Balkans. Cemetery: Doiran Memorial in Greece.

Villiers-Stuart, Charles Herbert. Rank; Major. Regiment or Service: Indian Army. Unit; 56th Punjabi Rifles (Frontier Force) attached to H. Q. Staff Australian and N. Z. Army Corps. Date of death; 17/05/1915. Age at death; 40. Killed in action. Son of Col. Villiers-Stuart, of Castletown, Carrick-on-Suir, Ireland; husband of Joan Villiers-Stuart, of Troquhain, Balmaclellan, Kirkcudbrightshire, Scotland. Munster Express, May 1915. Major Herbert Villiers Stuart. Killed in Action. Mrs Villiers Stuart, Castleane, Carrick-on-Suir, has been informed that her son, Major Herbert Villiers Stuart, was killed in action a few days ago at the Dardanelles. Deep sympathy is felt in Carrick and the adjoining districts for Mrs Villiers Stuart and the Misses Villiers Stuart in their bereavement. Tow other sons of Mrs Villers Stuart are on active service at the front. Munster Express, June, 1915. Late Major Villiers Stuart. On the proposition of Mr Morrissey, seconded by Mr Bowers, a resolution was unanimously adopted to Mrs Villiers Stuart and family, Castleane, Carrick-on-Suir, on the death of Major Herbert Villiers Stuart, who was killed at the Dardanelles. Mr Morrissey said the late Major

Villiers Stuart's father was for many years an active member of the board and a very kind hearted gentleman. Limerick Chronicle, May, 1915. Major Villiers Stewart, killed at the Dardanelles, was a son of the late Lieutenant-Colonel Villiers Stuart, Castlane, Carrick-on-Suir, Much sympathy is felt in the district with his mother and sisters, who have been always identified with charitable movements. Irish Independent; Major C H Villiers Stuart, of Castleane, Carrick-on-Suir, who was killed in action left property of the gross value of £2,313. 26/05/1915. Freeman's Journal. Killed in Action-Major Villiers Stuart, son of the late Lieutenant Colonel Villiers Stuart, Castlane Carrick-on-Suir, has been killed in action on the Dardanelles. Deep sympathy is felt in Carrick-on-Suir district for his mother, Mrs Villiers Stuart, and for his sisters, all of whom have always been prominently identified with every charitable movement in the town and district. Freeman's Journal, 26/05/1915. Killed in Action. -Major Villiers Stuart, son of the late Lieutenant Colonel Villiers Stuart, Castlane, Carrick-on-Suir, has been killed in action in the Dardanelles. Deep sympathy is felt in Carrick-on-Suir district for his mother, all of whom have always been prominently identified with every charitable movement in the town and district. Grave or Memorial Reference; I H 4. Cemetery: Beach Cemetery, Anzac, Turkey. He is also commemorated on the Great War Memorial in St Canice's Cathedral, Kilkenny…'To the Glory of God and in loving memory of the following members of the Diocese of Ossory who gave their lives for their country in the Great War 1914-1918'.

W

Waldron, Francis. Rank; Lance Corporal. Regiment or Service: Royal Irish Regiment. Unit; "A" Coy. 2nd Battalion. Service Number; 7780. Date of death; 14/07/1916. Age at death;19. Born; St John's, Kilkenny. Enlisted; Kilkenny. Killed in action. Son of Thomas and Anne Waldron, of Maudlin Street, Kilkenny. Grave or Memorial Reference; Pier and Face 3 A. Cemetery: Thiepval Memorial in France.

Walker, John. Rank; Private. Regiment or Service: Northumberland Fusiliers. Unit; No. 2 Coy. 25th (Tyneside Irish) Battalion. Service Number; 25/734. Date of death; 26/10/1916. Age at death; 34. Born; Kilkenny. Enlisted; Newcastle-on-Tyne. Killed in action. Son of Michael and Ellen Walker, of Coolbawn, Castlecomer, Co. Kilkenny; husband of Sarah Ann Walker, of 2, Stable Street, Cornsay Colliery, Co. Durham. Grave or Memorial Reference; IV A 20. Cemetery: Cite Bonjean Military Cemetery, Armentieres in France

Walker, Thomas. Rank; Private. Regiment or Service: Royal Dublin Fusiliers. Unit; 2nd Battalion. Service Number; 5596. Date of death; 28/06/1916. Born; Mallow, County Cork. Enlisted; Carlow. Residence; Kilkenny. Killed in action. Brother of William (4724) listed below. Grave or Memorial Reference; I D 29. Cemetery: Bard Cottage Cemetery in Belgium.

Walker, William. Rank; Private. Regiment or Service: Leinster Regiment. Unit; 2nd Battalion. Service Number; 4724. Date of death; 31/07/1917. Enlisted; Kilkenny. Residence; Kilkenny. Killed in action. Brother of Thomas (5596) listed above. Kilkenny People, March, 1918. The Home Fires Won't be Burning. When the Boys Come Home. Kate Walker, widow of the Callan Road, gave three sons to "fight for the liberty of small nations" in France and Belgium. If they were three munition workers in England they would now be earning an aggregate of about £20 per week, and they would be able to keep their widowed mother in luxury. They went out to fight, however, and according to the mother "she had lost one son in the war, another was missing since the 31st August." The third is in receipt of the magnificent stipend of 6s. 4d. per week. If she paid her rent punctually to her landlord Major Hanford, of Flood Hall, she would be a profiteer on 4s. 10d. per week, with the extra advantage of knowing that her three boys were "doing their bit," were "making the world safe for democracy," and particularly safe for Major Hanford, one of the wealthiest men in the county, and would be able to afford an occasional tear (the only thing she could afford) for the Belgian refugees turned out of their homes by the "Huns." She did not pay the rent, however, and when summoned for possession of her mansion before the petty sessions on Tuesday she made the ridiculous plea that "the war was the cause of her not being able to pay the rent." During the last three years we had countless "flag days" in Kilkenny, and fashionably dressed women went around rattling collection boxes for the Poles, and the Serbians and the Rumanians. None of the money appears to have gone the way of Mrs Walker, she being neither a Pole, a Serb nor a Rumanian. If she now has to take refuge in the workhouse she will probably come across a saying of Madame Roland; "Liberty, what crimes are committed in thy name!" Or perhaps she may happen along another wise saying attributed to another distinguished lady of the pre-Revolutionary period in France, who, when told that the people had no bread to eat, innocently inquired,"Then why don't they eat cake?" The following is the report of the case before a particular large bench of magistrates at the petty sessions;-Major R. T. H. Hanford, D. L., Flood Hall, sought a decree for possession of a house held by Kate Walker at the Callan Road at the weekly rent of 1s. 6d. Mr A. F. Watters, solicitor, apperared for Major Hanford. Defendant pleaded that the war was the cause of her not being able to pay the rent. Mr Joseph Bannan, agent, said this case was before the court 12 months ago, when the defendant gave an undertaking to pay up, but she hadn't made any effort to do so. Defendant said she had lost a son in the war, another was a prisoner of war and a third was missing since the 31st of last August. Mr Watters said that when the case was before the court previously the defendant promised to pay up the arrears when she received some "back" money that was coming to her from the War Office. The defendant said at that time she expected a sum of over £3 which one of her sons was signing over to her, but she never got it. Mr Watters—She has sixteen months in the house now without paying rent. Mayor—She ought to try and pay something. Defendant—I have nothing to pay it-if I had I would pay it. The couple of shillings I get go for a bit of coal and other things, and I don't have anything left. Mr Sullivan—I certainly think that Major Hanford has given you a good deal of latitude. Mr Watters—if she made any effort at all to pay we would not have pressed her. Mr Brennan—She has a son-in-law in the house with her and he won't work. I offered him work myself and he would not take it. Defendant's son-in-law said he had a house of his own from Mr Fenton for about the past twelve months. Mr Sullivan—You ought to assist your mother-in-law. Witness said he did assist her, and were it not for that she would have to go into the workhouse long ago. —A decree for possession was given. Grave or Memorial Reference; III M 8. Cemetery: Oxford Road Cemetery in Belgium.

Wall, James. Rank; Fireman. Regiment or Service: Mercantile Marine. Unit; S. S."Coningbeg" (Glasgow). Date of death; 18/12/1917. Age at death;42. Torpedoed by German Submarine U-62. There were no survivors. U62 surrendered in November 1918. Son of the late James and Johanna Wall; husband of Bridget Wall (nee Roche), of 13, Grange Terrace, Waterford, Ireland. Born at Slieverue Co. Kilkenny. Cemetery: Tower Hill Memorial in the UK. He is also listed on the Formby-Coningbeg Memorial, Adelphi Quay in Waterford City.

Wall, James. Rank; Private. Regiment or Service: Royal Dublin Fusiliers. Unit; 2nd Battalion. Service Number; 18951. Date of death; 21/03/1918. Born; Butt's, County Kilkenny. Enlisted; Kilkenny. Killed in action. Grave or Memorial Reference; Panel 79 and 80. Cemetery: Pozieres Memorial in France.

Wall, Mark. Rank; Private. Regiment or Service: Royal Irish Regiment. Unit; "C" Coy. 5th Battalion. Service Number; 7565. Date of death; 19/12/1917. Age at death;25. Born; Slieverue, County Kilkenny. Enlisted; Waterford. Died at home. Son of Thomas and Margaret Wall, of Hollow House, Abbey Lands, Ferry Bank, Waterford. Munster Express, January, 1918. Waterford Soldiers Death. The death occurred at the 2nd Southern General Hospital, Bristol, on the 129th December, of Private Mark Wall, Royal Irish Regiment. The deceased, who was aged 26 years, was a native of Sallypark, Waterford, and joined the army in 1915. His service was unbroken by any term of sickness until July last when he underwent a surgical operation and from which point his health seems to have broken down. He was marked for home and arrived at Bristol on the 22nd November. His condition became worse, so much so that his parents were summoned ad he breathed his last in the presence of his mother and sister. He was interred with military honours at Arnos Vale Cemetery, Bristol. Grave or Memorial Reference; Screen Wall. War Plot. C. 9. Cemetery: Bristol (Arnos Vale) Roman Catholic Cemetery, UK.

Wall, Michael. Rank; Lance Corporal. Regiment or Service: Household Cavalry and Cavalry of the line including the Yeomanry and Imperial Camel Corps. Unit; Unit; 6th Dragoons (Inniskilling). Service Number; 21207. Date of death; 01/02/1917. Born; Freshford, County Kilkenny. Enlisted; Kilkenny. Killed in action. Grave or Memorial Reference; Panel 1. Cemetery: Cambrai Memorial in Louveral in France

Wall, Patrick. Rank; Fireman. Regiment or Service: Mercantile Marine. Unit; Unit: S. S."Coningbeg" (Glasgow). Date of death; 18/12/1917. Torpedoed by German Submarine U-62. There were no survivors. of Catherine and the late Mark Wall; husband of Mary Catherine Wall (nee Connolly), of 94, Gracedieu Rd, Waterford, Ireland. Born in Co. Kilkenny. Cemetery: Tower Hill Memorial in the UK. He is also listed on the Formby-Coningbeg Memorial, Adelphi Quay in Waterford City.

Wallace, James. Rank; Private. Regiment or Service: Irish Guards. Unit; Reserve Battalion. Service Number; 4226. Born; Aughaviller, County Kilkenny. Enlisted; Kilkenny. Died at home. Son of Mrs Margaret Wallace, of Co. Kilkenny. In his Will, dated 14-August-1914, his effects and property were received by;- (Mother) Mrs Margaret Wallace, Hagginstown, Knocktopher, County Kilkenny, Ireland. Cemetery: Brookwood (United Kingdom 1914-18) Memorial, 30 Miles from London.

Wallace, William. Rank; Private. Regiment or Service: Royal Irish Regiment. Unit; 1st Battalion. Service Number; 8980. Date of death; 25/08/1915. Age at death;26. Born; Clough, County Kilkenny. Enlisted; Ballydaniel, County Kilkenny. Residence; Clough. Died of wounds. Son of Mrs. Katie Conville, of Clogh, Castlecomer, Co. Kilkenny. Grave or Memorial Reference; VIII B 75. Cemetery: Boulogne Eastern Cemetery in France.

Walsh, James. Rank; Private. Regiment or Service: Royal Irish Regiment. Unit; 1st Battalion. Service Number; 4202. Date of death; 16/03/1915. Born; Muckalee, County Kilkenny. Enlisted; Kilkenny. Residence; Coolcullen, County Kilkenny. Killed in action. Son of John and Margaret Walsh, of Seskin Rea, Old Leighlin, Bagenalstown, Co. Carlow. Tipperary Star, November, 1914. Urlingford & Johnstown Notes. Prisoners. Private James Walsh, 18th Royal Irish, Private John Fanning, 4th Hussars, are both prisoners in Germany. Fanning has four other brothers at the front. Patrick Norton of the 4th Royal Irish, has been wounded and is at present in Plymouth Hospital. At the present time there are 42 from Urlingford at the front. Grave or Memorial Reference; Panel 33. Cemetery: Ypres (Menin Gate) Memorial in Belgium.

Walsh, James. Rank; Private. Regiment or Service: Royal Munster Fusiliers. Unit; 8th Battalion. Service Number; 4771. Date of death; 26/05/1916. Age at death;38. Born; Kilkenny. Enlisted; Liverpool. Residence; Liverpool. Killed in action. Husband of Florence Webb (formerly Walsh), of 363. Longmoor Lane, Fazakerley, Liverpool. Grave or Memorial Reference; I E 5. Cemetery: Philosophe British Cemetery, Mazingarbe in France.

Walsh, John. Rank; Lance Corporal. Regiment or Service: Royal Dublin Fusiliers. Unit; "A" Coy. 2nd Battalion. Service Number; 43060. Date of death; 16/08/1917. Age at death; 21. Born; Gowran, County Kilkenny. Enlisted; Kilkenny. Residence; Ratheash, County Kilkenny. Killed in action. Son of William and Ellen Walsh, of Rathcash Clifden, Co. Kilkenny. Notes; Formerly he was with the Royal Irish Regiment where his number was 5386. Grave or Memorial Reference; Panel 144 to 145. Cemetery: Tyne Cot Memorial in Belgium.

Walsh, Michael. Rank; Private. Regiment or Service: Royal Irish Rifles. Unit; 7th Battalion. Service Number; 5930. Date of death; 08/03/1917. Born; Killarney, County Kerry. Enlisted; Tralee. Residence; Kilkenny. Killed in action. Grave or Memorial Reference; N 60. Cemetery: Kemmel Chateau Military Cemetery in Belgium.

Walsh, Michael Joseph. Rank; Private. Regiment or Service: Canadian Infantry (Western Ontario Regiment). Unit. Unit; 47th Battalion. Service Number; 2020170. Date of death; 16/02/1919. Age at death; 31. Son of the late Richard and Johanna Walsh, of Highrath, Callan, Co. Kilkenny, Ireland. Born, Highwrath, Callan, Kilkenny, Ireland. Address on enlistment; Edward Hotel, Vancouver, B. C. Occupation on enlistment, Labourer. Date of birth; -02-March-1886. Next of kin details; (sister) Helen Walsh, 6557, Langley Avenue. Chicago, USA. Place and date of enlistment, 12-December-1916, Vancouver. Height, 5 feet, 9 ½ inches. Complexion, fair. Eyes, grey. Hair, brown. Grave or Memorial Reference: K. 228. Cemetery: Epsom Cemetery, UK. Grave or Memorial Reference; K 228. Cemetery: Epsom Cemetery, UK.

Walsh, Nicholas. Rank; Regimental Sergeant Major. Regiment or Service: Canadian Infantry (Alberta Regiment). Unit; 49th Battalion. Service Number; 432178. Date of death; 24/09/1916. Age at death;48. Awards: M C, Mentioned in Despatches Next of kin listed as (father), James Walsh, Ireland. Place of birth, Baronsland, Bennettsbridge County Kilkenny. Date of birth, 12-June-1876. Occupation on enlistment, Clerk. Place and date of enlistment, 04-January-1915, Edmonton. Address on enlistment,. Height, 5 feet, 11 inches. Complexion, fair. Eyes, blue. Hair, brown. Previous military experience; 8 years with the Royal Dublin Fusiliers. Kilkenny People, September, 1916. Thomastown Soldier Dies of Wounds. On Monday morning last a telegram was received in Thomastown conveying the sad intelligence that Regimental Sergeant Major, Nicholas Walsh, 4th Canadian Battalion, Edmonton Regiment, had died of wounds received in action in France. The deceased soldier had only arrived in England and was it is stated on his way to the military hospital at Leeds in which city the sad event took place. He was a native of Baronsland, Thomastown, where his parents and relatives who are respected and well-to-do members of the farming community reside. Four months ago he married Miss Grace, Thomastown, while on six days leave from the front. Last April he was specially commended by his commanding officer and mentioned in despatches for gallantry and courageous conduct in rescuing wounded men from blown-in dug-outs and carrying them to a place of safety. He was subsequently awarded the D. C. M. The greatest sympathy is felt for his young widow, parents, brothers and sisters, in their bereavement. Kilkenny People, February, 1917. Posthumous Honours for Irish Soldier. On Wednesday in Cork, Major-General Doran presented to Mrs Walsh the Military Cross which had been awarded to her late husband, Regimental Sergeant Major Walsh, of the 49th Canadian Battalion, for conspicuous gallantry. The presentation was made at a parade of men of the Royal Field Artillery, Royal Dublin Fusiliers and Leinster Regiment, and was witnessed by a large number of the citizens, including the Lord Mayor and Lady Mayoress. Sergeant-Major Walsh was a native of Thomastown, County Kilkenny, and his widow at present resides in Cork. Grave or Memorial Reference; In the South West part. Cemetery: Bennetsbridge Catholic Churchyard, County Kilkenny.

Walsh, Patrick. Rank; Private. Regiment or Service: Royal Irish Regiment. Unit; C Company, 2nd Battalion. Service Number; 6906. Date of death; 24/05/1915. Age at death; 39. Born; Carrigeen, County Kilkenny. Enlisted; Waterford. Residence; Mooncoin, County Kilkenny. Killed in action. Son of John and Mary Walsh, of Ballygorey Cottage, Mooncoin, Co. Kilkenny. Enlisted August, 1914. Grave or Memorial Reference; Pier and Face 3 A. Cemetery: Thiepval Memorial in France.

Walsh, Patrick. Rank; Private. Regiment or Service: Irish Guards. Unit; 1st Battalion. Service Number; 10081/10061. Date of death; 24/09/1916. Age at death; 25. Born; Kilmacow, County Kilkenny. Enlisted; Waterford. Died of wounds. Son of Peter and Johanna Walsh, of Miltown, Kilmacow, Waterford. Munster Express October-14-1916;- Killed in Action. News was also received this week of the death of private P. Walsh, Irish Guards, who was killed in action last week. Before joining the army deceased lived at Miltown, Kilmacow, and was employed at the Greenville Roller Mils. Notes; Number listed as 10081 (CWGC), 10061 (SDGW). Grave or Memorial Reference; II C 56. Cemetery: Dartmoor Cemetery, Becordel-Becourt in France.

Walsh, Patrick. Rank; Private. Regiment or Service: Royal Irish Regiment. Unit; 1st Battalion. Service Number; 5134. Date of death; 29/01/1915. Born; St Patrick's, Waterford. Enlisted; Tipperary. Residence; Waterford. Died of wounds. Kilkenny Journal, February, 1915. Death of Kilkenny Soldier at the Front. It is also reported that Private Patrick Walsh, Royal Irish Regiment (son of the late Mr Andrew Walsh, Merchant, High Street,) has been killed in action. Grave or Memorial Reference; B 8. Cemetery: Dickiebusch New Military Cemetery in Belgium.

Walsh, Richard. Rank; Private. Regiment or Service: Irish Guards. Unit; "B" Coy. 1st Battalion. Service Number; 4250. Date of death; 10/12/1914. Age at death; 23. Born; Callan, County Kilkenny. Enlisted; Kilkenny. Died of wounds at home. Son of Patrick and Mary Walsh, of 9, Green Street, Callan, Co. Kilkenny. Kilkenny People, December 1914. Callan Soldier's Death. Widespread regret has been caused by the news of the death of Private Richard Walsh, Callan, who died on Friday last as a result of a gunshot wound, at Netley Abbey Hospital, to which he was transferred some time previous from Boulogne. The deceased, who was a splendid type of Irish manhood— he was 6 feet 2 inches in height—and a great athlete, joined the Irish Guards two years ago, and was a great favourite with his officers and comrades. At the outbreak of war he was sent to the front with his regiment, and was in many engagements, including the battle of Mons, where he received gunshot wounds to the legs and arms. The internment took place on Monday last with full military honours, in the military cemetery, Netley, the deceased's father, Mr Patrick Walsh, and sister, Miss Bridget Walsh, Green Street, being present. The Catholic Chaplain of the hospital read the burial service. The deceased was a member of the John Locke H. C., and played with the team which won the second division county championship and the semi-final of Leinster in 1912. On Monday the deceased's father received the following;--"Irish Guards Record Office, Buckingham Gate, S. W. —The King commands me to assure you of the true sympathy of His Majesty and the Queen in your sorrow. —Signed "KITCHENER."At a meeting of the John Locke H. C. a resolution was passed on the motion of Mr M. Joyce, seconded by Mr J. Fogarty expressing regret at the death of the deceased and tendering their sympathy to his bereaved parents. Grave or Memorial Reference; R C 822. Cemetery: Netley Military Cemetery, Hampshire, UK.

Walsh, Richard. Rank; Private. Regiment or Service: Royal Irish Regiment. Unit; 6th Battalion. Service Number; 11102. Date of death; 03/09/1916. Born; Green Hill, County Kilkenny. Enlisted; Kilkenny. Died of wounds. He won the Military Medal and is listed in the London Gazette. Grave or Memorial Reference; Pier and Face 3 A. Cemetery: Theipval Memorial in France.

Walsh, William. Rank; Private. Regiment or Service: Royal Irish Regiment. Unit; 2nd Battalion. Service Number; 6520. Date of death; 23/08/1914. Age at death; 34. Born; Callan, County Kilkenny. Enlisted; Kilkenny. Died of wounds at home. Son of William and Ellen Walsh, of Rathcash, Clyden, Co. Kilkenny. Grave or Memorial Reference; I A 9. Cemetery: St Symphorien Military Cemetery in Belgium.

Walsh, William. Rank; Private. Regiment or Service: Irish Guards. Unit; 1st Battalion. Service Number; 9636. Date of death; 14/12/1916. Born; Mooncoin, County Kilkenny. Enlisted; Waterford. Died of wounds. Grave or Memorial Reference; VI J 6. Cemetery: Sailly-Saillisel British Cemetery in France.

Walshe, Patrick. Rank; Private. Regiment or Service: Royal Irish Regiment. Unit; 2nd Battalion. Service Number; 3093. Date of death; 19/10/1914. Age at death; 29. Born; St Mary's, Kilkenny. Enlisted; Tipperary. Residence; Kilkenny. Killed in action. Son of Matthew and Bridget Walshe (nee Grotty), of 65 and 66, High Street, Kilkenny. Grave or Memorial Reference; Panel 11 and 12. Cemetery: Le Touret Memorial In France.

Walshe, James D. Rank; Lieutenant. Regiment or Service: Royal Welsh Fusiliers. Unit; 4th Battalion. Date of death; 06/04/1918. Age at death;26. Killed in action. Son of Nicholas Walshe, of Kilkenny; husband of Mildred Annie Walshe, of Bute Lodge, Northumberland Avenue, Laindon, Essex. Kilkenny People, April, 1918. Lieutenant James Walsh, Royal Irish Fusiliers, who was killed in action on April 6th, was the only son of Mr Nicholas Walsh, of Kilkenny, with whom deep sympathy is felt. Educated at the Christian Brothers Schools in this Coty, Lieutenant Walsh gained a post in the Valuation Office, Dublin, and passed into the Army at the outbreak of the war. He was given his commission two years ago. Grave or Memorial Reference; I F 42. Cemetery: Martinsart British Cemetery, Somme, France.

Walshe, William. Rank; Lance Corporal. Regiment or Service: Machine Gun Corps. Unit; Infantry, 64th Brigade. Service Number; 11589. Date of death; 26/09/1916. Born; Mooncoin, County Kilkenny. Enlisted; New Cross. Residence; Carrickbeg. Killed in action. Notes; Formerly he was with the Royal Irish Regiment where his number was 9687. Grave or Memorial Reference; Pier and Face 5C and 132C. Cemetery: Thiepval Memorial in France

Ward, Thomas. Rank; Private. Regiment or Service: Royal Irish Regiment. Unit; 1st Battalion. Service Number; 4072. Date of death; 24/04/1915. Age at death;22. Born; Callan, County Kilkenny. Enlisted; Callan. Killed in action. Son of Mr. and Mrs. Ward, of Haggards Green, Callan, Co. Kilkenny. After his death his effects and property were received by;- (Mother) Haggsart Green, Callan, County Kilkenny. Notes; Killed in Action at Saint Julien, France. Grave or Memorial Reference; Panel 33. Cemetery: Ypres (Menin Gate) Memorial in Belgium.

Watson, Charles Horace Samuel. Rank; Lance Corporal/Private. Regiment or Service: Royal Dublin Fusiliers. Unit; 1st Battalion. Service Number; 29938. Date of death; 21-February/March-1918. Age at death; 27. Born; Islington, Middlesex. Enlisted; Dublin. Residence; Finbury Park, London. Killed in action. Son of William Samuel and Elizabeth Watson, of Barnack, Stamford, Northants. Excise Officer, stationed in Ireland. De Ruvigny's Roll of Honour. 2nd son of William Samuel Watson, of 134, Corbyn Street, Finsbury Park, London, N., Forman Turner, Freeman of the City of London and freeman of the Turners Company, by his wife, Elizabeth Ann, daughter of the late Emanuel Moores, of Bourton, Co, Dorset; and brother to Private Ralph Watson (q. v.). Born at Islington, London, N., 25-July-1890. Educated at Montem Street, Tollington Park, N., and at the Clark's College, Holloway, N. Was Excise Officer in charge of the station at Rathdowney, Queen's County. Enlisted 19-April-1917. Served with the Expeditionary Force in France and Flanders from 02-January-1918, and was killed in action north of the Somme on the St Quentin-Cambrai line 21-February following. Buried in the Villers Faucon Communal Cemetery. An officer wrote; "Though your nson had not been with us long, it was sufficient for him to show the best qualities in a non-commissioned officer; hard-working, conscientious, his strong sense of duty made him entirely reliable, and young as he was he would have been quickly promoted to higher rank had he lived." He was unmarried. Notes; Date of death listed as 21-February-1918 (CWGC), 21-March-1918 (SDGW). Grave or Memorial Reference; I B 14. Cemetery: Villers-Faucon Communal Cemetery Extension, Somme, France.

Webb, Samuel Cecil. Rank; Lieutenant/Temporary Captain. Regiment or Service: Royal Munster Fusiliers. Unit; 6th Battalion. Date of death; 03/10/1916. Killed in action. Son of Charles and Louisa Webb, of Park Place, Tashinny, Co. Longford. De Ruvigny's Roll of Honour. . son of the late Charles Webb, of Park Place, Tashinny, County Longford, by his wife, Louisa, daughter of Ambrose Bole. Bor in Boyle, County Roscommon, 01-October-1886. Educated at bath College, Bromsgrove School and Trinity College, Dublin. Was a solicitor in Kilkenny. Obtained a commission as 2nd Lieutenant, The Royal Munster Fusiliers, 145-december-1914 and was promoted Lieutenant. Served with the Mediterranean Expeditionary Force at Gallipoli. Was wounded at Suvla bay in August-1915. proceeded to Salonika the following month, and was killed in action at the taking of the village of Jenikoi, Macedonia, 03-October-1916. Buried at Mekes. While at Trinity College he rowed in the sonior VIII, 1903-07, graduated B. A. in 1907 (Gold Medal in Legal and Political Science). L. L. B. (1st Class, Part 1.) in 1907, and passed the Solicitors Final Examination (1st Place and Silver Medal) in May, 1908. Samuel Webb is also listed in 'Wigs and Guns. '. Kilkenny Journal, September, 1915. The Roll of Honour. Captain H. D. O'Hara, R. D. F, who was wounded on the 11th ult., ad whose death has been annpunced, was the only son of W. J. O'Hara, R. M., and Cecilia, youngest daughter of the late Peter

Connellan, Esq., D. L., Coolmore, Thomastown. The many friends of Lieutenant S. C. Webb, R. M. F., whose name appears amongst the wounded, will be glad to learn that he is making speedy progress towards recovery, he was wounded during the landing and advance of the Irish Division under General Mahon on the shores of the Gallipoli Peninsula. Grave or Memorial Reference; III C 15. Cemetery: Struma Military Cemetery in Greece.

Webster, Robert. Rank; Private. Regiment or Service: Royal Irish Regiment. Unit; C Company 1st Battalion. Service Number; 10544. Date of death; 02/05/1915. Age at death; 26. Born; Gurtnahoe, County Tipperary. Enlisted; Clonmel. Residence; Gurtnahoe. Killed in action. Son of John and Ellen Webster, of Sallypark, Urlingford, Co. Kilkenny. Grave or Memorial Reference; Panel 11. Cemetery: Ypres (Menin Gate) Memorial in Belgium.

Wellwood, Robert. Rank; Reverend/Secretary. Regiment or Service: Young Men's Christian Association. Date of death; 19/05/1918. Age at death;54. Born; Callan, County Kilkenny. Enlisted; New York. Killed in action. Son of John Wellwood and Anne Calback. Rev Wellwood was the first man of the YMCA to be killed in action. Irish Independent; Rev R Wellwood, son of the late Mr J Wellwood, Ballykeefe, Kilmamagh, County Kilkenny, was Sec. of the American YMCA, and was killed by shrapnel. From"Summary of World War Work of the American Y. M. C. A. ; with the soldiers and sailors of America at home, on the seas, and overseas." 1920. Wellwood, Robert, New York City, N. Y., Missionary to China. Killed, May 19, 1918, in enemy air raid on British lines. Secretary, Chinese coolies, Blargies. Born 1864. Sailed, Jan. 27, 1918. Place of burial, Grave C6, Plot 1, Communal Cemetery, Blargies. Next of kin, Mrs Robert Wellwood, wife, care of A. B. M. S.,. Ford Building, Boston, Mass. Irish Times. Wellwood-May 19, Rev. Robert Wellwood, Secretary American Y. M. C. A., killed by shrapnel, son of the late John Wellwood, Esq., Ballykeefe, Kilmanagh, Kilkenny. The Weekly Irish Times. Ireland's Roll of Honour. June 29, 1918. Rev. Robert Wellwood, Secretary of the American Y. M. C. A., was killed by shrapnel. He was the fourth son of the late Mr John Wellwood, of Ballykeefe, Kilmanagh, County Kilkenny. Notes; Born 1864. Entered service from New York. Grave or Memorial Reference; Plot A, Row 6, Grave 13. Cemetery: Somme American Cemetery.

Welsh, Michael. Rank; Gunner. Regiment or Service: Royal Garrison Artillery. Unit; 287th Siege Battery. Service Number; 41807. Date of death; 22/11/1917. Age at death; 44. Born; Arls, Carlow, Queen's County. Enlisted; Reading. Residence; Ballyfoyle, Kilkenny. Killed in action. Son of John and Mary Ann Walsh, of Ballyfoyle, Maganey, Co. Kildare. Grave or Memorial Reference; III B 3. Cemetery: Ypres Reservoir Cemetery in Belgium. Also listed as WALSH on the Great War Memorial, Milford Street, Leighlinbridge, County Carlow.

Captain Wheeler, from 'Our Heroes.'

Wheeler, Charles Palliser. Rank; Captain. Regiment or Service: Royal Berkshire Regiment. Unit; "A" Coy. 1st Battalion. Date of death; 25/09/1915. Age at death;26. Killed in action. Son of Lt. Col. E. Wheeler (R. M. A.), and Mrs. Wheeler, of The Rocks, Kilkenny. 'Our Heroes'. was the only son of Colonel and Mrs Wheeler, The Rocks, Kilkenny, and nephew to the late Sir Charles D. Wheeler Cuffe, Bart., County Kilkenny. He was educated at Haileybury and Sandhurst, obtained his commission in the 1st Royal Berks in 1910, and became Captain in May, 1915. He was in the retreat from Mons, was wounded in the battle of the Aisne, and was killed instantaneously by a burst of shrapnel on the morning of September 26th last. Irish Independent; Captain C P Wheeler, Berks regt., killed on 25th ult., was the only son of Colonel Wheeler, The Rock, Kilkenny. Deceased, who was in the retreat from Mons, and wounded at the battale of the Aisne, was 26 years of age. Grave or Memorial Reference; II A 5. Cemetery: Vielle-Chapelle New Military Cemetery, Lacouture, Pas-de-Calais, France. He is commemorated on the Great War Memorial in St Canice's Cathedral, Kilkenny…'To the Glory of God and in loving memory of the following members of the Diocese of Ossory who gave their lives for their country in the Great War 1914-1918', and also listed on the Haileybury (College) Register.

Whelan, John. Rank; Private. Regiment or Service: Royal Dublin Fusiliers. Unit; 9th Battalion. Service Number; 17410. Date of death; 13/03/1916. Born; Kilkenny. Enlisted; Dublin. Residence; Kilkenny. Killed in action. Grave or Memorial Reference; Panels 127 to. Cemetery: Loos Memorial in France.

Whelan, Patrick. Rank; Private. Regiment or Service: Royal Irish Fusiliers. Unit; 7th Battalion. Service Number; 19806. Date of death; 09/09/1916. Born; Kilkenny. Enlisted; Kilkenny. Killed in action. Grave or Memorial Reference; XXI B 10. Cemetery: Delville Wood Cemetery, Longueval in France.

White, Aubrey Cecil. Rank; Second Lieutenant. Regiment or Service: York and Lancaster Regiment. Unit; 8th Battalion. Date of death; 01/07/1916. Age at death; 20. Killed in action. Son of Richard and Anna M. White (nee Croly), of Gowran, Co. Kilkenny. Educated Castle Park, Dalkey, Co. Dublin, and Trent College, Derbyshire. Waterford News. County Kilkenny Officer Killed. Mr Richard White, Gowran House, County Kilkenny, has received a telegram from the War Office informing him that his second son, Second Lieutenant Aubrey Cecil White, York and Lancaster Regiment, previously reported missing, was killed in action while leading his men in the battle of the Somme. Lieutenant White, who was 20 years old, was educated at Castle Park, Dalkey, and later at Trent College, Derbyshire. He was gazetted Second Lieutenant in October, 1914, and went out to France at the end of last year. He was grandson of the late Edward White, Fort Etna, Limerick, and of Henry Grey Croly, of 7 Merrion Square, Dublin. Irish Times. White-July 1, previously reported missing, now officially reported killed in action, Aubrey Cecil, York and Lanaster Regiment, son of Richard and Anna White, Gowran House, Kilkenny. Grave or Memorial Reference; II B 10. Cemetery: Lonsdale Cemetery, Authuile in France.

White, John. Rank; Lance Corporal. Regiment or Service: Irish Guards. Unit; 1st Battalion. Service Number; 2695. Date of death; 10/10/1917. Born; Wexford. Enlisted; Whitehall. Residence; Johnstown. Killed in action. He won the Military Medal and is listed in the London Gazette. In his Will, dated 01-April-1917, his effects and property were received by;- (Mother) Mrs B White, Post Office Johnstown, Kilkenny, Ireland. Irish Independent; White-In sad and loving memory of my dear son, John White, Johnstown, County Kilkenny (late Irish Guards), who was killed in action October 10, 1917. Sacred Heart of Jesus, have mercy upon his soul. Inserted by his sorrowing mother. Grave or Memorial Reference; VII F 17. Cemetery: Artillery Wood Cemetery in Belgium.

Private White, from De Ruvigny's Roll of Honour.

White, Robert Henry. Rank; Private. Regiment or Service: Canadian Infantry (Central Ontario Regiment) Unit. Unit; "C" Coy. 3rd Battalion. Service Number; 9733. Date of death; 23/04/1915. Age at death; 19. Son of the late Robert and Elizabeth White, of Roscrea, Co. Tipperary, Ireland. De Ruvigny's Roll of Honour. . 2nd son of the late Robert White, Master Roscrea (Ireland) Union, by his wife, Elizabeth (44, Dingwall Avenue, Toronto, Canada), daughter of William Proctor, of Glashare, County Kilkenny. Born in Roscrea, County Tipperary on 08-July-1895. Educated at the National School there. Went to Canada in May, 1914, and was a Sales Clerk. Volunteered on the outbreak of war and joined the Canadian Expeditionary Force at Toronto, about 20 August-1914. Left Vancouver for England with the first contingent 09-October-1914. Trained on Salisbury plain during the winter of 1914-15. Went to France early in February, and was killed in acton "in the field between St Julien and St Jean," 23-April-1915, being shot through the head and killed instantly. Grave or Memorial Reference; Panel 18 - 24 - 26 - 30. Cemetery: Ypres (Menin Gate) Memorial in Belgium.

Wholehouse, Francis. Rank; Private. Regiment or Service: Leinster Regiment. Unit; 2nd Battalion. Service Number; 3323. Date of death; 14/08/1915. Born; Callen, County Kilkenny. Enlisted; Kilkenny. Killed in action. Notes; Formerly he was with the Royal Irish Regiment where his number was 3802. Grave or Memorial Reference; Panel 44. Cemetery: Ypres (Menin Gate) Memorial in Belgium.

Lieutenant Wickham, from 'Our Heroes.'

Wickham, Anthony Theodore Clephane. Rank; Lieutenant. Regiment or Service: Connaught Rangers. Unit; 4th Battalion attached to the 2nd Battalion. Date of death; 04/11/1914. Killed in action. Son of the Rev. J. D. C. and Mrs. Wickham, of Holcomb Manor, Holcomb, Stratton-on-Fosse, Somerset. 'Our Heroes'. Gazetted to the 4th Battalion of the Connaught Rangers in October, 1907. He was the son of Mr and Mrs Wickham, of the Manor, Holcombe, near Bath. De Ruvigny's Roll of Honour. only son of the Reverend J. D. C. Wickham, of the Manor, Holcombe, Co. Somerset, J. P. Served with the Expeditionary Force in France and Flanders, and was killed in action 02-November-1914. Irish Independent; Captain T C Wickham, Connaught Rangers, of Annamuct, Kilkenny, was only son of the Rev. J D C Wickham, J. P., Holcombe, Somerset. Grave or Memorial Reference; IV E 7. Cemetery: Sanctuary Wood Cemetery, Ypres, Belgium.

Willoughby, Charles. Rank; Private. Regiment or Service: Royal Irish Regiment. Unit; 1st Battalion. Service Number; 1729. Date of death; 18/05/1915. Born; Coolcullen, County Kilkenny. Enlisted; Carlow. Killed in action. Grave or Memorial Reference; Panel 4. Cemetery: Le Touret Memorial in France. Also listed under Leighlinbridge/Old Leighlin on the Great War Memorial, Milford Street, Leighlinbridge, County Carlow.

Willows, John. Rank; Rifleman. Regiment or Service: Rifle Brigade. Unit; 11th Battalion. Service Number; B/410. Date of death; 27/02/1916. Age at death; 22. Born; Kilkenny. Enlisted; London. Residence; Kilkenny. Killed in action. Son of Henry and Ellen Willows, of The Castle, Stables, Kilkenny. In his Will, dated 11-August-1915, his effects and property were received by;- (Mother) Mrs H Willows, Archer Street, Kilkenny, Ireland. Waterford News;-Death of a Young Kilkenny Soldier. Mr Harry Willows, the esteemed head coachman at Kilkenny Castle, and Mrs Willows, Archer Street, Kilkenny, are informed of the death in action of their eldest son, Jack, of the 11th Rifle Brigade, who was killed in France during the night of February 27th-28th. He was hit by a shell, and died a few hours afterwards. The internment took place on the night of February 28th in a little cemetery north of Ypres, where his grave is marked by a cross. In a letter to Mrs Willows, the Rev Basil Churchward expressed the great sorrow he felt at the death of her gallant son and his sense of the great trial which his loss had brought to her."But," he added,"You will fee proud that your son is one of those who gave his very all for the safety and honour of those at home." Rifleman Willows, wow as about twenty years of age, was chauffeur to the Lady Constance Butler. He was in London with her ladyship in August, 1914, and a few days after the outbreak of war joined the Rifle Brigade. Grave or Memorial Reference; I S 16. Cemetery: La Brique Military Cemetery No 2, Ieper, West-Vlaanderen, Belgium. He is also commemorated on the Great War Memorial in St Canice's Cathedral, Kilkenny... 'To the Glory of God and in loving memory of the following members of the Diocese of Ossory who gave their lives for their country in the Great War 1914-1918'.

Willson, William T. Rank; Private. Regiment or Service: King Edward's Horse. Unit; 2nd Battalion. Service Number; 822. Date of death; 01/03/1919. Killed in action. Cemetery: Kilkenny (St John) Church of Ireland Churchyard, Kilkenny.

Willy, John James. Rank; Rifleman. Regiment or Service: Royal Irish Rifles. Unit; 2nd Battalion. Service Number; 7161. Date of death; 25/12/1915. Born; Kilkenny. Enlisted; Ballykinlar, County Down. Died at home. Grave or Memorial Reference; Screen Wall. G. B. 18. 135. Cemetery: Wandsworth (Earlsfield) Cemetery UK.

Woodgate, Thomas Joseph. Rank; Private Second Class. Regiment or Service: Royal Air Force. Unit; 23rd Training Squadron. Service Number; 297699. Date of death; 10/10/1918. Age at death;18. Son of Edward J. Woodgate, of Mill Street, Callan, Co. Kilkenny. Steamship Leinster was hit by a German Torpedo and sank with the loss of over 400 people. It was the greatest maritime disaster in Irish Waters. Date of Death: 18. 10-October-1918. Among the passengers were 14 RAF members, most of whom lost their lives. Thomas had joined the Royal Air Force seven months previously and was returning to duty with 23rd Training Squadron when he was lost. Grave or Memorial Reference; CE. New Plot. 752. Cemetery: Grangegorman Military Cemetery, Dublin.

Woodhams, Alfred Thomas. Rank; Lance Corporal. Regiment or Service: Yorkshire Regiment. Unit; 6th Battalion. Service Number; 15629. Date of death; 22/08/1915. Age at death; 20. Born; Kilkenny. Enlisted; Richmond, Yorkshire. Killed in Action in Gallipoli. Son of William and Eliza Woodhams, of 12, Skeeby Terrace, Richmond, Yorks. Grave or Memorial Reference; Panel 55 to 58. Cemetery: Helles memorial in Turkey.

Wright, Peter. Rank; Private. Regiment or Service: Royal Irish Regiment. Unit; 2nd Battalion. Service Number; 1781. Date of death; 21/03/1918. Born; Glenmore, County Kilkenny. Enlisted; Waterford. Killed in action. Grave or Memorial Reference; Panel 30 and 31. Cemetery: Pozieres Memorial in France.

X-Y-Z

Younge, Frederick George Patrick. Rank; Lieutenant. Regiment or Service: Leinster Regiment. Unit; 2nd Battalion. Date of death; 14/02/1915. Age at death; 22. Died of wounds. Son of Mr. J. M. and Mrs. J. Younge, of Oldtown, Rathdowney, Offaly. Grave or Memorial Reference; F 7. Cemetery: Bailleul Communal Cemetery (Nord) in France.

Younge, Lawrence. Rank; Private. Regiment or Service: Royal Irish Regiment. Unit; 1st Battalion. Service Number; 6390. Date of death; 06/07/1917. Born; Kilmacow, County Kilkenny. Enlisted; Waterford. Died at sea. Cemetery: Doiran Memorial in Greece.